AF770200

COMPUTER BASED NUMERICAL AND STATISTICAL TECHNIQUES

Computer Based Numerical and Statistical Techniques

Editor:

Maria Emilova Velinova, Ph.D.

ArclerPress

www.arclerpress.com

Computer Based Numerical and Statistical Techniques

Editor: Maria Emilova Velinova, Ph.D.

© 2017 Arcler Press LLC
708 3rd Avenue, 6th Floor
New York
NY 10017
United States of America
www.arclerpress.com

ISBN: 978-1-68094-451-8

Library of Congress Control Number: 2016951161

This book contains information obtained from highly regarded resources. Reprinted material sources are indicated. Copyright for individual articles remains with the authors as indicated. A Wide variety of references are listed. Reasonable efforts have been made to publish reliable data and views articulated in the chapters are those of the individual contributors, and not necessarily those of the editors or publishers. Editors or publishers are not responsible for the accuracy of the information in the published chapters or consequences of their use. The publisher believes no responsibility for any damage or grievance to the persons or property arising out of the use of any materials, instructions, methods or thoughts in the book. The editors and the publisher have attempted to trace the copyright holders of all material reproduced in this publication and apologize to copyright holders if permission has not been obtained. If any copyright holder has not been acknowledged, please write to us so we may rectify.

Notice: Registered trademark of products or corporate names are used only for explanation and identification without intent of infringement.

Arcler Press LLC publishes wide variety of books and eBooks. For more information about Arcler Press and its products, visit our website at www.arclerpress.com

About the Editor

Maria Emilova Velinova, Ph.D.

Maria Velinova is Ph.D. holder in Quantum chemistry at the University of Sofia since April 2012. Her major research experience is in the field of Computational Chemistry, especially in statistical mechanics methods applied to different sorts of biomolecules. Member of the Laboratory of Quantum and Computational Chemistry at the University of Sofia.

Contents

List of Contributors

Sankar Prasad Mondal
Department of Mathematics, National Institute of Technology, Agartala, Jirania, Tripura 799046, India

Susmita Roy
Department of Mathematics, National Institute of Technology, Agartala, Jirania, Tripura 799046, India

Biswajit Das
Department of Mechanical Engineering, National Institute of Technology, Agartala, Jirania, Tripura 799046, India

Hassam Nasarullah Chaudhry
School of Energy, Geoscience, Infrastructure and Society, Heriot-Watt University, Dubai, UAE

John Kaiser Calautit
School of Civil Engineering, University of Leeds, Leeds, United Kingdom

Ben Richard Hughes
School of Civil Engineering, University of Leeds, Leeds, United Kingdom

S. R. Mishra
Department of Mathematics, Institute of Technical Education and Research, Siksha 'O' Anusandhan University, Khandagiri, Bhubaneswar, Odisha 751030, India

S. Jena
Department of Mathematics, Centurion University of Technology and Management, Bhubaneswar, India

R. C. Mittal
Department of Mathematics, IIT Roorkee, Roorkee, Uttarakhand 247667, India

Rachna Bhatia
Department of Mathematics, IIT Roorkee, Roorkee, Uttarakhand 247667, India

Amir Tokić
[1]Faculty of Electrical Engineering, Tuzla University, 75000 Tuzla, Bosnia and Herzegovina

Ivo Uglešić
[2]Faculty of Electrical Engineering and Computing, Zagreb University, 11000 Zagreb, Croatia

Gorazd Štumberger
Faculty of Electrical Engineering and Computer Science, Maribor University, 2000 Maribor, Slovenia

Anton Beljaars
European Centre for Medium-Range Weather Forecasts, Shinfield Park, Reading, RG2 9AX, UK

Emanuel Dutra
European Centre for Medium-Range Weather Forecasts, Shinfield Park, Reading, RG2 9AX, UK

Gianpaolo Balsamo
European Centre for Medium-Range Weather Forecasts, Shinfield Park, Reading, RG2 9AX, UK

Zakieh Avazzadeh
State Key Laboratory of Hydrology-Water Resources and Hydraulic Engineering, College of Mechanics and Materials, Hohai University, Nanjing 210098, China

Mohammad Heydari
Young Researchers and Elite Club, Islamic Azad University, Ashkezar Branch, Ashkezar 8941613695, Iran

Wen Chen
State Key Laboratory of Hydrology-Water Resources and Hydraulic Engineering, College of Mechanics and Materials, Hohai University, Nanjing 210098, China

G. B. Loghmani
Department of Mathematics, Yazd University, Yazd, Iran

Rick Chartrand
Theoretical Division, MS B284, Los Alamos National Laboratory, Los Alamos, NM 87545, USA

Chunye Gong
College of Aerospace Science and Engineering, National University of Defense Technology, Changsha 410073, China
Science and Technology on Space Physics Laboratory, Beijing 100076, China
School of Computer Science, National University of Defense Technology, Changsha 410073, China

Weimin Bao
College of Aerospace Science and Engineering, National University of Defense Technology, Changsha 410073, China
Science and Technology on Space Physics Laboratory, Beijing 100076, China

Guojian Tang
College of Aerospace Science and Engineering, National University of Defense Technology, Changsha 410073, China

Yuewen Jiang
Department of Engineering Science, University of Oxford, Oxford OX2 0ES, UK

Jie Liu
School of Computer Science, National University of Defense Technology, Changsha 410073, China

Harald Atmanspacher
lnstitut ffir Grenzgebiete der Psychologie, Wilhelmstr. 3a, D-79098 Freiburg;
Max-Planck-Institut ffir extraterrestrische Physik, Giessenbachstr., D-85740 Garching;

Werner Ehm
lnstitut ffir Grenzgebiete der Psychologie, Wilhelmstr. 3a, D-79098 Freiburg;

Herbert Scheingraber
Max-Planck-Institut ffir extraterrestrische Physik, Giessenbachstr., D-85740 Garching;

Gerda Wiedenmann
Max-Planck-Institut ffir extraterrestrische Physik, Giessenbachstr., D-85740 Garching;
Nabios GmbH, Donnersberger Str. 41, D-80634 Mnchen

A. R. Messina
Graduate Studies Program in Electrical Engineering, The Center for Research and Advanced Studies, Avenida Científica 1145, Colonia El Bajío, Guadalajara, 45015 Jalisco, Mexico

P. Esquivel,
Graduate Studies Program in Electrical Engineering, The Center for Research and Advanced Studies, Avenida Científica 1145, Colonia El Bajío, Guadalajara, 45015 Jalisco, Mexico

F. Lezama
Graduate Studies Program in Electrical Engineering, The Center for Research and Advanced Studies, Avenida Científica 1145, Colonia El Bajío, Guadalajara, 45015 Jalisco, Mexico

Mohamed Abdolell
Department of Diagnostic Radiology, Dalhousie University, Halifax, NS, Canada B3H 2Y9
Department of Diagnostic Imaging, Capital District Health Authority, Halifax, NS, Canada B3H 2Y9
Division of Medical Education/Informatics, Dalhousie University, Halifax, NS, Canada B3H 2Y9

Kaitlyn Tsuruda
Department of Diagnostic Imaging, Capital District Health Authority, Halifax, NS, Canada B3H 2Y9

Gerry Schaller
Department of Diagnostic Radiology, Dalhousie University, Halifax, NS, Canada B3H 2Y9
Department of Diagnostic Imaging, Capital District Health Authority, Halifax, NS, Canada B3H 2Y9

Judy Caines
Nova Scotia Breast Screening Program, Halifax, NS, Canada B3H 2Y9
Department of Diagnostic Radiology, Dalhousie University, Halifax, NS, Canada B3H 2Y9
Department of Diagnostic Imaging, Capital District Health Authority, Halifax, NS, Canada B3H 2Y9

Zheng Xie
School of Computer Science, The University of Manchester, Manchester M13 9PL, UK

Doug Edwards
School of Computer Science, The University of Manchester, Manchester M13 9PL, UK

Jing Lin
Division of Operation and Maintenance Engineering, Luleå University of Technology, 97187 Luleå, Sweden
Luleå Railway Research Centre (JVTC), 97187 Luleå, Sweden

J.H. Lin
State Key Laboratory of Structural Analysis of Industrial Equipment, Dalian University of Technology, Dalian 116023, China

J. Wang
Department of Civil Engineering, SUNY at Buffalo, 109 Red Jacket Quard., Buffalo, NY 14261, USA

Y.H. Zhang
State Key Laboratory of Structural Analysis of Industrial Equipment, Dalian University of Technology, Dalian 116023, China

Monica W. K. Kan
Department of Physics and Materials Science, City University of Hong Kong, Tat Chee Avenue, Kowloon Tong, Hong Kong
Department of Oncology, Princess Margaret Hospital, Hong Kong

Peter K. N. Yu
Department of Physics and Materials Science, City University of Hong Kong, Tat Chee Avenue, Kowloon Tong, Hong Kong

Lucullus H. T. Leung
Department of Oncology, Princess Margaret Hospital, Hong Kong

Preface

Computer-based numerical and statistical techniques have the purpose to improve performance and minimize error in problem-solving application. For example, in signal processing that considers signals as stochastic processes, using their statistical properties; in climatology and climate monitoring to attempt for weather prediction and to reveal alterations in the environment; in demography where the statistical study of an entire population is performed, statistical methods can be applied to any kind of population character that varies over a time or space. For such reasons, the application of both numerical analysis and statistical sciences has become a fundamental knowledge of all the modern engineers and scientists.

The contents of this book cover several advanced applications of numerical and statistical procedures in many different fields. In particular, numerical stability analysis, numerical integration methods for differential and integral equations, numerical differentiation, time-series and images statistical analysis, and Monte Carlo methods.

In the first section of book, the search of numerical solutions of first-order linear Fuzzy differential equations, of PDEs in two different problems of fluid dynamics and heat transfer, of nonlinear Sine-Gordon equation by modified cubic B-spline collocation method, and of nonlinear models of electrical transformers is discussed. Moreover, enough space is given to the analysis of the numerical stability in weather and climate models, and of the exponential convergence of particular forms of integral equations. At last, the problems both of differentiating a noisy and nonsmooth function avoiding the noise amplification of finite-difference methods, and of the computational cost of several numerical methods applied for solving of fractional differential equations are considered.

In the second and last section of the book, different examples of statistical analysis and of application of Monte Carlo (MC) methods are shown in several fields. In particular, the statistical study of time series with scaling indices, and the application of wavelet-based analysis and a sliding window-based method for extracting spatiotemporal patterns are discussed. Moreover, the statistical evaluation both of a fully automated mammographic breast density algorithm, and of the effect of nano-CMOS spatial variability on integrated circuits is also studied. Lastly, three different examples of application of MC are provided: an integrated procedure for Bayesian inference using Markov chain MC methods; MC numerical simulations to solve non-stationary random responses of nonlinear multi-degrees-of-freedom Duffing systems subjected to evolutionary random excitations; and the comparison of classical MC methods and deterministic grid-based Boltzmann equation solvers implemented in a commercial treatment planning system for radiotherapy photon beam dose calculation.

Editor
Maria Emilova Velinova, Ph.D.

CHAPTER 1

NUMERICAL SOLUTION OF FIRST-ORDER LINEAR DIFFERENTIAL EQUATIONS IN FUZZY ENVIRONMENT BY RUNGE-KUTTA-FEHLBERG METHOD AND ITS APPLICATION

Sankar Prasad Mondal,[1] Susmita Roy,[1] and Biswajit Das[2]

[1]Department of Mathematics, National Institute of Technology, Agartala, Jirania, Tripura 799046, India

[2]Department of Mechanical Engineering, National Institute of Technology, Agartala, Jirania, Tripura 799046, India

ABSTRACT

The numerical algorithm for solving "first-order linear differential equation in fuzzy environment" is discussed. A scheme, namely, "Runge-Kutta-Fehlberg method," is described in detail for solving the said differential equation. The numerical solutions are compared with (i)-gH and (ii)-gH differential (exact solutions concepts) system. The method is also followed by complete error analysis. The method is illustrated by solving an example and an application.

INTRODUCTION

Fuzzy Differential Equation. In modeling of real natural phenomena, differential equations play an important role in many areas of discipline, exemplary in economics, biomathematics, science, and engineering. Many experts in such areas widely use differential equations in order to make some problems under study more comprehensible. In many cases, information about the physical phenomena related is always immanent with uncertainty.

Today, the study of differential equations with uncertainty is instantaneously growing as a new area in fuzzy analysis. The terms such as "fuzzy differential equation" and "fuzzy differential inclusion" are used interchangeably in mention to differential equations with fuzzy initial values or fuzzy boundary values or even differential equations dealing with functions on the space of fuzzy numbers. In the year 1987, the term "fuzzy differential equation (FDE)" was introduced by Kandel and Byatt [1]. There are different approaches to discuss the FDEs: (i) the Hukuhara derivative of a fuzzy number valued function is used, (ii) Hüllermeier [2] and Diamond and Watson [3–5] suggested a different formulation for the fuzzy initial value problems (FIVP) based on a family of differential inclusions, (iii) in [6, 7], Bede et al. defined generalized differentiability of the fuzzy number valued functions and studied FDE, and (iv) applying a parametric representation of fuzzy numbers, Chen et al. [8] established a new definition for the differentiation of a fuzzy valued function and used it in FDE.

Solution of Fuzzy Differential Equation by Numerical Techniques. Numerical methods are the methods by which we can find the solution of differential equation where the exact solution is critical to find. There exist various numerical methods for solving differential equation such as Setia et al. [9], Liu [10], and Setia et al. [11]. Our aim is to find the numerical techniques by which the solution of a linear or nonlinear first-order fuzzy differential equation comes easily and the solution is very close to the exact solution. There exist many techniques of

Citation: Sankar Prasad Mondal, Susmita Roy, and Biswajit Das, "Numerical Solution of First-Order Linear Differential Equations in Fuzzy Environment by Runge-Kutta-Fehlberg Method and Its Application," International Journal of Differential Equations, vol. 2016, Article ID 8150497, 14 pages, 2016. doi:10.1155/2016/8150497

numerical methods for finding the solution of fuzzy differential equation. Authors applied the method in certain types of fuzzy differential equation which shows that their techniques are best fit for that particular problem. The first paper on fuzzy differential equation and numerical analysis was published in 1999 by Ma et al. [12]. Allahviranloo et al. [13] apply the two-step method on fuzzy differential equations. Allahviranloo et al. [14] find the numerical solution by using predictor-corrector method. Allahviranloo et al. [15] find an algorithm for finding the solution *N*th-order fuzzy linear differential equations using numerical techniques. Pederson and Sambandham in [16] use characterization theorem on hybrid fuzzy initial value problem. A soft computing technique, namely, artificial neural network, is implicated for solving FDE by Effati and Pakdaman [17]. Duraisamy and Usha [18] used modified Euler's method. The extension principle method was compared by Euler's method in Saberi Najafi et al. [19] article. Rostami et al. [20] find a numerical algorithm for solving nonlinear fuzzy differential equations. Moghadam and Dahaghin [21] apply two-step methods for numerical solution of FDE. Batiha in [22] finds an iterative solution of multispecies predator-prey model by variational iteration method. Ahmad and Hasan [23] proposed a new fuzzy version of Euler's method for solving differential equations with fuzzy initial value. Nirmala and Chenthur Pandian [24] give an idea for improving the numerical result on FDE. Shafiee et al. [25] use predictor-corrector method for nonlinear fuzzy Volterra integral equations. Comparison results on some numerical techniques on first-order fuzzy differential equation are illustrated by Ghanbari [26]. The use of variational iteration method for solving *N*th-order fuzzy differential equations is shown by Jafari et al. [27]. Tapaswini and Chakraverty [28] discuss a new approach to fuzzy initial value problem by Improved Euler method. The solution of FIVP is compared by Least Square method and Adomian Decomposition method by Ahmed and Fadhel [29]. Solution of differential equation by Euler's method using fuzzy concept is developed by Saikia [30]. Ezzati et al. [31] find the numerical solution of Volterra-Fredholm integral equations with the help of inverse and direct discrete fuzzy transforms and collocation technique. The Adomian method is applied on second-order FDE by Wang and Guo [32]. Fard [33] uses iterative scheme to find the solution of generalized system of linear FDE, whereas Block method is used by Mehrkanoon et al. [34]. Asady and Alavi [35] apply a numerical method for solving *N*th-order linear fuzzy differential equation.

Solution of Fuzzy Differential Equation by Runge-Kutta Method. Runge-Kutta method is well known for finding the approximate or numerical solution. In the last decade Runge-Kutta method is applied in fuzzy differential equation for finding the numerical solution. The researchers are giving various types of view to apply these methods. Someone changes the order and someone applies different types on FDE, a comparison of another method to Runge-Kutta method. The details of published work done in Runge-Kutta method are summarized below.

Numerical Solution of Fuzzy Differential Equations by Runge-Kutta method of order three is developed by Duraisamy and Usha [36]. Solution techniques for fourth-order Runge-Kutta method with higher order derivative approximations are developed by Nirmala and Chenthur Pandian [37]. Runge-Kutta method of order five is developed by Jayakumar et al. [38]. The techniques extended Runge-Kutta-like formulae of order four are developed by Ghazanfari and Shakerami [39]. Third-order Runge-Kutta method is developed by Kanagarajan and Sambath [40]. Runge-Kutta-Fehlberg method for hybrid fuzzy differential equation is solved by Jayakumar and Kanagarajan [41]. A different approach followed by Runge-Kutta method is applied by Akbarzadeh Ghanaie and Mohseni Moghadam [42]. "Numerical Solution of Fuzzy IVP with Trapezoidal and Triangular Fuzzy Numbers by Using Fifth-Order Runge-Kutta Method" is solved by Ghanbari [43]. "New Multi-Step Runge-Kutta Method for Solving Fuzzy Differential Equations" is solved by Nirmala and Chenthur Pandian [44]. "Numerical Solution of Fuzzy Hybrid Differential Equation by Third Order Runge-Kutta Nystrom Method" is solved by Saveetha and Chenthur Pandian [45]. A new approach to solve fuzzy differential equation by using third-order Runge-Kutta method is developed by Deshmukh [46]. Runge-Kutta method of order four is developed by Duraisamy and Usha [47] and order five is developed by Jayakumar and Kanagarajan [48].

Application of Fuzzy Differential Equation. Fuzzy differential equations play a significant role in the fields of biology, engineering, and physics as well as among other fields of science, for example, in population models [49], civil engineering [50], bioinformatics and computational biology [51], quantum optics and gravity [52], modeling hydraulic [53], HIV model [54], decay model [55], predator-prey model [56], population dynamics model [57], friction model [58], growth model [59], bacteria culture model [60], bank account and drug concentration problem [61], barometric pressure problem [62], concentration problem [63], weight loss and oil production model [64], arm race model [65], vibration of mass [66], and fractional predator-prey equation [67].

Novelties. Although some developments are done, some new interest and new work have been done by ourselves which are mentioned below:

- Differential equation is solved in fuzzy environment by numerical techniques; that is, coefficients and initial condition both are taken as fuzzy number of a differential equation and solved by numerical techniques.
- The numerical solution is compared with the exact solution ((i)-gH and (ii)-gH both cases).
- Runge-Kutta-Fehlberg method for solving fuzzy differential equation is used.
- For application purpose a mixture problem is considered.
- The solutions are found using different step length for better accuracy of the result.
- The necessary algorithm for numerical solution is given.

Structure of the Paper. The paper is organized as follows: in Preliminary Concepts, the preliminary concepts and basic concepts on fuzzy number and fuzzy derivative are given. The method for finding the exact solution is discussed in Exact Solution of Fuzzy Differential Equation. In Numerical Solution of Fuzzy Differential Equation we proposed Runge-Kutta-Fehlberg method in fuzzy environment. The convergence of the said method and algorithm for finding the numerical results are also discussed in this section. Numerical Example shows a numerical example. In Application an important application, namely, mixture problem, is illustrated in fuzzy environment. Finally conclusions and future research scope of this paper are drawn in last section, Conclusion.

PRELIMINARY CONCEPTS

Definition 1 (fuzzy set). A fuzzy set $\tilde{A}$ is defined by $\tilde{A} = \{(x, \mu_{\tilde{A}}(x)) : x \in A, \mu_{\tilde{A}}(x) \in [0, 1]\}$. In the pair $(x, \mu_{\tilde{A}}(x))$ the first element x belongs to the classical set A and the second element $\mu_{\tilde{A}}(x)$ belongs to the interval [0, 1], called membership function.

Definition 2 (α-cut of a fuzzy set). The α-level set (or interval of confidence at level α or α-cut) of the fuzzy set $\tilde{A}$ of X is a crisp set A_α that contains all the elements of X that have membership values in A greater than or equal to α; that is, $A = \{x : \mu_{\tilde{A}}(x) \geq \alpha, x \in X, 0 < \alpha \leq 1\}$.

Definition 3 (fuzzy number). The basic definition of fuzzy number is as follows [30]: if we denote the set of all real numbers by $\mathscr{R}$ and the set of all fuzzy numbers on $\mathscr{R}$ is indicated by $\mathscr{R}_{\mathscr{F}}$ then a fuzzy number is mapping such that $u : \mathscr{R} \to [0, 1]$, which satisfies the following four properties:

- u is upper semicontinuous.
- u is a fuzzy convex; that is, $(\lambda x + (1 - \lambda)y) \geq \min\{u(x), u(y)\}$ for all $x, y \in \mathscr{R}$, $\lambda \in [0, 1]$.
- u is normal; that is, $\exists x_0 \in \mathscr{R}$ for which $(x_0)=1$.
- supp $u = \{x \in \mathscr{R} \mid u(x) > 0\}$ is support of u and the closure of (supp u) is compact.

Definition 4 (parametric form of fuzzy number [31]). A fuzzy number is represented by an ordered pair of functions $(u_1(\alpha), u_2(\alpha))$, $0 \leq \alpha \leq 1$, that satisfy the following condition:

- $u_1(\alpha)$ is a bounded left continuous nondecreasing function for any $\alpha \in [0, 1]$.
- $u_2(\alpha)$ is a bounded left continuous nonincreasing function for any $\alpha \in [0, 1]$.
- $u_1(\alpha) \leq u_2(\alpha)$ for any $\alpha \in [0, 1]$.

Note. If $u_1(\alpha) = u_2(\alpha) = \alpha$, then α is a crisp number

Definition 5 (generalized Hukuhara difference [20]). The generalized Hukuhara difference of two fuzzy numbers u, V $\in \mathscr{R}_{\mathscr{F}}$ is defined as follows:

$$u \ominus_{\text{gH}} v = w \Longleftrightarrow \begin{cases} \text{(i)} \ u = v \oplus w, \\ \text{or} \quad \text{(ii)} \ v = u \oplus (-1)\, w. \end{cases} \tag{1}$$

Consider $[w]\alpha = [w_1(\alpha), w_1(\alpha)]$; then $w_1(\alpha) = \min\{u_1(\alpha) - V_1(\alpha), u_2(\alpha) - V_2(\alpha)\}$ and $w_2(\alpha) = \max\{u_1(\alpha) - V_1(\alpha), u_2(\alpha) - V_2(\alpha)\}$

Here the parametric representation of a fuzzy valued function $: [a, b] \to \mathscr{R}_{\mathscr{F}}$ is expressed by $[f(t)]_\alpha = [f_1(t, \alpha), f_2(t, \alpha)]$, $t \in [a, b]$, $\alpha \in [0, 1]$.

Definition 6 (generalized Hukuhara derivative for first order [20]). The generalized Hukuhara derivative of a fuzzy valued function $f: (a, b) \to \mathscr{R}_{\mathscr{F}}$ at t_0 is defined as

$$f'(t_0) = \lim_{h \to 0} \frac{f(t_0 + h) \ominus_{\text{gH}} f(t_0)}{h}. \tag{2}$$

If $f'(t_0) \in \mathscr{R}_{\mathscr{F}}$ satisfying (2) exists, we say that f is generalized Hukuhara differentiable at t_0.

Also we say that (t) is (i)-gH differentiable at t_0 if

$$[f'(t_0)]_\alpha = [f_1'(t_0, \alpha), f_2'(t_0, \alpha)], \tag{3}$$

and $f(t)$ is (ii)-gH differentiable at t_0 if

$$[f'(t_0)]_\alpha = [f_2'(t_0, \alpha), f_1'(t_0, \alpha)]. \tag{4}$$

Definition 7 (see [6]). For arbitrary $u = (u_1, u_2)$ and V = $(V_1, V_2) \in E_1$, the quantity

$$D(u, v) = \left(\int_0^1 (u_1 - v_1)^2 + \int_0^1 (u_2 - v_2)^2 \right)^{1/2} \tag{5}$$

is the distance between fuzzy numbers u and V.

Definition 8 (triangular fuzzy number). A triangular fuzzy number (TFN) denoted by $\tilde{A}$ is defined as (a, b, c) where the membership function

$$\mu_{\tilde{A}}(x) = \begin{cases} 0, & x \leq a, \\ \dfrac{x-a}{b-a}, & a \leq x \leq b, \\ 1, & x = b, \\ \dfrac{c-x}{c-b}, & b \leq x \leq c, \\ 0, & x \geq c. \end{cases} \tag{6}$$

Definition 9 (α-cut of a fuzzy set $\tilde{A}$). The α-cut of $\tilde{A} = (a, b, c)$ is given by

$$A_\alpha = [a + \alpha(b - a), c - \alpha(c - b)], \quad \forall \alpha \in [0, 1]. \tag{7}$$

Definition 10 (fuzzy ordinary differential equation (FODE)). Consider a simple 1st-order linear ordinary differential equation as follows:

$$\frac{dx}{dt} = kx + x_0 \quad \text{with initial condition } x(t_0) = \gamma. \tag{8}$$

The above ordinary differential equation is called fuzzy ordinary differential equation if any one of the following three cases holds:

- Only γ is a fuzzy number (Type-I).
- Only k is a fuzzy number (Type-II).
- Both k and γ are fuzzy numbers (Type-III)

EXACT SOLUTION OF FUZZY DIFFERENTIAL EQUATION

Consider the fuzzy initial value problem

$$y'(t) = f(t, y(t)), \quad t \in I = [0, T] \text{ with } y(0) = y_0, \tag{9}$$

where f is a continuous mapping from $R_+ \times R$ into R and $y_0 \in E$ with r-level sets

$$[y_0]_r = [y_1(0; \alpha), y_2(0; \alpha)], \quad \alpha \in (0, 1]. \tag{10}$$

We write $(t, y) = [f_1(t, y), f_2(t, y)]$ and $f_1(t, y) = F[t, y_1, y_2]$, $f_2(t, y) = G[t, y_1, y_2]$.

Because of $y'(t) = f(t, y)$ we have the following.

When (t, y) is (i)-gH differentiable

$$y_1'(t, \alpha) = F[t; y_1(t; \alpha), y_2(t; \alpha)],$$
$$y_2'(t, \alpha) = G[t; y_1(t; \alpha), y_2(t; \alpha)]. \tag{11}$$

When (t, y) is (ii)-gH differentiable

$$y_2'(t,\alpha) = F\left[t; y_1(t;\alpha), y_2(t;\alpha)\right],$$
$$y_1'(t,\alpha) = G\left[t; y_1(t;\alpha), y_2(t;\alpha)\right], \tag{12}$$

where, by using extension principle, we have the membership function

$$f(t; y(t))(s) = \text{Sup}\left\{y(t)(\tau) \setminus s = f(t,\tau)\right\}, \ s \in R. \tag{13}$$

So fuzzy number is $(t; y(t))$. From this it follows that

$$[f(t; y(t))]_\alpha = [f_1(t, y(t);\alpha), f_2(t, y(t);\alpha)], \quad \alpha \in [0;1], \tag{14}$$

where

$$f_1(t, y(t);\alpha) = F\left[t; y_1(t;\alpha), y_2(t;\alpha)\right]$$
$$= \min\left\{f(t,u) \setminus u \in \left[y_1(t;\alpha), y_2(t;\alpha)\right]\right\},$$
$$f_2(t, y(t);\alpha) = G\left[t; y_1(t;\alpha), y_2(t;\alpha)\right]$$
$$= \max\left\{f(t,u) \setminus u \in \left[y_1(t;\alpha), y_2(t;\alpha)\right]\right\}. \tag{15}$$

Note. (1) Both cases ((i)-gH and (ii)-gH) can be applied to a FDE for finding exact solution.

(2) After taking α-cut of the given FDE, it transforms to system of ordinary differential equation.

NUMERICAL SOLUTION OF FUZZY DIFFERENTIAL EQUATION

Runge-Kutta-Fehlberg Method for Ordinary (Crisp) Differential Equation

Consider the initial value problem $y'(t) = (t, y(t))$; $y(t_0)=y_0$.

The Runge-Kutta-Fehlberg method (denoted as RKF45) is one way to try to resolve this problem.

The problem is to solve the initial value problem in above equation by means of Runge-Kutta methods of order 4 and order 5.

First we need some definitions:

$$k_1 = hf(t_i, y_i),$$
$$k_2 = hf\left(t_i + \frac{1}{4}h, y_i + \frac{1}{4}k_1\right),$$
$$k_3 = hf\left(t_i + \frac{3}{8}h, y_i + \frac{3}{32}k_1 + \frac{9}{32}k_2\right),$$
$$k_4 = hf\left(t_i + \frac{12}{13}h, y_i + \frac{1932}{2197}k_1 - \frac{7200}{2197}k_2 + \frac{7296}{2197}k_3\right),$$
$$k_5 = hf\left(t_i + h, y_i + \frac{439}{216}k_1 - 8k_2 + \frac{3680}{513}k_3 - \frac{845}{4104}k_4\right),$$
$$k_6 = hf\left(t_i + h, y_i - \frac{8}{27}k_1 + 2k_2 - \frac{3544}{2565}k_3 + \frac{1859}{4104}k_4 - \frac{11}{40}k_5\right). \tag{16}$$

Then an approximation to the solution of initial value problem is made using Runge-Kutta method of order 4:

$$y_{i+1} = y_i + \frac{25}{216}k_1 + \frac{1408}{2565}k_3 + \frac{2197}{4101}k_4 - \frac{1}{5}k_5. \tag{17}$$

A better value for the solution is determined using a RungeKutta method of order 5:

$$z_{i+1} = y_i + \frac{16}{135}k_1 + \frac{6656}{12{,}825}k_3 + \frac{28{,}561}{56{,}430}k_4 - \frac{9}{50}k_5 + \frac{2}{55}k_6. \tag{18}$$

The optimal step size sh can be determined by multiplying the scalar s times the step size h. The scalar s is

$$s = \left(\frac{\epsilon h}{2\left|z_{i+1} - y_{i+1}\right|}\right)^{1/4}$$
$$= 0.0840896\left(\frac{\epsilon h}{\left|z_{i+1} - y_{i+1}\right|}\right)^{1/4}, \tag{19}$$

where ϵ is the specified error control tolerance.

Note that RK4 requires 4 function evaluations and RK5 requires 6 evaluations, that is, 10 for RK4 and RK5. Fehlberg devised a method to get RK4 and RK5 results using only 6 function evaluations by using some of K values in both methods.

Runge-Kutta-Fehlberg Method for Solving Fuzzy Differential Equations

Let $Y = [Y_1, Y_2]$ be the exact solution and let $y = [y_1, y_2]$ be the approximated solution of the fuzzy initial value problem.

Let $[(t)]_\alpha = [Y_1(t,\alpha), Y_2(t,\alpha)]$, $[y(t)]_r = [y_1(t,\alpha), y_2(t,\alpha)]$.

Throughout this argument, the value of r is fixed. Then the exact and approximated solution at t_n are, respectively, denoted by

$$[Y(t_n)]_\alpha = [Y_1(t_n,\alpha), Y_2(t_n,\alpha)],$$
$$[y(t_n)]_\alpha = [y_1(t_n,\alpha), y_2(t_n,\alpha)]. \tag{20}$$

The grid points at which the solution is calculated are $h = (T - t_0)/N$, $t_i = t_0 + ih$, $0 \le i \le N$.

Then we obtained

$$y_1(t_{n+1},\alpha) = y_1(t_n,\alpha) + \frac{16}{135}K_1 + \frac{6656}{12{,}825}K_3 + \frac{28{,}561}{56{,}430}K_4 - \frac{9}{50}K_5 + \frac{2}{55}K_6, \tag{21}$$

where

$$K_1 = hF(t_n, y_1(t_n,\alpha), y_2(t_n,\alpha)),$$
$$K_2 = hF\left(t_n + \frac{1}{4}h, y_1(t_n,\alpha) + \frac{1}{4}K_1, y_2(t_n,\alpha) + \frac{1}{4}K_1\right),$$
$$K_3 = hF\left(t_n + \frac{3}{8}h, y_1(t_n,\alpha) + \frac{3}{32}K_1 + \frac{9}{32}K_2, y_2(t_n,\alpha) + \frac{3}{32}K_1 + \frac{9}{32}K_2\right),$$
$$K_4 = hF\left(t_n + \frac{12}{13}h, y_1(t_n,\alpha) + \frac{1932}{2197}K_1 - \frac{7200}{2197}K_2 + \frac{7296}{2197}K_3, y_2'(t_n,\alpha) + \frac{1932}{2197}K_1 - \frac{7200}{2197}K_2 + \frac{7296}{2197}K_3\right),$$

$$K_5 = hF\Big(t_n + h, y_1(t_n,\alpha) + \frac{439}{216}K_1 - 8K_2 + \frac{3680}{513}K_3 - \frac{845}{4104}K_4, y_2(t_n,\alpha) + \frac{439}{216}K_1 - 8K_2 + \frac{3680}{513}K_3 - \frac{845}{4104}K_4\Big),$$
$$K_6 = hF\Big(t_n + h, y_1(t_n,\alpha) - \frac{8}{27}K_1 + 2K_2 - \frac{3544}{2565}K_3 + \frac{1859}{4104}K_4 - \frac{11}{40}K_5, y_2(t_n,\alpha) - \frac{8}{27}K_1 + 2K_2 - \frac{3544}{2565}K_3 + \frac{1859}{4104}K_4 - \frac{11}{40}K_5\Big), \quad (22)$$

$$y_2(t_{n+1},\alpha) = y_2(t_n,\alpha) + \frac{16}{135}L_1 + \frac{6656}{12{,}825}L_3 + \frac{28{,}561}{56{,}430}L_4 - \frac{9}{50}L_5 + \frac{2}{55}L_6, \quad (23)$$

where

$$L_1 = hG(t_n, y_1(t_n,\alpha), y_2(t_n,\alpha)),$$
$$L_2 = hG\Big(t_n + \frac{1}{4}h, y_1(t_n,\alpha) + \frac{1}{4}L_1, y_2(t_n,\alpha) + \frac{1}{4}L_1\Big),$$
$$L_3 = hG\Big(t_n + \frac{3}{8}h, y_1(t_n,\alpha) + \frac{3}{32}L_1 + \frac{9}{32}L_2, y_2(t_n,\alpha) + \frac{3}{32}L_1 + \frac{9}{32}L_2\Big),$$
$$L_4 = hG\Big(t_n + \frac{12}{13}h, y_1(t_n,\alpha) + \frac{1932}{2197}L_1 - \frac{7200}{2197}L_2 + \frac{7296}{2197}L_3, y_2(t_n,\alpha) + \frac{1932}{2197}L_1 - \frac{7200}{2197}L_2 + \frac{7296}{2197}L_3\Big),$$
$$L_5 = hG\Big(t_n + h, y_1(t_n,\alpha) + \frac{439}{216}L_1 - 8L_2 + \frac{3680}{513}L_3 - \frac{845}{4104}L_4, y_2(t_n,\alpha) + \frac{439}{216}L_1 - 8L_2 + \frac{3680}{513}L_3 - \frac{845}{4104}L_4\Big),$$
$$L_6 = hG\Big(t_n + h, y_1(t_n,\alpha) - \frac{8}{27}L_1 + 2L_2 - \frac{3544}{2565}L_3 + \frac{1859}{4104}L_4 - \frac{11}{40}L_5, y_2(t_n,\alpha) - \frac{8}{27}L_1 + 2L_2 - \frac{3544}{2565}L_3 + \frac{1859}{4104}L_4 - \frac{11}{40}L_5\Big). \quad (24)$$

Convergence of Fuzzy Runge-Kutta-Fehlberg Method

The solution is calculated by grid points at $a = t_0 \le t_1 \le \cdots \le t_N = b$ and $h = (b - a)/N = t_{n+1} - t_n$.

Therefore, we have

$$Y_1(t_{n+1},\alpha) = Y_1(t_n,\alpha) + F(t_n, Y_1(t_n,\alpha), Y_2(t_n,\alpha)),$$
$$Y_2(t_{n+1},\alpha) = Y_2(t_n,\alpha) + G(t_n, Y_1(t_n,\alpha), Y_2(t_n,\alpha)),$$
$$y_1(t_{n+1},\alpha) = y_1(t_n,\alpha) + F(t_n, y_1(t_n,\alpha), y_2(t_n,\alpha)),$$
$$y_2(t_{n+1},\alpha) = y_2(t_n,\alpha) + G(t_n, y_1(t_n,\alpha), y_2(t_n,\alpha)). \quad (25)$$

Clearly, $y_1(t,\alpha)$ and $y_2(t,\alpha)$ converge to $Y_1(t,\alpha)$ and $Y_2(t,\alpha)$, respectively, whenever $h \to 0$; that is,

$$\lim_{h\to 0} y_1(t,\alpha) = Y_1(t,\alpha),$$
$$\lim_{h\to 0} y_2(t,\alpha) = Y_2(t,\alpha). \quad (26)$$

***Proof*.** Before we go to the main proof we need to know some results.

Lemma 11. Let the sequence of numbers $\{W\}_{n=0}^{N}$ satisfy

$$|W_{n+1}| \le A|W_n| + B, \quad 0 \le n \le N-1, \quad (27)$$

for some given positive constants A and B. Then

$$|W_n| \le A^n|W_0| + B\frac{A^n - 1}{A - 1}, \quad 0 \le n \le N. \quad (28)$$

Lemma 12. Let the sequence of numbers $\{W\}_{n=0}^{N}$ *and* $\{V\}_{n=0}^{N}$ satisfy

$$|W_{n+1}| \le |W_n| + A\max\{|W_n|, |V_n|\} + B,$$
$$|V_{n+1}| \le |V_n| + A\max\{|W_n|, |V_n|\} + B, \quad (29)$$

for some given positive constants A and B, and denote

$$U_n = |W_n| + |V_n|, \quad 0 \le n \le N. \quad (30)$$

Then

$$U_n \le \overline{A}^n U_0 + \overline{B}\frac{\overline{A}^n - 1}{\overline{A} - 1}, \quad 0 \le n \le N, \quad (31)$$

where $\overline{A} = 1 + 2A$ *and* $\overline{B} = 2B$.

Let (t, u, V) and $G(t, u, V)$ be obtained by substituting $[y_1(t,\alpha), y_2(t,\alpha)] = [u, V]$ in (21) and (23); that is,

$$F(t,u,v) = \frac{16}{135}K_1(t,u,v) + \frac{6656}{12{,}825}K_3(t,u,v) + \frac{28{,}561}{56{,}430}K_4(t,u,v) - \frac{9}{50}K_5(t,u,v) + \frac{2}{55}K_6(t,u,v),$$
$$G(t,u,v) = \frac{16}{135}L_1(t,u,v) + \frac{6656}{12{,}825}L_3(t,u,v) + \frac{28{,}561}{56{,}430}L_4(t,u,v) - \frac{9}{50}L_5(t,u,v) + \frac{2}{55}L_6(t,u,v). \quad (32)$$

The domain where F and G are defined is as

$$H = \{(t,u,v) \mid 0 \le t \le T, -\infty < v < \infty, -\infty < u \le v\}. \quad (33)$$

Theorem 13. Let (t, u, V) and $G(t, u, V)$ belong to $C^{p-1}(K)$ and let the partial derivative of F and G be bounded over K. Then for arbitrary fixed $0 \le \alpha \le 1$, the numerical solution of (9), $[y_1(t,\alpha), y_2(t,\alpha)]$ converges to the exact solution $[Y_1(t,\alpha), Y_2(t,\alpha)]$.

Proof (see [46]). By using Taylor's theorem we get

$$Y_1(t_{n+1},\alpha) = Y_1(t_n,\alpha) + hF(t_n, Y_1(t_n,\alpha), Y_2(t_n,\alpha)) + \frac{h^{p+1}}{(p+1)!}Y_1^{(p+1)}(\xi_{n,1}),$$
$$Y_2(t_{n+1},\alpha) = Y_2(t_n,\alpha) + hG(t_n, Y_1(t_n,\alpha), Y_2(t_n,\alpha)) + \frac{h^{p+1}}{(p+1)!}Y_2^{(p+1)}(\xi_{n,2}), \quad (34)$$

where $\xi_{n,1}, \xi_{n,2} \in (t_n, t_{n+1})$.

Now if we denote

$$W_n = Y_1(t_n, \alpha) - y_1(t_n, \alpha),$$

$$V_n = Y_2(t_n, \alpha) - y_2(t_n, \alpha), \quad (35)$$

then the above two expressions converted to

$$W_{n+1} = W_n + h\{F(t_n, Y_1(t_n,\alpha), Y_2(t_n,\alpha)) - F(t_n, y_1(t_n,\alpha), y_2(t_n,\alpha))\} + \frac{h^{p+1}}{(p+1)!} \cdot Y_1^{(p+1)}(\xi_{n,1}),$$

$$V_{n+1} = V_n + h\{G(t_n, Y_1(t_n,\alpha), Y_2(t_n,\alpha)) - G(t_n, y_1(t_n,\alpha), y_2(t_n,\alpha))\} + \frac{h^{p+1}}{(p+1)!} \cdot Y_2^{(p+1)}(\xi_{n,2}). \quad (36)$$

Hence we can write

$$|W_{n+1}| \le |W_n| + 2Lh \max\{|W_n|, |V_n|\} + \frac{h^{p+1}}{(p+1)!}M,$$

$$|V_{n+1}| \le |V_n| + 2Lh \max\{|W_n|, |V_n|\} + \frac{h^{p+1}}{(p+1)!}M, \quad (37)$$

where $M = \max\{\max|Y_1^{(p+1)}(t;\alpha)|, \max|Y_2^{(p+1)}(t;\alpha)|\}$ for $t \in [0, T]$ and $L>0$ is a bound for the partial derivative of F and G.

Therefore we can write

$$|W_n| \le (1+4Lh)^n |U_0| + \frac{2h^{p+1}}{(p+1)!}M\frac{(1+4Lh)^n - 1}{4Lh},$$

$$|V_n| \le (1+4Lh)^n |U_0| + \frac{2h^{p+1}}{(p+1)!}M\frac{(1+4Lh)^n - 1}{4Lh}, \quad (38)$$

where $|U_0| = |W_0| + |V_0|$.

In particular,

$$|W_N| \le (1+4Lh)^N |U_0| + \frac{2h^{p+1}}{(p+1)!}M\frac{(1+4Lh)^{T/h} - 1}{4Lh},$$

$$|V_N| \le (1+4Lh)^N |U_0| + \frac{2h^{p+1}}{(p+1)!}M\frac{(1+4Lh)^{T/h} - 1}{4Lh}. \quad (39)$$

Since $W_0 = V_0 = 0$, we have

$$|W_N| \le M\frac{e^{4LT} - 1}{2L(p+1)!}h^p,$$

$$|V_N| \le M\frac{e^{4LT} - 1}{2L(p+1)!}h^p. \quad (40)$$

Thus, if $h \to 0$, we get $W_N \to 0$ and $V_N \to 0$, which completes the proof.

Algorithm for Finding the Numerical Solution

Step 1. $(t, y_1, y_2) \leftarrow$ "Function to be supplied"

$(t, y_1, y_2) \leftarrow$ "Function to be supplied"

Step 2. Read (0), $y_1(0)$, $y_2(0)$, h, limit.

Step 3. For $i = 0(1)$ limit

$K_1 \leftarrow hF(t_i, y_1(t_i, r), y_2(t_i, r))$

$K_2 \leftarrow h \cdot F(t_i + (1/4)h, y_1(t_i, r) + (1/4)K_1, y_2(t_i, r) + (1/4)K_1)$

$K_3 \leftarrow h \cdot F(t_i + (3/8)h, y_1(t_i, r) + (3/32)K_1 + (9/32)K_2, y_2(t_i, r) + (3/32)K_1 + (9/32)K_2)$

$K_4 \leftarrow h \cdot F(t_i + (12/13)h, y_1(t_i, r) + (1932/2197)K_1 - (7200/2197)K_2 + (7296/2197)K_3, y_2(t_i, r) + (1932/2197)K_1 - (7200/2197)K_2 + (7296/2197)K_3)$

$K_5 \leftarrow hF(t_i + h, y_1(t_i, r) + (439/216)K_1 - 8K_2 + (3680/513)K_3 - (845/4104)K_4, y_2(t_i, r) + (439/216)K_1 - 8K_2 + (3680/513)K_3 - (845/4104)K_4)$

$K_6 \leftarrow hF(t_i + h, y_1(t_i, r) - (8/27)K_1 + 2K_2 - (3544/2565)K_3 + (1859/4104)K_4 - (11/40)K_5, y_2(t_i, r) - (8/27)K_1 + 2K_2 - (3544/2565)K_3 + (1859/4104)K_4 - (11/40)K_5)$

$L_1 \leftarrow h \cdot G(t_i, y_1(t_i, r), y_2(t_i, r))$

$L_2 \leftarrow hG(t_i + (1/4)h, y_1(t_i, r) + (1/4)L_1, y_2(t_i, r) + (1/4)L_1)$

$L_3 \leftarrow hG(t_i + (3/8)h, y_1(t_i, r) + (3/32)L_1 + (9/32)L_2, y_2(t_i, r) + (3/32)L_1 + (9/32)L_2)$

$L_4 \leftarrow hG(t_i + (12/13)h, y_1(t_i, r) + (1932/2197)L_1 - (7200/2197)L_2 + (7296/2197)L_3, y_2(t_i, r) + (1932/2197)L_1 - (7200/2197)L_2 + (7296/2197)L_3)$

$L_5 \leftarrow hG(t_i + h, y_1(t_i, r) + (439/216)L_1 - 8L_2 + (3680/513)L_3 - (845/4104)L_4, y_2(t_i, r) + (439/216)L_1 - 8L_2 + (3680/513)L_3 - (845/4104)L_4)$

$L_6 \leftarrow hG(t_i + h, y_1(t_i, r) - (8/27)L_1 + 2L_2 - (3544/2565)L_3 + (1859/4104)L_4 - (11/40)L_5, y_2(t_i, r) - (8/27)L_1 + 2L_2 - (3544/2565)L_3 + (1859/4104)L_4 - (11/40)L_5)$

Step 4.

$y_1(t_{i+1}, r) = y_1(t_i, r) + (16/135)K_1 + (6656/12{,}825)K_3 + (28{,}561/56{,}430)K_4 - (9/50)K_5 + (2/55)K_6$

Step 5.

$y_2(t_{i+1}, r) = y_2(t_i, r) + (16/135)L_1 + (6656/12{,}825)L_3 + (28{,}561/56{,}430)L_4 - (9/50)L_5 + (2/55)L_6$

Step 6. $t_{i+1} = t_i + h$. Write $y_1(t_{i+1}, r)$, $y_2(t_{i+1}, r)$, t_{i+1}.

Step 7. Next i

Step 8. End.

NUMERICAL EXAMPLE

Example. Solve $y' = -y + t + 1$ with initial condition (0) = (0.96, 1, 1.01). Then find the solution at $t = 0.1$.

Solution. For (i)-gH differentiable case the exact solution is

$$y_1(r,t) = t + (0.96 + 0.04r)e^{-t},$$

$$y_2(r,t) = t + (1.01 - 0.01r)e^{-t} \quad (41)$$

and for (ii)-gH differentiable case the exact solution is

$$y_1(r,t) = 1 + t + (-0.04 + 0.04r)e^{t},$$

$$y_2(r,t) = 1 + t + (0.01 - 0.01r)e^{t}. \quad (42)$$

Remark 14. From Figure 1 and Table 1 we conclude that the lower exact solution ((i)-gH case) is approximately equal to the numerical solution when we take the step length h = 0.01 (for h = 0.001 is nearly equal), whereas the lower exact solution ((ii)-gH case) is approximately equal to the numerical solution when we take the step length $h = 0.1$.

Remark 15. From Figure 2 and Table 1 we conclude that the upper exact solution ((i)-gH case) is approximately equal to the numerical solution when we take the step length $h = 0.001$ (for $h = 0.01$ is nearly equal), whereas the upper exact solution ((ii)-gH case) is approximately equal to the numerical solution when we take the step length $h = 0.1$.

APPLICATION

Problem. A tank initially contains 300 gals of brine which has dissolved in c lbs of salt. Coming into the tank at 3 gals/min is brine with concentration k lbs salt/gals and the well stirred mixture leaves at the rate 3 gals/min. Let (x)lbs be the salt in the tank at any time $t \geq 0$. Then $d(x)/dx + (1/100)y(x) = k$, $x \in [0, 0.5]$ with $y(0) = c$, if the initial condition is being modeled as fuzzy numbers $c = (1, 2, 3)$ and $k = (1, 2, 4)$. Find solution at $x = 0.4$.

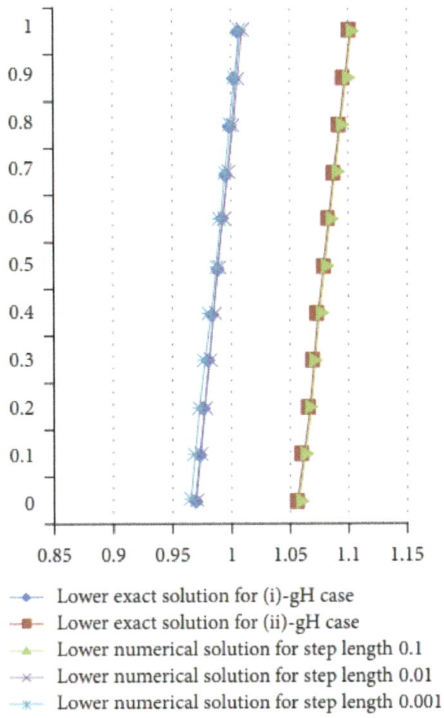

Figure 1: Comparison of lower exact solutions and numerical solution for different step lengths at $t = 0.1$

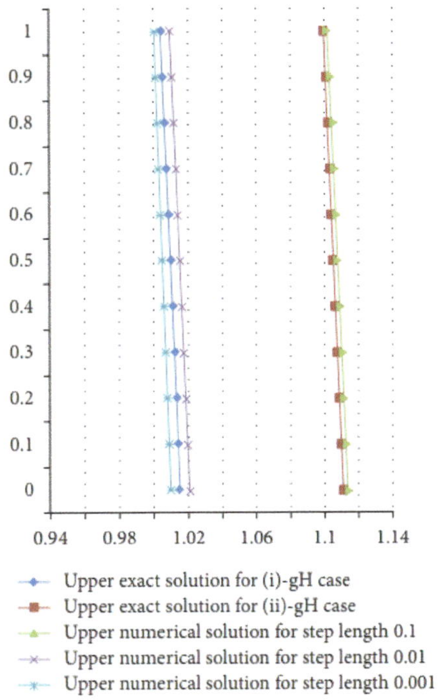

Figure 2: Comparison of upper exact solutions and numerical solution for different step lengths at $t = 0.1$.

Table 1: Comparison of the exact solutions and numerical solutions for different step lengths at $t = 0.1$

r	Exact solution for (i)-gH differentiable case		Exact solution for (ii)-gH differentiable case		Numerical solution for $h = 0.1$ by RKF method		Numerical solution for $h = 0.01$ by RKF method		Numerical solution for $h = 0.001$ by RKF method	
	Y_1	Y_2	Y_1	Y_2	y_1	y_2	y_1	y_2	y_1	y_2
0	0.9686	1.0139	1.0558	1.1111	1.0597	1.1149	0.9696	1.0201	0.9610	1.0110
0.1	0.9723	1.0130	1.0602	1.1099	1.0642	1.1138	0.9737	1.0191	0.9650	1.0100
0.2	0.9759	1.0121	1.0646	1.1088	1.0686	1.1127	0.9777	1.0181	0.9690	1.0090
0.3	0.9795	1.0112	1.0691	1.1077	1.0730	1.1116	0.9818	1.0171	0.9730	1.0080
0.4	0.9831	1.0103	1.0735	1.1066	1.0774	1.1105	0.9858	1.0161	0.9770	1.0070
0.5	0.9867	1.0094	1.0779	1.1055	1.0818	1.1094	0.9898	1.0151	0.9810	1.0060
0.6	0.9904	1.0085	1.0823	1.1044	1.0862	1.1083	0.9939	1.0141	0.9850	1.0050
0.7	0.9940	1.0076	1.0867	1.1033	1.0906	1.1072	0.9979	1.0131	0.9890	1.0040
0.8	0.9976	1.0066	1.0912	1.1022	1.0951	1.1061	1.0020	1.0121	0.9930	1.0030
0.9	1.0012	1.0057	1.0956	1.1011	1.0995	1.1050	1.0060	1.0110	0.9970	1.0020
1	1.0048	1.0048	1.1000	1.1000	1.1039	1.1039	1.0100	1.0100	1.0010	1.0010

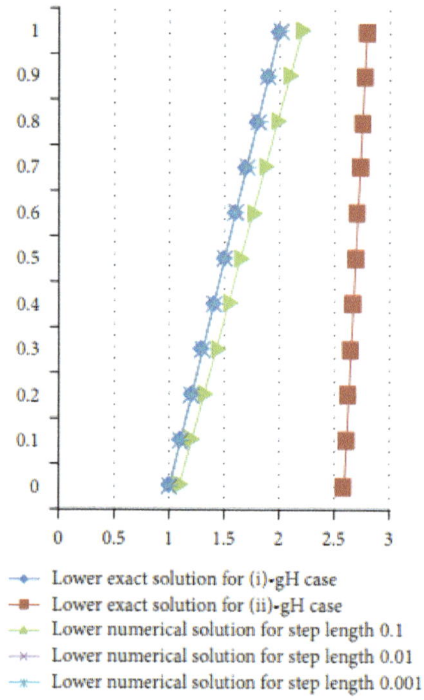

Figure 3: Comparison of lower exact solutions and numerical solution for different step lengths at $t = 0.4$

Solution. For (i)-gH differentiable case the exact solution is

$$y_1(x,\alpha) = \frac{(1+\alpha)}{100}\left(1 + 99e^{-(1/100)x}\right),$$

$$y_2(x,\alpha) = \frac{(2-\alpha)}{50} + \frac{(148-49\alpha)}{50}e^{-(1/100)x}. \quad (43)$$

For (ii)-gH differentiable case the exact solution is

$$\begin{aligned} y_1(x,\alpha) &= (149 - 149\alpha)\,e^{(1/100)x} \\ &\quad + (-248 + 50\alpha)\,e^{-(1/100)x} \\ &\quad + (100 + 100\alpha), \\ y_2(x,\alpha) &= -(149 - 149\alpha)\,e^{(1/100)x} \\ &\quad + (-248 + 50\alpha)\,e^{-(1/100)x} \\ &\quad + (400 - 200\alpha). \end{aligned} \quad (44)$$

Remark 16. From Figure 3 and Table 2 we conclude that the lower exact solution ((i)-gH case) is approximately equal to the numerical solution when we take the step length $h = 0.001$ (for $h = 0.01$ is nearly equal), whereas the lower exact solution ((ii)-gH case) is not equal to any numerical solution.

Remark 17. From Figure 4 and Table 2 we conclude that the upper exact solution ((i)-gH case) is approximately equal to the numerical solution when we take the step length of $h = 0.01$ and $h = 0.001$. For $h = 0.1$ it is nearly equal, whereas the upper exact solution ((ii)-gH case) is not equal to any numerical solution.

CONCLUSION

In this paper we applied Runge-Kutta-Fehlberg method for finding the numerical solution of first-order linear differential equation in fuzzy environment. The numerical solution is compared with the exact solution ((i)-gH and (ii)-gH both cases). The results presented in the contribution show that Runge-Kutta-Fehlberg method is a powerful mathematical tool for solving first-order linear differential equation in fuzzy environment. The convergence of Runge-Kutta-Fehlberg method has been discussed. The process method is applied to a mechanical problem in fuzzy environment which shows that it is a promising method to solve the said types of differential equation. In the future we can apply these methods for solving higher order linear and nonlinear differential equation in fuzzy environment.

Table 2: Comparison of the exact solutions and numerical solutions for different step lengths at $x = 0.4$

α	Exact solution for (i)-gH differentiable case		Exact solution for (ii)-gH differentiable case		Numerical solution for $h = 0.1$ by RKF method		Numerical solution for $h = 0.01$ by RKF method		Numerical solution for $h = 0.001$ by RKF method	
	Y_1	Y_2	Y_1	Y_2	y_1	y_2	y_1	y_2	y_1	y_2
0	0.9960	2.9882	2.5872	3.3928	1.1039	3.3117	1.0100	3.0301	1.0010	3.0030
0.1	1.0957	2.8886	2.6075	3.3326	1.2143	3.2013	1.1110	2.9291	1.1011	2.9029
0.2	1.1953	2.7890	2.6279	3.2723	1.3247	3.0909	1.2120	2.8281	1.2012	2.8028
0.3	1.2949	2.6894	2.6482	3.2121	1.4351	2.9805	1.3130	2.7271	1.3013	2.7027
0.4	1.3945	2.5897	2.6685	3.1519	1.5455	2.8701	1.4141	2.6261	1.4014	2.6026
0.5	1.4941	2.4901	2.6888	3.0916	1.6558	2.7597	1.5151	2.5251	1.5015	2.5025
0.6	1.5937	2.3905	2.7091	3.0314	1.7662	2.6493	1.6161	2.4241	1.6016	2.4024
0.7	1.6933	2.2909	2.7295	2.9711	1.8766	2.5390	1.7171	2.3231	1.7017	2.3023
0.8	1.7929	2.1913	2.7498	2.9109	1.9870	2.4286	1.8181	2.2221	1.8018	2.2022
0.9	1.8925	2.0917	2.7701	2.8507	2.0974	2.3182	1.9191	2.1211	1.9019	2.1021
1	1.9921	1.9921	2.7904	2.7904	2.2078	2.2078	2.0201	2.0201	2.0020	2.0020

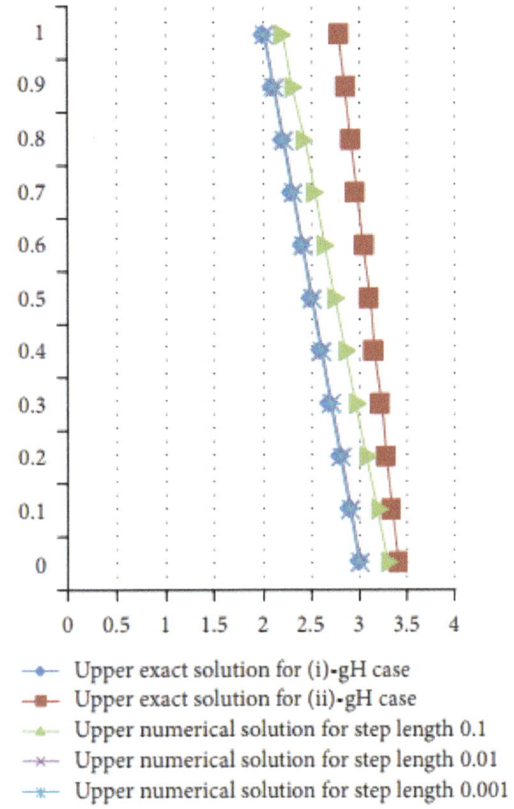

Figure 4: Comparison of upper exact solutions and numerical solution for different step lengths at $t = 0.4$.

REFERENCES

1. A. Kandel and W. J. Byatt, "Fuzzy differential equations," in Proceedings of the International Conference Cybernetics and Society, pp. 1213–1216, Tokyo, Japan, 1978.
2. E. Hüllermeier, "An approach to modelling and simulation of uncertain dynamical systems,"International Journal of Uncertainty, Fuzziness and Knowledge-Based Systems, vol. 5, pp. 117–137, 1997.
3. P. Diamond, "Time-dependent differential inclusions, cocycle attractors and fuzzy differential equations," IEEE Transactions on Fuzzy Systems, vol. 7, no. 6, pp. 734–740, 1999.
4. P. Diamond, "Stability and periodicity in fuzzy differential equations," IEEE Transactions on Fuzzy Systems, vol. 8, no. 5, pp. 583–590, 2000.
5. P. Diamond and P. Watson, "Regularity of solution sets for differential inclusions quasi-concave in a parameter," Applied Mathematics Letters, vol. 13, no. 1, pp. 31–35, 2000.
6. B. Bede and S. G. Gal, "Generalizations of the differentiability of fuzzy-number-valued functions with applications to fuzzy differential equations," Fuzzy Sets and Systems, vol. 151, no. 3, pp. 581–599, 2005. ·
7. B. Bede, I. J. Rudas, and A. L. Bencsik, "First order linear fuzzy differential equations under generalized differentiability," Information Sciences, vol. 177, no. 7, pp. 1648–1662, 2007.
8. M. Chen, C. Wu, X. Xue, and G. Liu, "On fuzzy boundary value problems," Information Sciences, vol. 178, no. 7, pp. 1877–1892, 2008. ·
9. A. Setia, Y. Liu, and A. S. Vatsala, "Numerical solution of fractional integro-differential equations with nonlocal boundary conditions," Journal of Fractional Calculus and Applications, vol. 5, no. 2, pp. 155–165, 2014.

10. Y. Liu, "An efficient algorithm for solving differential equations to facilitate modeling and simulation of aerospace systems," SAE Technical Paper 2015-01-2402, 2015.

11. A. Setia, Y. Liu, and A. S. Vatsala, "Solution of linear fractional Fredholm integro-differential equation by using second kind Chebyshev wavelet," in Proceedings of the 11th International Conference on Information Technology (ITNG '14), pp. 465–469, Las Vegas, Nev, USA, April 2014.

12. M. Ma, M. Friedman, and A. Kandel, "Numerical solutions of fuzzy differential equations," Fuzzy Sets and Systems, vol. 105, no. 1, pp. 133–138, 1999.

13. T. Allahviranloo, N. Ahmady, and E. Ahmady, "Two step method for fuzzy differential equations,"International Mathematical Forum, vol. 1, no. 17–20, pp. 823–832, 2006.

14. T. Allahviranloo, N. Ahmady, and E. Ahmady, "Numerical solution of fuzzy differential equations by predictor-corrector method," Information Sciences, vol. 177, no. 7, pp. 1633–1647, 2007.

15. T. Allahviranloo, E. Ahmady, and N. Ahmady, "Nth-order fuzzy linear differential equations,"Information Sciences, vol. 178, pp. 1309–1324, 2008.

16. S. Pederson and M. Sambandham, "Numerical solution of hybrid fuzzy differential equation IVPs by a characterization theorem," Information Sciences, vol. 179, no. 3, pp. 319–328, 2009.

17. S. Effati and M. Pakdaman, "Artificial neural network approach for solving fuzzy differential equations," Information Sciences, vol. 180, no. 8, pp. 1434–1457, 2010.

18. C. Duraisamy and B. Usha, "Another approach to solution of fuzzy differential equations by modified Euler's method," in Proceedings of the International Conference on Communication and Computational Intelligence (INCOCCI '10), pp. 52–55, Kongu Engineering College, Erode, India, December 2010.

19. H. Saberi Najafi, F. Ramezani Sasemasi, S. Sabouri Roudkoli, and S. Fazeli Nodehi, "Comparison of two methods for solving fuzzy differential equations based on Euler method and Zadehs extension," The Journal of Mathematics and Computer Science, vol. 2, no. 2, pp. 295–306, 2011.

20. M. Rostami, M. Kianpour, and E. bashardoust, "A numerical algorithm for solving nonlinear fuzzy differential equations," The Journal of Mathematics and Computer Science, vol. 2, no. 4, pp. 667–671, 2011.

21. M. Sh. Dahaghin and M. M. Moghadam, "Analysis of a two-step method for numerical solution of fuzzy ordinary differential equations," Italian Journal of Pure and Applied Mathematics, vol. 27, pp. 333–340, 2010.

22. K. Batiha, "Numerical solutions of the multispecies predator-prey model by variational iteration method," Journal of Computer Science, vol. 3, no. 7, pp. 523–527, 2007.

23. M. Z. Ahmad and M. K. Hasan, "A new fuzzy version of Euler's method for solving differential equations with fuzzy initial values," Sains Malaysiana, vol. 40, no. 6, pp. 651–657, 2011.

24. V. Nirmala and S. Chenthur Pandian, "A method to improve the numerical solution of fuzzy initial value problems," International Journal of Mathematical Archive, vol. 3, no. 3, pp. 1231–1240, 2012.

25. M. Shafiee, S. Abbasbandy, and T. Allahviranloo, "Predictor-corrector method for nonlinear fuzzy volterra integral equations," Australian Journal of Basic and Applied Sciences, vol. 5, no. 12, pp. 2865–2874, 2011.

26. M. Ghanbari, "Solution of the first order linear fuzzy differential equations by some reliable methods,"Journal of Fuzzy Set Valued Analysis, vol. 2012, Article ID jfsva-00126, 20 pages, 2012.

27. H. Jafari, M. Saeidy, and D. Baleanu, "The variational iteration method for solving n-th order fuzzy differential equations," Central European Journal of Physics, vol. 10, no. 1, pp. 76–85, 2012.

28. S. Tapaswini and S. Chakraverty, "A new approach to fuzzy initial value problem by improved Euler method," Fuzzy Information and Engineering, vol. 4, no. 3, pp. 293–312, 2012. ·

29. M. A. Ahmed and F. S. Fadhel, "Solution of fuzzy initial value problems using Least square and Adomian decomposition method," Journal of Kufa for Mathematics and Computer, vol. 1, no. 4, pp. 49–60, 2011.

30. R. K. Saikia, "Solution of differential equation by Euler's method using fuzzy concept," International Journal of Computer Technology & Applications, vol. 3, no. 1, pp. 226–230, 2012.

31. R. Ezzati, F. Mokhtari, and M. Maghasedi, "Numerical solution of volterra-fredholm integral equations with the help of inverse and direct discrete fuzzy transforms and collocation technique," International Journal of Industrial Mathematics, vol. 4, no. 3, pp. 221–229, 2012.

32. L. Wang and S. Guo, "Adomian method for second-order fuzzy differential equation," World Academy of Science, Engineering and Technology, vol. 76, pp. 979–982, 2011.

33. O. S. Fard, "An iterative scheme for the solution of generalized system of linear fuzzy differential equations," World Applied Sciences Journal, vol. 7, no. 12, pp. 1597–1604, 2009.

34. S. Mehrkanoon, M. Suleiman, and Z. A. Majid, "Block method for numerical solution of fuzzy differential equations," International Mathematical Forum, vol. 4, no. 46, pp. 2269–2280, 2009.

35. B. Asady and M. Alavi, "Numerical method for solving nth-order linear fuzzy differential equations,"Advances in Fuzzy Sets and Systems, vol. 6, no. 2, pp. 95–106, 2010.

36. C. Duraisamy and B. Usha, "Numerical solution of fuzzy differential equations by Runge-Kutta method of order three," International Journal of Advanced Scientific and Technical Research, vol. 1, no. 1, pp. 1–13, 2011.

37. V. Nirmala and S. Chenthur Pandian, "Numerical solution of fuzzy differential equation by fourth order Runge-Kutta method with higher order derivative approximations," European Journal of Scientific

Research, vol. 62, no. 2, pp. 198–206, 2011.

38. T. Jayakumar, D. Maheskumar, and K. Kanagarajan, "Numerical solution to fuzzy differential equations by Runge Kutta method of order five," Applied Mathematical Sciences, vol. 6, no. 57–60, pp. 2989–3002, 2012.

39. B. Ghazanfari and A. Shakerami, "Numerical solutions of fuzzy differential equations by extended Runge-Kutta-like formulae of order 4," Fuzzy Sets and Systems, vol. 189, pp. 74–91, 2012.

40. K. Kanagarajan and M. Sambath, "Numerical solution of fuzzy differential equations by third order Runge-Kutta method," International Journal of Applied Mathematics and Computation, vol. 2, no. 4, pp. 1–8, 2010.

41. T. Jayakumar and K. Kanagarajan, "Numerical solution for hybrid fuzzy differential equations by Ruge-Kutta Fehlberg method," International Journal of Mathematical Analysis, vol. 6, no. 53-56, pp. 2619–2632, 2012. ·

42. Z. Akbarzadeh Ghanaie and M. Mohseni Moghadam, "Solving fuzzy differential equations by Runge-Kutta method," The Journal of Mathematics and Computer Science, vol. 2, no. 2, pp. 208–221, 2011.

43. M. Ghanbari, "Solution of the first order linear fuzzy differential equations by some reliable methods,"Journal of Fuzzy Set Valued Analysis, vol. 2012, Article ID jfsva-00126, 20 pages, 2012.

44. V. Nirmala and S. Chenthur Pandian, "New multi-step Runge-Kutta method for solving fuzzy differential equations," Mathematical Theory and Modeling, vol. 1, no. 3, pp. 16–22, 2011.

45. N. Saveetha and S. Chenthur Pandian, "Numerical solution of fuzzy hybrid differential equation by third order Runge Kutta Nystrom method," Mathematical Theory and Modeling, vol. 2, no. 4, pp. 8–17, 2012.

46. N. M. Deshmukh, "A new approach to solve Fuzzy differential equation by using third order Runge-Kutta method," ISSN No-2031-5063, Vol. 1, Issue 3, pp. 1–4, 2011.

47. C. Duraisamy and B. Usha, "Numerical solution of fuzzy differential equations by Runge-Kutta method of order four," European Journal of Scientific Research, vol. 67, no. 2, pp. 324–337, 2012.

48. T. Jayakumar and K. Kanagarajan, "Numerical solution for hybrid fuzzy system by Runge Kutta method of order five," Applied Mathematical Sciences, vol. 6, no. 72, pp. 3591–3606, 2012.

49. J. J. Buckley, T. Feuring, and Y. Hayashi, "Linear systems of first order ordinary differential equations: fuzzy initial conditions," Soft Computing, vol. 6, no. 6, pp. 415–421, 2002.

50. M. Oberguggenberger and S. Pittschmann, "Differential equations with fuzzy parameters,"Mathematical and Computer Modelling of Dynamical Systems, vol. 5, no. 3, pp. 181–202, 1999.

51. J. Casasnovas and F. Rossell, "Averaging fuzzy biopolymers," Fuzzy Sets and Systems, vol. 152, no. 1, pp. 139–158, 2005.

52. M. S. El Naschie, "From experimental quantum optics to quantum gravity via a fuzzy Kähler manifold,"Chaos, Solitons & Fractals, vol. 25, no. 5, pp. 969–977, 2005.

53. A. Bencsik, B. Bede, J. Tar, and J. Fodor, "Fuzzy differential equations in modeling hydraulic differential servo cylinders," in Proceedings of the 3rd Romanian-Hungarian Joint Symposium on Applied Computational Intelligence (SACI '06), Timisoara, Romania, 2006.

54. H. Zarei, A. V. Kamyad, and A. A. Heydari, "Fuzzy modeling and control of HIV infection,"Computational and Mathematical Methods in Medicine, vol. 2012, Article ID 893474, 17 pages, 2012.

55. G. L. Diniz, J. F. R. Fernandes, J. F. C. A. Meyer, and L. C. Barros, "A fuzzy Cauchy problem modelling the decay of the biochemical oxygen demand in water," in Proceedings of the Joint 9th IFSA World Congress and 20th NAFIPS International Conference, IEEE, Vancouver, Canada, July 2001.

56. M. Z. Ahmad and B. De Baets, A Predator-Prey Model with Fuzzy Initial Populations, IFSA-EUSFLAT, 2009.

57. L. C. Barros, R. C. Bassanezi, and P. A. Tonelli, "Fuzzy modelling in population dynamics," Ecological Modelling, vol. 128, no. 1, pp. 27–33, 2000.

58. B. Bede, I. J. Rudas, and J. Fodor, "Friction model by using fuzzy differential equations," in Proceedings of the 12th International Fuzzy Systems Association World Congress (IFSA '07), Cancun, Mexico, June 2007, vol. 4529 of Lecture Notes in Computer Science, pp. 23–32, Springer, Berlin, Germany, 2007.

59. S. P. Mondal, S. Banerjee, and T. K. Roy, "First order linear homogeneous ordinary differential equation in fuzzy environment," International Journal of Pure and Applied Sciences and Technology, vol. 14, no. 1, pp. 16–26, 2013.

60. S. P. Mondal and T. K. Roy, "First order linear non homogeneous ordinary differential equation in fuzzy environment," Mathematical theory and Modeling, vol. 3, no. 1, pp. 85–95, 2013.

61. S. P. Mondal and T. K. Roy, "First order linear homogeneous ordinary differential equation in fuzzy environment based on laplace transform," Journal of Fuzzy Set Valued Analysis, vol. 2013, Article ID jfsva-00174, 18 pages, 2013.

62. S. P. Mondal and T. K. Roy, "First order linear homogeneous fuzzy ordinary differential equation based on lagrange multiplier method," Journal of Soft Computing and Applications, vol. 2013, Article ID jsca-00032, 17 pages, 2013.

63. S. P. Mondal and T. K. Roy, "First order linear non homogeneous ordinary differential equation in fuzzy environment based on Laplace transform," Journal of Mathematics and Computer Science, vol. 3, no. 6, pp. 1533–1564, 2013.

64. S. Prasad Mondal and T. Kumar Roy, "First order homogeneous ordinary differential equation with initial value as triangular intuitionistic fuzzy number," Journal of Uncertainty in Mathematics Science, vol. 2014, Article ID jums-00003, 17 pages, 2014.

65. S. P. Mondal and T. K. Roy, "System of differential equation with initial value as triangular intuitionistic

fuzzy number and its application," International Journal of Applied and Computational Mathematics, vol. 1, no. 3, pp. 449–474, 2015.

66. S. Chakraverty and S. Tapaswini, "Standerd orthogonal polynomial based solution of fuzzy differential equation," The International Journal of Fuzzy Computation and Modelling, vol. 1, no. 1, 2014.

67. S. Tapaswini and S. Chakraverty, "Numerical solution of fuzzy arbitrary order predator-prey equations," Applications & Applied Mathematics, vol. 8, no. 2, pp. 647–672, 2013.

CHAPTER 2 NUMERICAL ANALYSIS OF THE INTEGRATION OF WIND TURBINES INTO THE DESIGN OF THE BUILT ENVIRONMENT

Hassam Nasarullah Chaudhry[1], John Kaiser Calautit[2] and Ben Richard Hughes[2]

[1] School of Energy, Geoscience, Infrastructure and Society, Heriot-Watt University, Dubai, UAE

[2] School of Civil Engineering, University of Leeds, Leeds, United Kingdom

ABSTRACT

The effect of wind distribution on the architectural domain of the Bahrain Trade Centre was numerically analysed using Computational Fluid Dynamics (CFD). Using the numerical data, the power generation potential of the building integrated wind turbines was determined in response to the prevailing wind direction. Simulating a reference wind speed of 6 m/s, the findings from the study quantified an estimate power generation of 6.4 kW indicating a capacity factor of 2.9% for the computational model. At the windward side of the building, it was observed that the layers of turbulence intensified in inverse proportion to the height of the building with an average value of 0.45 J/kg. The air velocity was found to gradually increase in direct proportion to the elevation with the turbine located at higher altitude receiving maximum exposure to incoming wind. This study highlighted the potential of using advanced computational fluid dynamics in order to factor wind into the design of any architectural environment.

INTRODUCTION

Building energy is part of a complex system that includes transport and urban planning and has major social consequences as well as climate change impacts. The energy mix is also important in determining carbon dioxide emissions. Buildings worldwide account for a surprisingly high 40% of global energy consumption and the resulting carbon footprint, significantly exceeding those of all transportation combined. Energy consumption of the Gulf Cooperation Council (GCC) countries is driven largely by residential use, with almost 47% of the electricity being consumed by the residential sector. Large and attractive opportunities exist to reduce building's energy use at lower costs and higher returns than other sectors. At the same time, substantial investments will be required to achieve this target. These will require the combination of actions called for in this report, including building energy codes, investment subsidies, labelling and reporting mechanisms, increased and trained workforce capacity and evolving energyefficiency designs and technologies. To achieve an energy-efficient world, governments, businesses and individuals must transform the building sector through a multitude of actions, which include increasing energy awareness globally.

Despite the renewable energy generation potential of wind turbines, their integration into high rise building structures has not advanced significantly. Apart from the lack of architectural appeal, the turbulence and wind shadowing effects represent a risk for uptake of the technology in the built environment

Citation: Chaudhry, HN, Calautit, JK and Hughes, BR (2014) Numerical analysis of the integration of wind turbines into the design of the built environment. American Journal of Engineering and Applied Sciences, 7 (4). 363 - 373 (10). ISSN 1941-7020

(Muller et al., 2008). Figure 1 displays examples of existing wind turbines integrated to commercial high rise buildings. In 2007, the Bahrain World Trade Centre introduced the world's first building integrated wind turbines (Fig. 1c). This was the first instance that a commercial development integrated large-scale wind turbines within its design to harness the power of the wind. The three turbines, measuring 29 meters in rotor diameter were supported by bridges spanning between the complex's two towers. Through its positioning and the unique aerodynamic design of the towers, the prevailing onshore Gulf breeze is intended to be funnelled into the path of the turbines, helping to create power generation efficiency. The anticipated benefits determined that once the system was operational, the wind turbines delivered approximately 11-15% of the energy needs of the building, or 1,100 to 1,300 megawatt-hours per year (Killa and Smith, 2008).

There are currently two major types of operational wind turbine technologies which can be used for building integration. These are classified as the Horizontal Axis Wind Turbines (HAWT) and the Vertical Axis Wind Turbines (VAWT). Horizontal axis wind turbines are the more common type of wind turbines in demand. In these turbines, the focus rotor shaft is pointed parallel to the direction of wind while the blades move perpendicular to that direction, thus providing high overall efficiency. On the other hand, the vertical axis wind turbines orientate on vertical axis where the focus rotor shaft is aligned vertically. A twodimensional 'not-to-scale' design modeling based on the two wind turbine technologies is shown in Fig. 2. The schematic provides the essential information on the individual situation of the major components in the wind turbine structure (Killa and Smith, 2008).

Theoretically, the air velocity incrimination is directly proportional to increasing elevation, as it is unaffected by the urban environment and surrounding topography. Thus, installing wind turbines on top of buildings allows for taking advantage of this height efficiently (Hughes et al., 2011). However, in many cases, the building geometry and its aerodynamic features can further assist in enhancing wind turbine performance by inducing a higher volume of air than the macro-climate (Hughes and Chaudhry, 2011).

Numerical analyses involving Computational Fluid Dynamics (CFD) are often carried out for evaluating building design and energy performances. In the past few years, CFD has been playing an increasingly important role in the design of buildings. The information provided by CFD assists in investigating the impact of building technologies, quantifying indoor environment quality and in integrating renewable energy systems. In this study, the CFD modeling approach is used out in order to determine the influence of building morphology on the efficiency of building-integrated wind turbines.

(a)

(b)

(c)

Figure 1: (a) Wind turbines on the roof of twelve west building; (b) the Strata tower with three building-integrated wind turbines; (c) Bahrain World Trade Centre

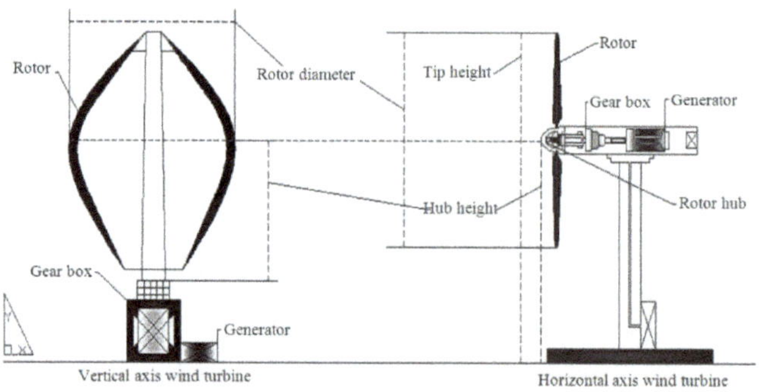

Figure 2: Structural comparison between the horizontal axis wind turbines and vertical axis wind turbines (Chaudhry and Hughes, 2011)

PREVIOUS RELATED WORKS

Work related to implementation of renewable energy as power sources in buildings, in particular wind energy is rapidly increasing. Following is a concise assessment of previous work related to this investigation.

Chong et al. (2013) conducted a study on the design of a wind turbine generator for the purpose of energy consumption in buildings. Two VAWTs in cross-wind orientation were integrated with an enclosure were installed above a cooling tower in order to harness the discharged wind for electricity generation. The tests were conducted with and without the VAWTs on the performance of the system. From the laboratory testing, it was observed that installing VAWTs at a correct position above the exhaust air system did not indicate any significant negative impacts on the performance of the cooling tower model. The performance of the cooling tower model was improved by the increment of intake air speed and the reduction off the motor power consumption. The rotational speed of the VAWTs were very high (>400 rpm) while the tip speed ratios were in the range of 1.28- 1.29, making it preferable for electricity generation.

Sharpe and Proven (2010) carried out detailed work on the concept and early development of a building integrated wind turbine in Scotland. The Crossflex proposal used in this investigation is based on the Darrieus turbines approach, consisting of two or more flexible aero foil blades attached to both the top and bottom of a vertical rotating shaft. The blade design incorporated low solidity and low mass materials for its construction. Although the development of this technology is still in its early stage, the study has outlined the remaining tasks of its work. The subsequent stages will involve supplementary computer modeling using CFD analysis to model airflow over the cowling to establish the nature of augmentation and flow stability that may occur and to optimise the design in respect of these.

Lu and Sun (2014) presented an integrated method of both macro (weather data and domain topography) and micro aspect (CFD) analysis in order to design wind turbines around numerous high-rise buildings with predominant wind in Hong Kong. Long-term wind data were compared at dense urban island and small island stations. The mean wind speeds for the urban locations were estimated at 2.93 m/s at 25 m above ground level. The study's findings determined that the wind power density at 4m above the building roof was enhanced numerously by 1.3-5.4 times with 5-7 m/s inlet velocity.

Mithraratne (2009) investigated the performance of wind turbines mounted on roof-tops, used for microgeneration in municipal houses in New Zealand. The research focused on energy consumption over a lifetime of the wind turbine with respect to the energy generation and Green House Gas (GHG) emissions at various circumstances in the life cycle. The work concluded that the feasibility level of roof-top wind turbines is generally poor as compared to large scale wind turbines for micro-generation.

Li et al. (2013) investigated the wind loads on the Pearl River Tower building in China to determine the power generation potential of wind turbines using wind tunnel testing. The Pearl River Tower, located in Guangzhou has 71 stories and rises about 310 m from the ground, which features four open holes (tunnels) equipped with four wind turbines at mechanical floors on two height levels. The objective of this study was to evaluate the wind speed amplifications in the tunnels for wind-power generation through the installation of wind turbines and to gain a better understanding of the wind effects on such a high-rise building with open holes. The findings from the analyses indicated that the bell-mouthed shape of the wind tunnels with contracted inner sections were useful in increasing the wind velocities at the location of the turbines. In addition, the work revealed that the presence of surrounding buildings influences wind speed amplifications and wind loads on the building structure.

In this study, the effect of wind distribution on the architectural domain of the Bahrain Trade Centre is numerically analysed using CFD. Individual parameters including air velocity distribution, pressure profiles and turbulence kinetic energy were computationally investigated to illustrate the variations in relation to increasing altitude. The power generation potential of the building integrated wind turbines were then determined using the study's findings.

COMPUTATIONAL METHODOLOGY

The computational domain comprised of the building geometry, which was designed according to the actual specifications of the high-rise tower and the specific wind turbines. The two 50 storey sail shaped towers are reported to measure to a height of 240 m and support three horizontal-axis wind turbines incorporating a rotor diameter of 29 m (Muller et al., 2008).

The three-dimensional Reynolds-Averaged NavierStokes (RANS) equations along with the momentum and continuity equations were solved using the commercial CFD code for the velocity and pressure field simulations. The model employs the control-volume technique and the Semi-Implicit Method for Pressure-Linked Equations (SIMPLE) velocity-pressure coupling algorithm with the second order upwind discretisation. The standard k-e transport model which is frequently used for incompressible flows was used to define the turbulence kinetic energy and flow dissipation rate within the model (Launder and Spalding, 1972). The use of the standard k-e transport model on building configurations has been found in previous works of (Calautit et al., 2013a; 2013b; Hughes et al., 2012)]. The turbulence kinetic energy, k and its rate of dissipation, e, are obtained from the following transport equations formulated in Equation 1 and 2:

$$\frac{\partial}{\partial t}(\rho k)+\frac{\partial}{\partial x_i}(\rho k u_i)=\frac{\partial}{\partial x_j}\left[\left(\mu+\frac{\mu_t}{\sigma k}\right)\frac{\partial k}{\partial x_j}\right]$$
$$+G_k+G_b-\rho\in-Y_M+S_k \qquad (1)$$

$$\frac{\partial}{\partial t}(\rho e)+\frac{\partial}{\partial x_i}(\rho e u_i)=\frac{\partial}{\partial x_j}\left[\left(\mu+\frac{\mu_t}{\sigma_e}\right)\frac{\partial k}{\partial x_j}\right]$$
$$+C_{1e}\frac{e}{k}(G_k+C_{3e}G_b)-C_{2\in}\rho\frac{e^2}{k}+S_e \qquad (2)$$

Where:

G_k = Represents the generation of turbulence kinetic energy due to the mean velocity gradients

G_b = Represents the generation of turbulence kinetic energy due to buoyancy

Y_M = Represents the contribution of fluctuating dilatation in compressible turbulence to the overall dissipation rate

C_{1e}, C_{2e} and C_{3e} = Constants

σ_k and σ_e = The turbulent Prandtl numbers for k and e

Mesh Generation

Mesh generation is one of the most important processes in CFD simulation. The quality of the mesh plays an important role on the accuracy of results and the stability of the solution. For the investigated computational domain, patch independent CFD tetrahedron meshing technique was applied on the geometry wherein the boundary conditions were applied on the edges and faces. The patch independent mesh algorithm for tetrahedron elements is based on the subsequent spatial subdivision algorithm which ensures refinement of the mesh where essential, but retains larger elements where feasible, therefore allowing faster computing times. The meshed model comprised of 2,013,428 nodes and 10,849,999 elements as displayed in Fig. 2. The minimum face angle was 5.67°C while the maximum edge length and element volume ratios were 9.9 and 44.6. Figure 3 and. 4 displays the schematic of the geometry along with the meshed model.

Grid Independency

In order to verify the accuracy of the numerical models, a grid independency test was carried out to determine the variation in results over increasing mesh sizes. Basic concepts associated with mesh refinement deals with the refinement and evaluation of elements where the posterior error indicator is larger than the preset criterion, while mesh enrichment considers running higher order polynomials till the solution is expected to improve with a fixed mesh (Chung, 2002). Grid verification was carried out using mesh refinements (h-method) in order to optimise the distribution of mesh size h over a finite element.

The area-weighted average value of the static pressure on the three wind turbines located on the building façade was taken as the error indicator, as the grid was refined from 1,519,000 to 10,849,999 elements with the average pressure value being 4.36 Pa. The grid was evaluated and refined until the posterior estimate error became insignificant between the number of elements and the posterior error indicator. The discretisation error was found to be the lowest at over ten million elements for both indicated variables and the mesh was thus selected to achieve a balance between accuracy and computational time. The y+ values at the wall varied between 5 and 61. Fig. 5 displays the wall y+ values and variation in discretisation error at increasing number of meshed elements.

Boundary Conditions

The applied boundary conditions (Table 1) comprised of a reference velocity (u_{ref}) of 6 m/s at a height of 300 m (z_{ref}) approaching directly perpendicular to the building façade (Kubik et al., 2011). The geometry was modeled as a solid zone while the enclosure was modeled as a fluid zone for the analyses. The boundary conditions were kept identical throughout the numerical investigation for all analysed models.

Wind Energy Potential in Bahrain

Figure 6 displays the wind days per month and wind direction distribution in Bahrain (WWSBA, 2014). The predominant wind direction was observed to be from the North West. Evidently, the building structure was oriented in the direction of the dominant prevailing wind in order to allow the turbines to operate at maximum efficiency.

In order to estimate how much energy a specific turbine will be expected to produce at a given location, the wind resource at that location must be identified. A wind turbine works by extracting kinetic energy out of the wind and converting it to mechanical and then electrical energy. The power that is available in the wind to be converted to electrical energy is defined in Equation 3:

$$P_{wind} = \frac{1}{2}\rho A U^3 \qquad (3)$$

Where:

P_{wind} = Power available in the wind

ρ = Density of air

A = Swept area of the turbine

U = Wind speed approaching the wind turbine

Table 1: Boundary conditions

Parameter	Type
Geometry	Solid zone
Enclosure	Fluid zone
Operating Pressure	Atmospheric
Viscous model	k-epsilon (2 Equation)
Near-wall treatment	Standard wall functions
Velocity formulation	Absolute
Solver type	Pressure-based
Time	Steady
Gravity	-9.81 m/s^2

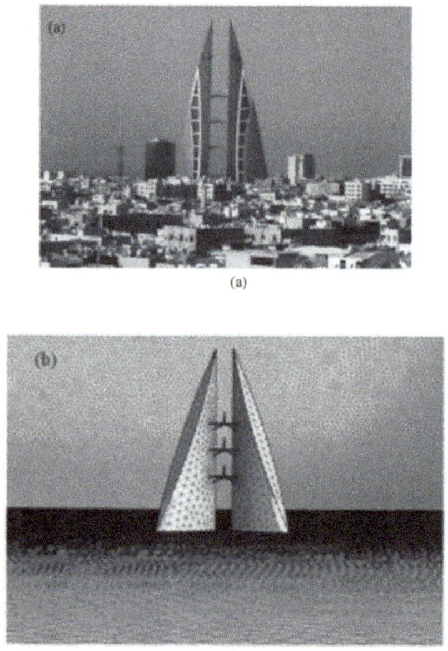

Figure 3: (a) Actual building configuration (b) meshed model

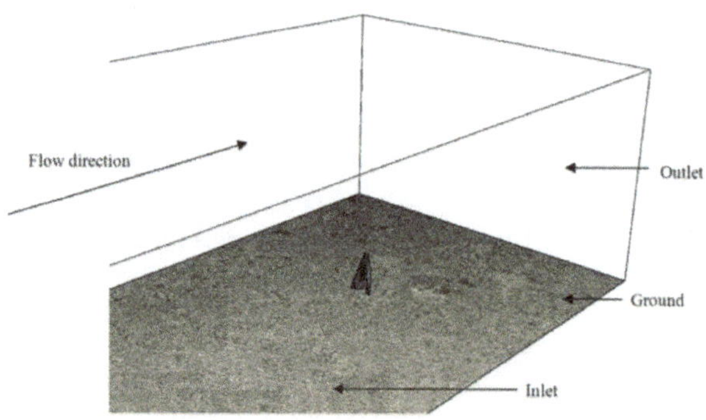

Figure 4: Representation of the flow domain

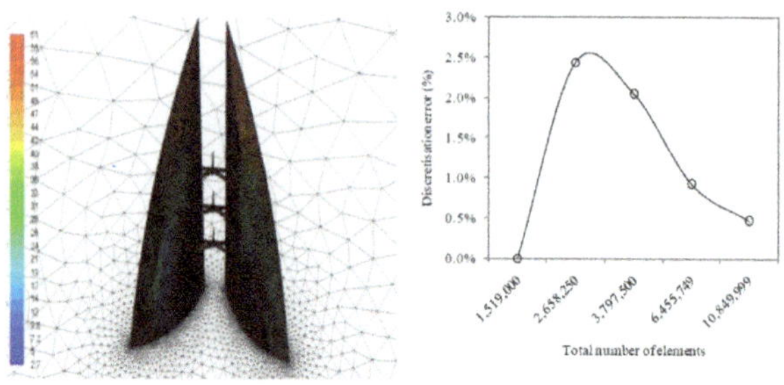

Figure 5: Variation in discretisation error at increasing number of elements

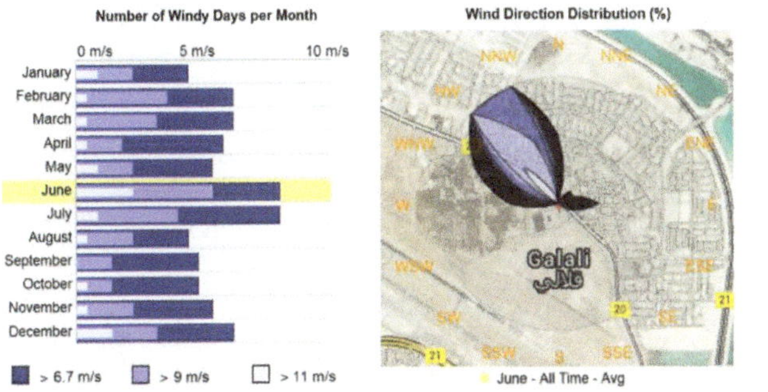

Figure 6: (a) Wind days per month and (b) wind direction distribution in Bahrain (WWSBA, 2014)

Large-scale integration of wind turbines into buildings requires extensive research and development for it to operate at high efficiencies in order to balance out the high cost of installation. The specification of the wind turbines used in this study was mapped on the ones installed on the Bahrain Trade Centre. The fixed horizontal axis wind turbine comprised of a conventional nacelle design containing an enclosure with the gearbox, cooling system and the associated control system. The nominal electrical power rating of the turbine was 225 kW with the rotor diameter measuring 29 m. The rotor speed at full load was 38 rpm. The cut-in wind speed for the wind turbine operation was 4 m/s while the cut-out speed was 20 m/s (Muller et al., 2008).

Since the potential power production is proportional to the wind speed cubed, the annual mean wind power density cannot be defined by strictly using the mean annual wind speed. However, some knowledge of the wind distribution must be known to estimate the power density. The power density ($P_{density}$) can be used as a function of the power divided by the area and the expression is displayed in Equation 4:

$$P_{density} = \frac{1}{2}\rho U^3 \tag{4}$$

Using the computational domain, a representation of velocity boundary layer profile and turbulence intensity (I) at the windward side of the building is shown in Fig. 7 wherein the wind speed is taken from the direction of the sea. The thickness of boundary layer of the atmosphere varies with wind speed, turbulence level and the type of surface. The power law is an empirical equation expressed in Equation 5. For neutral stability conditions, α is approximately 1/7, or 0.143, regarded as a reasonable but conservative estimate (Kubik et al., 2011):

$$u = u_{ref}\left(\frac{z}{z_{ref}}\right)^{\alpha} \tag{5}$$

Where:

u = Speed at a particular point

u_{ref} = Reference speed

z = Height at a particular point

z_{ref} = Reference height

RESULTS AND DISCUSSION

Pressure, Velocity and Turbulence Profiles

Using the building model, Fig. 8 displays the contour levels for static pressure as the air comes in contact with the building. A positive airside pressure was created as the air stream came in direct contact with the building façade. This was due to the force being directly perpendicular to the area of interaction. As a result, a negative pressure was created on the opposite end at the immediate downstream of the building where the air velocity increased due to the streamlined body of the structure. The maximum positive pressure was estimated at 20 Pa while the maximum negative pressure was observed to be -14 Pa. The analysis showed that a total pressure differential of 34 Pa was created for the entire geometry.

Figure 9 and 10 displays the contour levels of velocity and turbulence kinetic energy, upstream and downstream of the building model. The findings displayed that the air velocity gradually increased to 7.1 m/s from a reference velocity of 6 m/s. At the windward side of the building, it was observed that the layers of turbulence intensified in inverse proportion to the height of the building with an average value of 0.45 J/kg. The turbulence kinetic energy was however found to increase (maximum value of 1.35 J/kg) at the leeward side of the building as the wind came in contact and sheared away towards the sides of the structure.

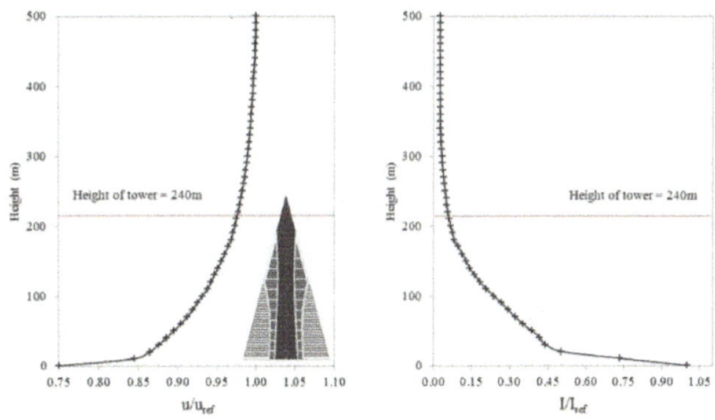

Figure 7: Representation of the boundary layer profile and turbulence intensity

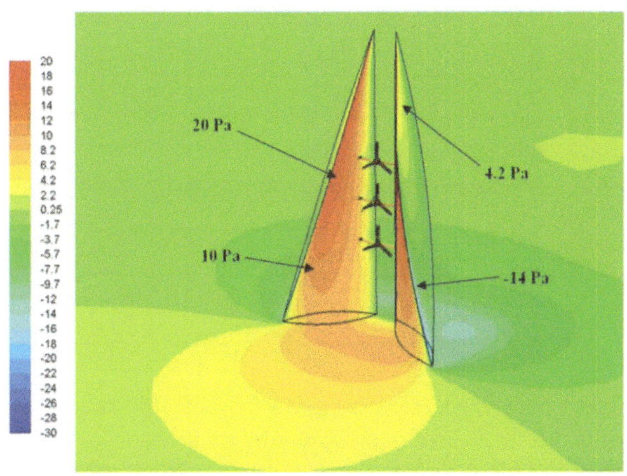

Figure 8: Contour levels of static pressure on the surface of the building and ground

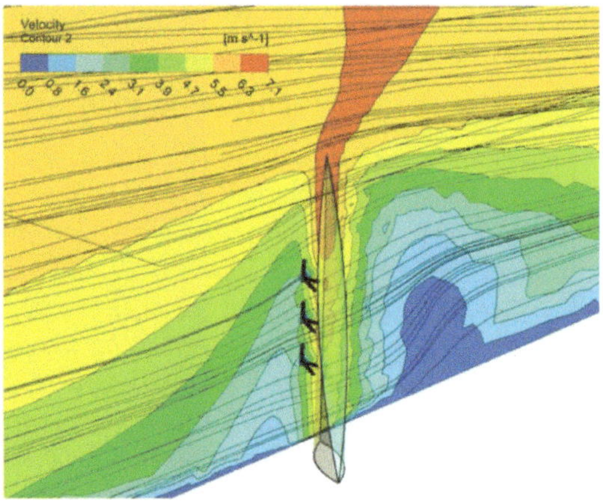

Figure 9: Streamlines and contour levels of velocity magnitude formation upstream and downstream of the building

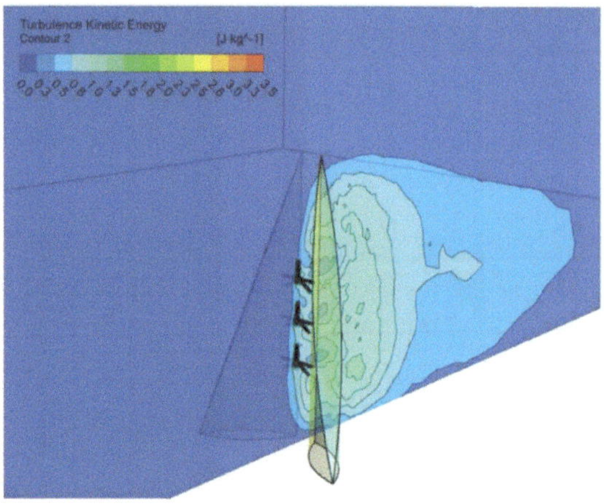

Figure 10: Contour levels of turbulence kinetic energy upstream and downstream of the building

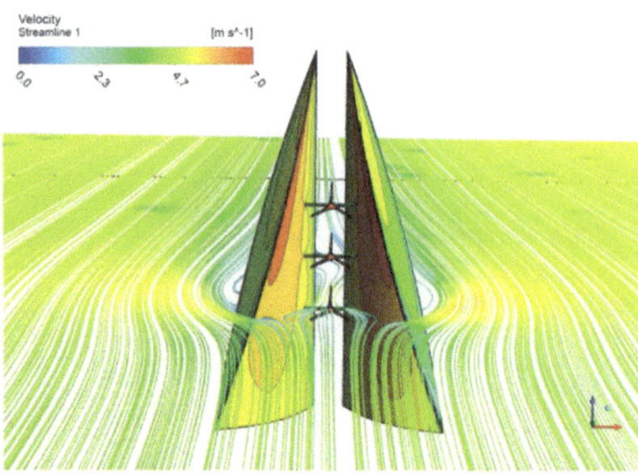

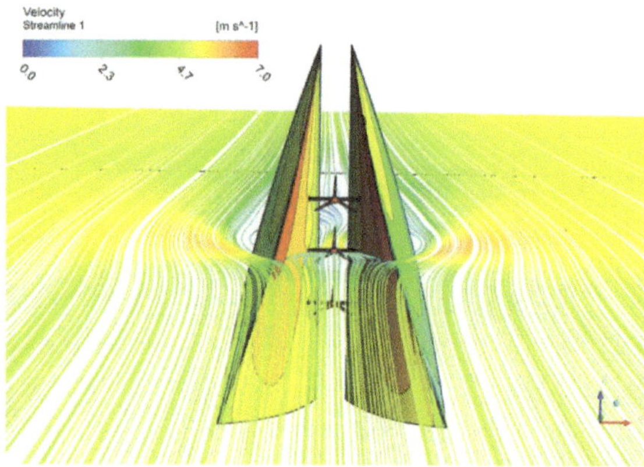

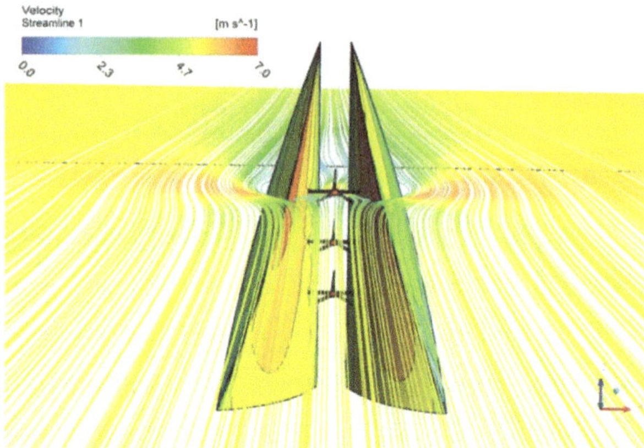

Figure 11: Velocity streamlines formation around the three levels (low-altitude, mid-altitude and high-altitude) of wind turbines

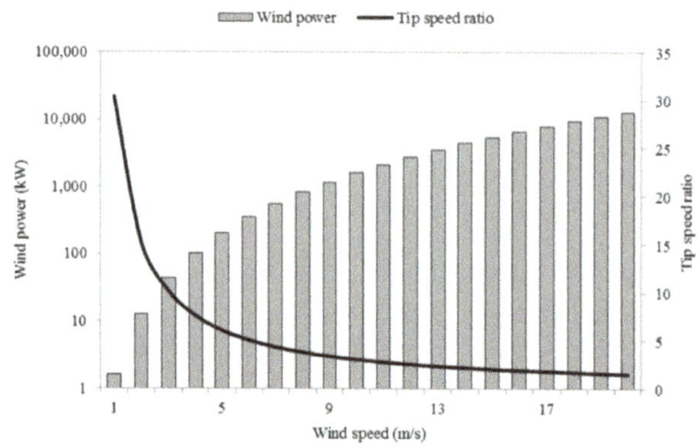

Figure 12: Analytical relationship between wind power and tip speed ratio at increasing wind speeds

Table 2: Estimated power density and capacity factor

Turbine	Velocity (m/s)	Estimated power (W)	Power density (W/m2)	Capacity factor (%)
1	2.6	-	-	-
2	3.3	-	-	-
3	4.1	6,430	43.1	2.9%

Figure 11 displays the formation of velocity streamlines around the three levels (low-altitude, midaltitude and high-altitude) of wind turbines. As observed, the air velocity on approach increases by 17% when it comes in contact with the wind turbine located at the highest altitude in relation to the wind turbine located at the lowest level.

Power Density and Turbine Capacity Factor

Following the numerical investigation, an estimation of the wind power characteristics was calculated theoretically. Using the rotor diameter of 29 m for the wind turbine used in the Bahrain Trade Centre, an analytical comparison between power in the wind and the tip speed ratio is illustrated in Fig.

12. Wind turbines are designed to operate at their optimum tip speed ratio in order to extract as much power possible from the air stream. For a grid connected wind turbine with three rotor blades, the optimum tip speed ratio is recommended between 6 and 8 (Cetin et al., 2005). While a linear increase in wind power was obtained with increasing wind speeds, the recommended tip speed ratio values were found to be at 4 and 5 m/s respectively.

Using the wind speeds obtained from the CFD models, the conservative figures of estimated power generation capability of wind turbines for all analysed cases is displayed in Table 2. Three wind turbines were used on the buildings which were categorised as Turbine 1 (low-altitude), Turbine 2 (mid-altitude) and Turbine 3 (high-altitude). Using the computational model, the study quantified an estimate power generation of 6.4 kW indicating a capacity factor of 2.9%.

CONCLUSION

In this study, the feasibility of implementing building-integrated wind turbines was determined by investigating the effect of structural morphology on the extraction of prevailing inlet wind. The power generation capacity of wind turbines was determined using the specifications of the Bahrain Trade Centre. The threedimensional Reynolds-averaged Navier-Stokes (RANS) equations along with the momentum and continuity equations were solved using the commercial CFD code for velocity and pressure field simulations. Using a reference wind speed of 6 m/s, the findings revealed an increase of 15.4% in velocity obtained at the top of the tower. The study quantified an estimate power generation of 6.4 kW indicating a capacity factor of 2.9% for the building model. This study highlighted the potential of using advanced computational techniques in order to factor the effect of wind distribution into the design of any architectural environment.

AUTHOR'S CONTRIBUTIONS

The authors performed the CFD modelling, simulation and analysis of the integration of the wind turbine into the building. Following the CFD investigation, the team estimated the power density and capacity factor of each turbine.

REFERENCES

1. Calautit, J.K., B.R. Hughes and S.A. Ghani, 2013a. Numerical investigation of the integration of heat transfer devices into wind towers. Chem. Eng. Trans., 34: 43-48. DOI: 10.3303/CET1334008
2. Calautit, J.K., B.R. Hughes and S.A. Ghani, 2013b. A Numerical investigation into the feasibility of integrating green building technologies into row houses in the Middle East. Architectural Sci. Rev., 56: 279-296. DOI: 10.1080/00038628.2012.686433
3. Cetin, N.S., M.A., Yurdusev, R. Ata and A. Ozdemir, 2005. Assessment of optimum tip speed ratio of wind turbines. Math. Comput. Applic., 10: 147-154.
4. Chaudhry, H.N. and B.R. Hughes, 2011. Computational analysis of dynamic architecture. J. Power Energy, 225: 85-95. DOI: 10.1177/09576509JPE1056
5. Chong, W.T., S.Y. Yip, A. Fazlizan, S.C. Poh and W.P. Hew et al., 2013. Design of an exhaust air energy recovery wind turbine generator for energy conservation in commercial buildings. Renewable Energy, 67: 252-256. DOI: 10.1016/j.renene.2013.11.028
6. Chung, T.J., 2002. Computational Fluid Dynamics. 1st Edn., Cambridge University Press.
7. Hughes, B.R. and H.N. Chaudry, 2011. Power generation potential of dynamic architecture. World Acad. Sci., Eng. Technol., 5: 01-24.
8. Hughes, B.R., J.K. Calautit and S.A. Ghani, 2012. The development of commercial wind towers for natural ventilation: A review. Applied Energy, 92: 606-627. DOI: 10.1016/j.apenergy.2011.11.066
9. Hughes, B.R., H.N. Chaudhry and S.A. Ghani 2011. A review of sustainable cooling technologies in buildings. Renewable Sustainable Energy Rev., 15: 3112-3120. DOI: 10.1016/j.rser.2011.03.032
10. Killa, S. and R.F. Smith, 2008. Harnessing energy in tall buildings: Bahrain world trade center and beyond. Proceedings of the Council of Tall Buildings and Urban Habitat (CTBUH) 8th World Congress, Mar. 3-5, Dubai, UAE.
11. Kubik, M.L., P.J. Coker and C. Hunt, 2011. Using meteorological wind data to estimate turbine generation output: A sensitivity analysis. Proceedings of the World Renewable Energy Congress, May 8-13, Linkoping, Sweden, pp: 4074-4081.
12. Launder, B. and D.B. Spalding, 1972. Lectures in Mathematical Models of Turbulence. 1st Edn., Academic Press, London, England, ISBN-10: 0124380506, pp: 169.
13. Li, Q.S., F.B. Chen, Y.G. Li and Y.Y. Lee, 2013. Implementing wind turbines in a tall building for power generation: A study of wind loads and wind speed amplifications. J. Wind Eng. Indus. Aerodynam., 116: 70-82. DOI: 10.1016/j.jweia.2013.03.004
14. Lu, L. and K. Sun, 2014. Wind power evaluation and utilization over a reference high-rise building in urban area. Energy Build., 68: 339-350. DOI: 10.1016/j.enbuild.2013.09.029
15. Mithraratne, N., 2009. Roof-top wind turbines for microgeneration in urban houses in New Zealand. Energy Build., 41: 1013-1018. DOI: 10.1016/j.enbuild.2009.05.003
16. Muller, G., F. Jentsch Mark and E. Stoddart, 2008. Vertical axis resistance type wind turbines for use in buildings. Renewable Energy, 34: 1407-1412. DOI: 10.1016/j.renene.2008.10.008
17. Sharpe, T. and G. Proven, 2010. Crossflex: Concept and early development of a true building integrated wind turbine. Energy Build., 42: 2365-2375. DOI: 10.1016/j.enbuild.2010.07.032
18. WWSBA, 2014. Wind and weather statistics Bahrain Airport. Windfinder.

CHAPTER 3

NUMERICAL SOLUTION OF BOUNDARY LAYER MHD FLOW WITH VISCOUS DISSIPATION

S. R. Mishra[1] and S. Jena[2]

[1]Department of Mathematics, Institute of Technical Education and Research, Siksha 'O' Anusandhan University, Khandagiri, Bhubaneswar, Odisha 751030, India

[2]Department of Mathematics, Centurion University of Technology and Management, Bhubaneswar, India

ABSTRACT

The present paper deals with a steady two-dimensional laminar flow of a viscous incompressible electrically conducting fluid over a shrinking sheet in the presence of uniform transverse magnetic field with viscous dissipation. Using suitable similarity transformations the governing partial differential equations are transformed into ordinary differential equations and then solved numerically by fourth-order Runge-Kutta method with shooting technique. Results for velocity and temperature profiles for different values of the governing parameters have been discussed in detail with graphical representation. The numerical evaluation of skin friction and Nusselt number are also given in this paper.

INTRODUCTION

The study of flow and heat transfer over a stretching/shrinking sheet receives considerable attention from many researchers due to its variety of applications in industries such as extrusion of a polymer in a melt spinning process, manufacturing of plastic films, wire drawing, hot rolling, and glass fibre production. Crane [1] first considered the steady laminar boundary layer flow of a Newtonian fluid caused by a linearly stretching flat sheet and found an exact similarity solution in closed analytical form. Chiam [2] investigated the steady two-dimensional stagnation point flow towards a stretching surface in the case when the stretching velocity is identical to the free stream velocity. Hiemenz [3] studied the steady two-dimensional boundary layer flows near the forward stagnation point on an infinite wall using a similarity transformation. Sakiadis [4, 5] reported the flow field analysis where the stretched surface was assumed to move with uniform velocity, and similarity solutions were obtained for the governing equations. The solution is later improved by Howrath [6]. Gupta and Gupta [7] have studied the effect of mass transfer on a stretching sheet with suction or blowing for linear surface velocity subject to uniform temperature. Wang [8] investigated the three-dimensional flow due to the stretching surface. The uniqueness of the solution obtained by Crane [1] was established by McLeod and Rajagopal [9]. Some important contributions in stretching sheet flow were made by Chakrabarti and Gupta [10], Andersson [11], Dirks et al. [12], Jat and Chaudhary [13–17] and Bhattacharyya and Layek [18], and many other authors.

The flow of incompressible fluid due to a shrinking sheet is gaining attention of modern day researchers because of its increasing application to many engineering problems. Lok et al. [19] studied oblique stagnation point flow of Newtonian flow towards a stretching surface. They reported that the

Citation: S. R. Mishra and S. Jena, "Numerical Solution of Boundary Layer MHD Flow with Viscous Dissipation," The Scientific World Journal, vol. 2014, Article ID 756498, 5 pages, 2014. doi:10.1155/2014/756498

position of the stagnation point depends on stretching sheet parameters and the angle of incidence. Hayat et al. [20] reported an analytical solution of MHD flow of a second-grade fluid over a shrinking sheet. Fang and Zhang [21] obtained a closed form analytical solution for steady MHD flow over a porous shrinking sheet subjected to mass suction. Wang [22] studied the stagnation point flow towards a shrinking sheet. Unsteady two-dimensional hydromagnetic flow and heat transfer of an incompressible viscous fluid were investigated by Adhikary and Mishra [23]. Ali et al. [24] investigated the unsteady viscous flow over a shrinking sheet with mass transfer in a rotating fluid. Recently, Bhattacharyya [25] studied the effects of heat source/sink on MHD flow and heat transfer over a shrinking sheet with mass suction.

Realizing the increasing technical application of MHD effects, the present paper studies the effects of magnetic parameter on the boundary layer flow and heat transfer over a porous shrinking sheet with mass suction and viscous dissipation. The physical quantities of interest such as skin friction Cf and Nusselt number Nu are calculated. The numerical results are plotted in some figures and the variations in physical characteristics of the flow dynamics and heat transfer for several parameters involved in the equations are discussed in detail.

FORMULATION OF THE PROBLEM

Consider a steady two-dimensional laminar flow of a viscous incompressible electrically conducting fluid over a permeable shrinking sheet which coincides with the plane y=0 and the flow is confined in the region y>0. The x- and y-axes are taken along and perpendicular to the sheet, respectively. Two equal and opposite forces are applied along the x- axis so that the sheet is stretched keeping the origin fixed. A uniform magnetic field of strength B_0 is assumed to be applied normal to the sheet. The magnetic Reynolds number is taken to be small and therefore the induced magnetic field is neglected. All the fluid properties are assumed to be constant throughout the motion. Under the usual boundary layer approximations the basic governing equations with viscous dissipation are

$$\frac{\partial u}{\partial x} + \frac{\partial v}{\partial y} = 0, \tag{1}$$

$$u\frac{\partial u}{\partial x} + v\frac{\partial u}{\partial y} = v\frac{\partial^2 u}{\partial y^2} - \frac{\sigma B_0^2 u}{\rho}, \tag{2}$$

$$u\frac{\partial T}{\partial x} + v\frac{\partial T}{\partial y} = \frac{\kappa}{\rho c_p}\frac{\partial^2 T}{\partial y^2} + \frac{Q_0}{\rho c_p}(T - T_\infty) + \frac{\mu}{\rho c_p}\left(\frac{\partial u}{\partial y}\right)^2 + \frac{\sigma B_0^2 u^2}{\rho c_p}, \tag{3}$$

where u and V are velocity components in x- and y-directions, respectively,] = μ/ρ is the kinematic viscosity, ρ is the density, μ is the coefficient of viscosity, σ is the electrical conductivity of the fluid, T is the temperature, T_∞ is the free stream temperature, κ is the thermal conductivity of the fluid, c_p is the specific heat at constant pressure, and Q_0 is the volumetric rate of heat generation or absorption.

The boundary conditions are

$$y = 0 : u = U_w = -cx, \quad v = -v_w, \quad T = T_w,$$
$$y \longrightarrow \infty : u \rightarrow 0, \quad T \longrightarrow T_\infty, \tag{4}$$

where c > 0, (0 < c < 1) is the shrinking constant, T_w is temperature of the sheet, and V_w(> 0) is a prescribed distribution of wall mass suction through the porous sheet.

The impact of the magnetic parameter M on the velocity and temperature is very significant in practical point of view.

In Figure 1, the variations in velocity field for several values of M are presented. It is observed that the velocity increases with increasing values of M. Accordingly, the thickness of the momentum boundary layer decreases. This happens due to the Lorentz force arising from the interaction of magnetic and electric fields during the motion of the electrically conducting fluid.

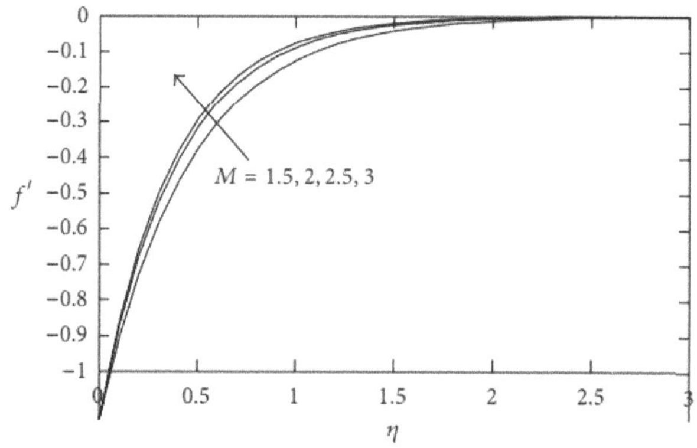

Figure 1: Velocity profile against η for various values of M when S = 2.0.

Figure 2 shows the effects of mass suction parameter S on the velocity profile for a fixed value of M. It is noted that, for a fixed value of η, velocity profile increases as applied suction increases and it makes the boundary layer thickness thinner.

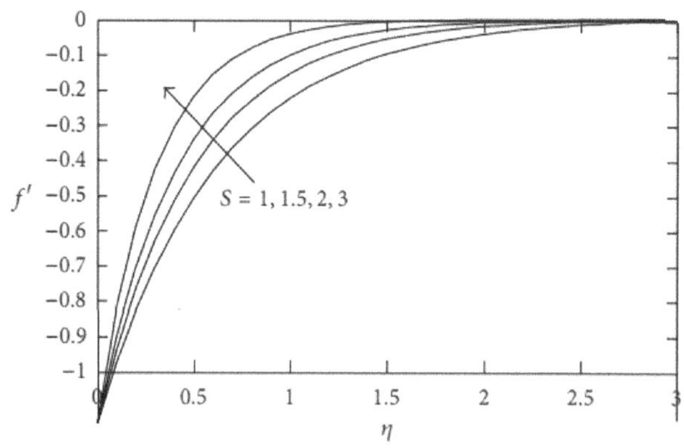

Figure 2: Velocity profile against η for various values of S when M = 2.0.

MATHEMATICAL ANALYSIS

The equation of continuity (1) is identically satisfied if we take the stream function (x, y) such that

$$u = \frac{\partial \psi}{\partial y}, \quad v = -\frac{\partial \psi}{\partial x}. \tag{5}$$

The momentum and energy equations (2) and (3) can be transformed into the corresponding ordinary differential equations by introducing the following similarity transformations:

$$\psi(x, y) = \sqrt{c\nu}xf(\eta),$$
$$\frac{T - T_\infty}{T_w - T_\infty} = \theta(\eta), \quad (6)$$

where

$$\eta = y\sqrt{\frac{c}{\nu}}. \quad (7)$$

The momentum and energy equations (2) and (3) are transformed to

$$f''' + ff'' - f'^2 - Mf' = 0,$$
$$\theta'' + \Pr\left(f\theta' + \lambda\theta\right) + \Pr\mathrm{Ec}f''^2 + M\Pr\mathrm{Ec}f'^2 = 0, \quad (8)$$

where $M = \sigma_e B_0^2/\rho c$ is the magnetic parameter, $\Pr = \mu c_p/\kappa$ is the Prandtl number, $\lambda = Q_0/\rho c_p c$ is the heat source ($\lambda < 0$) or sink ($\lambda > 0$) parameter, and $\mathrm{Ec} = U_w^2/c_p(T_w - T_\infty$ is the Eckert number.

The corresponding boundary conditions are

$$\eta = 0 : f = S, \quad f' = -1, \quad \theta = 1,$$
$$\eta \longrightarrow \infty : f' \longrightarrow 0, \quad \theta \longrightarrow 0, \quad (9)$$

where $S = v_w/\sqrt{c\nu}\ (> 0)$ is the mass suction parameter.

The physical quantities of interest of the problem are the skin-friction coefficient Cf and the Nusselt number Nu, which can be expressed, respectively, as

$$C_f = \frac{\mu(\partial u/\partial y)_{y=0}}{(\rho U^2/2)} = \frac{2}{\sqrt{\mathrm{Re}}}f''(0),$$
$$\mathrm{Nu} = -\frac{x(\partial T/\partial y)_{y=0}}{(T_w - T_\infty)} = -\sqrt{\mathrm{Re}}\,\theta'(0), \quad (10)$$

where Re = $(U_w x)/]$ is the local Reylolds number.

RESULTS AND DISCUSSION

The set of nonlinear differential equations (8) with boundary conditions (9) were solved numerically using RungeKutta fourth-order algorithm with a systematic guessing of shooting technique until the boundary condition at infinity is satisfied. The computations were done by a programme which uses a symbolic and computational computer language, Matlab. Numerical computations are performed for various values of the physical parameters involved, for example, the magnetic parameter M, the mass suction parameter S, the Prandtl number Pr, the Eckert number Ec, and the heat source/sink parameter λ.

In order to assure the accuracy of the applied numerical scheme the computed values of skin-friction are compared with the available results of Muhaimin et al. [26] in Table 1 and have been found to be in very good agreement. The variation of the temperature gradient at the sheet, that is, $-\theta'(0)$, which is significant in evaluating the rate of heat transfer from the sheet, is presented in Tables 2 and 3.

Table 1: Skin friction coefficient $f''(0)$ for different values of S with $M = 2.0$.

S	Present study	Muhaimin et al. [26]
2	2.414476	2.414214
3	3.302813	3.302776
4	4.236071	4.236068

Table 2: $-\theta'(0)$ for various values of Pr when M=2, S=2, and Ec = 0.1.

λ	Pr = 0.1	Pr = 0.71
−0.2	0.428487	1.229785
−0.1	0.418625	1.179859
0	0.408646	1.127127
0.1	0.398547	1.071191
0.2	0.388325	1.011564

Table 3: $-\theta'(0)$ for various values of Ec when M=2, S=2, and Pr = 0.71.

λ	Ec = 0.1	Ec = 0.71
−0.2	1.229785	0.50059
−0.1	1.179859	0.443616
0	1.127127	0.383339
0.1	1.071191	0.319285
0.2	1.011564	0.250881

Figure 3 shows the effects of magnetic parameter M on the temperature distribution. Here it is noticed that the temperature (η) decreases with increasing values of M. The temperature field for various values of Prandtl number Pr is represented in Figure 4. With increasing Pr the thermal boundary layer thickness quickly decreases. The temperature field for various values of heat source or sink parameter λ is exhibited in Figure 5. It is noted that, for a fixed value of η, temperature (η) decreases as λ decreases. Figure 6 shows the effects of Eckert number Ec on temperature (η). It is observed that, for any fixed value of η, temperature (η) decreases as Ec decreases.

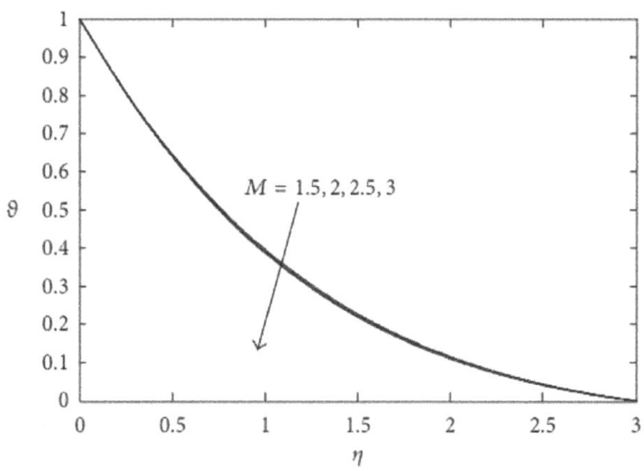

Figure 3: Temperature profile against η for various values of M when S = 2.0, Pr = 0.71, and Ec = 0.1.

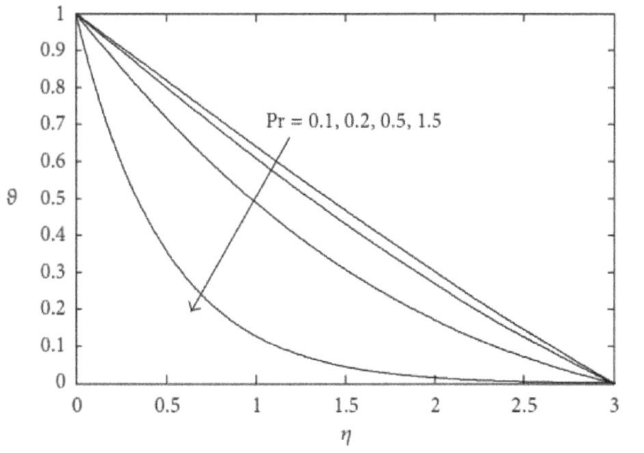

Figure 4: Temperature profile against η for various values of Pr when $M = 2.0$, $S = 2.0$, and Ec = 0.1.

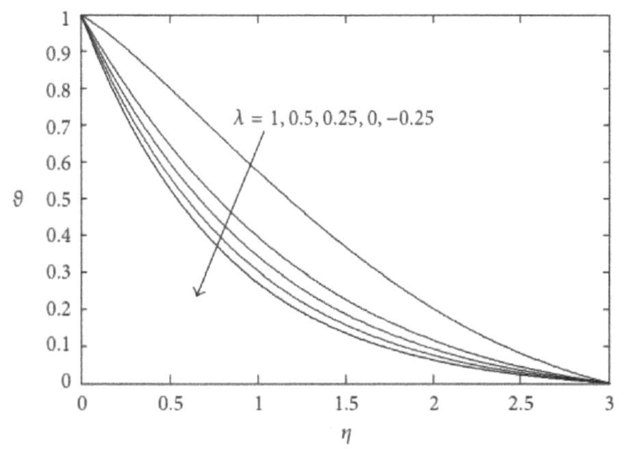

Figure 5: Temperature profile against η for various values of λ when $M = 2.0$, $S = 2.0$, Pr = 0.7, and Ec = 0.

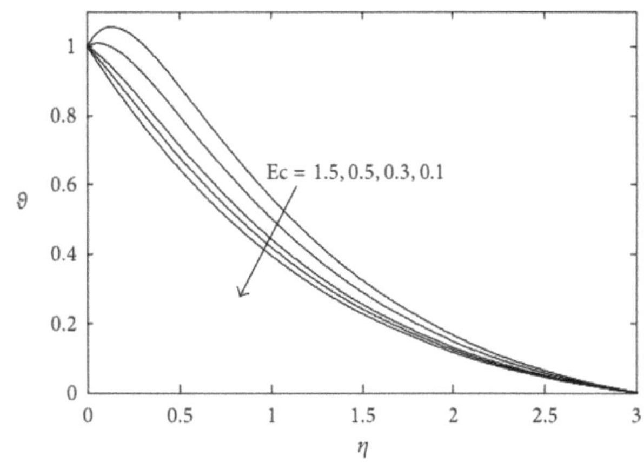

Figure 6: Temperature profile against η for various values of Ec when $M = 2.0$, $S = 2.0$, and Pr = 0.7.

CONCLUSION

The effects of magnetic parameter M on the boundary layer flow and heat transfer over a shrinking sheet subject to strong mass suction are studied.The self similar equations are obtained using similarity transformations. The study shows that, due to increase of the magnetic parameter M and the mass suction parameter S, the momentum boundary layer thickness decreases. Also, the dimensionless temperature profile as well as the thermal boundary layer thickness quickly reduces as Pr increases. Similarly thermal boundary layer thickness decreases as Ec decreases. For some higher values of heat source parameter heat absorption occurs at the sheet. The rate of heat transfer increases with Prandtl number.

REFERENCES

1. L. J. Crane, "Flow past a stretching plate," Zeitschrift für Angewandte Mathematik und Physik, vol. 21, no. 4, pp. 645–647, 1970.
2. T. C. Chiam, "Stagnation-point flow towards a stretching plate," Journal of the Physical Society of Japan, vol. 63, no. 6, pp. 2443–2444, 1994.
3. K. Hiemenz, "Die grenzchicht in einem in dem gleichformingen flussigkeitsstrom eingetauchten gerade kreiszlinder," Dingler Polytech Journal, vol. 326, p. 321, 1911.
4. B. C. Sakiadis, "Boundary-layer behavior on continuous solid surfaces: I. Boundary-layer equations for two-dimensional and axisymmetric flow," AIChE Journal, vol. 7, no. 1, pp. 26–28, 1961.
5. B. C. Sakiadis, "Boundary-layer behavior on continuous solid surfaces: II. The boundary layer on a continuous flat surface," AIChE Journal, vol. 7, no. 2, pp. 221–225, 1961.
6. L. Howrath, "On the calculation of steady flow in the boundary layer near the surface of a cylinder in a stream," Tech. Rep. 1632, Arcrm, 1935.
7. P. S. Gupta and A. S. Gupta, "Heat and mass transfer on a stretching sheet with suction or blowing," The Canadian Journal of Chemical Engineering, vol. 55, no. 6, pp. 744–746, 1977.
8. C. Y. Wang, "The three-dimensional flow due to a stretching flat surface," Physics of Fluids, vol. 27, no. 8, pp. 1915–1917, 1984.
9. J. B. McLeod and K. R. Rajagopal, "On the uniqueness of flow of a Navier-Stokes fluid due to a stretching boundary," Archive for Rational Mechanics and Analysis, vol. 98, no. 4, pp. 385–393, 1987. ·
10. A. Chakrabarti and A. S. Gupta, "Hydromagnetic flow and heat transfer over a stretching sheet,"Quarterly Journal of Mechanics and Applied Mathematics, vol. 37, no. 1, pp. 73–78, 1979.
11. H. I. Andersson, "MHD flow of a viscoelastic fluid past a stretching surface," Acta Mechanica, vol. 95, no. 1–4, pp. 227–230, 1992.
12. C. A. Dirks, M. Gouverneur, L. McCullum et al., "A note on MHD flow over a stretching permeable surface," Mechanics Research Communications, vol. 25, no. 3, pp. 263–269, 1998. ·
13. R. N. Jat and S. Chaudhary, "MHD stagnation flows with slip," Il Nuovo Cimento B, vol. 122, no. 8, pp. 823–831, 2007.
14. R. N. Jat and S. Chaudhary, "Magnetohydrodynamic boundary layer flow near the stagnation point of a stretching sheet," Il Nuovo Cimento B, vol. 123, no. 5, pp. 555–566, 2008.

15. R. N. Jat and S. Chaudhary, "MHD flow and heat transfer over a stretching sheet," Applied Mathematical Sciences, vol. 3, no. 25–28, pp. 1285–1294, 2009.

16. R. N. Jat and S. Chaudhary, "Unsteady magnetohydrodynamic boundary layer flow over a stretching surface with viscous dissipation and Joule heating," Il Nuovo Cimento B, vol. 124, no. 1, pp. 53–59, 2009.

17. R. N. Jat and S. Chaudhary, "Radiation effects on the MHD flow near the stagnation point of a stretching sheet," Zeitschrift für Angewandte Mathematik und Physik, vol. 61, no. 6, pp. 1151–1154, 2010.

18. K. Bhattacharyya and G. C. Layek, "Chemically reactive solute distribution in MHD boundary layer flow over a permeable stretching sheet with suction or blowing," Chemical Engineering Communications, vol. 197, no. 12, pp. 1527–1540, 2010. ·

19. Y. Y. Lok, N. Amin, and I. Pop, "Non-orthogonal stagnation point flow towards a stretching sheet,"International Journal of Non-Linear Mechanics, vol. 41, no. 4, pp. 622–627, 2006.·

20. T. Hayat, Z. Abbas, and M. Sajid, "On the analytic solution of magnetohydrodynamic flow of a second grade fluid over a shrinking sheet," Journal of Applied Mechanics, vol. 74, no. 6, pp. 1165–1171, 2007. ·

21. T. Fang and J. Zhang, "Closed-form exact solutions of MHD viscous flow over a shrinking sheet,"Communications in Nonlinear Science and Numerical Simulation, vol. 14, no. 7, pp. 2853–2857, 2009. ·

22. C. Y. Wang, "Stagnation flow towards a shrinking sheet," International Journal of Non-Linear Mechanics, vol. 43, no. 5, pp. 377–382, 2008.

23. S. D. Adhikary and J. C. Mishra, "Unsteady two-dimensional hydromagnetic flow and heat transfer of a fluid," International Journal of Applied Mathematics and Mechanics, vol. 7, no. 4, pp. 1–20, 2011.

24. F. M. Ali, R. Nazar, N. M. Arifin, and I. Pop, "Unsteady shrinking sheet with mass transfer in a rotating fluid," International Journal for Numerical Methods in Fluids, vol. 66, no. 11, pp. 1465–1474, 2011.

25. K. Bhattacharyya, "Effects of heat source/sink on mhd flow and heat transfer over a shrinking sheet with mass suction," Chemical Engineering Research Bulletin, vol. 15, no. 1, pp. 12–17, 2011.

26. M. Muhaimin, R. Kandasamy, and A. B. Khamis, "Effects of heat and mass transfer on nonlinear MHD boundary layer flow over a shrinking sheet in the presence of suction," Applied Mathematics and Mechanics, vol. 29, no. 10, pp. 1309–1317, 2008.

CHAPTER 4

NUMERICAL SOLUTION OF NONLINEAR SINE-GORDON EQUATION BY MODIFIED CUBIC B-SPLINE COLLOCATION METHOD

R. C. Mittal and Rachna Bhatia

Department of Mathematics, IIT Roorkee, Roorkee, Uttarakhand 247667, India

ABSTRACT

Modified cubic B-spline collocation method is discussed for the numerical solution of one-dimensional nonlinear sine-Gordon equation. The method is based on collocation of modified cubic B-splines over finite elements, so we have continuity of the dependent variable and its first two derivatives throughout the solution range. The given equation is decomposed into a system of equations and modified cubic B-spline basis functions have been used for spatial variable and its derivatives, which gives results in amenable system of ordinary differential equations. The resulting system of equation has subsequently been solved by SSP-RK54 scheme. The efficacy of the proposed approach has been confirmed with numerical experiments, which shows that the results obtained are acceptable and are in good agreement with earlier studies.

INTRODUCTION

In this paper we consider the one-dimensional sine-Gordon equation

$$\frac{\partial^2 u}{\partial t^2} = \frac{\partial^2 u}{\partial x^2} - \sin(u), \quad x \in (L_1, L_2), \ t \geq 0, \tag{1}$$

with initial conditions

$$u(x,0) = \phi_1(x), \qquad u_t(x,0) = \phi_2(x). \tag{2}$$

The Dirichlet boundary conditions are given by

$$u(L_1,t) = \psi_1(t), \qquad u(L_2,t) = \psi_2(t), \quad t \geq 0. \tag{3}$$

Citation: R. C. Mittal and Rachna Bhatia, "Numerical Solution of Nonlinear Sine-Gordon Equation by Modified Cubic B-Spline Collocation Method," International Journal of Partial Differential Equations, vol. 2014, Article ID 343497, 8 pages, 2014. doi:10.1155/2014/343497

The nonlinear sine-Gordon equation arises in many different applications such as propagation of fluxion in Josephson junctions [1], differential geometry, stability of fluid motion, nonlinear physics, and applied sciences [2]. The sine-Gordon equation (1) is a particular case of Klein-Gordon equation, which plays a significant role in many scientific applications such as solid state physics, nonlinear optics and quantum field theory [3], given by

$$\frac{\partial^2 u}{\partial t^2} - \alpha\frac{\partial^2 u}{\partial x^2} + g(u) = f(x,t), \tag{4}$$

where $g(u)$ is a nonlinear force and α is a constant

In the literature several schemes have been developed for the numerical solution of sine-Gordon equation. Ben-Yu et al. [4] proposed two difference schemes; Bratsos and Twizell [5] used method of lines to transform the initial/boundary value problem associated with (1) into a first order nonlinear initial value problem. Mohebbi and Dehghan [6] presented a combination of a compact finite difference approximation of fourth order and a fourth-order A-stable DIRKN method. Kuang and Lu [7] proposed two classes of finite difference method for generalized sine-Gordon equation; Bratsos and Twizell [8] presented a family of finite difference method, in which time and space derivatives are replaced by finite-difference approximations and then the equation is converted into a linear algebraic system. Wei [9] used the discrete singular convolution algorithm for the integration of (1). A variational iteration method to obtain approximate analytical solution of the sine-Gordon equation without any discretization has been developed by Batiha et al. [10]. Zheng [11] presented a numerical solution of sine-Gordon equation defined on the whole real axis. Bratsos [12] used a fourth-order rational approximation to the matrix exponential term in a threetime level recurrence relation for the numerical solution of (1). Dehghan and Shokri [13] solved the equation using collocation points and approximate the solution using radial basis functions; Dehghan and Mirzaei [14] used a boundary integral equation method; Rashidinia and Mohammadi [15] developed two implicit finite difference schemes, by using spline function approximations. Li-Min and Zong-Min [16] presented a meshless scheme by using a multiquadric quasiinterpolation without solving a large-scale linear system of equations, but a polynomial was needed to improve the accuracy of the scheme, while Jiang and Wang [17] proposed meshless approach by directly using high accuracy MQ quasiinterpolation without using any polynomial. A modified decomposition method for explicit and numerical solutions of the sine-Gordon equation in the form of convergent power series has been proposed by Kaya [18]. Uddin et al. [19] proposed a meshfree approach based on radial basis function for numerical solution of (1).

The B-spline possesses several properties such as minimal compact support and smoothness, which makes them suitable for the numerical solution of linear and nonlinear partial differential equations. B-spline with collocation provides a very simple solution procedure of differential equations.They also produce a spline function which is useful to obtain the solution at any point of the domain, while in finite difference methods [4, 6–8, 15], we can find the solution only at the selected knots. In the present method, approximate solutions of sine-Gordon equation are obtained using a modified cubic B-spline collocation method (MCBCM) in space and strong stability preserving Runge-Kutta (SSP-RK54) scheme [20] in time. The equation is converted into a system of partial differential equations and then, using MCBCM, it reduces into a system of ordinary differential equations. Finally we use SSP-RK54 scheme to solve the obtained system of ODEs. Numerical solution of nonlinear sine-Gordon equation has been obtained without using any transformation or without linearizing the nonlinear term.

The paper is organized as follows. In Section 2, cubic Bspline collocation method is explained. In Section 3, modified cubic B-spline basis functions are introduced and how to find the solution of (1)–(3) using these basis functions is explained. Initial vectors have been computed in Section 4. Numerical experiments are conducted in Section 5, to demonstrate the viability and the efficiency of the proposed method computationally, and results are compared with some previous results. Finally, brief conclusions drawn from the present study are presented in Section 6.

DESCRIPTION OF METHOD

The solution domain $L_1 \leq x \leq L_2$ is partitioned into a mesh of uniform length $h=x_{j+1}-x_j$, where $j = 0, 1, 2, \ldots, N-1, N$, such that $L_1 = x_0 < x_1 < \cdots < x_{N-1} < x_N = L_2$.

In the cubic B-spline collocation method the approximate solution can be written as the linear combination of cubic B-spline basis functions for the approximation space under consideration. Our numerical treatment for solving (1) using the collocation method with cubic B-Spline is to find an approximate solution $U_N(x, t)$ to the exact solution $u(x, t)$ in the form

$$U_N(x,t) = \sum_{j=-1}^{N+1} c_j(t) B_j(x), \tag{5}$$

where $c_j(t)$ are the time dependent quantities to be determined from boundary conditions and collocation from the differential equation.

The cubic B-spline $B(x)$ at the knots is given by

$$B_j(x) = \frac{1}{h^3} \begin{cases} (x - x_{j-2})^3 & x \in [x_{j-2}, x_{j-1}), \\ (x - x_{j-2})^3 - 4(x - x_{j-1})^3 & x \in [x_{j-1}, x_j), \\ (x_{j+2} - x)^3 - 4(x_{j+1} - x)^3 & x \in [x_j, x_{j+1}), \\ (x_{j+2} - x)^3 & x \in [x_{j+1}, x_{j+2}), \\ 0 & \text{otherwise}, \end{cases} \tag{6}$$

where the set of functions $\{B_{-1}, B_0, B_1, \ldots, B_{N-1}, B_N, B_{N+1}\}$ forms a basis for the function defined over the region $L_1 \leq x \leq L_2$ with the obvious adjustment of the boundary base functions to avoid undefined knots. Each cubic B-spline covers four elements so that an element is covered by four cubic B-splines. The values of $B(x)$ and its derivatives are tabulated in Table 1.

Table 1: The values of $B(x)$ and its derivatives.

x	x_{j-2}	x_{j-1}	x_j	x_{j+1}	x_{j+2}
$B_j(x)$	0	1	4	1	0
$B'_j(x)$	0	$\frac{3}{h}$	0	$-\frac{3}{h}$	0
$B''_j(x)$	0	$\frac{6}{h^2}$	$-\frac{12}{h^2}$	$\frac{6}{h^2}$	0

Then, using approximate function (5) and Table 1, the approximate values of $U(x, t)$ and its two derivatives at the knots are determined in terms of the time parameters c_j as follows:

$$\begin{aligned} U_j &= c_{j-1} + 4c_j + c_{j+1}, \\ U'_j &= \frac{3}{h}\left(c_{j+1} - c_{j-1}\right), \\ U''_j &= \frac{6}{h^2}\left(c_{j-1} - 2c_j + c_{j+1}\right). \end{aligned} \tag{7}$$

NUMERICAL SCHEME

We have used the following modified form of cubic B-spline basis functions [21] in the combination with collocation, to solve the sine-Gordon equation. Modified cubic B-spline basis functions have been used for handling the Dirichlet boundary conditions and finally we obtain a diagonally dominant system of differential equations. The procedure for modifying the basis functions is given as follows:

$$\tilde{B}_0(x) = B_0(x) + 2B_{-1}(x),$$
$$\tilde{B}_1(x) = B_1(x) - B_{-1}(x),$$
$$\tilde{B}_j(x) = B_j(x), \quad \text{for } j = 2,\ldots,N-2,$$
$$\tilde{B}_{N-1}(x) = B_{N-1}(x) - B_{N+1}(x),$$
$$\tilde{B}_N(x) = B_N(x) + 2B_{N+1}(x). \tag{8}$$

To find the numerical solution of sine-Gordon equation (1), first it is rewritten as a pair of coupled equations using the following transformation:

$$u_t(x,t) = v(x,t). \tag{9}$$

Then (1) transforms into a coupled system of equations as

$$u_t = v,$$
$$v_t = u_{xx} - \sin u. \tag{10}$$

Now for solving the couple of (10), using collocation method with modified cubic B-spline basis functions, first we assume our solution as the linear combination of modified cubic B-spline basis functions:

$$U_N(x,t) = \sum_{j=0}^{N} c_j(t)\,\tilde{B}_j(x). \tag{11}$$

Using the approximate solution (11), the approximate value of $U(x)$ can be written as

$$U_t(x) = \sum_{j=0}^{N} \dot{c}_j(t)\,\tilde{B}_j(x), \tag{12}$$

where $\dot{c}_j(t)$ is the derivative of $c_j(t)$ with respect to time t.

Using modified basis function (8) and Table 1 in (12), the value of $U(x)$ at different knots can be written as

$$U_t(x_0) = 6\dot{c}_0, \quad j = 0,$$
$$U_t(x_j) = \dot{c}_{j-1} + 4\dot{c}_j + \dot{c}_{j+1}, \quad j = 1,2,\ldots,N-1,$$
$$U_t(x_N) = 6\dot{c}_N, \quad j = N. \tag{13}$$

Using (11) in coupled system (10) and imposing the boundary conditions (3) at the boundary points, we have

$$U_t(x_0) = \dot{\psi}_1(t), \quad j = 0,$$
$$U_t(x_j) = v_j, \quad j = 1,2,\ldots,N-1,$$
$$U_t(x_N) = \dot{\psi}_2(t), \quad j = N,$$
$$v_t(x_0) = \dot{g}_1(t), \quad \text{for } j = 0, \tag{14}$$

$$v_t(x_j) = \sum_{j=0}^{N} c_j \tilde{B}_j''(x) - \sin(U_j), \quad \text{for } j = 1,2,\ldots,N-1,$$
$$v_t(x_N) = \dot{g}_2(t), \quad \text{for } j = N, \tag{15}$$

where $g_1(t)$ and $g_2(t)$ are $\dot{\psi}_1(t)$ and $\dot{\psi}_2(t)$, respectively.

Now using (13) in (14) and (8) and Table 1 in (15), we get the following system of equations:

$$6\dot{c}_0 = \dot{\psi}_1(t), \quad j = 0,$$
$$\dot{c}_{j-1} + 4\dot{c}_j + 4\dot{c}_{j+1} = v_j, \quad j = 1,2,\ldots,N-1,$$
$$6\dot{c}_N = \dot{\psi}_2(t), \quad j = N,$$
$$\dot{v}_0 = \dot{g}_1(t), \quad j = 0,$$
$$\dot{v}_j = \frac{6}{h^2}\left(c_{j-1} - 2c_j + c_{j+1}\right) - \sin\left(c_{j-1} + 4c_j + c_{j+1}\right),$$
$$j = 1,2,\ldots,N-1,$$
$$\dot{v}_N = \dot{g}_2(t), \quad j = N. \tag{16}$$

The systems (16) represent a system of first order differential equations and can be written as

$$\begin{bmatrix} 6 & 0 & \cdots & \cdots & 0 \\ 1 & 4 & 1 & \cdots & 0 \\ & \cdots & \cdots & \cdots & \\ & \cdots & \cdots & \cdots & \\ & & 1 & 4 & 1 \\ & & & 0 & 6 \end{bmatrix} \begin{bmatrix} \dot{c}_0 \\ \dot{c}_1 \\ \cdots \\ \cdots \\ \dot{c}_{N-1} \\ \dot{c}_N \end{bmatrix} = \begin{bmatrix} F_0 \\ F_1 \\ \cdots \\ \cdots \\ F_{N-1} \\ F_N \end{bmatrix}, \tag{17}$$

$$\begin{bmatrix} \dot{v}_0 \\ \dot{v}_1 \\ \cdots \\ \cdots \\ \dot{v}_{N-1} \\ \dot{v}_N \end{bmatrix} = \begin{bmatrix} G_0 \\ G_1 \\ \cdots \\ \cdots \\ G_{N-1} \\ G_N \end{bmatrix}, \tag{18}$$

where

$$F_0 = \dot{\psi}_1(t), \quad G_0 = \dot{g}_1(t), \quad F_j = v_j,$$
$$G_j = \frac{6}{h^2}\left(c_{j-1} - 2c_j + c_{j+1}\right) - \sin\left(c_{j-1} + 4c_j + c_{j+1}\right),$$
$$j = 1,2,\ldots,N-1,$$
$$F_N = \dot{\psi}_2(t), \quad G_N = \dot{g}_2(t). \tag{19}$$

Once the vector c^n has been determined at a specific time level, using (7), we can compute the approximate solution at the required knots. So first we solve system (17) for vector $\dot{c}$, by using Thomas algorithm only once at each time level $t>0$. Then the obtained system with the system (18) will give $(2N+2)$ first order ordinary differential equations and finally $(2N+2)$ first order ordinary differential equations have been solved by SSP-RK54 [20] scheme and consequently the approximate solution $U_N(x, t)$ is computed.

COMPUTATION OF INITIAL VECTOR

To find the solution at specific time level $t>0$, we need the initial vectors c^0 and v^0.

Using initial conditions (2), we have the following.

Initial Vector c^0

Consider the following:

$$U(x_j, 0) = \psi_1(0), \quad j = 0,$$
$$U(x_j, 0) = \phi_1(x_j), \quad j = 1,\ldots,N-1,$$
$$U(x_j, 0) = \psi_2(0), \quad j = N. \tag{20}$$

System (20) is a $(N+1) \times (N+1)$ tridiagonal system of equations, which can be written as

$$Ac^0 = B, \tag{21}$$

where

$$A = \begin{bmatrix} 6 & 0 & \cdots & \cdots & 0 \\ 1 & 4 & 1 & \cdots & 0 \\ & \cdots & \cdots & \cdots & \\ & \cdots & \cdots & \cdots & \\ & & 1 & 4 & 1 \\ & & & 0 & 6 \end{bmatrix}, \quad c^0 = \begin{bmatrix} \dot{c}_0 \\ \dot{c}_1 \\ \cdots \\ \cdots \\ \dot{c}_{N-1} \\ \dot{c}_N \end{bmatrix},$$

$$B = \begin{bmatrix} \psi_1(0) \\ \phi_1(x_1) \\ \cdots \\ \cdots \\ \phi_1(x_{N-1}) \\ \psi_2(0) \end{bmatrix}. \tag{22}$$

A is tridiagonal matrix. Using Thomas algorithm the solution of (20) can be easily found.

Initial Vector $\mathbf{v}^0$

Using the initial condition

$$U_t(x,0) = \phi_2(x), \tag{23}$$

we have

$$v(x_j,0) = \phi_2(x_j), \quad j = 0,1,\ldots,N-1,N, \tag{24}$$

which gives the initial vector $\mathbf{v}^0$.

NUMERICAL EXPERIMENTS

In this section, we consider four numerical examples to validate the proposed scheme. The accuracy of the scheme is verified by calculating L_2, L_∞, and root mean square errors and results are also compared with some published work.

L_2, L_∞, and RMS error norms are given by the following formulae:

$$L_2 = \|u - U_N\|_2 = \sqrt{h\sum_{j=0}^{N}\left|u_j - (U_N)_j\right|^2},$$

$$L_\infty = \|u - U_N\|_\infty = \max_j \left|u_j - (U_N)_j\right|,$$

$$\text{RMS error} = \frac{1}{N+1}\sqrt{\sum_{j=0}^{N}\left|u_j - (U_N)_j\right|^2}. \tag{25}$$

Example 1. In this example the numerical solutions of (1) are obtained in the computational domain $x \in [-a, a]$ with the initial conditions

$$u(x,0) = 0, \qquad u_t(x,0) = 4\operatorname{sech}(x). \tag{26}$$

The exact solution [6, 15, 16] is given as

$$u(x,t) = 4\arctan(t\operatorname{sech}(x)). \tag{27}$$

The boundary conditions (3) are obtained from the exact solution.

Case I (when a=1). First we solve the above example in the computational domain [−1, 1] with Δt = .0001 and for space step sizes h = .02, .04. In Table 2, we report the L_2 and L_∞ errors and compare them with those given in Dehghan and Shokri [13]. We see that our results are in good agreement with [13], when we take h = .04. For h = .02 our results are better than the result of [13] in terms of L_2 error. In Table 3, absolute errors, are reported at t = .01, .1, 1, with h = .02. A graph comparing the exact and numerical solutions at t=1 with h = .02 and Δt = .0001 is depicted in Figure 1.

Table 2: L_2 and L_∞ errors of Example 1 in the domain [−1, 1] at different time levels.

t	Present Scheme h = .04		Present Scheme h = .02		Dehghan and Shokri [13] h = .04	
	L_2	L_∞	L_2	L_∞	L_2	L_∞
.25	1.18×10^{-5}	2.32×10^{-5}	3.71×10^{-6}	8.20×10^{-6}	3.91×10^{-5}	5.89×10^{-6}
.50	4.19×10^{-5}	4.11×10^{-5}	1.34×10^{-5}	1.62×10^{-5}	1.30×10^{-4}	2.01×10^{-5}
.75	7.78×10^{-5}	1.02×10^{-4}	2.40×10^{-5}	2.54×10^{-5}	2.35×10^{-4}	3.63×10^{-5}
1	1.30×10^{-4}	1.64×10^{-4}	3.00×10^{-5}	4.14×10^{-5}	3.27×10^{-4}	5.07×10^{-5}

Table 3: Absolute errors of Example 1 at different time levels with h = .02, Δt = .0001.

x	t = .01	t = .1	t = 1
−.80	4.19×10^{-11}	4.24×10^{-8}	1.11×10^{-5}
−.60	1.72×10^{-11}	1.94×10^{-8}	6.17×10^{-7}
−.40	3.32×10^{-11}	3.01×10^{-8}	1.47×10^{-5}
0	1.15×10^{-10}	1.09×10^{-7}	4.13×10^{-5}
.40	3.32×10^{-11}	3.01×10^{-8}	1.47×10^{-5}
.60	1.72×10^{-11}	1.94×10^{-8}	6.17×10^{-7}
.80	4.19×10^{-11}	4.24×10^{-8}	1.11×10^{-5}

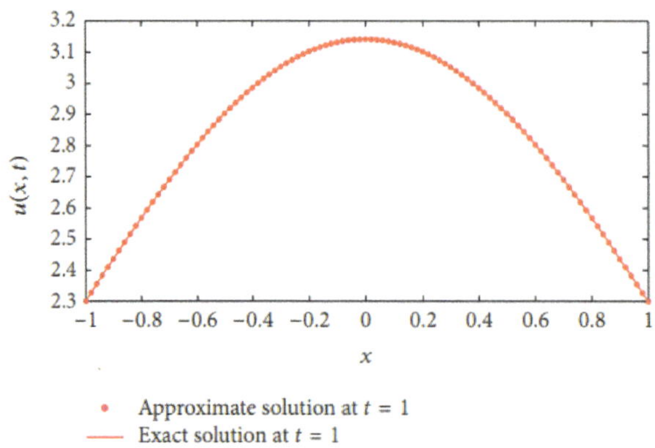

Figure 1: Approximate and exact solution at t=1 with h = .02 and Δt = .0001.

Case II. In the domain [−2, 2], the solutions of Example 1 are obtained with $\Delta t = .01$ and $h = .01$. In Table 4, we report the $L\infty$ and RMS errors at different time levels and results are compared with those of Li-Min and Zong-Min [16]. We noticed that our results are in good agreement with [16] in terms of $L\infty$ error and in terms of RMS error our results are better than [16]. Figure 2 depicts the comparison of exact and numerical solution at t=1.

Table 4: L_∞ and RMS errors of Example 1 in the domain [−2, 2] with $h = .01$, $\Delta t = .01$ at different time levels

t	Present Scheme		Li-Min and Zong-Min [16]	
	L_∞	RMS	L_∞	RMS
.1	7.20×10^{-6}	6.53×10^{-8}	1.54×10^{-6}	7.43×10^{-6}
.2	2.26×10^{-5}	2.69×10^{-7}	9.25×10^{-5}	1.76×10^{-5}
.3	4.54×10^{-5}	6.36×10^{-7}	9.02×10^{-5}	3.60×10^{-5}
.4	7.52×10^{-5}	1.19×10^{-6}	1.62×10^{-4}	1.62×10^{-4}
.5	1.12×10^{-4}	1.96×10^{-6}	2.58×10^{-4}	1.10×10^{-4}
.6	1.55×10^{-4}	2.96×10^{-6}	3.73×10^{-4}	1.65×10^{-4}
.7	2.04×10^{-4}	4.21×10^{-6}	4.98×10^{-4}	2.29×10^{-4}
.8	2.59×10^{-4}	5.72×10^{-6}	6.24×10^{-4}	2.98×10^{-4}
.9	3.19×10^{-4}	7.50×10^{-6}	7.44×10^{-4}	3.69×10^{-4}
1	3.84×10^{-4}	9.56×10^{-6}	8.49×10^{-4}	4.37×10^{-4}

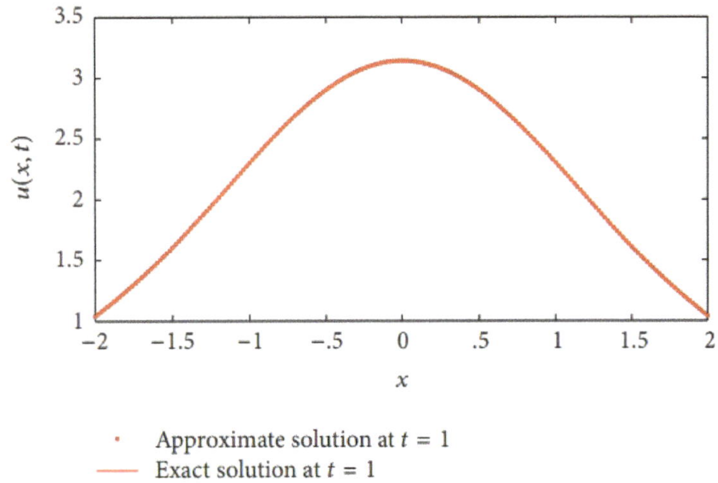

Figure 2: Approximate and exact solution at t=1 with $h = .01$ and $\Delta t = .01$.

Example 2. In this example we consider (1) in the computational domain $x \in [-3, 3]$ with the initial conditions.

$$u(x,0) = 4\arctan\left(\exp\left(\frac{x}{\sqrt{1-c^2}}\right)\right),$$

$$u_t(x,0) = \frac{-4c\gamma\exp(\gamma x)}{1+\exp(2\gamma x)}, \tag{28}$$

and the exact solution [6, 15] is given by

$$u(x,t) = 4\arctan(\exp(\gamma(x-ct))), \tag{29}$$

where c is the velocity of solitary wave and $\gamma = 1/\sqrt{1-c^2}$.

In Table 5, we report L_2 and L_∞ errors, for different values of h with $c = .5$ and $\Delta t = .0001$. We also compare our results with those of Dehghan and Shokri [13]. From Table 5, it is clear that our scheme and that of [13] have approximately similar $L2$ errors, for $h = .04$. For $h = .02$ our results are better than [13] in terms of $L2$ errors and approximately similar in terms of $L\infty$ error norm. We also compute L_2, L_∞ error norm for different values of h with $\Delta t = .0001$ at t=1 and calculate order of convergence, which is shown in Table 7.The absolute errors, for $t = .01$, .1, 1, are also reported in Table 6. Figure 3 depicts the graph between exact and numerical solutions at t=1.The boundary conditions (3) can be obtained from the exact solution.

Table 5: L_2 and L_∞ errors of Example 2 with $c = .5$ at different time levels

t	Present Scheme				Dehghan and Shokri [13]	
	$h = .04$		$h = .02$		$h = .04$	
	L_2	L_∞	L_2	L_∞	L_2	L_∞
.25	3.66×10^{-5}	4.90×10^{-5}	9.26×10^{-6}	1.21×10^{-6}	1.76×10^{-5}	4.95×10^{-6}
.50	9.00×10^{-5}	7.55×10^{-5}	2.24×10^{-5}	1.89×10^{-5}	4.31×10^{-5}	8.42×10^{-6}
.75	1.60×10^{-4}	1.43×10^{-4}	3.98×10^{-5}	3.57×10^{-5}	8.25×10^{-5}	1.65×10^{-5}
1	2.27×10^{-4}	2.10×10^{-4}	5.66×10^{-5}	5.25×10^{-5}	1.27×10^{-4}	2.51×10^{-5}

Table 6: Absolute errors of Example 2 at different time levels with $h = .02$, $\Delta t = .0001$.

x	$t = .01$	$t = .1$	$t = 1$
−2.5	6.05×10^{-10}	5.96×10^{-8}	5.28×10^{-6}
−2	8.76×10^{-10}	8.69×10^{-8}	1.21×10^{-6}
−1.5	5.64×10^{-10}	5.89×10^{-8}	9.16×10^{-8}
−1	2.68×10^{-9}	2.53×10^{-7}	2.02×10^{-5}
0	5.80×10^{-11}	5.64×10^{-8}	2.51×10^{-5}
1	2.72×10^{-9}	2.92×10^{-7}	4.82×10^{-5}
1.5	5.57×10^{-10}	5.08×10^{-8}	1.27×10^{-5}
2	8.78×10^{-10}	8.81×10^{-8}	2.21×10^{-6}
2.5	6.07×10^{-10}	6.15×10^{-8}	3.41×10^{-6}

Table 7: Errors and order of convergence for Example 2 at t=1

h	L_2	Order of convergence	L_∞	Order of convergence
.08	9.08×10^{-4}		8.40×10^{-4}	
.04	2.27×10^{-4}	2	2.10×10^{-4}	2
.02	5.66×10^{-5}	2.003	5.25×10^{-5}	2
.01	1.40×10^{-5}	2.015	1.31×10^{-5}	2.002
.005	3.65×10^{-6}	1.939	3.28×10^{-6}	1.998

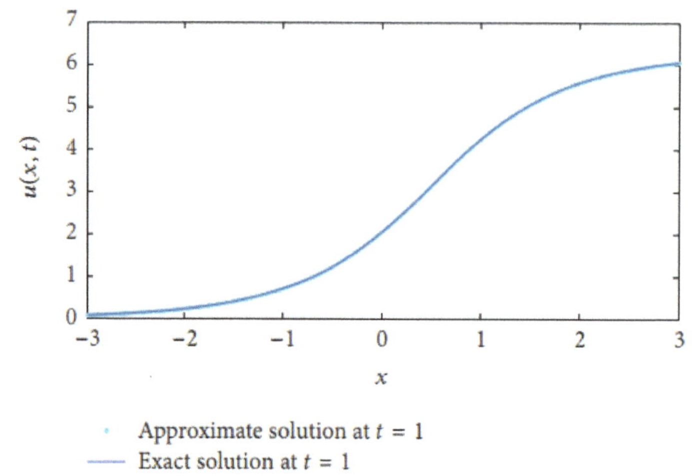

Figure 3: Approximate and exact solution at t=1 with $h = .02$ and $\Delta t = .0001$.

Example 3. In this example we consider nonlinear sineGordon equation in the computational domain $x \in [-10, 10]$ with the initial conditions

$$u(x,0) = 0, \qquad u_t(x,0) = \frac{4}{\sqrt{1+c^2}}\operatorname{sech}\left(\frac{x}{\sqrt{1+c^2}}\right). \tag{30}$$

The exact solution [12, 19] is given as

$$u(x,t) = 4\arctan\left(c^{-1}\sin(\bar{\gamma}ct)\operatorname{sech}(\bar{\gamma}x)\right), \tag{31}$$

where c is the velocity of solitary wave and $\bar{\gamma} = 1/\sqrt{1+c^2}$.

The boundary conditions (3) can be obtained from the exact solution.

We solve Example 3 with $c = .5$, $h = .01$, and $\Delta t = .001$. Computed L_2 and L_∞ errors are reported in Table 8 and compared with Uddin et al. [19] and Bratsos [12]. As we see from Table 8, our results are better. In Table 9, we report L_2 and L_∞ error norms for different values of h with $\Delta t = .001$ at $t = 20$, and using them we compute the order of convergence. It is clear that the present method is of second order of convergence. In Figure 4, we show the space-time graph of approximate solution for $t \leq 20$ with $h = .01$ and $\Delta t = .001$.

Table 8: L_2 and L_∞ errors of Example 3 with $c = .5$, $h = .01$, $\Delta t = .001$ at different time levels.

t	Present Scheme		Bratsos [12]	Uddin et al. [19]
	L_2	L_∞	L_∞	L_∞
1	7.448×10^{-6}	7.029×10^{-6}	$.98816 \times 10^{-3}$	1.474×10^{-3}
10	3.999×10^{-5}	2.226×10^{-5}	$.16291 \times 10^{-2}$	9.215×10^{-3}
20	6.467×10^{-4}	3.567×10^{-4}	$.10379 \times 10^{-2}$	3.038×10^{-1}

Table 9: Errors and order of convergence for Example 3 at $t = 20$.

h	L_2	Order of convergence	L_∞	Order of convergence
.08	4.171×10^{-2}		2.302×10^{-2}	
.04	1.038×10^{-2}	2.006	5.729×10^{-3}	2.006
.02	2.593×10^{-3}	2.001	1.430×10^{-3}	2.002
.01	6.467×10^{-4}	2.003	3.567×10^{-4}	2.003

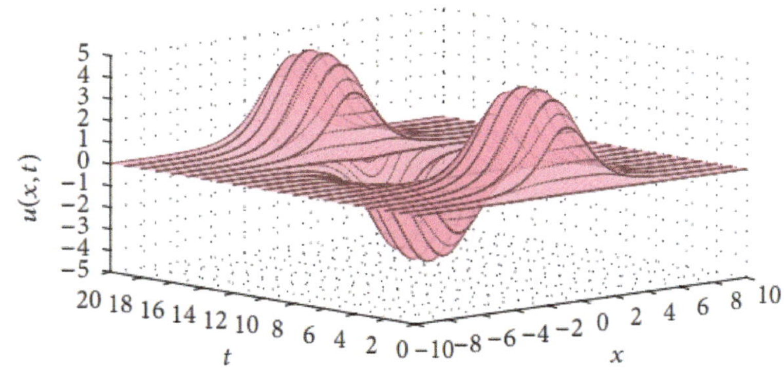

Figure 4: The graph of approximate solution up to $t = 20$, in domain $-10 \leq x \leq 10$..

Example 4. Now we consider (1) in the computational domain $x \in [-20, 20]$ with the initial conditions

$$u(x,0) = 4\arctan\left(c\sinh\left(\frac{x}{\sqrt{1-c^2}}\right)\right), \quad u_t(x,0) = 0. \tag{32}$$

The exact solution [12, 19] is given as

$$u(x,t) = 4\arctan\left(c\sinh(\gamma x)\operatorname{sech}(\gamma ct)\right), \tag{33}$$

where c is the velocity of solitary wave and $\gamma = 1/\sqrt{1-c^2}$.. The boundary conditions (3) can be obtained from the exact solution

We solve Example 4 with $c = .5$, $h = .01$, and $\Delta t = .001$ and results are reported in Table 10. We compare our results with those given in Uddin et al. [19] and Bratsos [12] in terms of L_∞ errors and found them better. In Table 11, we report the L_2 and L_∞ error norms for different values of h, with $\Delta t = .001$ at $t = 20$, and using them compute the order of convergence of the method. Figure 5 depicts the space-time graph of approximate solution for $t \leq 20$ with $h = .01$ and $\Delta t = .001$.

Table 10: L_2 and L_∞ errors of Example 4 with $c = .5$ at different time levels

t	Present Scheme $h = .01$ L_2	Present Scheme $h = .01$ L_∞	Bratsos [12] $h = .01$ L_∞	Uddin et al. [19] $N = 201$ L_∞
2	2.564×10^{-5}	1.818×10^{-5}	$.12760 \times 10^{-3}$	1.568×10^{-3}
10	8.850×10^{-5}	5.228×10^{-5}	$.19115 \times 10^{-3}$	3.151×10^{-3}
20	1.713×10^{-4}	9.438×10^{-5}	$.25189 \times 10^{-3}$	1.828×10^{-2}

Table 11: Errors and order of convergence for Example 4 at $t = 20$.

h	L_2	Order of convergence	L_∞	Order of convergence
.08	1.094×10^{-2}		6.025×10^{-3}	
.04	2.740×10^{-3}	1.997	1.509×10^{-3}	1.997
.02	6.851×10^{-4}	1.999	3.775×10^{-4}	1.999
.01	1.713×10^{-4}	1.999	9.438×10^{-5}	1.999

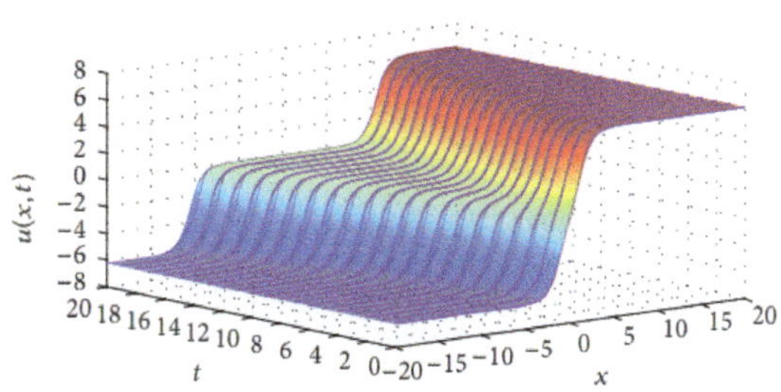

Figure 5: The graph of approximate solution up to $t = 20$, in domain $-20 \leq x \leq 20$.

CONCLUSIONS

This paper investigates the application of B-spline collocation method to represent the solution of sine-Gordon equation with Dirichlet's boundary conditions, by reducing it into coupled system of equations. The combination of modified cubic B-spline basis function in space and SSP-RK54 in time successfully worked to give reliable and accurate solutions of sine-Gordon equation. The numerical approximate solutions have been computed without using any transformation and linearization process. To demonstrate the accuracy and usefulness of the present scheme, four numerical experiments are carried out and results are compared with some earlier work. It is observed that the proposed method produces good results in comparison to those available in the literature. From the order of convergence calculated in Tables 7, 9, and 11, the method is shown to have a second order of convergence. The results reveal that the present method is an applicable technique and approximates the solutions very well.

REFERENCES

1. J. K. Perring and T. H. R. Skyrme, "A model unified field equation," Nuclear Physics, vol. 31, pp. 550–555, 1962.
2. A. Barone, F. Esposito, C. J. Magee, and A. C. Scott, "Theory and applications of the sine-Gordon equation," La Rivista del Nuovo Cimento, vol. 1, no. 2, pp. 227–267, 1971.
3. M. Dehghan and A. Shokri, "Numerical solution of the nonlinear Klein-Gordon equation using radial basis functions," Journal of Computational and Applied Mathematics, vol. 230, no. 2, pp. 400–410, 2009. ·
4. G. Ben-Yu, P. J. Pascual, M. J. Rodriguez, and L. Vázquez, "Numerical solution of the sine-Gordon equation," Applied Mathematics and Computation, vol. 18, no. 1, pp. 1–14, 1986.
5. A. G. Bratsos and E. H. Twizell, "The solution of the sine-Gordon equation using the method of lines,"International Journal of Computer Mathematics, vol. 61, no. 3-4, pp. 271–292, 1996.·
6. A. Mohebbi and M. Dehghan, "High-order solution of one-dimensional sine-Gordon equation using compact finite difference and DIRKN methods," Mathematical and Computer Modelling, vol. 51, no. 5-6, pp. 537–549, 2010.
7. J. X. Kuang and L. H. Lu, "Two classes of finite-difference methods for generalized sine-Gordon equations," Journal of Computational and Applied Mathematics, vol. 31, no. 3, pp. 389–396, 1990.
8. A. G. Bratsos and E. H. Twizell, "A family of parametric finite-difference methods for the solution of the sine-Gordon equation," Applied Mathematics and Computation, vol. 93, no. 2-3, pp. 117–137, 1998. ·
9. G. W. Wei, "Discrete singular convolution for the sine-Gordon equation," Physica D, vol. 137, no. 3-4, pp. 247–259, 2000.
10. B. Batiha, M. S. M. Noorani, and I. Hashim, "Numerical solution of sine-Gordon equation by variational iteration method," Physics Letters A, vol. 370, no. 5-6, pp. 437–440, 2007. ·
11. C. Zheng, "Numerical solution to the sine-Gordon equation defined on the whole real axis," SIAM Journal on Scientific Computing, vol. 29, no. 6, pp. 2494–2506, 2007.
12. A. G. Bratsos, "A fourth order numerical scheme for the one-dimensional sine-Gordon equation,"International Journal of Computer Mathematics, vol. 85, no. 7, pp. 1083–1095, 2008.·
13. M. Dehghan and A. Shokri, "A numerical method for one-dimensional nonlinear sine-Gordon equation using collocation and radial basis functions," Numerical Methods for Partial Differential Equations, vol. 24, no. 2, pp. 687–698, 2008.
14. M. Dehghan and D. Mirzaei, "The boundary integral equation approach for numerical solution of the one-dimensional sine-Gordon equation," Numerical Methods for Partial Differential Equations, vol. 24, no. 6, pp. 1405–1415, 2008.
15. J. Rashidinia and R. Mohammadi, "Tension spline solution of nonlinear sine-Gordon equation,"Numerical Algorithms, vol. 56, no. 1, pp. 129–142, 2011.·
16. M. Li-Min and W. Zong-Min, "A numerical method for one-dimensional nonlinear sine-Gordon equation using multiquadric quasi-interpolation," Chinese Physics B, vol. 18, no. 8, pp. 3099–3103, 2009.
17. Z.-W. Jiang and R.-H. Wang, "Numerical solution of one-dimensional Sine-Gordon equation using high accuracy multiquadric quasi-interpolation," Applied Mathematics and Computation, vol. 218, no. 15, pp. 7711–7716, 2012.
18. D. Kaya, "A numerical solution of the sine-Gordon equation using the modified decomposition method," Applied Mathematics and Computation, vol. 143, no. 2-3, pp. 309–317, 2003.
19. M. Uddin, S. Haq, and G. Qasim, "A meshfree approach for the numerical solution of nonlinear sine-Gordon equation," International Mathematical Forum, vol. 7, no. 21–24, pp. 1179–1186, 2012.
20. S. Gottlieb, C.-W. Shu, and E. Tadmor, "Strong stability-preserving high-order time discretization methods," SIAM Review, vol. 43, no. 1, pp. 89–112 (electronic), 2001.
21. R. C. Mittal and R. Bhatia, "Numerical solution of second order one dimensional hyperbolic telegraph equation by cubic B-spline collocation method," Applied Mathematics and Computation, vol. 220, pp. 496–506, 2013.

CHAPTER 5 SIMULATIONS OF TRANSFORMER INRUSH CURRENT BY USING BDF-BASED NUMERICAL METHODS

Amir Tokić,[1] Ivo Uglešić,[2] and Gorazd Štumberger[3]

[1]Faculty of Electrical Engineering, Tuzla University, 75000 Tuzla, Bosnia and Herzegovina

[2]Faculty of Electrical Engineering and Computing, Zagreb University, 11000 Zagreb, Croatia

[3]Faculty of Electrical Engineering and Computer Science, Maribor University, 2000 Maribor, Slovenia

ABSTRACT

This paper describes three different ways of transformer modeling for inrush current simulations. The developed transformer models are not dependent on an integration step, thus they can be incorporated in a state-space form of stiff differential equation systems. The eigenvalue propagations during simulation time cause very stiff equation systems. The state-space equation systems are solved by using A- and L-stable numerical differentiation formulas (NDF2) method. This method suppresses spurious numerical oscillations in the transient simulations. The comparisons between measured and simulated inrush and steady-state transformer currents are done for all three of the proposed models. The realized nonlinear inductor, nonlinear resistor, and hysteresis model can be incorporated in the EMTP-type programs by using a combination of existing trapezoidal and proposed NDF2 methods.

INTRODUCTION

The transformer represents one of the essential elements in power systems. Proper modeling of the transformer is very important in different transient and steady-state power systems simulations.The nonlinearity of the transformer iron core is the most important parameter in simulations of lowfrequency transients, such as transformer inrush current, ferroresonance, temporary overvoltages during transformer energizations, load rejections, and harmonic analysis. All these transients belong to a frequency range of up to 1 kHz [1] for which it is not necessary to take into account frequency dependencies of the transformer parameters. A standard Steinmetz T equivalent circuit model of a two-winding single-phase transformer is shown in Figure 1. In addition, there is an analogous Π-shaped equivalent model.This model is rarely used due to the fact that the detailed transformer construction has to be known for determining the parameters of the Π equivalent model.

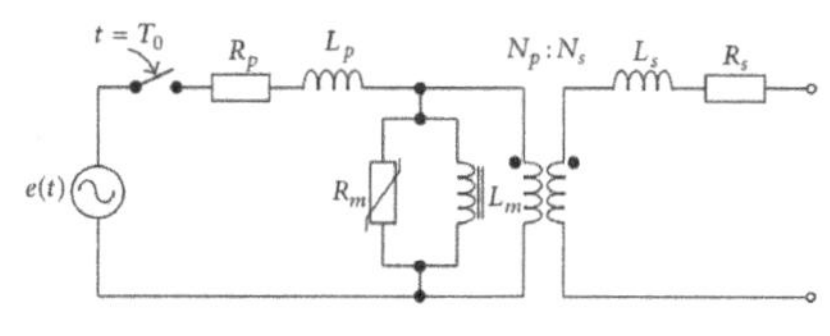

Figure 1: Standard T equivalent transformer circuit model.

Different types of T transformer models will be used in this paper in the first place. Transformer parameters can be divided into two basic groups: winding and ironcore parameters. In Figure 1, R_p and R_s represent the serial winding resistances that generally include the Joule and eddy current losses in the windings, whilst L_p and L_s represent the serial

Citation: Amir Tokić, Ivo Uglešić, and Gorazd Štumberger, "Simulations of Transformer Inrush Current by Using BDF-Based Numerical Methods," Mathematical Problems in Engineering, vol. 2013, Article ID 215647, 10 pages, 2013. doi:10.1155/2013/215647

leakage inductances divided amongst primary and secondary windings. The shunt branch parameters describe iron core behavior, where the resistance R_m represents the core eddy current losses, whilst inductance L_m represents the saturation or hysteresis phenomena in the transformer core. The winding parameters are linear, whilst the iron core parameters describe nonlinear phenomena during the analysis of low-frequency transformer transients.

In general, there are three different approaches when modeling transformer iron-core nonlinearities:

(a) linear resistor R_m and nonlinear inductor L_m,

(b) nonlinear resistor R_m and nonlinear inductor L_m,

(c) linear resistor R_m and nonlinear hysteresis inductor L_m.

During the analysis of low-frequency transformer transients such as inrush current and ferroresonance, the more used model is the model (a) because of its simplicity; relatively rare used models are (b), and (c). For example, [2–10] use the (a) based model of transformer, [11–14] use the (b) but [15–18] use the (c) based model of the transformer.

Typical procedures for obtaining an instantaneous nonlinear magnetizing curve and nonlinear curve of core losses, by the separation technique of losses from the magnetizing curve, are described in [19, 20].

The modeling of nonlinear or hysteresis inductor and nonlinear core loss resistor can be done by using the curve fitting procedure for the approximation of nonlinearity or by using piecewise linear representation of the nonlinear curve. The well-known curve fitting approximations are obtained by using the polynomial, exponential, arctg, and hyperbolic functions. The polynomial approximation was suggested by Mayergoyz in [21]. Exponential approximation was introduced by Trutt et al. in [22]. Arctg approximation was started by Karlqvist in [23], and the hyperbolic functions were introduced by Takacs in [24] and refined by Takacs in [25].

The piecewise linearization of a nonlinear curve for the modeling of nonlinear or hysteretic inductor, on the other hand, is used in [7–10]. Linearization of a nonlinear curve has certain advantages and disadvantages. Successful control of the numerical stability properties of the applied numerical methods is the main advantage [26–28]. Also, another advantage of this linearization is the improved speed compared to those classical methods used in calculations within nonlinear algebraic-differential equation systems. On the other hand, piecewise linearization has disadvantages related to overshooting effects [27].

TRANSFORMER IRON CORE MODELING

The original way of modeling nonlinear transformer iron core in low-frequency transient analysis, using three mentioned models, is derived in this paper.

Modeling of Nonlinear Core Inductor

The nonlinear core inductor can be described using a magnetizing curve: magnetizing current versus magnetic flux, as shown in Figure 2.

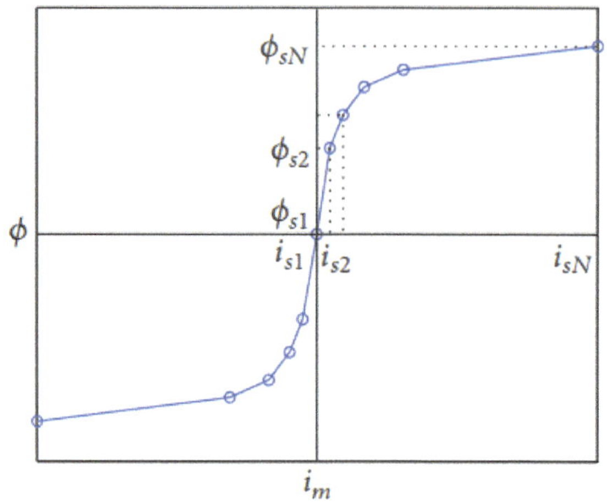

Figure 2: Nonlinear curve of core inductor.

When this curve is piecewise linear, the results are the input vectors magnetizing currents $I_{L_m} = [i_{s_1}, i_{s_2}, \ldots, i_{s_N}]^T$ and magnetic fluxes $\Phi_{L_m} = [\phi_{s_1}, \phi_{s_2}, \ldots, \phi_{s_N}]^T$, whereas N is the total number of magnetizing curve regions. The magnetizing current for the kth linear region of the magnetizing curve, $k = 1, 2, \ldots, (N - 1)$, is calculated using the equation

$$i_{m_k} = \frac{1}{L_{m_k}}\phi + \text{sign}(\phi)\, I_{s_k} = \frac{1}{L_{m_k}}\phi + S_{\phi_k}, \tag{1}$$

where

$L_{m_k} = (\phi_{s_{k+1}} - \phi_{s_k})/(i_{s_{k+1}} - i_{s_k})$ and $I_{s_k} = i_{s_k} - (1/L_{m_k})\phi_{s_k}$.

Based on (1), it is possible to create a nonlinear inductor equivalent model using a linear inductor and a corresponding current source, Figure 3. This model is functionally dependent on the position of the operating point k. At the same time, contrary to EMTP-based equivalent models, the inductor model is not dependent on the integration step.

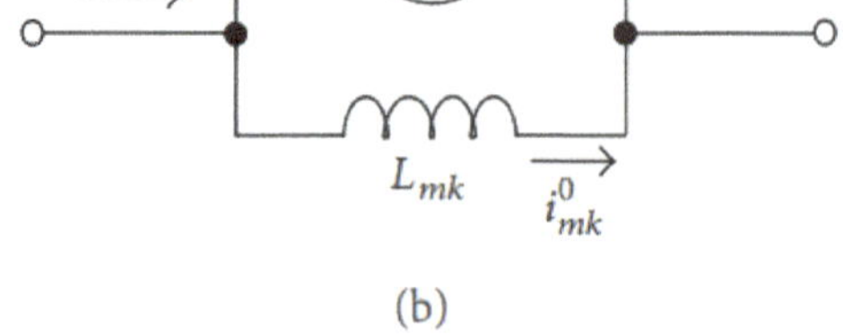

Figure 3: (a) Nonlinear inductor and (b) equivalent model.

Modeling of Nonlinear Core Resistor

Analogous to the nonlinear core inductor, the nonlinear core resistor can be described using the curve: resistor current versus corresponding resistor voltage, as shown in Figure 4.

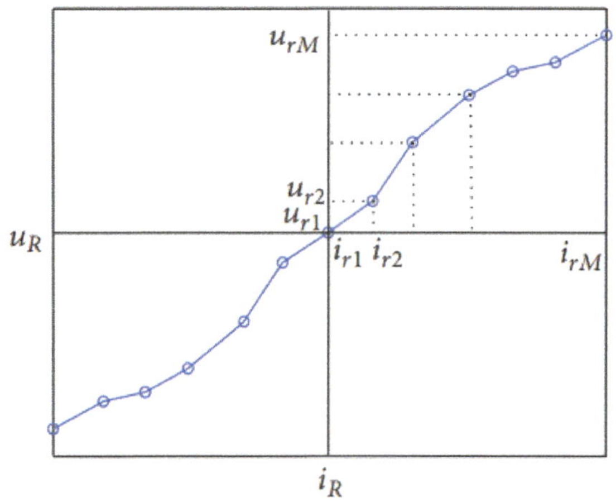

Figure 4: Nonlinear curve of core resistor.

In this case, the input vectors are the resistor currents $I_{R_m} = [i_{r_1}, i_{r_2}, \ldots, i_{r_M}]^T$ and resistor voltages $U_{R_m} = [u_{r_1}, u_{r_2}, \ldots, u_{r_M}]^T$, where M is the total number of resistor curve regions. The resistor current for the kth linear region of the resistor curve, $k = 1, 2, \ldots, (M - 1)$, is calculated using the equation

$$i_{R_k} = \frac{1}{R_{m_k}} u_R + \operatorname{sign}(u_R) I_{r_k} = \frac{1}{R_{m_k}} u_R + S_{r_k},$$

where $R_{m_k} = (u_{r_{k+1}} - u_{r_k})/(i_{r_{k+1}} - i_{r_k})$ and $I_{r_k} = i_{r_k} - (1/R_{m_k}) u_{r_k}$.

In the same way, it is possible to create a nonlinear resistor equivalent model using a linear resistor and a corresponding current source, Figure 5.

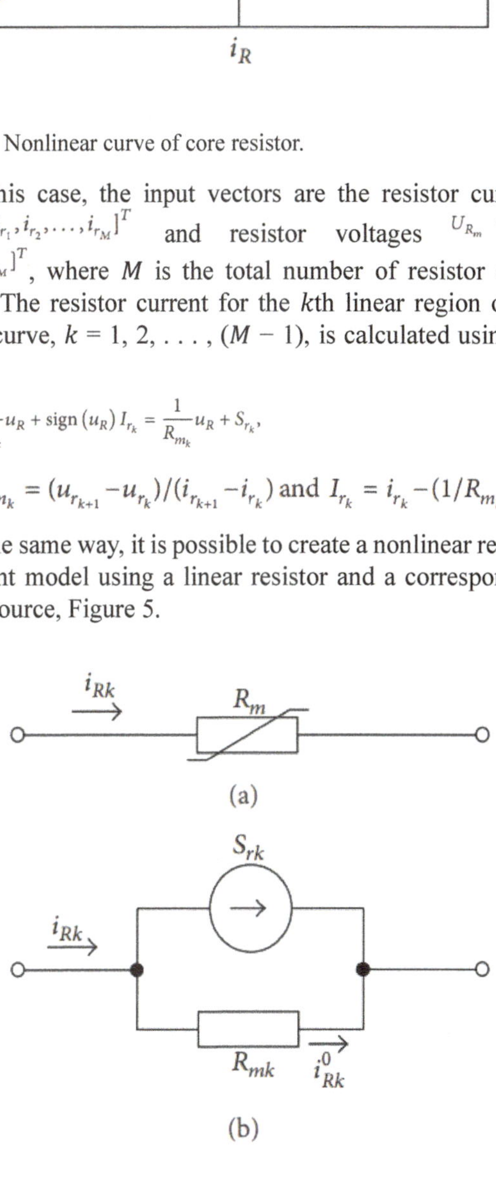

Figure 5: (a) Nonlinear resistor and (b) equivalent model.

Modeling of Hysteresis Core Inductor

By definition, the major loop is the largest possible loop whose end points reach the technical saturation. Beyond the saturation points the hysteresis is a single-valued function. Symmetrical or asymmetrical minor hysteresis loops lie within the major loop. The following is assumed, based on experimental results, for hysteresis modeling (Figure 6) (a) the operating point trajectories lie within the major hysteresis loop, (b) in the direction of the flux increase (decrease), the operating point heads towards the lower (upper) branch of the major loop, and (c) after the flux reversal points are detected (1, 2, 3), the operating point trajectories will head towards the previous reversal point.

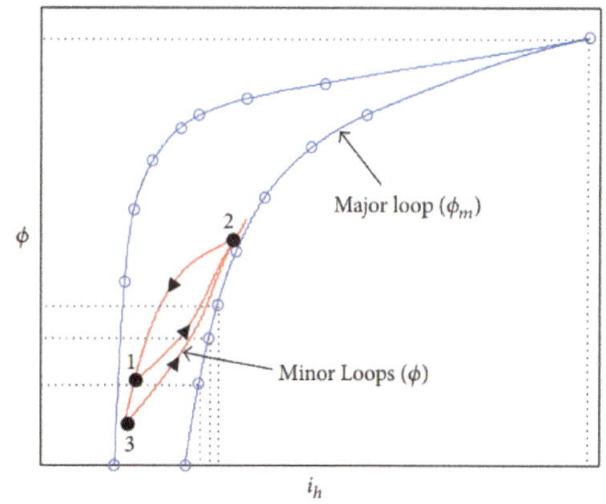

Figure 6: Major and minor hysteresis loops.

Therefore, following the symmetry, the major hysteresis loop is defined by the points of the lower (or upper) half of the major hysteresis loops, that is, by input vectors are: hysteresis currents $I_{L_h} = [i_{h_1}, i_{h_2}, \ldots, i_{h_P}]^T$ and magnetic fluxes $\Phi_{L_h} = [\phi_{h_1}, \phi_{h_2}, \ldots, \phi_{h_P}]^T$, where P is the total number of the major hysteresis loops.

The expression for the hysteresis current of the kth piecewise region in terms of the main flux ϕ_m, $k = 1, 2, \ldots, (P-1)$, Figure 6, can be stipulated as.

$$i_{h_k} = \frac{1}{L_{m_k}} \phi_m + \operatorname{sign}(\Delta\phi_m) I_{h_k}, \tag{3}$$

where $\Delta\phi_m = \phi_m(t_j) - \phi_m(t_{j-1})$, $j = 1, 2, 3, \ldots, J_{\max}$, $L_{m_k} = (\phi_{h_{k+1}} - \phi_{h_k})/(i_{h_{k+1}} - i_{h_k})$, and $I_{h_k} = i_{h_k} - (1/L_{m_k})\phi_{h_k}$.

In the general case, if it is assumed that the distance between the operating point and the major loop is a linear function of the magnetic flux, for both the ascending and descending trajectory, the next equation is valid:

$$d = \mu_k \phi + \eta_k = \operatorname{sign}(\Delta\phi)(\phi - \phi_m). \tag{4}$$

The unknown coefficients μ_k and η_k are determined on condition that the two successive reversal points ($\phi_{\text{rev1}}, d_{\text{rev1}}$) and ($\phi_{\text{rev2}}, d_{\text{rev2}}$) lie on this line.

Based on relations (3)-(4) it can be proved that the expression for the hysteresis current of the kth linear region that describes the trajectory of the actual operating point is noting that $\Delta L_{m_k} = (\operatorname{sign}(\Delta\phi)\mu_k/(\operatorname{sign}(\Delta\phi)\mu_k - 1)) L_{m_k}$ and $\Delta I_k = (1/L_{m_k})\eta_k$.

$$i_{h_k} = \frac{1}{L_{m_k} - \Delta L_{m_k}} \phi + \operatorname{sign}(\Delta\phi) \cdot (I_{h_k} - \Delta I_k), \tag{5}$$

In this way the hysteresis inductor L_h in Figure 3(a) can be modeled by introducing a linear inductor L_{h_k} in parallel connection with a current source S_{h_k}, both functionally dependent on the actual linear region k, Figure 7 as follows:

$$L_{h_k} = L_{m_k} - \Delta L_{m_k},$$

$$S_{h_k} = \operatorname{sign}(\Delta\phi) \cdot (I_{h_k} - \Delta I_k). \tag{6}$$

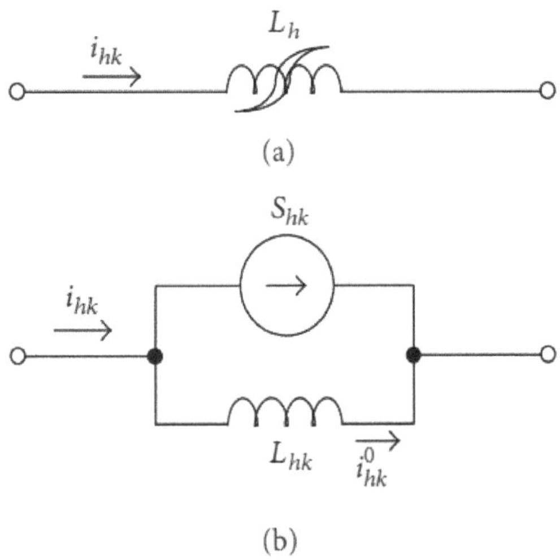

Figure 7: (a) Hysteresis inductor and (b) equivalent model.

It is noted that all three developed models has a special routine for eliminating the possible overshooting effect [26–28].

INRUSH CURRENT MODELING AND NUMERICAL METHODS

The transformer inrush current is a well-known transient response to the energization of a transformer iron core. During transformer energization, depending on the value of the remanent flux, the magnetization curve and the breaker switching instant, the iron core magnetic flux can reach a twice higher value than the nominal operating value. In the case when the remanent flux is nearly as high as the saturation, then the inductance is reduced to near zero. The only initial impedance is the small ohmic resistance of the primary coil. As a result, the transformer iron core is driven into a saturation, and inrush current is produced. The transformer inrush current, which could be many times higher than the operational current, may cause irreparable damages to the circuit without taking into account the design stage.

The developed models for the nonlinear inductor, nonlinear resistor, and hysteresis inductor are very suitable for formulation state-space equations that describe low- frequency transformer transients such as transformer energization, Figure 8.

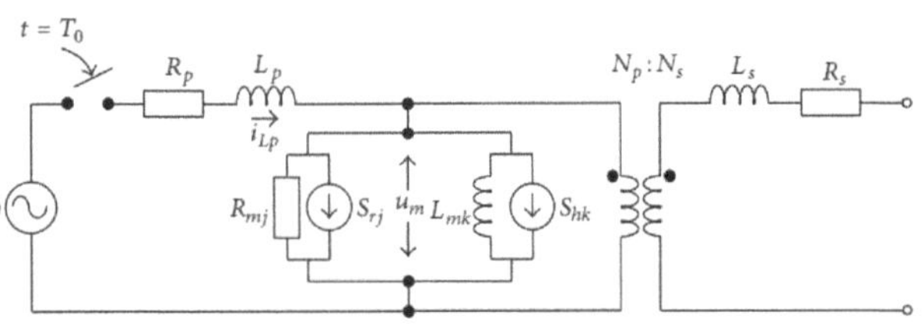

Figure 8: Equivalent transformer model for inrush current simulations.

An arbitrary numerical method could be applied in such a state-space form. In the EMTP-type of programs, the elements are strongly dependent on the integration step; this fact becomes apparent when a trapezoidal numerical method is applied to the relevant branch. The general algorithm procedure for generating state-space matrixes is shown in [27]. According to this procedure, a state-space equation is developed that describes transformer transients during inrush current analysis:

$$\frac{dX(t)}{dt} = A_{j,k}X(t) + B_{j,k}U(t) = F(X,t), \tag{7}$$

where the state-space vector and input vector are:

$$X(t) = \left[i_{L_p} \;\; \phi\right]^T,$$

$$U(t) = \left[e(t) \;\; S_{\phi_k} \;\; S_{r_j}\right]^T. \tag{8}$$

System matrixes are, respectively as follows:

$$A_{j,k} = \begin{bmatrix} -\dfrac{R_p + R_{m_j}}{L_p} & \dfrac{R_{m_j}}{L_p L_{m_k}} \\ R_{m_j} & -\dfrac{R_{m_j}}{L_{m_k}} \end{bmatrix},$$

$$B_{j,k} = \begin{bmatrix} \dfrac{1}{L_p} & 0 \\ \dfrac{R_{m_j}}{L_p} & -R_{m_j} \\ \dfrac{R_{m_j}}{L_p} & -R_{m_j} \end{bmatrix}^T. \tag{9}$$

It is very important to discover whether the demonstrated system is a stiff system. Stiff systems are categorized as those different components of solutions which evolve on very different time scales occurring simultaneously, that is, the rates of change of the various components of the solutions which differ markedly. Stiffness is a property of system with strong implications for its practical solution using numerical methods. The stiffness of system is defined by two factors: stiffness ratio $\xi_{j,k}$ and stiffness index $\zeta_{j,k}$ for all state matrixes $A_{j,}$.:

$$\xi_{j,k} = \frac{\max_i \left|\mathrm{Re}\left(\lambda_{j,k}^{(i)}\right)\right|}{\min_i \left|\mathrm{Re}\left(\lambda_{j,k}^{(i)}\right)\right|},$$

$$\zeta_{j,k} = \max_i \left|\mathrm{Re}\left(\lambda_{j,k}^{(i)}\right)\right|, \tag{10}$$

where $\lambda_{j,k}^{(i)}, i = 1, 2, \ldots, \dim(A_{j,k})$ are eigenvalues of all state matrixes $A_{j,k}$.. In the case for $\xi_{j,k} \gg 1$ it is a stiff system, and in the case for $\zeta_{j,k} \to \infty$ it is a very stiff system

The state equations (7) are traditionally solved using the implicit *A*-stable, second-order trapezoidal method [7]:

$$X_{n+1} = X_n + \frac{\Delta t}{2}\left[F(X_n, t_n) + F(X_{n+1}, t_{n+1})\right], \quad n = 1, 2, 3, \ldots. \tag{11}$$

The trapezoidal method is suitable for nonstiff and moderate stiff systems; however for a very stiff system this method could be inaccurate, and other techniques should be used [26–30]. Indeed, the trapezoidal method is not *L*- stable, such that, for state matrixes $A_{j,}$ with eigenvalues containing large negative real parts, this method produces unwanted numerical oscillations. In addition, the classical explicit numerical methods are not applicable for stiff or very stiff systems due to finite regions of numerical stability.

On the other hand, the Backward Differentiation Formulas (BDFp) methods of pth order, $p \leq 5$, as introduced by Gear in 1971, have the following form [29, 30]:

$$\sum_{m=1}^{p} \frac{1}{m} \nabla^m X_{n+1} = \Delta t F\left(X_{n+1}, t_{n+1}\right). \tag{12}$$

The order of the truncation errors for the BDFp methods is Δt^{p+1} [29, 30]. The BDFp methods are (α)- and L- stable, with stability angles ranging between 90∘ , 90∘ , 86∘ , 73∘ , and 51∘ [25]. The L-stability properties of the BDFp methods lead to the suppression of numerical oscillations, whereas the trapezoidal method is not free from numerical oscillations [29, 30]. In addition, Numerical Differentiation Formulas (NDFp), as suggested by Klopfenstein in 1971, are a modification of the BDFp's methods with the next relations [31, 32]:

$$\sum_{m=1}^{p} \frac{1}{m} \nabla^m X_{n+1} = \Delta t F\left(X_{n+1}, t_{n+1}\right) + \kappa \gamma_p \left(X_{n+1} - X_{n+1}^{[0]}\right), \tag{13}$$

where the coefficients are $\gamma_p = \sum_{m=1}^{p}(1/m)$, the predicted value is $X_{n+1}^{[0]} = \sum_{m=0}^{p} \nabla^m X_n$, and parameter κ was introduced by Shampine and Reichelt [32], which is a compromise made in balancing efficiency in step size and stability angle of the NDFp. These methods are also (α)- and L-stable [32]. Compared with the BDFp's, the NDFp methods achieve the same accuracy as BDFp methods with a bigger stepsize percents 26%, 26%, 26%, 12%, and 0%, respectively. This implies improvements in the efficiency of the methods. However, the percent changes in the stability angle are 0%, 0%, −7%, −10%, and 0%, respectively. It can be concluded the NDFp methods are more precise than the BDFp but not more stable. The other modifications of original BDFp methods are the extended BDF methods as proposed by Cash in [33], the generalized A-BDF methods as introduced by Fredebeul in [34], the diagonalizable extended BDF methods as suggested by Frank and van der Houwen in [35], a predictor modification to the extended BDF methods as introduced by Alberdi and Anza in [36], and the block BDF methods developed by Yatim et al. in [37].

The main aim of this paper was to explore the types of differential equation systems describing the energization of a transformer, using appropriate numerical method for the correct simulations of equations. In general, for simulating electrical systems, the priority is that the numerical method is A-stable, has a high accuracy, and successfully solves a (very) stiff system.

In regard to these requirements, the conclusion is that methods BDF1 and -2 and NDF1 and -2 are A- and L-stable. They are generally well suited for simulations of nonlinear electrical systems. This paper realizes an algorithm for the solution of (7) based on the usages of the NDF2 or BDF2 methods. These methods were selected because of the fact that they have the same truncation errors of order Δt^3 , like a trapezoidal method, and they are A- and L-stable. On the other hand, it is shown that it is possible to combine these methods using the widely used trapezoidal method for simulating electrical systems.

INRUSH CURRENT MEASUREMENTS AND SIMULATIONS

Three developed single-phase transformer models were tested on an example of a transformer inrush current transient.

The system and transformer parameters are

(i) system voltage: $e(t) = 328 \cos(\omega t - 39∘)$;
(ii) nominal transformer power: $S_{tr} = 300$ VA;
(iii) primary/secondary voltage: $U_p = 220/24$ V;
(iv) short circuit voltage: $u_k\% = 5.45\%$;
(v) primary winding resistance: $R_p = 3.75\ \Omega$;
(vi) primary winding leakage inductance: $L_p = 2.54$ mH;
(vii) core loss resistance: $R_m = 3826\ \Omega$.

The nonlinear magnetizing curve with a major hysteresis loop is shown in Figure 9. A nonlinear curve of an iron core losses resistor is shown in Figure 10.

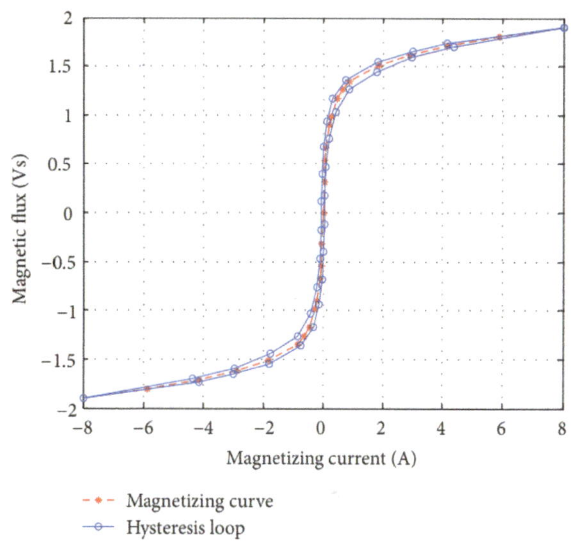

Figure 9: Magnetizing curve and hysteresis loop.

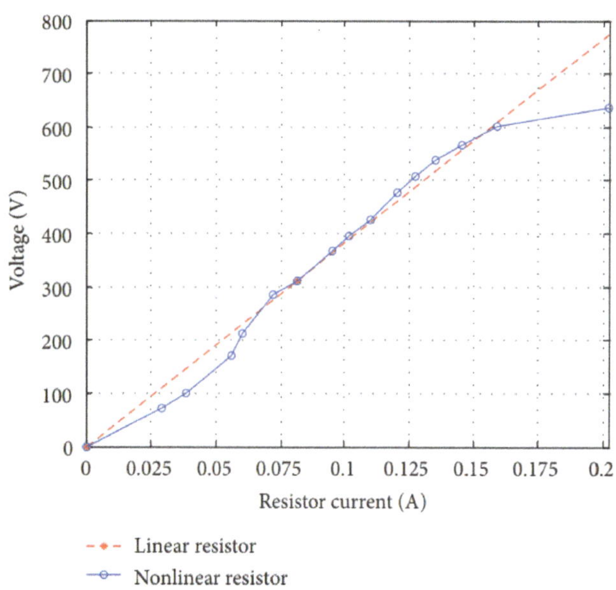

Figure 10: Nonlinear core loss resistor curve.

Figures 11 and 12 present the results of measurement of transformer inrush and steady-state current. In addition, harmonic analysis of the transformer inrush current for the first four harmonic components is realized, Figure 13.

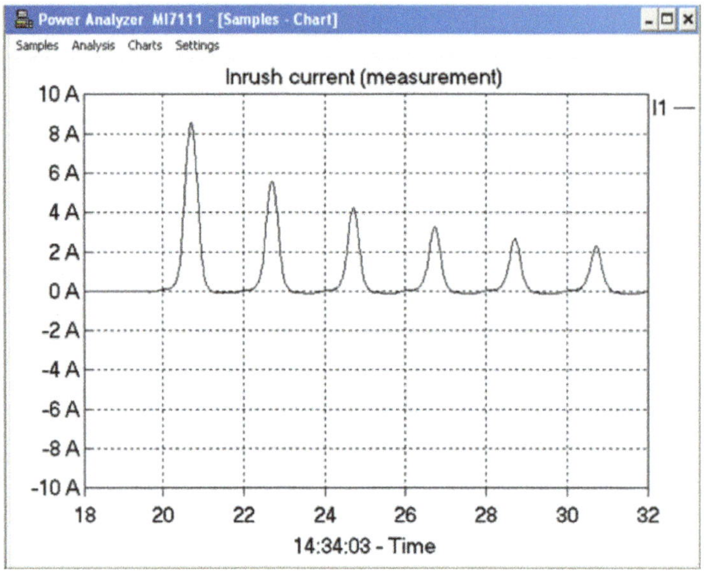

Figure 11: Measured transformer inrush current.

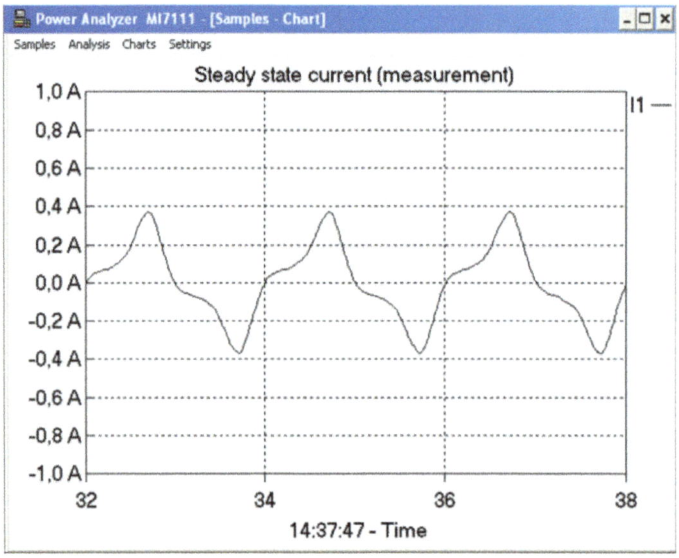

Figure 12: Measured transformer steady-state current.

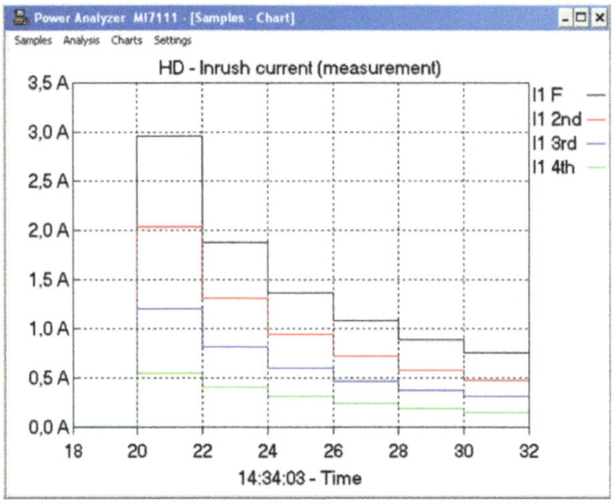

Figure 13: Harmonic content of measured inrush current.

Figure 14 shows the simulation results of the developed algorithm for Model 3 realized using the classical trapezoidal method with integration step $\Delta t = 100\ \mu sec$.

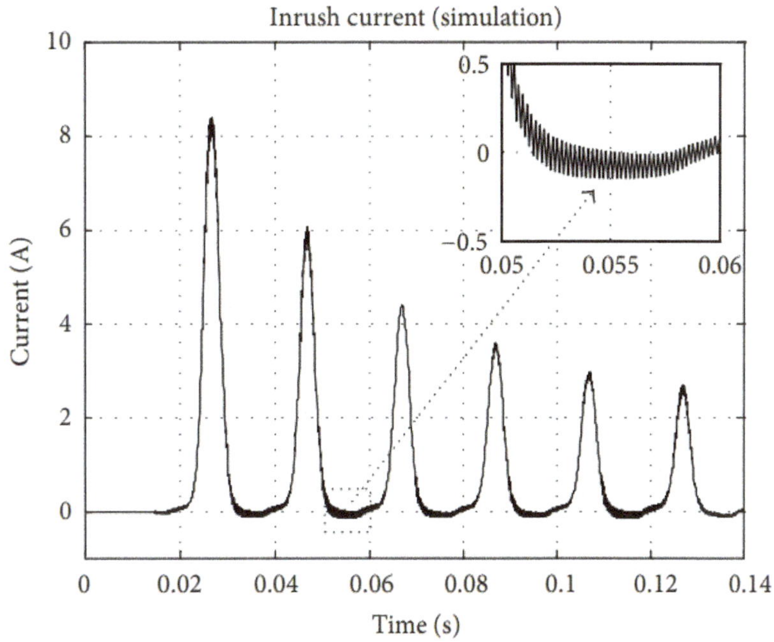

Figure 14: Inrush current simulation, Model 3, trapezoidal method, $\Delta t = 100\ \mu sec$.

Figure 14 clearly shows the existence of numerical oscillations during the trapezoidal method's usage. Otherwise, any simulations of the developed models (Model 1, Model 2, or Model 3), using trapezoidal method, clearly showed the existence of unwanted numerical oscillations.

In order to investigate the causes of numerical oscillations during simulation of maximum and minimum eigenvalues, stiffness ratios and stiffness indexes were calculated at each integration step. Figure 15 shows the results of the calculated maximum and minimum eigenvalues during the simulation times.

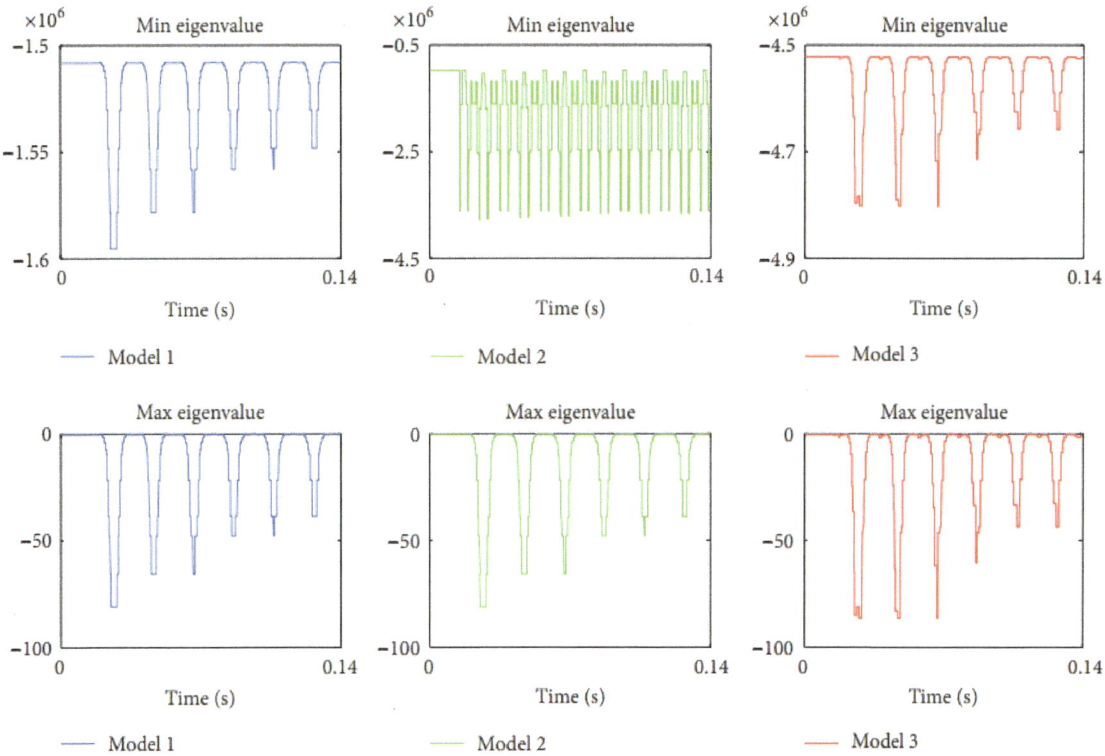

Figure 15: Eigenvalue propagation during the simulation time: all three models.

Table 1 shows the borders of the analyzed stiffness parameters. It is obvious that they are very stiff systems for all three cases.

Table 1: Stiffness ratios and stiffness indexes of the system.

Model 1	$1.508 \cdot 10^6 \leq \zeta_{j,k} \leq 1.596 \cdot 10^6$ $1.965 \cdot 10^4 \leq \xi_{j,k} \leq 4.949 \cdot 10^4$
Model 2	$0.964 \cdot 10^6 \leq \zeta_{j,k} \leq 3.775 \cdot 10^6$ $1.256 \cdot 10^4 \leq \xi_{j,k} \leq 1.183 \cdot 10^7$
Model 3	$4.521 \cdot 10^6 \leq \zeta_{j,k} \leq 4.784 \cdot 10^6$ $4.622 \cdot 10^4 \leq \xi_{j,k} \leq 1.566 \cdot 10^7$

It is interesting that the extreme values of parameters $\xi_{j,}$ rose in the unsaturated regions of the magnetizing (hysteresis) curve, and the extreme values of parameter $\zeta_{j,k}$ rose in the saturated region of this curve. Also, it is interesting that the time function of parameter $\zeta_{j,}$ is an analog to the inrush current waveform in all three cases.

In view of the mentioned reasons, the BDF2 and NDF2 methods were used for simulation of transformer inrush current. Figures 16 and 17 show the results when comparing the measured and simulated inrush current and steady-state transformer current by usage of the NDF2 method with an integration step of $\Delta t = 100\ \mu$sec.

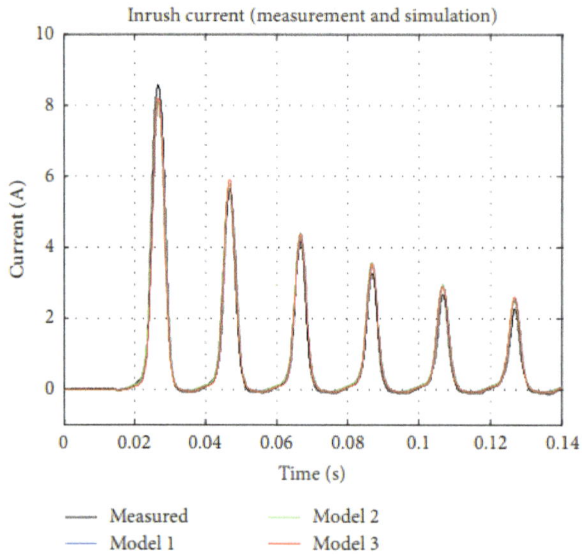

Figure 16: Measured and simulated transformer inrush current, NDF2 method, $\Delta t = 100\ \mu$sec.

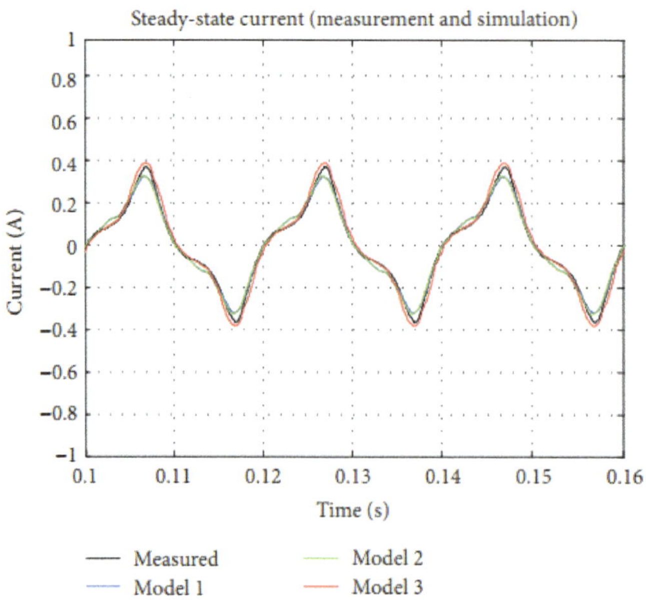

Figure 17: Measured and simulated transformer steady-state current, NDF2 method, $\Delta t = 100\ \mu$sec.

Figure 18 shows the peak values for the inrush currents errors for all three models. It is necessary to note that the maximum error when using Models 1 and 2 was 5.29%, whilst when using Model 3, the maximum error was 4.30%.

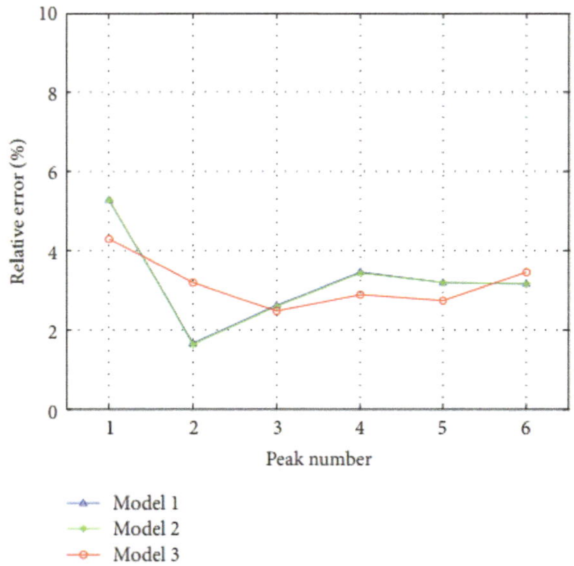

Figure 18: Relative error of peak values of inrush current.

Table 2 shows the error in peak value for the transformer steady-state current. Minimum error was in Model 3.

Table 2: Peak error of steady-state current.

Model	Model 1	Model 2	Model 3
Peak error [%]	13.18%	11.98%	4.56%

In addition, a comparison of the harmonic contents between the measured and simulated inrush current is realized, Figure 19. This figure shows that the best results were for Model 3, whilst Models 1 and 2 provided mostly identical simulation results.

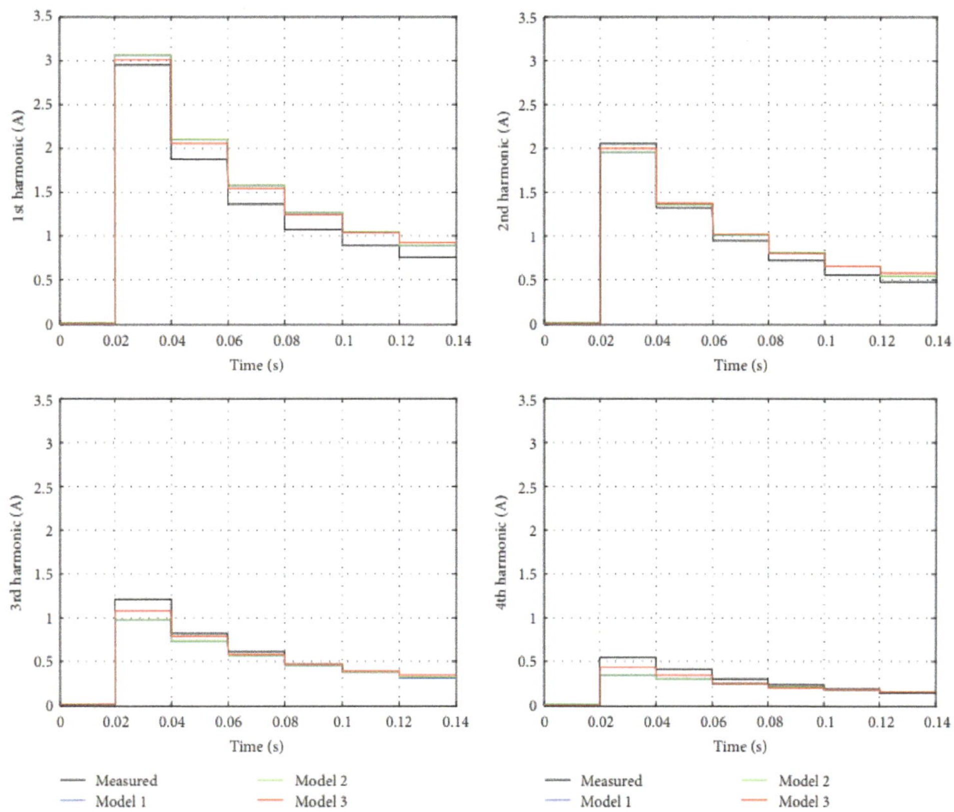

Figure 19: Harmonic content of measured and simulated inrush currents.

On the basis of all the aforementioned, it is possible to suggest the hybrid numerical method as a linear combination of the traditional trapezoidal method and the proposed BDF2 (NDF2) method. In [38] a hybrid method was proposed by Tadeusiewicz and Halgas in 2005 that presented a linear combination of the trapezoidal and BDF2 method in the form

$$X_{n+1} = \left(1+\frac{\theta}{3}\right)X_n - \frac{\theta}{3}X_{n-1} + (1-\theta)\frac{\Delta t}{2}F(X_n,t_n) + \left(1+\frac{\theta}{3}\right)\frac{\Delta t}{2}F(X_{n+1},t_{n+1}). \quad (14)$$

In expression (14), θ=0 leads to the trapezoidal method, whereas θ=1 leads to the BDF2 method.

In the same way, we have proposed a hybrid method that represents a linear combination of the trapezoidal and NDF2 methods in the form

$$X_{n+1} = \left(1+\frac{\theta}{5}\right)X_n - \frac{3\theta}{10}X_{n-1} + (1-\theta)\frac{\Delta t}{2}F(X_n,t_n) + \left(1+\frac{\theta}{5}\right)\frac{\Delta t}{2}F(X_{n+1},t_{n+1}) + \frac{\theta}{10}X_{n+1}^{[0]}. \quad (15)$$

In the expression (15), θ=0 leads to the trapezoidal method, whereas θ=1 leads to the NDF2 method. This method overcomes all the eventual problems during the usage of the standard trapezoidal method.

CONCLUSIONS

This paper investigates the different models and numerical methods that could be implemented for the simulations of inrush current in a single-phase transformer. Various core models of a transformer are developed in the paper: a model with a nonlinear inductor and a linear resistor, a model with a nonlinear inductor and a nonlinear resistor, and a model with a hysteresis inductor and a linear resistor. In addition, the paper investigates eigenvalues propagations during simulation time for all three models. The defined stiffness parameters, the stiffness ratios and the stiffness indexes, indicated that very stiff systems should be solved for all three developed models. The state-space equation system is solved by using proposed *A*- and *L*-stable numerical differentiation formulas (NDF2) (BDF2) method. The proposed method has the same order as a trapezoidal method; however this method overcomes the main drawback of the trapezoidal method (numerical oscillations). In the case where the numerical oscillations are generated by use of the trapezoidal method, the NDF2 (BDF2) method efficiently suppresses them. Comparisons between the measured and simulated inrush and steady-state currents of a transformer are conducted for all three proposed models. The best simulation results were obtained by using the developed Model 3, which incorporates hysteresis inductor. The developed Models 1 and 2 gave almost identical simulation results. The realized nonlinear inductor, nonlinear resistor, and hysteresis model can be incorporated within the EMTP-type of programs by using a combination of the existing trapezoidal and proposed NDF (BDF) method of order 2. In this way, the suggested numerical method could be used in the simulation of electrical networks with nonlinear elements. The future work will investigate the propagation of eigenvalues of a system in simulations of inrush currents in a three-phase power transformer

REFERENCES

1. CIGRE Working Group SC 33.02, "Guidelines for representation of network elements when calculating transients," CIGRE Brochure, vol. 39, pp. 1–29, 1990.
2. D. A. N. Jacobson, P. W. Lehn, and R. W. Menzies, "Stability domain calculations of period-1 ferroresonance in a nonlinear resonant circuit," IEEE Transactions on Power Delivery, vol. 17, no. 3, pp. 865–871, 2002.
3. G. Štumberger, S. Seme, B. Štumberger, B. Polajžer, and D. Dolinar, "Determining magnetically nonlinear characteristics of transformers and iron core inductors by differential evolution," IEEE Transactions on Magnetics, vol. 44, no. 6, pp. 1570–1573, 2008.
4. C. Pérez-Rojas, "Fitting saturation and hysteresis via arctangent functions," IEEE Power Engineering Review, vol. 20, no. 11, pp. 55–57, 2000.
5. X. Zhang, "An efficient algorithm for transient calculation of the electric networks including magnetizing branches," Mathematical Problems in Engineering, vol. 2011, Article ID 479626, 11 pages, 2011.
6. A. Ben-Tal, V. Kirk, and G. Wake, "Banded chaos in power systems," IEEE Transactions on Power Delivery, vol. 16, no. 1, pp. 105–110, 2001.
7. H. W. Dommel, Electromagnetic Transients Program, Reference Manual, (EMTP Theory Book), Bonneville Power Administration, Portland, Ore, USA, 1986.
8. C. E. Lin, C. L. Cheng, C. L. Huang, and J. C. Yeh, "Investigation of magnetizing inrush current in transformers—part I: numerical simulation," IEEE Transactions on Power Delivery, vol. 8, no. 1, pp. 246–254, 1993.
9. E. H. Badawy and R. D. Youssef, "Representation of transformer saturation," Electric Power Systems Research, vol. 6, no. 4, pp. 301–304, 1983.
10. S. Seker, T. C. Akinci, and S. Taskin, "Spectral and statistical analysis for ferroresonance phenomenon in electric power systems," Electrical Engineering, vol. 94, no. 2, pp. 117–124, 2012.
11. I. Clavería, M. García-Gracia, M. Á. García, and L. Montañes, "A time domain small transformer model under sinusoidal and non-sinusoidal supply voltage," European Transactions on Electrical Power, vol. 15, no. 4, pp. 311–323, 2005.
12. J. R. Lucas, P. G. McLaren, W. W. L. Keerthipala, and R. P. Jayasinghe, "Improved simulation models for current and voltage transformers in relay studies," IEEE Transactions on Power Delivery, vol. 7, no. 1, pp. 152–159, 1992.
13. Y. Baghzouz and X. D. Gong, "Voltage-dependent model for teaching transformer core nonlinearity,"IEEE Transactions on Power Systems, vol. 8, no. 2, pp. 746–752, 1993.
14. T. Tran-Quoc and L. Pierrat, "Efficient non linear transformer model and its application to ferroresonance study," IEEE Transactions on Magnetics, vol. 31, no. 3, pp. 2060–2063, 1995.
15. A. D. Theocharis, J. Milias-Argitis, and T. Zacharias, "Single-phase transformer model including magnetic

hysteresis and eddy currents," Electrical Engineering, vol. 90, no. 3, pp. 229–241, 2008.

16. J. Faiz and S. Saffari, "Inrush current modeling in a single-phase transformer," IEEE Transactions on Magnetics, vol. 46, no. 2, pp. 578–581, 2010.
17. H. Akçay and D. G. Ece, "Modeling of hysteresis and power losses in transformer laminations," IEEE Transactions on Power Delivery, vol. 18, no. 2, pp. 487–492, 2003.
18. S.-R. Huang, S. C. Chung, B.-N. Chen, and Y.-H. Chen, "A harmonic model for the nonlinearities of single-phase transformer with describing functions," IEEE Transactions on Power Delivery, vol. 18, no. 3, pp. 815–820, 2003.
19. W. L. A. Neves and H. W. Dommel, "On modelling iron core nonlinearities," IEEE Transactions on Power Systems, vol. 8, no. 2, pp. 417–422, 1993.
20. A. Tokić, I. Uglešić, V. Milardić, and G. Štumberger, "Conversion of RMS to instantaneous saturation curve: inrush current and ferroresonance cases," in Proceedings of the 14th International IGTE Symposium on Numerical Field Calculation in Electrical Engineering, pp. 1–4, Graz, Austria, 2010.
21. I. D. Mayergoyz, Mathematical Models of Hysteresis and Their Applications, Academic Press, Elsevier, New York, NY, USA, 2003.
22. F. C. Trutt, E. A. Erdelyi, and R. E. Hopkins, "Representation of the magnetization characteristic of DC machines for computer use," IEEE Transactions on Power Apparatus and Systems, vol. 87, no. 3, pp. 665–669, 1968.
23. O. Karlqvist, Calculation of the Magnetic Field in the Ferromagnetic Layer of a Magnetic Drum, vol. 86 of Transactions of the Royal Institute of Technology, Elanders boktr., Stockholm, Sweden, 1954.
24. J. Takâcs, "A phenomenological mathematical model of hysteresis," COMPEL: The International Journal for Computation and Mathematics in Electrical and Electronic Engineering, vol. 20, no. 4, pp. 1002–1014, 2001.
25. J. Takâcs, "The Everett integral and its analytical approximation," in Advanced Magnetic Materials, pp. 203–230, Intech Publication, 2012.
26. A. Tokić, V. Madžarević, and I. Uglešić, "Numerical calculations of three-phase transformer transients,"IEEE Transactions on Power Delivery, vol. 20, no. 4, pp. 2493–2500, 2005.
27. A. Tokić and I. Uglešić, "Elimination of overshooting effects and suppression of numerical oscillations in transformer transient calculations," IEEE Transactions on Power Delivery, vol. 23, no. 1, pp. 243–251, 2008.
28. A. Tokić, V. Madžarević, and I. Uglešić, "Hysteresis model in transient simulation algorithm based on BDF numerical method," in Proceedings of the IEEE Power Tech Conference, pp. 1–6, St. Petersburg, Russia, 2005.
29. E. Hairer and G. Wanner, Solving Ordinary Differential Equations. II: Stiff and Differential-Algebraic Problems, vol. 14 of Springer Series in Computational Mathematics, Springer, Berlin, Germany, 1991.
30. C. W. Gear, Numerical Initial Value Problems in Ordinary Differential Equations, Prentice-Hall, Englewood Cliffs, NJ, USA, 1971.
31. R. W. Klopfenstein, "Numerical differentiation formulas for stiff systems of ordinary differential equations," RCA Review, vol. 32, no. 3, pp. 447–462, 1971.
32. L. F. Shampine and M. W. Reichelt, "The MATLAB ODE suite," SIAM Journal on Scientific Computing, vol. 18, no. 1, pp. 1–22, 1997.
33. J. R. Cash, "On the integration of stiff systems of O.D.E.s using extended backward differentiation formulae," Numerische Mathematik, vol. 34, no. 3, pp. 235–246, 1980.
34. C. Fredebeul, "A-BDF: a generalization of the backward differentiation formulae," SIAM Journal on Numerical Analysis, vol. 35, no. 5, pp. 1917–1938, 1998.
35. J. E. Frank and P. J. van der Houwen, "Diagonalizable extended backward differentiation formulas," BIT Numerical Mathematics, vol. 40, no. 3, pp. 497–512, 2000.
36. E. Alberdi and J. J. Anza, "A predictor modification to the EBDF method for Stiff systems," Journal of Computational Mathematics, vol. 29, no. 2, pp. 199–214, 2011.
37. S. A. M. Yatim, Z. B. Ibrahim, K. I. Othman, and M. B. Suleiman, "A quantitative comparison of numerical method for solving stiff ordinary differential equations," Mathematical Problems in Engineering, vol. 2011, Article ID 193691, 12 pages, 2011.
38. M. Tadeusiewicz and S. Hałgas, "Transient analysis of nonlinear dynamic circuits using a numerical-integration method," COMPEL: The International Journal for Computation and Mathematics in Electrical and Electronic Engineering, vol. 24, no. 2, pp. 707–719, 2005.

CHAPTER 6 ON THE NUMERICAL STABILITY OF SURFACE-ATMOSPHERE COUPLING IN WEATHER AND CLIMATE MODELS

Anton Beljaars, Emanuel Dutra, and Gianpaolo Balsamo

European Centre for Medium-Range Weather Forecasts, Shinfield Park, Reading, RG2 9AX, UK

ABSTRACT

Coupling the atmosphere with the underlying surface presents numerical stability challenges in cost-effective model integrations used for operational weather prediction or climate simulations. These are due to the choice of large integration time-step, aiming at reducing computational burden, and to an explicit flux coupling formulation, often preferred for its simplicity and modularity. The atmospheric models therefore use the surface-layer temperatures (representative of the uppermost soil, snow, ice, water, etc.,) at previous integration time-step in all surface-atmosphere heat-flux calculations and prescribe fluxes to be used in the surface models' integrations. Although both models may use implicit formulations for the time stepping, the explicit flux coupling can still lead to instabilities.

In this study, idealized simulations with a fully coupled implicit system are performed to derive an empirical relation between surface heat flux and surface temperature at the new time level. Such a relation mimics the fully implicit formulation by allowing to estimate the surface temperature at the new time level without solving the surface heat diffusion problem. It is based on similarity reasoning and applies to any medium with constant heat diffusion and heat capacity parameters. The advantage is that modularity of the code is maintained and that the heat flux can be computed in the atmospheric model in such a way that instabilities in the snow or ice code are avoided. Applicability to snow/ice/soil models with variable density is discussed, and the loss of accuracy turns out to be small.

INTRODUCTION

Coupling atmospheric models to the underlying surface model, involves both scientific and technical issues. Models of the atmospheric circulation tend to be computer intensive and therefore often employ long time steps (up to one hour), which is a challenge for stability and accuracy (Beljaars et al., 2004). The turbulent diffusion part of these codes provides the coupling to the surface, has short physical time scales near the surface and therefore needs implicit numerics for stability. The surface may be vegetation, soil, snow, ice, or a combination of these in a tile scheme. Best et al. (2004) propose a coupling strategy to the surface that has a clean interface between atmosphere and surface code, and allows to include the surface or the top part of the surface in the implicit computations. This is often necessary for stability if the physical time scale of e.g. vegetation, soil, snow or ice surface is short compared to the model time step.

Citation: Beljaars, A., Dutra, E., and Balsamo, G.: On the numerical stability of surface-atmosphere coupling in weather and climate models, Geosci. Model Dev. Discuss., doi:10.5194/gmd-2016-96, in review, 2016

The ideal solution for stability is to combine the boundary layer heat diffusion and e.g. the snow or ice layer diffusion in a single implicit solver. However, modularity of the code and the complication of additional processes like phase changes and water percolation make this less practical. The standard solution is to compute fluxes at the surface on the basis of the old time level surface temperature. It is often called "explicit flux coupling". To improve stability and accuracy, West et al. (2016) recently proposed to move the flux coupling level one level down i.e. just below the surface. This has the advantage of including the fast responding surface layer in the fully implicit computations, which is beneficial for stability and accuracy.

Ongoing work at ECMWF on snow modelling raised similar issues. The existing single layer snow model (see e.g. Dutra et al., 2010), has already a minor stability issue when the snow layer becomes very thin. This was addressed by introducing some empirical implicitness in the coupling by making an educated guess of the future snow temperature. Initial experimentation with a multilayer snow model (Dutra et al., 2012) showed even more frequent instabilities, so more implicitness in the coupling is required for stability

In this paper, we propose a solution, that has the simplicity and modularity of the explicit flux coupling, but still has the stability of the fully implicit system. To derive simple solutions, the fully implicit coupled system is used as a reference. It is shown that the tri-diagonal set of equations corresponding to the discretized diffusion equation (for snow, ice or soil) can be converted to a relation between temperature and heat flux at the surface. The coefficients in this relation are then parameterized dependent on properties of the medium, time step and vertical discretization. The coefficients are put in dimensionless form, which makes the empirical coefficients universal and applicable to any medium and any discretization.

The experimental environment in this paper, is a simple model of a near surface air layer coupled to a snow pack by turbulent exchange. The atmosphere (e.g. at a height of 10 m, typical for atmospheric models) is assumed to have a diurnal cycle, and the response of temperature in the snow pack is considered. Although the following sections refer to snow only, the dimensionless framework ensures that the outcome is valid for any medium

The following two sections (2 and 3) describe the equations for the discretized snow layer and the turbulent coupling between atmosphere and snow. Sections 4, 5 and 6 describe the numerical solution for an idealized diurnal cycle, the parametrization of the coefficients that relate heat flux and top layer snow temperature and the testing of the proposed scheme. Finally, the results and their applicability are briefly discussed in the concluding section. Also the implications of non-uniform snow density are discussed.

IMPLICIT NUMERICAL SOLUTION OF THE DIFFUSION EQUATION

We consider the diffusion equation for temperature in snow

$$\rho C\frac{\partial T}{\partial t} = \frac{\partial G}{\partial z}, \qquad (1)$$

$$G = K\frac{\partial T}{\partial z}, \qquad (2)$$

where ρ (kgm^{-3}) is density, C ($Jkg^{-1}K^{-1}$) is heat capacity, T (K) is temperature, G (Wm^{-2}) is heat flux, and K ($Wm^{-1}K^{-1}$) is the diffusion coefficient for heat. The boundary conditions are:

$$G = G_0 \; for \; z = 0, \qquad (3)$$

$$G = 0 \; for \; z \rightarrow -\infty. \qquad (4)$$

For numerical stability with long time steps it is necessary to use an implicit scheme. With a vertical grid defined as in Fig. 1, the equation can be discretized as follows

$$(\rho C)_j\frac{T_j^{n+1}-T_j^n}{\Delta t} = \frac{1}{\Delta z_j}\left(K_{j-1/2}\frac{T_{j-1}^{n+1}-T_j^{n+1}}{\Delta z_{j-1/2}} - K_{j+1/2}\frac{T_j^{n+1}-T_{j+1}^{n+1}}{\Delta z_{j+1/2}}\right), \qquad (5)$$

with boundary conditions

$$(\rho C)_1\frac{T_1^{n+1}-T_1^n}{\Delta t} = \frac{1}{\Delta z_1}\left(G_0 - K_{1+1/2}\frac{T_1^{n+1}-T_2^{n+1}}{\Delta z_{1+1/2}}\right), \qquad (6)$$

$$(\rho C)_{NL}\frac{T_{NL}^{n+1}-T_{NL}^n}{\Delta t} = -\frac{1}{\Delta z_{NL}}\left(K_{NL-1/2}\frac{T_{NL-1}^{n+1}-T_{NL}^{n+1}}{\Delta z_{NL-1/2}}\right). \qquad (7)$$

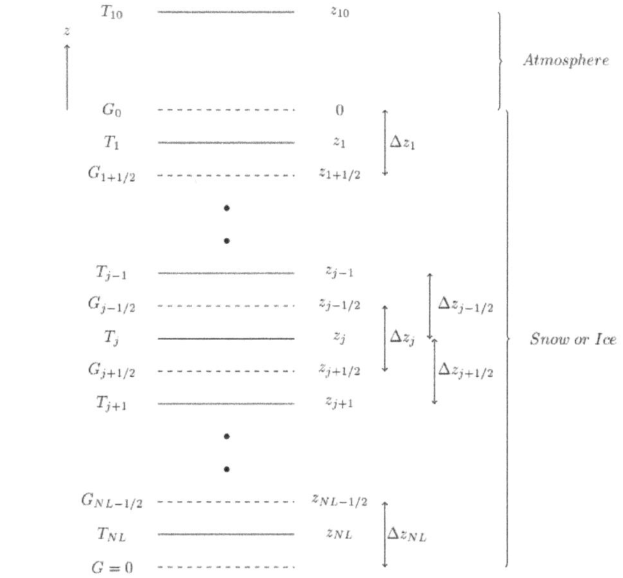

Figure 1: The numerical grid is defined by the position of the half levels, i.e. the thickness of the layers. The full levels are in the middle of the layers, i.e. $z_j = (z_{j-1/2} + z_{j+1/2})/2$. The surface is at z = 0. The bottom level is defined by the accumulated depth of all the layers. The temperature is defined on full levels and the heat fluxes are defined on half levels.

This set of equations forms a tri-diagonal system, with diagonals A, B and C (the coefficients are defined in Appendix A). The matrix equations can be solved by successive elimination of the C-coefficients from the bottom upward. At the same time, the equations are scaled such that the B-coefficients become equal to 1. Arriving at the top, it provides a solution for T_1^{n+1}. The solution for the other layers can be found by successive back-substitution of the temperatures going from top to bottom.

In case G_0 is not known, the elimination provides a linear relation between G_0 and T_1^{n+1}

$$T_1^{n+1} = \alpha G_0 + \beta. \qquad (8)$$

This relation can be used to achieve fully implicit coupling with the air/surface interaction formulation.

COUPLING TO THE LOWEST MODEL LEVEL OF THE ATMOSPHERE

The heat flux into the snow layer can be related to the air / surface temperature difference in the following way

$$G_0 = \rho_a c_p C_H |U| (T_a - T_{sk}), \tag{9}$$

where G_0 is the heat flux into the snow pack, ρ_a is air density, c_p is air heat capacity, C_H is the transfer coefficient between the atmospheric level and the surface, |U| is absolute wind speed, T_a is air temperature, and T_{sk} is temperature of the snow surface (skin temperature).

The coupling through a transfer coefficient is standard and represents the integral profile function according to Monin Obukhov (MO) similarity (see e.g. Brutsaert, 1982). The transfer coefficient in neutral conditions is related to the height of the atmospheric level, and the surface roughness lengths of momentum and heat

$$C_H = \frac{\kappa^2}{ln(z_a/z_{om}) ln(z_a/z_{oh})}, \tag{10}$$

where κ is the VonKarman constant (0.4), z_a is the height of the atmospheric level, z_{om} is the surface roughness length for momentum, and z_{oh} is the surface roughness length for heat. Stability can be included by extending the logarithmic terms with the integral MO stability functions

In the vertically discretized snow (see Fig. 1), the temperature of layer 1 is assumed to be at the midpoint which is different from the skin temperature. Therefore, the total conductivity between the atmosphere and the first snow layer (λ_t) is composed of two components: the turbulent transfer in the air above the surface (λ_a) and the conductivity of half of the top snow layer (λ_{sk}). The two conductivities are in parallel, because the inverse of conductivities (resistances) are in series, leading to the following formulation for the heat flux into the snow

$$G_0 = \lambda_t (T_a - T_1), \tag{11}$$

with

$$\lambda_t = \frac{\lambda_a \lambda_{sk}}{\lambda_a + \lambda_{sk}},$$
$$\lambda_a = \rho_a c_p C_H |U|,$$
$$\lambda_{sk} = \frac{2K_{1-1/2}}{\Delta z_1}.$$

Two different time stepping procedures are considered:

i. Explicit flux coupling. This is the traditional approach where the expression for the surface flux uses the previous time level of the surface temperature leading to the following discretization of Eq. (11)

$$G_0 = \lambda_t (T_a^{n+1} - T_1^n). \tag{12}$$

With the explicit specification of the flux at the surface flux, the tridiagonal system can be solved directly.

ii. Implicit flux coupling. The discretization of Eq. (11) reads

$$G_0 = \lambda_t (T_a^{n+1} - T_1^{n+1}), \tag{13}$$

With this fully implicit formulation, the surface heat flux cannot be specified explicitly, so it has to be found as part of the coupled atmosphere/surface system. For that purpose the tri-diagonal problem is solved in two steps. First, the elimination part is performed resulting in a solution for α and β in Eq. (8). Together with Eq. (13), T_1^{n+1} and G_0 can be computed:

$$T_1^{n+1} = \frac{\alpha \lambda_t T_a^{n+1} + \beta}{1 + \alpha \lambda_t}, \tag{14}$$

$$G_0 = \frac{\lambda_t (T_1^{n+1} - \beta)}{1 + \alpha \lambda_t}. \tag{15}$$

Finally the entire temperature profile can be resolved by performing the back-substitution in the tri-diagonal solver.

SOLUTIONS WITH A SIMPLE MULTILAYER SNOW MODEL

In this section, solutions are considered for a 1 m thick snow layer with constant heat capacity and heat diffusion coefficients. Idealized temperature forcing from the atmosphere is prescribed as a sinusoidal diurnal cycle. The choice of constants is documented in Table 1. The initial temperature profile at t = 0 is set to −5 °C, and a single sinusoidal diurnal cycle with an amplitude of 1 °C is imposed at the 10m level in the atmosphere

Table 1: List of parameters used in the idealized simulation of a snow layer

Parameter	Description	Value	Units
ρ	snow density	150	$kg\,m^{-3}$
ρ_{ice}	ice density	920	$kg\,m^{-3}$
C	snow (and ice) heat capacity	2228	$J\,kg^{-1}K^{-1}$
K_{ice}	ice heat diffusion coefficient	2.2	$W m^{-1} K^{-1}$
K	snow heat diffusion coefficient	$K_{ice}(\rho/\rho_{ice})^{1.88}$	$W m^{-1} K^{-1}$
ρ_a	air density	1.2	$kg\,m^{-3}$
c_p	air heat capacity	1005	$J\,kg^{-1}K^{-1}$
$\lvert U \rvert$	absolute wind speed	4	$m\,s^{-1}$
z_{om}	roughness length for momentum	0.0001	m
z_{oh}	roughness length for heat	0.0001	m
z_a	height atmospheric forcing level	10	m
κ	VonKarman constant	0.4	–
D	total depth of snow layer	1	m

$$T_{10} = -5 + sin(\frac{2\pi t}{3600. * 24.}) . \quad (16)$$

The simulations are performed with different uniform vertical discretizations and different time steps. Fig. 2 shows time series of the snow skin temperature (left column) and the ground heat flux (right column), with the two schemes. The fairly long time step of 3600 seconds is selected to illustrate stability and time truncation issues, and a short time step of 100 seconds for comparison. In the latter case time truncation errors are small for both schemes (convergence was verified). The three rows in Fig. 2 are for different vertical discretizations: 0.2, 0.02 and 0.002 m.

The first thing to note is that amplitude and phase of the skin temperature diurnal cycle only have a small dependence on vertical resolution. This is surprising because the amplitude of diurnal cycle of layer 1 with $\Delta z = 0.2$ is only 20% of the amplitude with $\Delta z = 0.02$. The reason that the skin temperature is still reasonable is due to the conductivity between the middle of the layer and the top (much lower with $\Delta z = 0.2$ than with $\Delta z = 0.02$). So at low vertical resolution, a substantial part of the temperature signal at the snow skin is due to the "interpolation" between air and middle of the first snow layer making use of the air conductivity (λ_a) and the snow conductivity of half the top layer (λ_{sk}). One might interpret this result as a justification for rather low vertical resolution. However, it should be realized that the forcing has the diurnal time scale only. With faster time scales e.g. due to moving clouds and frontal passages, a relatively thick near surface layer will not be able to respond.

The second result is that the fully implicit solution with $\Delta t = 3600$ is very close to short time step solution with $\Delta t = 100$, so the long time step does not compromise accuracy in this case, although the time stepping is first order accurate only. However, the solution with explicit coupling deviates visibly from the implicit and very short time step solutions (compare the red solid curve in middle/left panel of Fig. 2 with the blue curve). Apparently, it is the mismatch of time levels in the flux computation that is detrimental to accuracy. The error is particularly visible as a phase error.

Finally, the explicit coupling turns out to be unstable for very thin snow layers (see lower panels in Fig. 2 for $\Delta z = 0.002$. Also for this case the long time step solution with implicit coupling is fairly accurate as it is very close to the short time step solution.

Because of the good stability and accuracy characteristics, we develop in the next section a parametric form of α and β in Eq. (8).

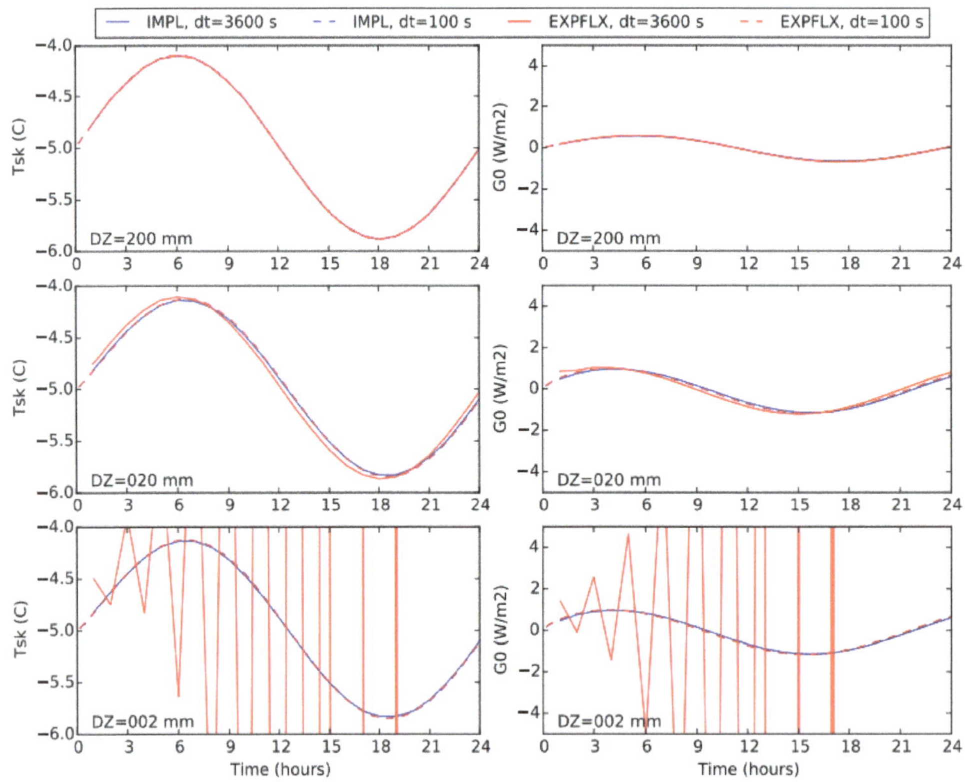

Figure 2: Diurnal cycle time series of snow skin temperature (left column) and surface heat flux (right column). The simulations were made with 0.2, 0.02 and 0.002 m vertical resolution (top, middle and bottom panels). The blue curves refer to the fully implicit solution(IMPL); the red curves indicate the solutions with explicit flux coupling (EXPFLX). The solid curves are with a time step of 3600 seconds and the dashed curves with 100 seconds.

SCALING RELATIONS FOR α AND β

As suggested above, it is desirable to have all the flux formulations (also for the atmosphere/surface exchange at the new time level n + 1. This implies the fully implicit option as described in sections 2 and 3. It also requires to perform the elimination part of the tri-diagonal solver to find the relation between T_1^{n+1} and G_0 according to Eq. (8). Because of code modularity it is desirable to make a reasonable estimate of the heat flux into the snow, before the snow code is executed. Therefore, an educated guess is made of the coefficients α and β in Eq. (8) without solving the tri-diagonal system, i.e. α and β are parameterized.

For that purpose, we make use of similarity theory for the diffusion equation with constant coefficients. If we think of an infinite medium (thick snow layer) with uniform temperature T_0 and make a jump at the surface to T_{new} at t = 0, we have to consider the following basic variables: temperature T at time t, T_0, Tnew, K/(ρC), and depth z. According to the Buckingham Pi Theorem (Stull, 1988), 5 variables with 3 dimensions (m, s, and K), lead to two independent dimensionless groups: $(T - T_0)/(T_{new} - T_0)$ and z/δ, where

$$\delta = \left(\frac{K\Delta t}{\rho C}\right)^{1/2}. \tag{17}$$

Length scale δ is the natural length scale of the medium for time scale t after which the temperature change at the surface was applied. From the physical point of view, δ is the typical depth to which the perturbation of the surface temperature has propagated at time t. The implication is that $(T - T_0)/(T_{new} - T_0)$ is a universal function of z/δ. At this stage we do not care about the form, although the solution can be easily found by transforming the equation to the new coordinate z/δ, which allows to separate the time dependence and the depth dependence leading to an ordinary differential equations which can be solved analytically (Carslaw and Jaeger, 1959).

Similarly, we can apply an external forcing by suddenly applying a heat flux G_0 at time 0 and look for the temperature response. Instead of scaling the temperature with $T_{new} - T_0$, we convert G_0 into a temperature scale and obtain

$$\frac{K(T-T_0)}{\delta G_0} = h\left(\frac{z}{\delta}\right), \tag{18}$$

where h is a universal function. If we are interested in the surface temperature only (i.e. z = 0), the left hand side becomes a constant, which we will call h_0 (which is order 1).

This line of reasoning can also be applied to the evolution of the surface temperature during a single time step of the diffusion problem with discrete equations. Equation (18) can be written as Eq. (8), with $t = \Delta t,\ T = T_1^{n+1},\ T_0 = T_1^n$, and Eq. (17) for δ, resulting in

$$T_1^{n+1} = h_0\left(\frac{\Delta t}{K\rho C}\right)^{1/2} G_0 + T_0^n. \tag{19}$$

Therefore we expect the following scaling behavior for α

$$\alpha \sim \left(\frac{\Delta t}{K\rho C}\right)^{1/2}. \tag{20}$$

It indicates the surface temperature response to a 1 W/m² heat flux forcing over a finite time step Δt. The scaling arguments above apply to the continuous system. For the discretized system, the scaling behavior of α also depends on Δz. For a very fine grid (Δz << δz), the discrete system behaves like the continuous system and Eq. (20) applies. For a very thick top layer (Δz >> δ), the heat flux is simply distributed over the top layer and the following applies

$$\alpha = \frac{\Delta t}{\Delta z\rho C}. \tag{21}$$

In general the dimensionless α should be a universal function of δ/Δz, i.e.

$$\alpha\left(\frac{K\rho C}{\Delta t}\right)^{1/2} = f\left(\frac{\delta}{\Delta z}\right) = f\left(\frac{(K\Delta t)^{1/2}}{\Delta z(\rho C)^{1/2}}\right). \tag{22}$$

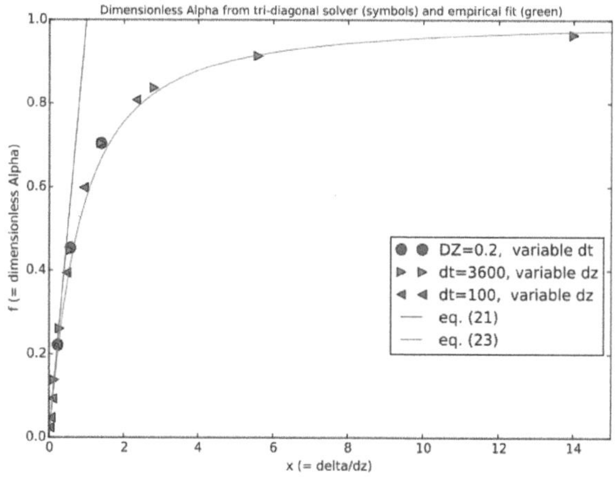

Figure 3: Dimensionless function $f = \alpha(K\rho C/\Delta t)^{1/2}$ as a function of x = δ/Δz. The circles and triangles are for different combinations of Δz and Δt. The blue line is the asymptotic limit for small δ/Δz. The green curve is the empirical fit according to Eq. (23).

The empirical function can be "measured" by running the numerical model as in the previous section for a range of time steps and vertical discretizations. Note that α remains constant during the time stepping and does not depend on the temperature profile. It is just a property of the tri-diagonal matrix which only contains properties of the medium, the time step and the level thickness. The results are shown in Fig. 3. Time steps range from 100 s to 3600 s, and layer thicknesses are used from 0.002 m to 0.2 m, with a total snow depth of 1 m for all simulations.

For small ratios of δ/Δz, the universal function should scale with Eq. (21) and for large values with (20). Surprisingly, coefficient h0 turns out to be 1. An empirical fit is proposed that makes a smooth transition between the two regimes according to (see Fig. 3)

$$f(x) = \frac{x}{(1+x^{1.3})^{1/1.3}}. \tag{23}$$

The exponent of 1.3 has been optimized to obtain a reasonable representation of the numerical data in the transition regime.

The second parameter for which an empirical formulation is needed is β. The physical meaning of β is clear from Eq. (8): it is the temperature of the top snow layer at the new time level T_1^{n+1} in case of zero heat flux. A simple approximation would be to select the temperature of the previous time level, but this is only valid for a uniform temperature profile. For a non-uniform temperature profile, heat diffusion will homogenize temperature, which will make β different from T_1^n at the old time level. Following the scaling arguments above, we know that information propagates vertically over a distance δ during time step Δ.

Therefore, we conjecture that the temperature of the old profile at depth δ is a better approximation for β than the temperature at level 1, i.e. T_δ^n is better than T_1^n. Fig. 4 indeed confirms that the temperature at depth δ is a reasonable approximation. The temperature at z = −δ has been obtained by linear interpolation between levels, except when δ < 0.5Δz. In the latter case, temperature T n 1 is selected. Note that, unlike α, β does change with temperature and does evolve during the integration.

From Figs. 3 and 4, it is concluded that reasonable estimates can be made of α and β without actually solving the tri-diagonal matrix. Depth scale δ and the thickness of the top layer Δz are crucial scales to characterize the temperature evolution of the top snow layer over a time step.

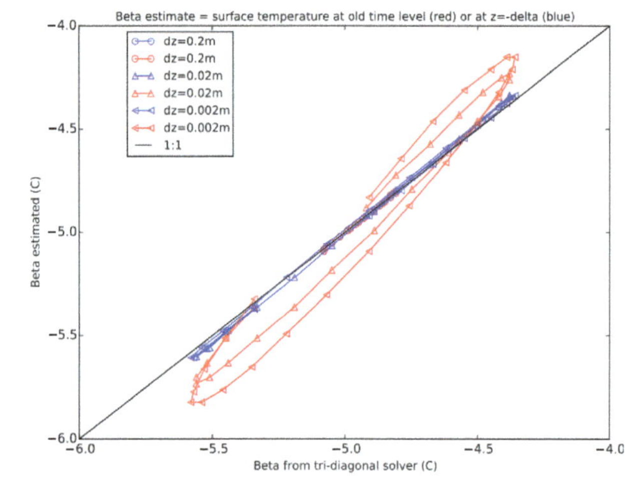

Figure 4: Empirical estimates of parameter β as a function of the value found from the tri-diagonal solver. The red curve represents the estimate according to T_1^n and the blue curve is the temperature at z = −δ, also at the previous time level n. The symbols (connected by lines) indicate the successive time steps in the diurnal cycle. Results are plotted for vertical resolutions of 0.2, 0.02 and 0.002 m.

SIMULATIONS WITH THE EMPIRICAL FORMULATION

With the empirical formulations for α and β, it is possible now to repeat the simulations of section 4. Instead of generating the fully implicit solution by solving the tri-diagonal matrix in the standard way, α and β are replaced by the empirical formulation between the elimination and back-substitution phase. If the formulation is perfect, the solution should be the same as the fully implicit solution. Results are shown in Fig. 5 for the temperature of the top layer and the heat flux. Layer thicknesses of 0.2, 0.02 and 0.002 m are shown as different rows in Fig. 5. In this case, the top layer temperature is shown instead of the skin temperature. The implication is that the amplitude of the diurnal cycle increases with the refinement of the vertical discretization, simply because with high vertical resolution, the top layer becomes a better approximation of the skin temperature. The figure confirms that the diurnal temperature cycle of the fully implicit solution (blue curve, IMPL) is well reproduced by the solution with parameterized α and β (black solid cure, IMPPAR). The differences between blue and black curves are very small.

Finally, the scheme was further simplified by using the parametric form for α only and estimating β by putting it equal to T_1^n. The advantage is that no interpolation to z = −δ is needed, but that stability of the coupling is still maintained. However, it is clear that numerical errors are increased for thin snow layers (see dashed black curve). Such errors have to be seen in the context of other model errors, so the use of a parameterized α only, to ensure stability, may still be sufficient for many applications.

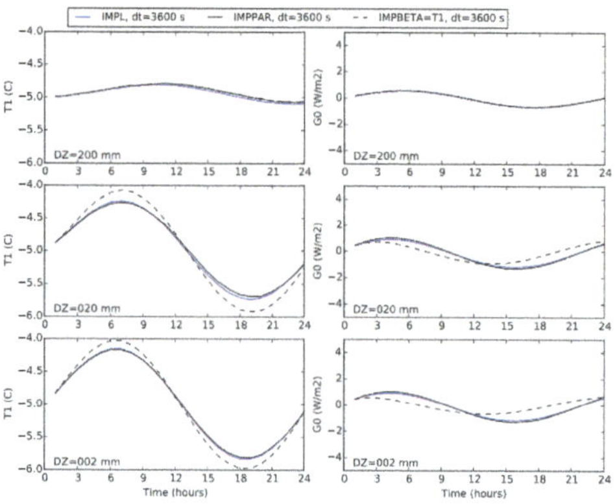

Figure 5: Diurnal cycle series of top layer snow temperature (left columns) and surface heat flux (right columns). The simulations were made with 0.2, 0.02 and 0.002 m resolution (top, middle and bottom panels). The blue curve refers to the fully implicit solution(IMPL); the black solid curve is the solution with parameterized α and β. The black dashes curve refers to the solution where α is parameterized and β is set equal to the temperature of level 1 at the previous time (n). The time step is 3600 seconds.

DISCUSSION AND CONCLUSION

For absolute numerical stability it is necessary to have a fully implicit coupling of the heat diffusion between atmosphere and surface (e.g. snow). It leads to a tri-diagonal problem in which atmosphere and surface are solved simultaneously. In practice, often so-called explicit flux coupling is applied: the atmospheric model uses the surface temperature of the previous time level to compute the surface heat flux, which is used later as boundary condition for the heat diffusion in the surface. Explicit surface coupling puts stability limits on the thickness of the top snow layer and on the time step. Explicit flux coupling is also desirable from the code modularity point of view.

Although the atmosphere / surface heat diffusion leads to a single tri-diagonal matrix problem, one can also break it up in different steps. It is shown that the elimination part of the solver of the snow heat diffusion problem leads to a linear relation between surface temperature and surface heat flux. This relation can be used together with the atmosphere / surface interaction formulation to solve for the surface heat flux.

A simple method has been developed to approximate the coefficients in this linear relation. The coefficients are scaled with the characteristic scales of the diffusion equation. This makes the result universal and applicable to an arbitrary medium e.g.snow, ice or soil. The depth scale that characterizes the penetration of a perturbation over a time step, turns out to play a crucial role. In this paper the relevant empirical function is "measured" by solving the diffusion equation for a range of vertical resolutions and time steps.

Finally, the empirical functions are used to solve for the coupled diffusion problem and compared with the fully implicit computations. The results are very close. The advantage of the method is that the surface fluxes can be computed without calling any surface code, and behaves like explicit flux coupling. The only difference is that the surface heat flux expression has a damping term depending on the time step. This damping term is the result of the change of surface temperature related to the heat flux, and stabilizes the result.

The scaling argument used above, only applies for a diffusion equation with constant properties of the medium. However, in reality there may a profile of e.g. snow density as snow becomes more and more compact in deeper layers. As a simple test, a case was selected where the profile of density is 150 kgm^{-3} at the surface, increases linearly to 250 kgm^{-3} at a depth of 0.5 m, and remains constant below 0.5 m. The characteristic depth is again computed as in section 5, and to non-dimensionalize, the snow properties are taken from the middle of the top snow layer. For this case the dimensionless α and characteristic temperature β are shown in Figs. 6 and 7. They are very close to the figures for constant snow properties (Figs. 3 and 4), which suggests that the sensitivity to snow properties is fairly small. In general, it is to be expected that the snow properties very close to the surface control the relation between flux and temperature over a short time step, because the penetration depth δ is small.

We conclude that making an estimate of the relation between heat flux and surface temperature is a practical solution to support explicit flux coupling and to combine numerical stability for long time steps with a modular code structure. The similarity framework makes the method applicable to any medium, e.g. snow, ice or soil. It is also worth noting that the method does not compromise conservation: the heat flux that is computed by the atmospheric model is later used by the surface model as boundary condition.

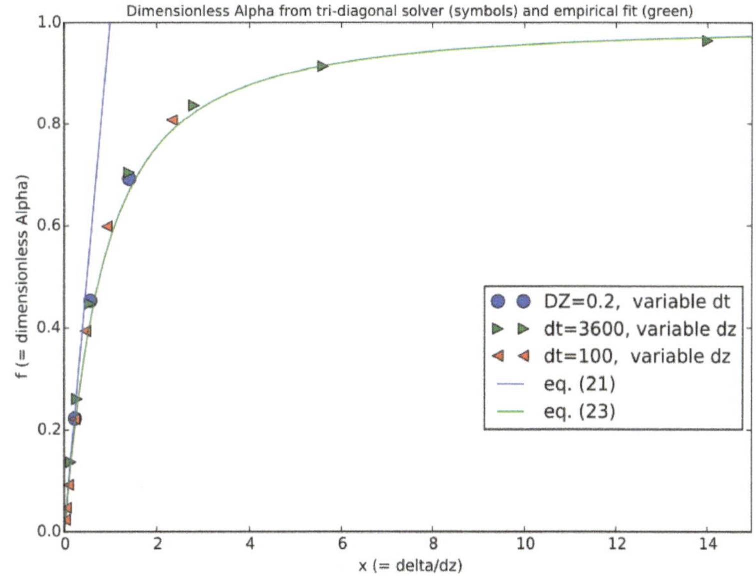

Figure 6: Dimensionless α as in Fig. 3, but for non-uniform snow density. The snow density is 150 kgm^{-3} at the surface, increases linearly to 250 kgm^{-3} at a depth of 0.5 m, and remains constant below 0.5 m.

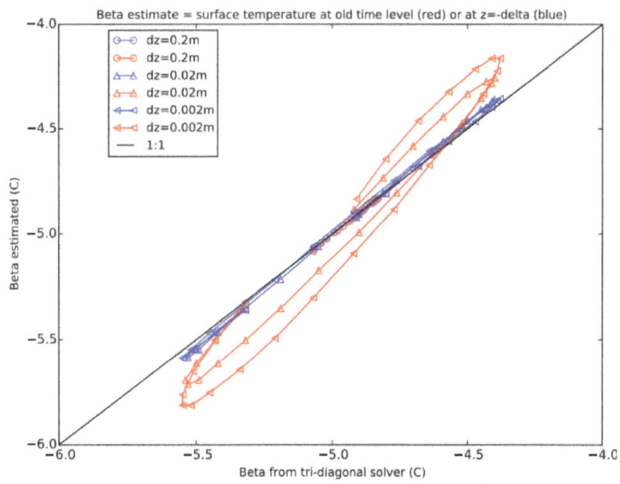

Figure 7: Dimensionless β as in Fig. 4, but for non-uniform snow density. The snow density is 150 kgm^{-3} at the surface, increases linearly to 250 kgm^{-3} at a depth of 0.5 m, and remains constant below 0.5 m.

APPENDIX A

The set of equations discussed in section 2 leads to the following tri-diagonal system

$$\begin{pmatrix} B_1 & C_1 & 0 & 0 & \cdots & 0 \\ A_2 & B_2 & C_2 & 0 & \cdots & 0 \\ 0 & A_3 & B_3 & C_3 & \cdots & 0 \\ \ddots & \ddots & \ddots & \ddots & & \ddots \\ 0 & \cdots & A_{NL-2} & B_{NL-2} & C_{NL-2} & 0 \\ 0 & \cdots & 0 & A_{NL-1} & B_{NL-1} & C_{NL-1} \\ 0 & \cdots & 0 & 0 & A_{NL} & B_{NL} \end{pmatrix} \begin{pmatrix} T_1^{n+1} \\ T_2^{n+1} \\ T_3^{n+1} \\ \vdots \\ T_{NL-2}^{n+1} \\ T_{NL-1}^{n+1} \\ T_{NL}^{n+1} \end{pmatrix} = \begin{pmatrix} R_1 \\ R_2 \\ R_3 \\ \vdots \\ R_{NL-2} \\ R_{NL-1} \\ R_{NL} \end{pmatrix}$$

(A1)

where

$$\begin{aligned} A_j &= -\frac{K_{j-1/2}}{\Delta z_j \Delta z_{j-1/2}}, \\ B_j &= \frac{(\rho C)_j}{\Delta t} + \frac{K_{j-1/2}}{\Delta z_j \Delta z_{j-1/2}} + \frac{K_{j+1/2}}{\Delta z_j \Delta z_{j+1/2}}, \\ C_j &= -\frac{K_{j+1/2}}{\Delta z_j \Delta z_{j+1/2}}, \\ R_j &= \frac{(\rho C)j}{\Delta t} T_j^n, \end{aligned} \tag{A2}$$

with boundary condition at the surface

$$\begin{aligned} A_1 &= 0, \\ B_1 &= \frac{(\rho C)_1}{\Delta t} + \frac{K_{1+1/2}}{\Delta z_1 \Delta z_{1+1/2}}, \\ C_1 &= -\frac{K_{1+1/2}}{\Delta z_1 \Delta z_{1+1/2}}, \\ R_1 &= \frac{G_0}{\Delta z_1} + \frac{(\rho C)_1}{\Delta t} T_1^n, \end{aligned} \tag{A3}$$

and the no-flux condition at the bottom

$$\begin{aligned} A_{NL} &= -\frac{K_{NL-1/2}}{\Delta z_{NL} \Delta z_{NL-1/2}}, \\ B_{NL} &= \frac{(\rho C)_{NL}}{\Delta t} + \frac{K_{NL-1/2}}{\Delta z_{NL} \Delta z_{NL-1/2}}, \\ C_{NL} &= 0, \\ R_{NL} &= \frac{(\rho C)_{NL}}{\Delta t} T_{NL}^n. \end{aligned} \tag{A4}$$

Data availability

The data that is used in this paper has been produced with a dedicated stand-alone fortran program. ECMWF's data policy does not allow open access to software. However, the code can be obtained from the first author subject to license. The license implies non-commercial use i.e. for research and education only.

REFERENCES

1. Beljaars, A., Bechtold, P., Koehler, M., Morcrette, J.-J., Tompkins, A., Viterbo, P., and Wedi, N.: The numerics of physical parametrization, in: Proc. of ECMWF Seminar on Recent developments in numerical methods for atmosphere and ocean modelling, pp. 113–134, 6-10 Sept., ECMWF, Reading, UK, 2004.
2. Best, M., Beljaars, A., Polcher, J., and Viterbo, P.: A proposed structure for coupling tiled surfaces with the planetary boundary layer, J. Hydrometeor., 5, 1271–1278, 2004.
3. Brutsaert, W.: Evaporation into the atmosphere, Springer, 1982.
4. Carslaw, H. and Jaeger, J.: Conduction of heat in solids, Springer, 1959.
5. Dutra, E., Balsamo, G., Viterbo, P., Miranda, P., Beljaars, A., Sch ar, C., , and Elder, K.: An improved snow scheme for the ECMWF land surface model: description and offline validation, J. Hydrometeor., 11, 899–916, 2010.
6. Dutra, E., Viterbo, P., Miranda, P., and Balsamo, G.: Complexity of snow schemes in a climate model and its impact on surface energy and hydrology, J. Hydrometeor., 13, 521–538, 2012.
7. Stull, R. B.: An introduction to boundary layer meteorology, Kluwer Academic Publishers, 1988
8. West, A. E., McLaren, A. J., Hewitt, H. T., and Best, M. J.: The location of the thermodynamic atmosphere-ice interface in fully coupled models-a case study using JULES and CICE, Geoscientific Model Development, 9, 1125, 2016.

CHAPTER 7

EXPONENTIAL CONVERGENCE FOR NUMERICAL SOLUTION OF INTEGRAL EQUATIONS USING RADIAL BASIS FUNCTIONS

Zakieh Avazzadeh,[1] Mohammad Heydari,[2] Wen Chen,[1], and G. B. Loghmani[3]

[1]State Key Laboratory of Hydrology-Water Resources and Hydraulic Engineering, College of Mechanics and Materials, Hohai University, Nanjing 210098, China

[2]Young Researchers and Elite Club, Islamic Azad University, Ashkezar Branch, Ashkezar 8941613695, Iran

[3]Department of Mathematics, Yazd University, Yazd, Iran

ABSTRACT

We solve some different type of Urysohn integral equations by using the radial basis functions. These types include the linear and nonlinear Fredholm, Volterra, and mixed Volterra-Fredholm integral equations. Our main aim is to investigate the rate of convergence to solve these equations using the radial basis functions which have normic structure that utilize approximation in higher dimensions. Of course, the use of this method often leads to ill-posed systems. Thus we propose an algorithm to improve the results. Numerical results show that this method leads to the exponential convergence for solving integral equations as it was already confirmed for partial and ordinary differential equations.

INTRODUCTION

Integral equations have been solved by many different methods [1, 2]. In [3] integral equations and methods of their solving are classified. This reference includes some traditional methods for solving integral equations. But some recent methods are Adomian decomposition method (ADM) [4], homotopy perturbation method (HPM) [5], He's variational iteration methods [6], optimal control [7], wavelets [8–11], neural networks [12], simulation method [13], block-pulse method [14], and so forth. Also, there are many other articles which contain new approaches in solving integral equations [15–18]. It is necessary to recall that most of the mentioned methods are not easy for solving integral equations in higher dimensions [19–24] and also for solving the mixed Volterra-Fredholm cases [6, 25–27]. However, in the present paper, we restrict ourselves to the method of radial basis functions (RBFs).

The RBF methodology was introduced by Hardy [28]. At first, it was popular in multivariate interpolation [29–34]. In 1990, Kansa introduced a way to use these functions for solving parabolic, hyperbolic, and elliptic partial differential equations [35]. After that, radial basis functions have been widely applied in numerous fields. In spite of many other applications of RBFs, we only focus on the use of RBFs for solving integral equations.

In 1992, Makroglou [36] applied the collocation technique to solve various linear and nonlinear integral equations. In 2002, Galperin and Kansa [37] applied RBFs for solution of weakly singular Volterra integral equations by global optimization. In 2007, Alipanah and Dehghan [38] used RBFs for solving one-dimensional nonlinear Fredholm integral equations without optimization technique and via quadrature integration methods. In [39], this method is generalized for two dimensions

Citation: Zakieh Avazzadeh, Mohammad Heydari, Wen Chen, and G. B. Loghmani, "Exponential Convergence for Numerical Solution of Integral Equations Using Radial Basis Functions," Journal of Applied Mathematics, vol. 2014, Article ID 710437, 9 pages, 2014. doi:10.1155/2014/710437

problems and the accuracy of the method is compared with the traditional spectral method in [40]. Also, Avazzadeh et al. used the RBFs for solving partial integrodifferential equations [41–43].

In [38, 39], the method was applied for Fredholm integral equations. In this paper, we describe the method for solving more different types of integral equations such as Volterra and mixed Volterra-Fredholm equations. In fact, some singular types of integral equations can be solved by this method. Therefore, the method can solve linear and nonlinear Fredholm, Volterra, and mixed Volterra-Fredholm equations even in higher dimensions.

The paper is organized in the following way. In Section 2, the radial basis functions as a tool for approximation are introduced. In Section 3, we recall the method of the solution of Fredholm integral equation [38, 39] and then the Volterra and mixed Volterra-Fredholm integral equations will be solved by using radial basis functions. In Section 4, some illustrating examples are presented. The last section includes conclusion and some ideas for future work.

RADIAL BASIS FUNCTIONS

Definition 1. Consider a given set of n distinct data points $\{p_j\}_{j=0}^{n}$ and the corresponding data values $\{f_j\}_{j=0}^{n}$, the basic RBF interpolant is given by

$$s(p) = \sum_{j=0}^{n} c_j\phi\left(\|p - p_j\|\right), \tag{1}$$

where $\|\cdot\|$ is the Euclidean norm, p, $p_j \in \mathbb{R}_d$ (d is a positive finite integer), and f_j is scalar. Also (r), $r \geq 0$, is some radial basis functions. The coefficient c_j is determined from the interpolation $(p_j) = f_j$, $j = 0, 1, \ldots, n$, which leads to the following symmetric linear system:

$$A\underline{c} = \underline{f}, \tag{1}$$

where the entries of $\underline{c}$, $\underline{f}$, and A are given by

$$\underline{c} = [c_0, \ldots, c_n]^T, \quad \underline{f} = [f_0, \ldots, f_n]^T,$$
$$a_{jk} = \phi\left(\|p_k - p_j\|\right), \quad k, j = 0, 1, \ldots, n. \tag{2}$$

Sometimes, $\{p_j\}_{j=0}^{n}$ are called center points. Every basis is directly related to one center point. Since these points are chosen arbitrarily, we have a mesh-free method [44–46].

The sufficient conditions for (r) in (3) to guarantee nonsingularity of the matrix are given in [47]. Also, Micchelli [33] showed that a larger class of functions could be considered, and thus the RBF method is uniquely solvable.

There are two kinds of radial basis functions, the piecewise smooth and the infinitely smooth radial functions. For infinitely smooth radial functions, we have a shape parameter ϵ. The parameter ϵ is a free parameter for controlling the shape of functions. As $\epsilon \to 0$ the radial functions become flatter [48, 49].

Some piecewise smooth RBFs are r^3 (Cubic) and $r^2 \log r$ (Thin plate spline) and some common infinitely smooth examples of the $\phi(r)$ that lead to a uniquely solvable method are in the following forms:

linear: r,

Gaussian (GA): $e^{-(\epsilon r)2}$,

Multiquadric (MQ): $(1 + (\epsilon r)^2)^{\alpha/2}$, $(\alpha \neq 0, \alpha \neq 2N)$,

inverse multiquadric (IMQ): $(1 + (\epsilon r)^2)^{-1/2}$,

inverse quadric (IQ): $(1 + (\epsilon r)^2)^{-1}$.

Madych and Nelson have proved exponential convergence property of multiquadratic approximation [31, 50]. He has shown that under certain conditions the interpolation error is $\varepsilon = O(\lambda^{c/h})$ (note that MQ RBF has been redefined from Hardy's original definition by the transformation $c = 1/\epsilon$), h is the mesh size, and $0<\lambda<1$ is a constant. As is said in [51], this implies that there are two ways to improve the approximation: either by reducing the size of h or by increasing the magnitude of c. It means that if $c \to \infty$ then $\varepsilon \to 0$. While reducing h leads to the heavy computations, increasing c is without the extra computational cost. However, according to "uncertainty principle" of Schaback [52], as the error becomes smaller, the matrix becomes more illconditioned; hence the solution will break down as c becomes too large. Nevertheless, there exists a wide range of c that high accurate results can be produced. So, if we could solve the illconditioned system, we could increase c and obtain the best approximation [50].There are some experimental trials about the shape parameter, ill-conditioning, and convergence [53– 55].

There are some methods for trade-off between c and error [56, 57]. The golden section algorithm [56] as a new method for finding a good shape parameter can be effective but often it is expensive. Baxter [58] investigated the preconditioned conjugate gradient technique. Casciola et al. [59] regularized the solutions with changing the Euclidean norm to the anisotropic norm. Karageorghis et al. [60] applied the matrix decomposition algorithm for improving 3D elliptic problems. Also, there are the regularization techniques for solving ill-conditioned systems such as truncated singular value decomposition (TSVD) and Tikhonov regularization method. Reader can see details in [58–60] and the references there in.

INTEGRAL EQUATION

Fredholm Integral Equation

Consider the following Fredholm integral equation of the Urysohn form:

$$u(x) - \lambda \int_a^b G(x, t, u(t))\, dt = f(x), \tag{4}$$

where λ is constant; $f(x)$ and $G(x, t, u(t))$ are assumed to be defined on the interval $a \leq x, t \leq b$. Let (x) be a radial basis function and we approximate $u(x)$ with the following interpolant function:

$$u(x) \simeq \sum_{j=0}^{n} c_j\phi\left(\|x - x_j\|\right) = C^T\Psi(x), \tag{5}$$

where $C^T = [c_0, c_1, \ldots, c_n]$ and $\Psi(x) = [\phi(\|x - x_0\|), \phi(\|x - x_1\|), \ldots, \phi(\|x - x_n\|)]^T$. Now, by replacing (5) in (4) we obtain

$$C^T\Psi(x) - \lambda \int_a^b G\left(x, t, C^T\Psi(t)\right) dt \simeq f(x). \tag{6}$$

In the above equation, c_j, $j = 0, 1, \ldots, n$, are unknown. For computing them, we collocate the points x_i, $i = 0, 1, \ldots, n$, as follows:

$$C^T\Psi(x_i) - \lambda \int_a^b G(x_i, t, C^T\Psi(t))\, dt \simeq f(x_i). \tag{7}$$

By applying the Legendre quadrature integration formula [61], (5) can be changed to the following form:

$$C^T\Psi(x_i) - \lambda \sum_{j=0}^{N} w_j G(x_i, t_j, C^T\Psi(t_j))\, dt \simeq f(x_i). \tag{8}$$

This is a nonlinear system of equations that can be solved by Newton's iterative method to obtain the unknown vector C^T.

Similarly, for the two-dimensional integral equation, consider the Fredholm integral equation as follows:

$$u(x,y) - \lambda \int_c^d \int_a^b G(x,y,s,t,u(s,t))\, ds\, dt$$
$$= f(x,y), \quad (x,y) \in [a,b] \times [c,d], \tag{9}$$

where $G(x, y, s, t, u(s, t))$ and $f(x, y)$ are given analytic functions. According to (1) the function (x, y) may be represented by approximate series as

$$u(p) \simeq \sum_{\gamma=0}^{n} c_\gamma \phi(\|p - p_\gamma\|) = C^T\Psi(p), \tag{10}$$

where n is any natural number, $p = (x,y) \in \mathbb{R}^2$, and $p_\gamma = (x_i, y_j) \in {}^2$. Noting the previous section, it is clear that the collocation points $\{p_\gamma\}_{\gamma=0}^{n}$ can be chosen as the centers. However, the selection process of the center points can affect accuracy; sometimes the uniform points or random points are preferred.

Replacing (10) in (9) we have

$$C^T\Psi(x,y) - \lambda \int_c^d \int_a^b G(x,y,s,t,C^T\Psi(s,t))\, ds\, dt$$
$$\simeq f(x,y), \quad (x,y) \in [a,b] \times [c,d]. \tag{11}$$

In the above equation, only $c_\gamma (\gamma = 0, 1, \ldots, n)$ are unknowns and it is an interesting technical advantage in using of RBFs. It means the process of solving is no more complicated in spite of increasing the dimension of the given problem.

Now we substitute the given collocation points in the above equation. Collocation points can be the same center points or any other arbitrary points:

$$C^T\Psi(x_i,y_j) - \lambda \int_c^d \int_a^b G(x_i,y_j,s,t,C^T\Psi(s,t))\, ds\, dt$$
$$\simeq f(x_i,y_j). \tag{12}$$

By applying the quadrature integration formula, (12) can be changed to the following form:

$$C^T\Psi(x_i,y_j) - \sum_{l=0}^{N}\sum_{k=0}^{N} w_l w_k G(x_i,y_j,s_k,t_l,C^T\Psi(s_k,t_l))$$
$$\simeq f(x_i,y_j). \tag{13}$$

This is a nonlinear system of equations that can be solved by Newton's iterative method to obtain the unknown vector C^T. We recall that the obtained linearized system by Newton's method is ill-conditioned and the use of regularization methods is efficient. Also, we can apply some other iterative regularization methods for solving an ill-conditioned nonlinear system of equations [62].

The mentioned method for solving Fredholm integral equation was discussed in [38, 39] and in the current paper it is generalized for solving Volterra and Volterra-Fredholm integral equations.

Volterra Integral Equation

Consider the following Urysohn Volterra integral equation:

$$u(x) - \lambda \int_a^x G(x,t,u(t))\, dt = f(x), \tag{14}$$

where λ is constant; $f(x)$ and $G(x, t, u(t))$ are assumed to be defined on the interval $a \leq x, t \leq b$. Similar to the previous section, we substitute (5) in (14) and collocate the points x_i, $i = 0, 1, \ldots, n$. So we have

$$C^T\Psi(x_i) - \lambda \int_a^{x_i} G(x_i,t,C^T\Psi(t))\, dt \simeq f(x_i). \tag{15}$$

Using the linear transform as follows,

$$t = \mu(s) = \frac{x_i - a}{2}s + \frac{x_i + a}{2}, \tag{16}$$

reduces (15) to the following integral equation:

$$C^T\Psi(x_i)$$
$$-\lambda \frac{x_i - a}{2} \int_{-1}^{1} G(x_i,\mu(s),C^T\Psi(\mu(s)))\, ds \simeq f(x_i). \tag{17}$$

Now, by applying a quadrature integration formula, we approximate the integral in (17) and thus we have a nonlinear system of equations that can be solved by Newton's iterative method to obtain the unknown vector C^T.

It is easy to use that the proposed method for solving the two-dimensional Volterra integral equation gives

$$F(u(x,y)) - \lambda \int_c^y \int_a^x G(x,y,s,t,u(s,t))\, ds\, dt$$
$$= f(x,y), \quad (x,y) \in [a,b] \times [c,d], \tag{18}$$

where $G(x, y, s, t, u(s, t))$ and $f(x, y)$ are given analytic functions. Similarly, we substitute (10) in (18) and collocate the points (x_i, y_j), $i, j = 0, 1, \ldots, n$. So we have

$$F(C^T\Psi(x_i,y_j)) - \lambda \int_0^{y_j} \int_0^{x_i} G(x_i,y_j,s,t,C^T\Psi(s,t))\, ds\, dt$$
$$\simeq f(x_i,y_j). \tag{19}$$

In the above equation, let the linear transforms

$$s = \mu(\xi) = \frac{x_i - a}{2}\xi + \frac{x_i + a}{2},$$
$$t = \nu(\tau) = \frac{y_j - c}{2}\tau + \frac{y_j + c}{2}. \tag{20}$$

Therefore, (19) is reduced to the integral equation which can be solved easily:

$$F(C^T\Psi(x_i,y_j)) - \lambda \frac{(x_i - a)(y_j - c)}{2}$$
$$\times \int_{-1}^{1}\int_{-1}^{1} G(x_i,y_j,\mu(\xi),$$
$$\nu(\tau), C^T\Psi(\mu(\xi),\nu(\tau)))\, d\xi\, d\tau$$
$$\simeq f(x_i,y_j). \tag{21}$$

Now, by applying a quadrature integration formula, we approximate the obtained integrals; then the nonlinear system of equations can be solved by Newton's iterative method to obtain the unknown vector C^T.

The Mixed Volterra-Fredholm Integral Equation

In general, Volterra-Fredholm integral equations can be classified into different types [6, 26]. We will only investigate the mixed Volterra-Fredholm integral equations in the following form:

$$F(u(x,y)) - \lambda \int_c^y \int_a^b G(x,y,s,t,u(s,t))\,ds\,dt$$
$$= f(x,y), \quad (x,y) \in [a,b] \times [c,d], \tag{22}$$

where $G(x, y, s, t, u)$ and $f(x, y)$ are given analytic functions. Similarly, we must substitute (10) in (22) and collocate the points (x_i, y_j), $i, j = 0, 1, \ldots, n$. After that, let the linear transforms

$$s = \mu(\xi) = \frac{b-a}{2}\xi + \frac{b+a}{2},$$
$$t = \nu(\tau) = \frac{y_j - c}{2}\tau + \frac{y_j + c}{2}, \tag{23}$$

and apply the quadrature integration formula corresponding to $[-1, 1]$. Similar to the previous section, we get the following system of equations:

$$F\left(C^T\Psi(x_i, y_j)\right)$$
$$- \lambda \frac{y_j - c}{2} \sum_{l=0}^{N} \sum_{k=0}^{N} w_k w_l G\left(x_i, y_j, \mu(\xi_k),\right.$$
$$\left.\nu(\tau_l), C^T\Psi\left(\mu(\xi_k), \nu(\tau_l)\right)\right)$$
$$= f(x_i, y_j). \tag{24}$$

The obtained nonlinear system of equations can be solved by Newton's iterative method to fulfill the unknown vector C^T.

NUMERICAL EXAMPLE

In this section, some examples are given to show validity and efficiency of the mentioned method. In this paper, the computations have been done using the Maple 13 with 100 digits precision. Note that digits are important factor because the obtained systems are ill-conditioned. For improving the results we have two ways: increasing digits and applying a regularization method. Since decreasing of digits leads to intensive decreasing of accuracy [54], we preferred to use high digits instead of applying complicated regularization methods. It can be a trade-off between increasing of complexity of mathematical operations in applying a regularization algorithm and increasing digits.

In our practical experiments with 100 digits, even applying SVD, QR, and iterative refinement methods did not affect the results for solving the linear systems. It must be mentioned that although it occurred in our experiments, it can be related to the rate of ill-conditioning. Hence, we reported the result of solving the obtaining nonlinear systems by Newton's iteration method without applying any regularization method. In this study, the criterion of accuracy is the value of infinity norm of the error function.

Example 1. Consider the following Volterra integral equation [63]:

$$u(x,y) - \int_0^y \int_0^x \left(xt^2 + \cos s\right) u(s,t)\,ds\,dt$$
$$= x \sin y - \frac{1}{4}x^5 + \frac{1}{4}x^5 \cos y - \frac{1}{4}x^2 \sin\left(y^2\right), \tag{25}$$

where $(x, y) \in [0, 1]^2$ and the exact solution is $u(x, y) = x \sin y$. The error for some radial basis functions and for different values of n is given in Table 1.

As it is mentioned, the interpolation error is $\varepsilon = O(\lambda^{c/h})$, h is the mesh size, $c = 1/\epsilon$, and $0<\lambda<1$ is a constant [50]. However the proof is for an interpolant function [50] and we are involved with a nonlinear integral equation; since we apply the collocation method, the error of the approximation and interpolation techniques are nearly the same.

Now we investigate how n affects error. Note that ε is directly related to n because n is inversely related to mesh size:

$$\frac{1}{h} \propto n \Longrightarrow \varepsilon \propto n. \tag{26}$$

So, we expect increasing of n decreases ε exponentially [44, 50]. In Figure 1, we show how n affects error. Also, we show the effect of c on error in Figure 2. We must note the obtained system is nonlinear. Therefore, although we expect the exponential trend, the nature of nonlinearity has negative effect on the rate of convergence which is different for each problem.

Table 1: Numerical results of different RBFs for Example 1. The roots of Legendre polynomial are chosen as center points

n	GA	MQ	IQ
4	7.6×10^{-3}	9.0×10^{-3}	7.5×10^{-3}
9	2.1×10^{-4}	2.0×10^{-4}	1.6×10^{-4}
16	1.6×10^{-5}	1.1×10^{-5}	1.4×10^{-5}
25	3.0×10^{-7}	7.0×10^{-7}	2.6×10^{-7}
36	6.6×10^{-8}	4.9×10^{-8}	6.2×10^{-8}
49	2.5×10^{-10}	3.7×10^{-10}	2.8×10^{-10}

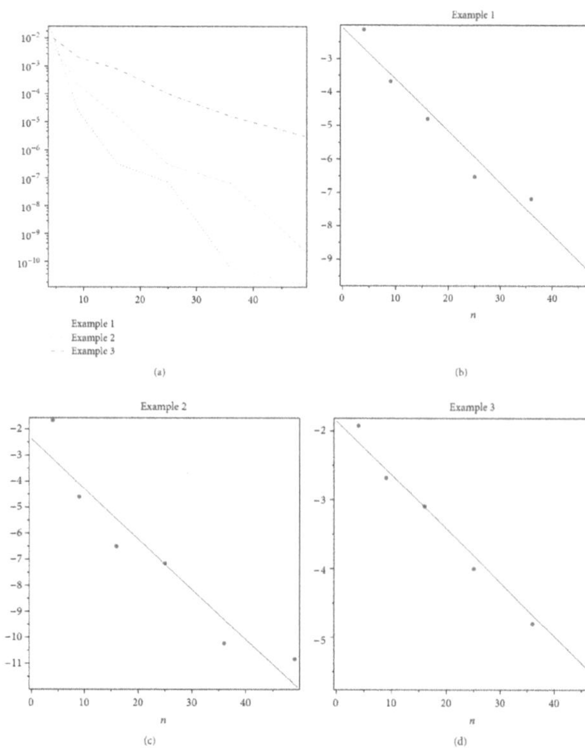

Figure 1: The horizontal axis is related to c or shape parameter and the vertical axis shows the corresponding error values where $n = 49$.

The relation between c and log (error) is linear in the interval (0, 10). Although the trend is changed, the graph confirms c can affect error exponentially. In brief, the error function is sensitive to c intensively. The data is related to Example 1.

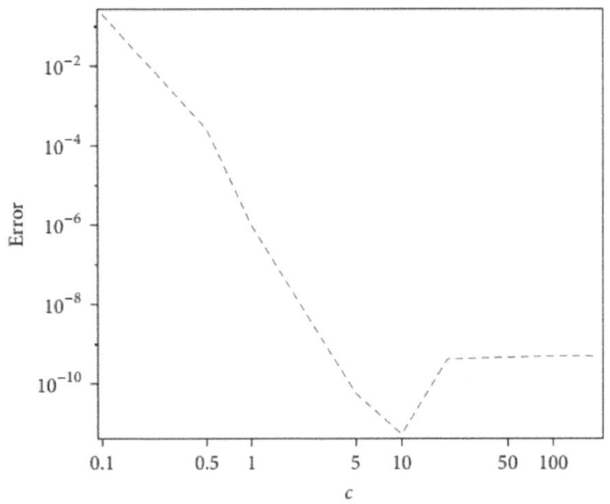

Figure 2: The horizontal axis is related to c or shape parameter and the vertical axis shows the corresponding error values where $n = 49$. The relation between c and log (error) is linear in the interval (0, 10). Although the trend is changed, the graph confirms c can affect error exponentially. In brief, the error function is sensitive to c intensively. The data is related to Example 1.

Example 2. Consider the following Volterra nonlinear integral equation [20]:

$$u(x,y) - \int_0^y \int_0^x [u(s,t)]^2 \, ds\, dt = x^2 + y^2 - \frac{1}{5}x^5 y + \frac{2}{9}x^3 y^3 - \frac{1}{5}xy^5, \quad (x,y) \in [0,1]^2, \tag{27}$$

with the exact solution $u(x, y) = x^2 + y^2$. Error for some radial basis functions for different values of n is given in Table 2.The effect of n on error is shown in Figure 1.

Table 2: Numerical results of different RBFs for Example 2. The roots of Legendre polynomial are chosen as center points

n	GA	MQ	IQ
4	2.2×10^{-2}	2.6×10^{-2}	2.2×10^{-2}
9	2.5×10^{-4}	1.2×10^{-4}	5.2×10^{-4}
16	3.2×10^{-7}	3.0×10^{-7}	4.4×10^{-7}
25	7.1×10^{-8}	7.4×10^{-8}	8.0×10^{-8}
36	6.0×10^{-11}	5.1×10^{-11}	5.9×10^{-11}
49	1.5×10^{-11}	2.1×10^{-11}	2.0×10^{-11}

Example 3. Consider the following Volterra-Fredholm integral equation of Urysohn type [24]:

$$u(x,y) - \int_0^y \int_0^1 \frac{x(1-t^2)}{(1+y)(1+s^2)} \left(1 - \exp^{-u(s,t)}\right) ds\, dt = -\ln\left(1 + \frac{xy}{1+y^2}\right) + \frac{xy^2}{8(1+y)(1+y^2)}, \tag{28}$$

where $(x, y) \in [0, 1]^2$ and the exact solution is $u(x, y) = -\ln(1 + xy/(1 + y^2))$. Error for some radial basis functions for different values of n is given in Table 3. The exponential effect of n on error is shown in Figure 1.

So far we compute the errors in the infinity norm that are shown in Tables 1, 2, and 3. Now, we compute the root mean square residual errors by the formula

$$\sqrt{\frac{\sum_{i=1}^{N} \delta_{ij}^2}{N}}, \tag{29}$$

where

$$\delta(x,y) = \hat{u}(x,y) - \iint G(x,y,s,t,\hat{u}(s,t))\, ds\, dt - f(x,y), \tag{30}$$

such that $\hat{u}$ is the approximated solution, N is a large number, and (x_i, y_j) are points uniformly distributed over the domain. This criterion shows tolerance of error in the solution region.

Table 3: Numerical results of different RBFs for Example 3. The roots of Legendre polynomial are chosen as the center points

n	GA	MQ	IQ
4	1.2×10^{-2}	1.7×10^{-2}	1.2×10^{-2}
9	2.1×10^{-3}	2.4×10^{-4}	2.4×10^{-3}
16	8.0×10^{-4}	7.7×10^{-4}	6.5×10^{-4}
25	1.0×10^{-4}	3.1×10^{-4}	3.4×10^{-4}
36	1.6×10^{-5}	2.8×10^{-5}	1.4×10^{-5}
49	5.2×10^{-6}	4.9×10^{-6}	7.2×10^{-6}

The results for Examples1, 2, and 3 are reported in Table 4 for the Gaussian radial basis function with $N = 400$. In fact, if we have the exact solution, we can compute the absolute maximum of error or infinity norm of error function; otherwise, we must compute the root mean square residual error which is defined in (29). The comparison between Tables 1, 2, 3, and 4 confirms the strong correlation between the absolute maximum of errors and the root of mean square of residual errors. So, even without having the exact solution we still will be able to estimate the error of approximation.

Table 4: Value of the root of mean square of residual errors that is computed by (29). The results for Examples 1, 2, and 3 are reported for Gaussian radial basis functions and $N = 400$. Comparison between Tables 1, 2, and 3 and following results confirms the strong correlation between absolute maximum of error and the root of mean square of residual errors. In brief, the estimation error of approximation is possible by (29) even as the exact solution is not given.

n	Example 1	Example 2	Example 3
4	1.0×10^{-3}	9.3×10^{-3}	1.2×10^{-3}
9	1.8×10^{-5}	8.9×10^{-5}	2.1×10^{-4}
16	1.8×10^{-5}	1.4×10^{-7}	8.3×10^{-4}
25	1.4×10^{-6}	3.1×10^{-8}	7.5×10^{-6}
36	8.5×10^{-8}	2.0×10^{-11}	5.9×10^{-6}
49	6.8×10^{-9}	5.2×10^{-12}	8.2×10^{-7}

CONCLUSION

First, we exploit some technical methods that can be used to improve results.

Supplementary Techniques

Quadrature Integration Methods. we applied the generalized Gauss-Lobatto quadrature on interval $[a, b]$ where the boundaries of the interval coincide with the collocation points.

Since $x_0 = a$ and $x_n = b$ in Gauss-Lobatto quadrature, we can improve the approximation on boundaries and the results are stable on boundary.

Regularization. We suggest applying the regularization methods for solving the resulting linear and particularly nonlinear systems. Considering there is no guarantee that Newton's method leads to the convergent solution, using of the regularization methods such as Tikhonov or Landweber is definitely recommended for ill-conditioned nonlinear system [62].

Partitioning. As mentioned the obtained systems by the collocation points are ill-conditioned. Moreover, the ill-conditioning is worse by increasing the number of collocation points. Therefore, to avoid the ill-conditioning we can partition domain of problems to the smaller area. This technique gives the smaller systems that can be solved easier. The numerical experiments show that performance of this technique can be effective when it is not possible to improve the tools of computation.

Finding the accurate solution of the two-dimensional integral equations is usually difficult. In this work, the linear and nonlinear, Fredholm, Volterra, and mixed Volterra-Fredholm integral equations of the second kind are solved by applying the radial basis functions (RBFs) method. The illustrative examples confirm the exponential convergence rate for integral equations similar to rate of convergence for solving partial and ordinary deferential equations using RBF method reported in [53].

ACKNOWLEDGMENTS

The work described in this paper was supported by the National Basic Research Program of China (973 Project no. 2010CB832702), the National Science Funds for Distinguished Young Scholars of China (1077403), NSFC Funds (no. 11372097), the 111 project under Grant B12032. Also, the authors greatly appreciate the precious time of Professor Mahdi Dehghan (from Amirkabir University, Iran) who help them generously.

REFERENCES

1. K. E. Atkinson, The Numerical Solution of Integral Equations of the Second Kind, Cambridge University Press, Cambridge, UK, 1997.
2. A. J. Jerri, Introduction to Integral Equations with Applications, John Wiley & Sons, New York, NY, USA, 1999.
3. A. D. Polyanin and A. V. Manzhirov, Handbook of Integral Equations, Chapman & Hall/CRC, 2008.
4. A.-M. Wazwaz, A First Course in Integral Equations, World Scientific, Singapore, 1997.
5. S. Abbasbandy, "Application of He's homotopy perturbation method to functional integral equations,"Chaos, Solitons & Fractals, vol. 31, no. 5, pp. 1243–1247, 2007.
6. S. A. Yousefi, A. Lotfi, and M. Dehghan, "He's variational iteration method for solving nonlinear mixed Volterra-Fredholm integral equations," Computers & Mathematics with Applications, vol. 58, no. 11-12, pp. 2172–2176, 2009.
7. S. A. Belbas, "A new method for optimal control of Volterra integral equations," Applied Mathematics and Computation, vol. 189, no. 2, pp. 1902–1915, 2007.
8. Y. Mahmoudi, "Wavelet Galerkin method for numerical solution of nonlinear integral equation,"Applied Mathematics and Computation, vol. 167, no. 2, pp. 1119–1129, 2005.
9. K. Maleknejad, R. Mollapourasl, and M. Alizadeh, "Numerical solution of Volterra type integral equation of the first kind with wavelet basis," Applied Mathematics and Computation, vol. 194, no. 2, pp. 400–405, 2007.
10. G. Vainikko, A. Kivinukk, and J. Lippus, "Fast solvers of integral equations of the second kind: wavelet methods," Journal of Complexity, vol. 21, no. 2, pp. 243–273, 2005.
11. S. Yousefi and M. Razzaghi, "Legendre wavelets method for the nonlinear Volterra-Fredholm integral equations," Mathematics and Computers in Simulation, vol. 70, no. 1, pp. 1–8, 2005.
12. A. Golbabai, M. Mammadov, and S. Seifollahi, "Solving a system of nonlinear integral equations by an RBF network," Computers & Mathematics with Applications, vol. 57, no. 10, pp. 1651–1658, 2009.
13. M. H. Kalos and P. A. Whitlock, Monte Carlo Methods, Wiley-Blackwell, Weinheim, Germany, 2nd edition, 2004.
14. K. Maleknejad, M. Shahrezaee, and H. Khatami, "Numerical solution of integral equations system of the second kind by block-pulse functions," Applied Mathematics and Computation, vol. 166, no. 1, pp. 15–24, 2005.
15. Z. Avazzadeh, M. Heydari, and G. B. Loghmani, "Numerical solution of Fredholm integral equations of the second kind by using integral mean value theorem," Applied Mathematical Modelling, vol. 35, no. 5, pp. 2374–2383, 2011.
16. K. Maleknejad and H. Derili, "Numerical solution of integral equations by using combination of spline-collocation method and Lagrange interpolation," Applied Mathematics and Computation, vol. 175, no. 2, pp. 1235–1244, 2006. ·
17. E. Mammen and K. Yu, "Nonparametric estimation of noisy integral equations of the second kind,"Journal of the Korean Statistical Society, vol. 38, no. 2, pp. 99–110, 2009.
18. H. K. Pathak, M. S. Khan, and R. Tiwari, "A common fixed point theorem and its application to nonlinear integral equations," Computers & Mathematics with Applications, vol. 53, no. 6, pp. 961–971, 2007.
19. S. A. Belbas, "Optimal control of Volterra integral equations in two independent variables," Applied Mathematics and Computation, vol. 202, no. 2, pp. 647–665, 2008.
20. H. Guoqiang, K. Hayami, K. Sugihara, and W. Jiong, "Extrapolation method of iterated collocation solution for two-dimensional nonlinear Volterra integral

equations," Applied Mathematics and Computation, vol. 112, no. 1, pp. 49–61, 2000.

21. G. Han and J. Wang, "Extrapolation of Nystrom solution for two dimensional nonlinear Fredholm integral equations," Journal of Computational and Applied Mathematics, vol. 134, no. 1-2, pp. 259–268, 2001. ·
22. M. Heydari, Z. Avazzadeh, H. Navabpour, and G. B. Loghmani, "Numerical solution of Fredholm integral equations of the second kind by using integral mean value theorem II. High dimensional problems," Applied Mathematical Modelling, vol. 37, no. 1-2, pp. 432–442, 2013.
23. K. Maleknejad, S. Sohrabi, and B. Baranji, "Application of 2D-BPFs to nonlinear integral equations,"Communications in Nonlinear Science and Numerical Simulation, vol. 15, no. 3, pp. 527–535, 2010. ·
24. A. M. Wazwaz, "A reliable treatment for mixed Volterra-Fredholm integral equations," Applied Mathematics and Computation, vol. 127, no. 2-3, pp. 405–414, 2002.
25. M. A. Abdou, K. I. Mohamed, and A. S. Ismail, "On the numerical solutions of Fredholm-Volterra integral equation," Applied Mathematics and Computation, vol. 146, no. 2-3, pp. 713–728, 2003.
26. A. A. Badr, "Numerical solution of Fredholm-Volterra integral equation in one dimension with time dependent," Applied Mathematics and Computation, vol. 167, no. 2, pp. 1156–1161, 2005.
27. A. Yildirim, "Homotopy perturbation method for the mixed Volterra-Fredholm integral equations,"Chaos, Solitons and Fractals, vol. 42, no. 5, pp. 2760–2764, 2009.
28. R. L. Hardy, "Multiquadratic equation of topology and other irregular surface," Journal of Geophysical Research, vol. 76, pp. 1905–1915, 1971.
29. M. D. Buhmann, "Multivariate interpolation in odd-dimensional Euclidean spaces using multiquadrics," Constructive Approximation, vol. 6, no. 1, pp. 21–34, 1990.
30. M. D. Buhmann and C. A. Micchelli, "Multiquadric interpolation improved," Computers & Mathematics with Applications, vol. 24, no. 12, pp. 21–25, 1992.
31. W. R. Madych and S. A. Nelson, "Multivariate interpolation and conditionally positive definite functions, II," Mathematics of Computation, vol. 54, no. 189, pp. 211–230, 1990.
32. W. R. Madych and S. A. Nelson, "Multivariate interpolation and conditionally positive definite functions," Approximation Theory and its Applications, vol. 4, no. 4, pp. 77–89, 1988.
33. C. A. Micchelli, "Interpolation of scattered data: distance matrices and conditionally positive definite functions," Constructive Approximation, vol. 2, no. 1, pp. 11–22, 1986.
34. G. B. Wright, Radial basis function interpolation: numerical and analytical developments [Ph.D. Dissertation], University of Colorado, 2003.
35. E. J. Kansa, "Multiquadrics—a scattered data approximation scheme with applications to computational fluid-dynamics—II solutions to parabolic, hyperbolic and elliptic partial differential equations," Computers & Mathematics with Applications, vol. 19, no. 8-9, pp. 147–161, 1990.
36. A. Makroglou, "Radial basis functions in the numerical solution of Fredholm integral and integro-differential equations," in Advances in Computer Methods for Partial Differential Equations, VII, R. Vichnevetsky, D. Knight, and G. Richter, Eds., pp. 478–484, Karen Hahn Imacs, New Brunswick, NJ, USA, 1992.
37. E. A. Galperin and E. J. Kansa, "Application of global optimization and radial basis functions to numerical solutions of weakly singular Volterra integral equations," Computers & Mathematics with Applications, vol. 43, no. 3–5, pp. 491–499, 2002.
38. A. Alipanah and M. Dehghan, "Numerical solution of the nonlinear Fredholm integral equations by positive definite functions," Applied Mathematics and Computation, vol. 190, no. 2, pp. 1754–1761, 2007. ·
39. A. Alipanah and S. Esmaeili, "Numerical solution of the two-dimensional Fredholm integral equations using Gaussian radial basis function," Journal of Computational and Applied Mathematics, vol. 235, no. 18, pp. 5342–5347, 2011. ·
40. Z. Avazzadeh, M. Heydari, and G. B. Loghmani, "A comparison between solving two dimensional integral equations by the traditional collocation method and radial basis functions," Applied Mathematical Sciences, vol. 5, no. 21–24, pp. 1145–1152, 2011.
41. Z. Avazzadeh, M. Heydari, W. Chen, and G. Loghmani, "Smooth solutio of partial integro-differential equations using radial basis functions," The Journal of Applied Analysis and Computation, vol. 4, no. 2, pp. 115–127, 2014.
42. Z. Avazzadeh, Z. Beygi Rizi, F. M. Maalek Ghaini, and G. B. Loghmani, "A semi-discrete scheme for solving nonlinear hyperbolic-type partial integro-differential equations using radial basis functions,"Journal of Mathematical Physics, vol. 52, no. 6, Article ID 063520, 15 pages, 2011.
43. Z. Avazzadeh, Z. Beygi Rizi, F. M. Maalek Ghaini, and G. B. Loghmani, "A numerical solution of nonlinear parabolic-type Volterra partial integro-differential equations using radial basis functions,"Engineering Analysis with Boundary Elements, vol. 36, no. 5, pp. 881–893, 2012.
44. M. D. Buhmann, Radial Basis Functions, Cambridge University Press, 2003.
45. M. D. Buhmann, Multivariable interpolation using radial basis functions [Ph.D. Dissertation], University of Cambridge, 1989.
46. W. Cheney and W. Light, A Course in Approximation Theory, William Allan, New York, NY, USA, 1999.
47. I. J. Schoenberg, "Metric spaces and completely monotone functions," Annals of Mathematics, vol. 39, no. 4, pp. 811–841, 1938.
48. T. A. Driscoll and B. Fornberg, "Interpolation in the limit

of increasingly flat radial basis functions,"Computers & Mathematics with Applications, vol. 43, no. 3–5, pp. 413–422, 2002.

49. B. Fornberg, G. Wright, and E. Larsson, "Some observations regarding interpolants in the limit of flat radial basis functions," Computers & Mathematics with Applications, vol. 47, no. 1, pp. 37–55, 2004. ·

50. W. R. Madych, "Miscellaneous error bounds for multiquadric and related interpolators," Computers & Mathematics with Applications, vol. 24, no. 12, pp. 121–138, 1992.

51. J. Li, A. H.-D. Cheng, and C.-S. Chen, "A comparison of efficiency and error convergence of multiquadric collocation method and finite element method," Engineering Analysis with Boundary Elements, vol. 27, no. 3, pp. 251–257, 2003.

52. R. Schaback, "Error estimates and condition numbers for radial basis function interpolation," Advances in Computational Mathematics, vol. 3, no. 3, pp. 251–264, 1995.

53. A. H. Cheng, M. A. Golberg, E. J. Kansa, and G. Zammito, "Exponential convergence and H-cmultiquadric collocation method for partial differential equations," Numerical Methods for Partial Differential Equations, vol. 19, no. 5, pp. 571–594, 2003.

54. C.-S. Huang, C.-F. Lee, and A. H.-D. Cheng, "Error estimate, optimal shape factor, and high precision computation of multiquadric collocation method," Engineering Analysis with Boundary Elements, vol. 31, no. 7, pp. 614–623, 2007.

55. Z.-C. Li and H.-T. Huang, "Study on effective condition number for collocation methods," Engineering Analysis with Boundary Elements, vol. 32, no. 10, pp. 839–848, 2008.

56. C. H. Tsai, J. Kolibal, and M. Li, "The golden section search algorithm for finding a good shape parameter for meshless collocation methods," Engineering Analysis with Boundary Elements, vol. 34, no. 8, pp. 738–746, 2010. ·

57. J. G. Wang and G. R. Liu, "On the optimal shape parameters of radial basis functions used for 2-D meshless methods," Computer Methods in Applied Mechanics and Engineering, vol. 191, no. 23-24, pp. 2611–2630, 2002.

58. B. J. Baxter, "Preconditioned conjugate gradients, radial basis functions, and Toeplitz matrices,"Computers & Mathematics with Applications, vol. 43, no. 3–5, pp. 305–318, 2002.

59. G. Casciola, L. B. Montefusco, and S. Morigi, "The regularizing properties of anisotropic radial basis functions," Applied Mathematics and Computation, vol. 190, no. 2, pp. 1050–1062, 2007.

60. A. Karageorghis, C. S. Chen, and Y. S. Smyrlis, "Matrix decomposition RBF algorithm for solving 3D elliptic problems," Engineering Analysis with Boundary Elements, vol. 33, no. 12, pp. 1368–1373, 2009. ·

61. P. K. Kythe and M. R. Schäferkotter, Handbook of Computational Method for Integration, Chapman & Hall/CRC Press, 2005.

62. B. Kaltenbacher, A. Neubauer, and O. Scherzer, Itera tive Regularization Methods for Nonlinear Ill-Posed Problems, Walter de Gruyter, 2008.

63. A. Tari, M. Y. Rahimi, S. Shahmorad, and F. Talati, "Solving a class of two-dimensional linear and nonlinear Volterra integral equations by the differential transform method," Journal of Computational and Applied Mathematics, vol. 228, no. 1, pp. 70–76, 2009.

CHAPTER 8

NUMERICAL DIFFERENTIATION OF NOISY, NONSMOOTH DATA

Rick Chartrand

Theoretical Division, MS B284, Los Alamos National Laboratory, Los Alamos, NM 87545, USA

ABSTRACT

We consider the problem of differentiating a function specified by noisy data. Regularizing the differentiation process avoids the noise amplification of finite-difference methods. We use total-variation regularization, which allows for discontinuous solutions. The resulting simple algorithm accurately differentiates noisy functions, including those which have a discontinuous derivative.

INTRODUCTION

In many scientific applications, it is necessary to compute the derivative of functions specified by data. Conventional finite-difference approximations will greatly amplify any noise present in the data. Denoising the data before or after differentiating does not generally give satisfactory results (see an example in Section4).

A method which does give good results is to regularize the differentiation process itself. This guarantees that the computed derivative will have some degree of regularity, to an extent that is often under control by adjusting parameters. A common framework for this is Tikhonov regularization [1] of the corresponding inverse problem. That is, the derivative of a function f, say on [0,], is the minimizer of the functional

$$(u)=\alpha R(u)+DF(Au-f) \qquad (1.1)$$

where $R(u)$ is a regularization or penalty term that penalizes irregularity in u, $Au(x) = \int_0^x u$ is the operator of antidifferentiation, $DF(Au-f)$ is a data fidelity term that penalizes discrepancy between Au and f, and α is a regularization parameter that controls the balance between the two terms.

The data fidelity term DF is most commonly the square of the L^2 norm, $DF = \int_0^L |\cdot|^2$, as is appropriate if $f$has additive, white Gaussian noise [2]. Other data fidelity terms can be used if the noise has a different, known distribution; see [3] for an alternative in the case of Poisson noise, and [4] for a more general approach.

In [1], the regularization term is the squared L^2 norm; this controls the size of u, without forcing minimizers to be regular. Tikhonov regularization was first applied to numerical differentiation by Cullum [5], where the regularization is the squared H^1 norm, $R(u) = \int_0^L |u'|^2$. This forces minimizers to be continuous, as is required for the H^1 norm to be finite. This prevents the accurate differentiation of functions with singular points.

Citation: Rick Chartrand, "Numerical Differentiation of Noisy, Nonsmooth Data," ISRN Applied Mathematics, vol. 2011, Article ID 164564, 11 pages, 2011. doi:10.5402/2011/164564

Other variational methods have the same drawback of forcing smoothness. An approach that penalizes the L^2 norm of u'' forces the minimizer to be a cubic spline (see [6–8]). The variational approach of Knowles and Wallace [9] does not fall into the category of Tikhonov regularization, but explicitly assumes that u is smooth.

TOTAL-VARIATION REGULARIZATION

We propose to use total-variation regularization in (1.1). We will thus compute the derivative of f on [0,] as the minimizer of the functional

$$F(u) = \alpha \int_0^L |u'| + \frac{1}{2}\int_0^L |Au - f|^2. \quad (2.1)$$

We assume $f \in L^2$ (an empty assumption in the discrete case), and for convenience that (0)=0 (in practice we simply subtract $f(0)$ from f). The functional F is defined on $B[0,L]$, the space of functions of bounded variation. It is in fact continuous on BV, as BV is continuously embedded in L^2, and A is continuous on L^2(being an integral operator with bounded kernel). Existence of a minimizer for F follows from the compactness of BV in L^2 [10, page 152] and the lower semicontinuity of the BV seminorm [10, page 120]. This and the strict convexity of F are sufficient to guarantee that F has a unique minimizer u^*.

Use of total variation accomplishes two things. It suppresses noise, as a noisy function will have a large total variation. It also does not suppress jump discontinuities, unlike typical regularizations. This allows for the computation of discontinuous derivatives, and the detection of corners and edges in noisy data.

Total-variation regularization is due to Rudin et al. in [11]. It has since found many applications in image processing. Replacing A in the two-dimensional analog of (2.1) with the identity operator gives a method for denoising an image f; see [12, 13] for an example where A is the Abel transform, giving a method for regularizing Abel inversion.

NUMERICAL IMPLEMENTATION

A simple approach to minimizing (2.1) is gradient descent. This amounts to evolving to stationarity the PDE obtained from the Euler-Lagrange equation:

$$u_t = \alpha \frac{d}{dx}\frac{u'}{|u'|} - A^T(Au - f), \quad (3.1)$$

where $A^T v(x) = \int_x^L v$ is the L^2-adjoint of A. Replacing the $|u'|$ in the denominator with $\sqrt{(u')^2 + \epsilon}$ for some small $\epsilon>0$ avoids division by zero. Typically, (3.1) is implemented with explicit time marching, with u_t discretized as $(u_{n+1}-u_n)/\Delta t$ for some fixed Δt.

The problem with (3.1) is that convergence is slow. A faster algorithm is the lagged diffusivity method of Vogel and Oman [14]. The idea is to replace at each iteration of (3.1) the nonlinear differential operator $u \mapsto (d/dx)(u'/|u'|)$ with the linear operator $u \mapsto (d/dx)(u'/|u_n'|)$. The algorithm has been proven to converge to the minimizer of F [15].

We consider two discrete implementations of the lagged diffusivity algorithm. The first uses explicit matrix constructions, and is faster for smaller problems, but becomes impractical for data of more than a few thousand points. We assume that u is defined on a uniform grid $\{x_i\}_0^L = \{0, \Delta x, 2\Delta x, \ldots, L\}$. Derivatives of $u$are computed halfway between grid points as centered differences, $Du(x_i+\Delta x/2) = u(x_{i+1})-u(x_i)$. This defines our $L\times(L+1)$ differentiation matrix D. This approach avoids the consideration of boundary conditions for differentiation, and we find it gives better algorithmic results at the boundary. Integrals of u are likewise computed halfway between grid points, using the trapezoid rule to define an $L\times(L+1)$ matrix A. Let E_n be the diagonal matrix whose ith entry is $((u_n(x_i) - u_n(x_{i-1}))^2 + \epsilon)^{-1/2}$. Let $L_n = \Delta x D^T E_n D$, $H_n = K^T K + \alpha L_n$. The matrix H_n is an approximation of the Hessian of F at u_n. The update $s_n=u_{n+1}-u_n$ is the solution to $H_n s_n=-g_n$, where $g_n=K(Ku_n-f)+\alpha L_n u_n$, and we solve the equation using MATLAB's backslash operator. For further algorithm details, see [16].

For larger problems, we use a modified version that avoids explicit matrices and uses simpler numerics. The differentiation matrix D is constructed as the square, sparse matrix for simple forward differences, with periodic boundary conditions. We use a function handle for A, simply using MATLAB's cumulative sum operator, as well as for A^T. It is important that the discretization of A^T be consistent with the discretization of A, in the sense that if one were to use the function handles to construct matrices, then they would be transposes of each other. In other respects, the algorithm is as above, except the definition of E_n now uses periodic boundary conditions, and the equation $H_n s_n=-g_n$ is solved using preconditioned conjugate gradient. For the preconditioner, we perform incomplete-Cholesky factorization on the sum of αL_n and the diagonal matrix whose entries are the row sums of $A^T A$, these sums being computable analytically.

Less straightforward is the choice of the regularization parameter α. One approach is to use the discrepancy principle: the mean-squared difference between Au^* and f should equal the variance of the noise in f. This has the effect of choosing the most regular solution of the ill-posed inverse problem $Au=f$ that is consistent with the data f. In practice, the noise in f is not generally known, but the noise variance can be estimated by comparing f with a smoothed version of f. The other approach is simply to use trial and error, adjusting α to obtain the desired balance between suppression of oscillations and fidelity to the data. In the next section, we will see an example showing the effect of the value of α.

EXAMPLES

A Simple Nonsmooth Example

Let $f_0(x)=|x-1/2|$, defined at 100 evenly spaced points in [0,1]. We obtain f by adding Gaussian noise of standard deviation 0.05. Figure 1 shows the resulting f. First, we show in Figure 2 the result of computing f' by simple centered differencing. The noise has been greatly amplified, so much that denoising the result is hopeless.

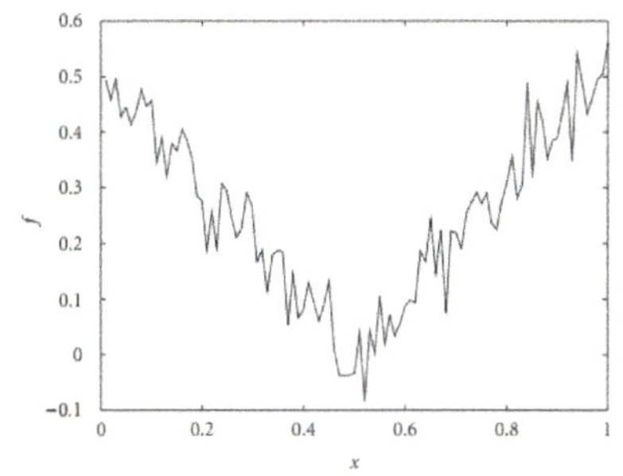

Figure 1: The function f, obtained from $|x-1/2|$ by adding Gaussian noise of standard deviation 0.05.

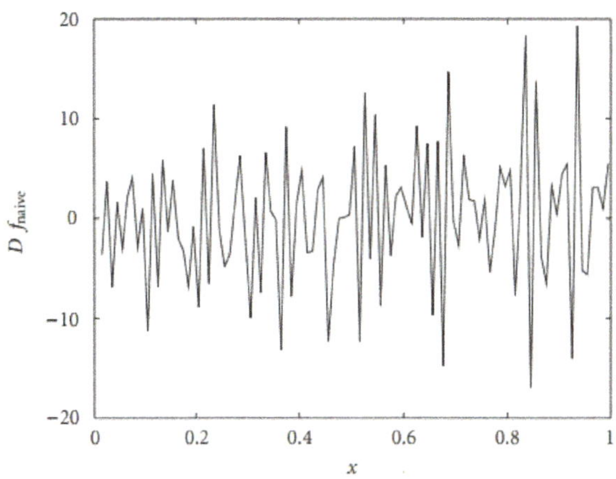

Figure 2: Computing f' with finite differences greatly amplifies noise.

We compare this with the result in Figure 3 of denoising f before computing f' by differencing. The denoising is done by H^1 regularization, minimizing

$$\alpha \int_0^L |u'|^2 + \frac{1}{2}\int_0^L |u-f|^2, \tag{4.1}$$

an appropriate denoising mechanism for continuous functions. We use α=3.5×10^{-3}, using the discrepancy principle, as this results in the L^2 norm of u^*-f being 0.5, the expected value of the L^2 norm of the noise vector $f-f_0$. The residual noise in the denoised f is still amplified enough by the differentiation process to give an unsatisfactory result.

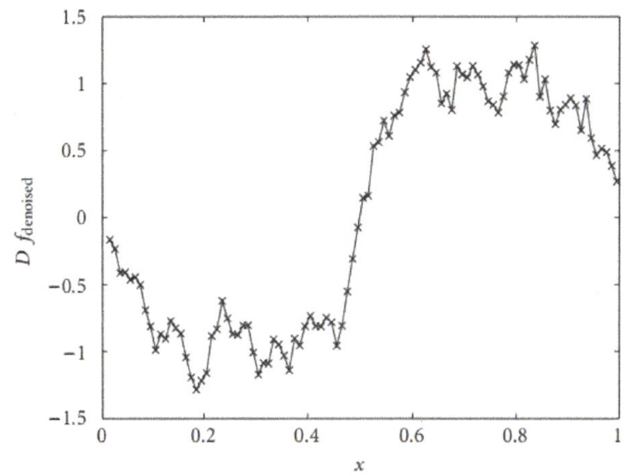

Figure 3: The function f is denoised, then differentiated with finite differences. The result is noisy and inaccurate.

Now, we implement our total-variation regularized differentiation, (2.1). We use the matrix-based version described above, using α=0.2 and ϵ=10^{-6}, initializing with the naive derivative (specifically [0; diff(f); 0], to obtain a vector of the appropriate size). Although convergence is nearly complete after 100 iterations, the points closest to the jump move much more slowly, adopting their final positions after 7000 iterations. This takes just 13.1 s, running on a conventional dual-core desktop. The result is in Figure 4. The overall shape of f_0' is captured almost perfectly. The jump is correctly located. The one inaccuracy is the size of the jump: there is a loss of contrast, which is typical of total-variation regularization in the presence of noise. Decreasing the size of the jump reduces the penalty term in (2.1), at the expense of increasing the data-fidelity term.

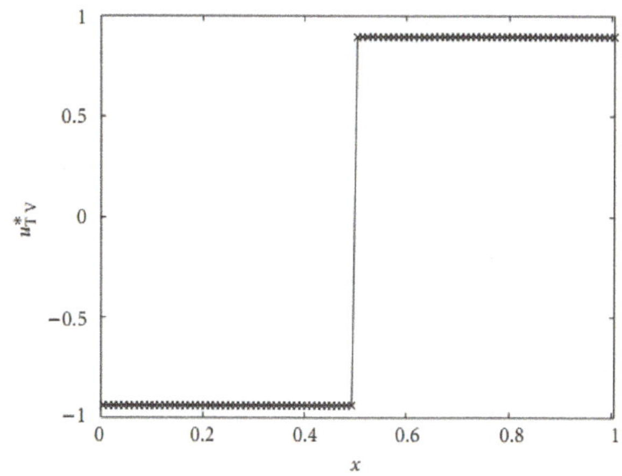

Figure 4: Regularizing the differentiation process with total-variation produces a noiseless derivative with a correctly located, sharp jump. The discrepancy of the values from ±1 are due to contrast loss, an artifact of total variation methods in the presence of noise.

We also show the result of applying the antidifferentiation operator to the computed f', and compare with f_0 in Figure 5. The corner is sharp and the lines are straight, though a little too flat.

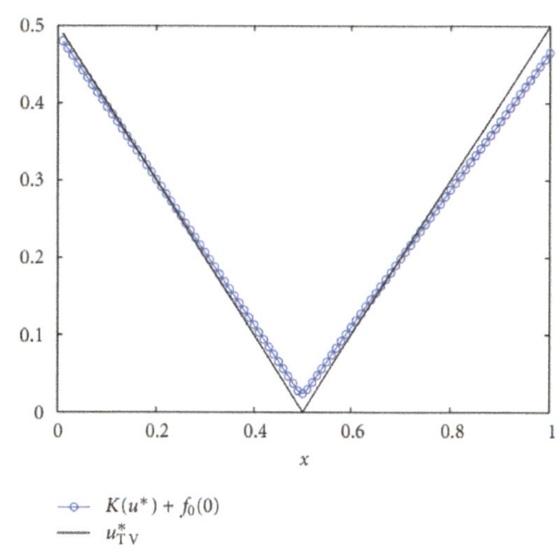

Figure 5: The function $f0$ (solid line) and the antidifferentiated numerical derivative (circles). The numerically computed function is very similar to the exact one.

Respirometry Data

Now, we consider data obtained from a whole-room calorimeter, courtesy of Edward L. Melanson of the University of Colorado Denver. The metabolic rate of a subject within the calorimeter can be determined via respirometry, the measurement of oxygen consumption, and carbon dioxide production within the room. The raw data traces need to undergo response corrections in order to be useful, which involves differentiation. Quoting [17]:

In essence, the first derivative of the trace is calculated, multiplied by a constant derived from the volume of the room and the volumetric flow rate, and added to the original data. Because of the long time constant of the room (5 h), the multiplicative constant is very large. Consequently, any significant noise in the derivatized data will overwhelm the original trace.

Thus, we see the need to regularize the differentiation process for this application.

In Figure 6 there is an example of the raw data for the oxygen consumption rate, which needs to be differentiated for the purposes of response correction. The data consists of samples taken every second for most of a day, for a total of 82,799 samples. In Figure 7 there is the result of computing the unregularized, finite-difference derivative. If restricted to the same vertical range as the following plots, the plot would be a solid black rectangle.

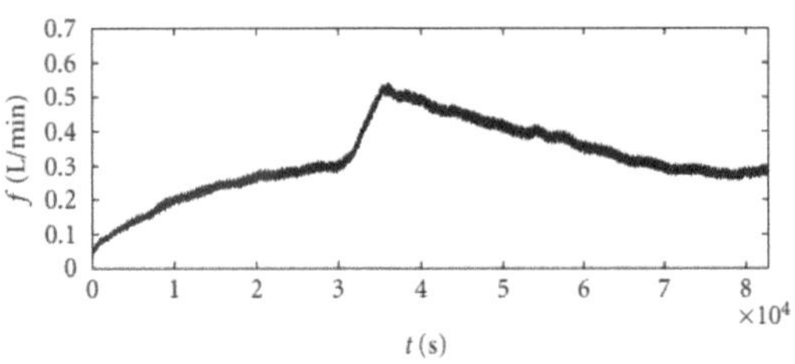

Figure 6: The trace of raw oxygen consumption data, consisting of 82,799 samples, one per second.

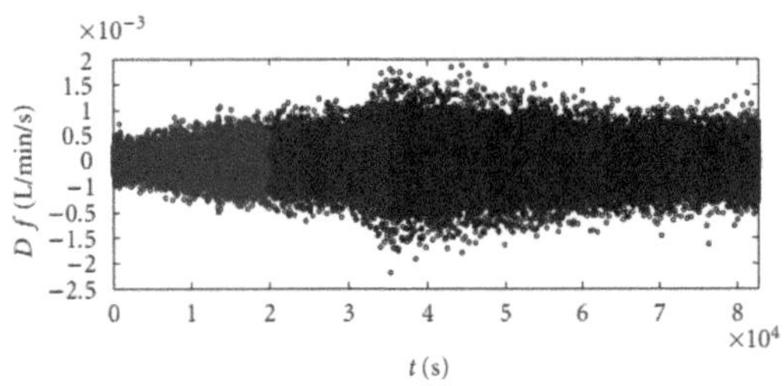

Figure 7: Computing the derivative with finite differences gives a useless result.

The data size is much too large for the explicit-matrix implementation, so we use the implicit approach. In each case, we use 60 iterations, taking about 5 minutes. We compare the total-variation regularized derivative with that computed with H^1 regularization, for two different regularization strengths. First, a stronger regularization, with a value of α=0.1 for the TV case. The result is in Figure 8. We then adjust the parameter for H^1 regularization until the curve matches the TV result away from the large bump, namely, α=500; see Figure 9. A value of ϵ=10−8 was used in both cases. The TV regularization is much more tolerant of rapid rises and falls while the H^1 result smooths away this information. We also compare the results of antidifferentiating the derivative and comparing with the original trace, with Figure 10 displaying a zoomed-in portion. The H^1 curve is unable to conform to the peak, as the H^1 regularization term heavily penalizes what would be the curvature of the curve in this figure. Away from the peak, the integrated derivatives follow the original trace, but not too closely, ignoring small-scale fluctuations. This is the effect of the regularization, with the choice of α serving to determine the scale of fluctuation that is considered insignificant.

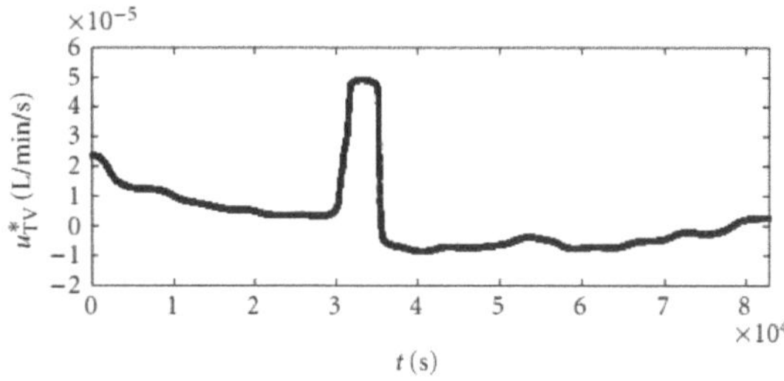

Figure 8: The derivative computed with strong TV regularization. Despite the heavy smoothing, the rapid rise and fall in the derivative is captured well.

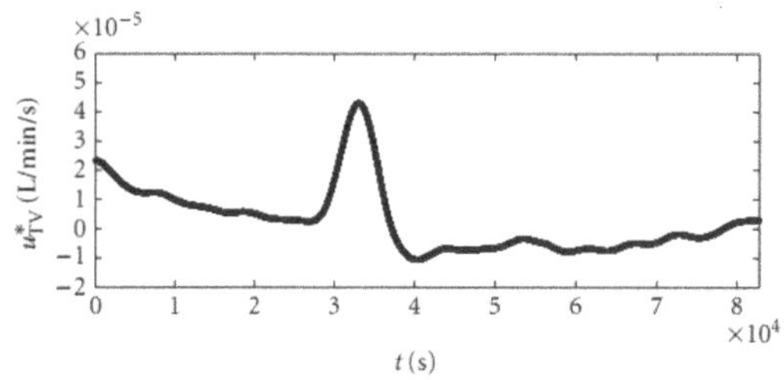

Figure 9: Using H^1 regularization, the jumps in the derivative are smoothed away.

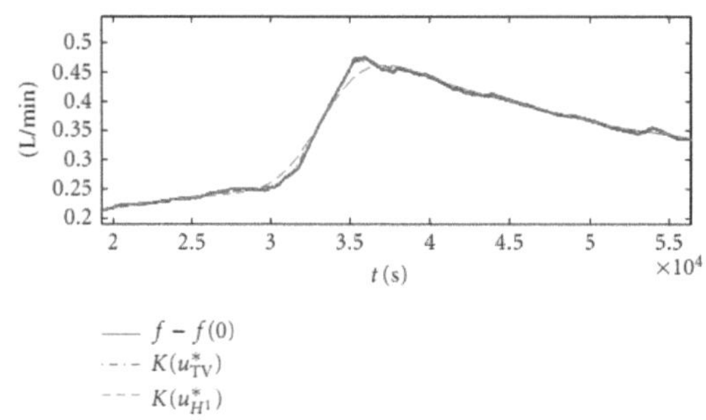

Figure 10: Integrating the derivatives and comparing with the original function, we find the TV result follows the curve more closely near the peak. Both curves follow the curve away from the peak, but ignore small fluctuations, to a degree determined by α.

The above result would be appropriate if the rapid rise and fall in the derivative corresponded to the only feature of interest. Now, we examine the result of weaker regularization, so as to preserve smaller-scale features. In this instance, we use $\alpha=10^{-3}$ for the TV regularization. As before, we choose α for the H^1regularization so that the result matches the TV result over most of the time period, in this case α=1. This time a slightly larger value of $\epsilon=10^{-6}$ was required, in order to offset the poorer conditioning of the linear system solved in the lagged diffusivity algorithm when α is smaller (in general, there is a tradeoff between better conditioning with larger values of ϵ and greater accuracy with smaller values).

Figures 11 and 12 show the results. Both derivatives capture more oscillations, including more structure in the rapid rise and fall. But the TV result is able to capture a discontinuity in the derivative that the H^1 result smooths away. When we compare the antiderivatives with the original function (Figure 13), we find that they follow the trace much more closely, conforming to smaller-scale fluctuations. Zooming in further, we see the greater curvature penalty on the H^1 curve prevents it from following the sharp corner, thus missing the discontinuous drop in the derivative.

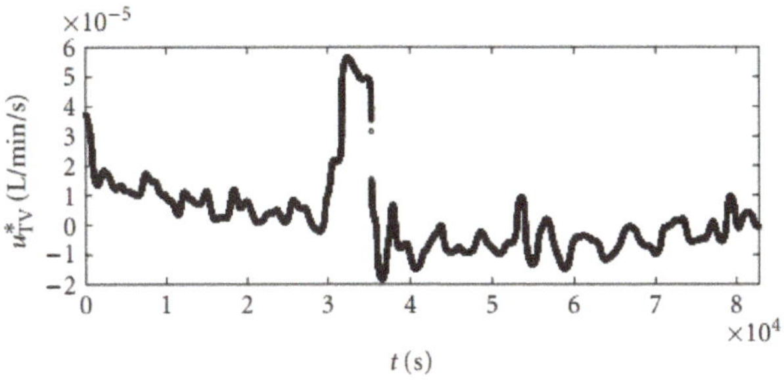

Figure 11: The derivative computed with lesser TV regularization, preserving more structure, including a discontinuity in the derivative.

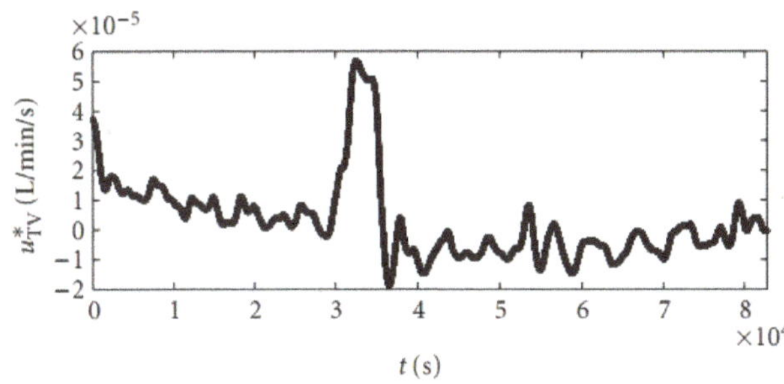

Figure 12: Using H^1 regularization, the discontinuity in the derivative is smoothed away.

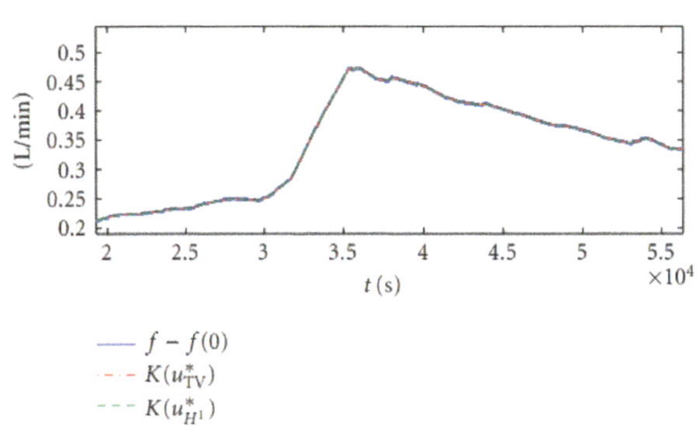

Figure 13: Integrating the derivatives and comparing with the original function, we find that with the weaker regularization, the integrals follow the curve closely, effectively considering much lesser fluctuations to be significant.

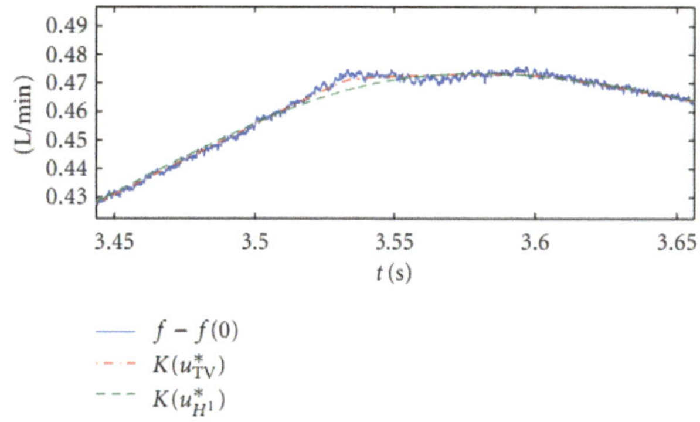

Figure 14: A closer look reveals that unlike the TV result, the H^1 curve cannot follow the high curvature at the corner, preventing the computed derivative from dropping discontinuously.

CONCLUSIONS

We presented a method for regularizing the numerical derivative process, using total-variation regularization. Unlike previously developed methods, the TV method allows for discontinuities in the derivatives, as desired when differentiating data corresponding to nonsmooth functions. We used the lagged diffusivity algorithm, which enjoys proven convergence properties, with one implementation that works rapidly for small problems, and a second more suitable for large problems. The TV regularization allows the derivative to capture more features of the data, while adjusting the regularization parameter controls the scale of fluctuations in the data that are ignored.

ACKNOWLEDGMENTS

This paper was supported by the U.S. Department of Energy through the LANL/LDRD Program. The authors wishes to thank John Lighton of Sable Systems International and Edward L. Melanson of the University of Colorado Denver for the data used in the examples.

REFERENCES

1. A. N. Tikhonov, "Regularization of incorrectly posed problems," Soviet Mathematics-Doklady, vol. 4, pp. 1624–1627, 1963.
2. M. Green, "Statistics of images, the TV algorithm of Rudin-Osher-Fatemi for image denoising and an improved denoising algorithm," Tech. Rep. 02-55, UCLA Computational and Applied Mathematics, 2002.
3. T. Le, R. Chartrand, and T. J. Asaki, "A variational approach to reconstructing images corrupted by Poisson noise," Journal of Mathematical Imaging and Vision, vol. 27, no. 3, pp. 257–263, 2007.
4. R. Chartrand and V. Staneva, "Total variation regularisation of images corrupted by non-Gaussian noise using a quasi-Newton method," IET Image Processing, vol. 2, no. 6, pp. 295–303, 2008.
5. J. Cullum, "Numerical differentiation and regularization," SIAM Journal on Numerical Analysis, vol. 8, pp. 254–265, 1971.

6. I. J. Schoenberg, "Spline functions and the problem of graduation," Proceedings of the National Academy of Sciences of the United States of America, vol. 52, pp. 947–950, 1964.·
7. C. H. Reinsch, "Smoothing by spline functions. I, II," Numerische Mathematik, vol. 10, pp. 177–183, 1967.
8. M. Hanke and O. Scherzer, "Inverse problems light: numerical differentiation," The American Mathematical Monthly, vol. 108, no. 6, pp. 512–521, 2001. ·
9. I. Knowles and R. Wallace, "A variational method for numerical differentiation," Numerische Mathematik, vol. 70, no. 1, pp. 91–110, 1995.
10. L. Ambrosio, N. Fusco, and D. Pallara, Functions of Bounded Variation and Free Discontinuity Problems, Oxford Mathematical Monographs, The Clarendon Press Oxford University Press, New York, NY, USA, 2000.
11. L. I. Rudin, S. Osher, and E. Fatemi, "Nonlinear total variation based noise removal algorithms,"Physica D, vol. 60, no. 1–4, pp. 259–268, 1992.
12. T. J. Asaki, R. Chartrand, K. R. Vixie, and B. Wohlberg, "Abel inversion using total-variation regularization," Inverse Problems, vol. 21, no. 6, pp. 1895–1903, 2005.
13. T. J. Asaki, P. R. Campbell, R. Chartrand, C. E. Powell, K. R. Vixie, and B. E. Wohlberg, "Abel inversion using total variation regularization: applications," Inverse Problems in Science and Engineering, vol. 14, no. 8, pp. 873–885, 2006.
14. C. R. Vogel and M. E. Oman, "Iterative methods for total variation denoising," SIAM Journal on Scientific Computing, vol. 17, no. 1, pp. 227–238, 1996. ·
15. D. C. Dobson and C. R. Vogel, "Convergence of an iterative method for total variation denoising,"SIAM Journal on Numerical Analysis, vol. 34, no. 5, pp. 1779–1791, 1997.
16. C. R. Vogel, Computational Methods for Inverse Problems, vol. 23 of Frontiers in Applied Mathematics, Society for Industrial and Applied Mathematics (SIAM), Philadelphia, Pa, USA, 2002.
17. E. L. Melanson, J. P. Ingebrigtsen, A. Bergouignan, K. Ohkawara, W. M. Kohrt, and J. R. B. Lighton, "A new approach for flow-through respirometry measurements in humans," American Journal of Physiology, vol. 298, no. 6, pp. R1571–R1579, 2010.

CHAPTER 9

COMPUTATIONAL CHALLENGE OF FRACTIONAL DIFFERENTIAL EQUATIONS AND THE POTENTIAL SOLUTIONS: A SURVEY

Chunye Gong,[1,2,3] Weimin Bao,[1,2] Guojian Tang,[1] Yuewen Jiang[4], and Jie Liu[3]

[1]College of Aerospace Science and Engineering, National University of Defense Technology, Changsha 410073, China

[2]Science and Technology on Space Physics Laboratory, Beijing 100076, China

[3]School of Computer Science, National University of Defense Technology, Changsha 410073, China

[4]Department of Engineering Science, University of Oxford, Oxford OX2 0ES, UK

ABSTRACT

We present a survey of fractional differential equations and in particular of the computational cost for their numerical solutions from the view of computer science. The computational complexities of time fractional, space fractional, and space-time fractional equations are $O(N^2M)$, $O(NM^2)$, and $O(NM(M + N))$ compared with $O(MN)$ for the classical partial differential equations with finite difference methods, where M, N are the number of space grid points and time steps. The potential solutions for this challenge include, but are not limited to, parallel computing, memory access optimization (fractional precomputing operator), short memory principle, fast Fourier transform (FFT) based solutions, alternating direction implicit method, multigrid method, and preconditioner technology. The relationships of these solutions for both space fractional derivative and time fractional derivative are discussed. The authors pointed out that the technologies of parallel computing should be regarded as a basic method to overcome this challenge, and some attention should be paid to the fractional killer applications, high performance iteration methods, high order schemes, and Monte Carlo methods. Since the computation of fractional equations with high dimension and variable order is even heavier, the researchers from the area of mathematics and computer science have opportunity to invent cornerstones in the area of fractional calculus.

INTRODUCTION

The idea of fractional is natural. If $\partial u/\partial x$ and $\partial^2 u/\partial x^2$ exist, $\partial^{1.5}u/\partial x^{1.5}$ maybe exists too. Fractional equations can be used to describe some physical phenomena more accurately than the classical integer order differential equation [1]. Fractional differential equations (FDEs) provide a powerful instrument for the description of memory and hereditary properties of different substances. The fractional diffusion equations play an important role in dynamical systems of semiconductor research, hydrogeology, bioinformatics, finance [2], and other research areas [3–6]. Rajeev and Kushwaha [7] presented a mathematical model describing the time fractional anomalous diffusion process of a generalized Stefan problem which is a limiting case of a shoreline problem. Space fractional advection-diffusion equations arise when velocity variations are heavy tailed and describe particle motion that account for variation in the flow field over the entire system [8]. FDEs may be divided into two fundamental types: time fractional differential equations and space fractional differential equations. For the fractional ordinary equations and fractional order control systems are also studied [9, 10]. The stability of

Citation: Chunye Gong, Weimin Bao, Guojian Tang, Yuewen Jiang, and Jie Liu, "Computational Challenge of Fractional Differential Equations and the Potential Solutions: A Survey," Mathematical Problems in Engineering, vol. 2015, Article ID 258265, 13 pages, 2015. doi:10.1155/2015/258265

fractional order control systems attracts many attentions [11, 12]. For example, Laguerre continued fraction expansion of the Tustin fractional discrete-time operator was investigated by Maione [13].

Some analytical methods were proposed for fractional differential equation [14, 15]. Saha Ray [16] presented the analytical solutions of the space fractional diffusion equations by two-step Adomian decomposition method. Momani and Odibat [17] gave a comparison between the homotopy perturbation method and the variational iteration method for linear fractional partial differential equations. By using initial conditions, the explicit solutions of the equations have been presented in the closed form and then their solutions have been represented graphically. Because most of fractional problems cannot be solved analytically, more and more works focus on their numerical solutions. There are many numerical solutions proposed for fractional equations [18], such as finite difference method (FDM) [18]. FDM is intuitive to understand and easy to learn for inexperienced researcher from the areas rather than mathematics. So this survey focuses on FDM for fractional equations.

For the numerical solutions of different differential equations, the area of mathematics pays much attention to approximating the equation more accurately and faster (accuracy and speed). The area of computer science mainly focuses on the runtime (speed) and code reuse (software). The numerical methods (mathematic area) have eternal value and may exist along with the existence of human culture [19–21]. The implementations (computer area) are closer to the human society and the real applications but vary quickly along with the computer architecture [22–28]. The computational cost of the numerical solutions for fractional equations is much heavier than that for the traditional integer order equations. In the near future, the fractional problems with high dimension, long time iterations, and huge grid points will need to be solved. These problems are real challenge for today's computer technologies and algorithms.

FRACTIONAL DIFFERENTIAL EQUATIONS

Origins

In 1695, L'Hopital wrote to Leibniz asking him about a particular notation he had used in his publications for the nth-derivative of the linear function $(x) = x$, $D^n x/Dx^n$ [29, 30]. L'Hopital's posed the question to Leibniz: what would the result be if $n = 1/2$? Leibniz's response was "An apparent paradox, from which one day useful consequences will be drawn." In these words fractional calculus was born [31]. Later, Fourier, Euler, and Laplace dabbled with fractional calculus [32]

A Short Summary of FDE

There are mainly three kinds of FDEs:

1. time fractional [33, 34],
2. space fractional [35],
3. space-time fractional [36]

One of the main challenges in fractional differential equation is the nonlocality of the fractional operator. In the case of a time fractional derivative, one needs to store all the history, whereas in the case of a space fractional derivative, one needs to deal with almost-dense matrices.

The partial differential equations (PDEs) mainly have three categories: parabolic, hyperbolic, and elliptic. There are corresponding FDEs to deal with the fractional conditions. There are various FDEs listed below:

- the parabolic, widely studied fractional diffusion equation [37, 38],
- the hyperbolic Telegraph equation [39],
- the elliptic fractional Laplace equation [40],
- fractional Black-Scholes equation in computational finance [41],
- fractional wave equation for sound, light, and water waves [42],
- fractional Fokker-Planck equations describing the time evolution of the probability density function of the velocity of a particle [43],
- fractional Euler equations and fractional Navier-Stokes equations [44] for fluid dynamics [45],
- fractional kinetic equations for motion of objects [46],
- the perfect, fractional Maxwell's equations for electrodynamics [47],
- fractional Boltzmann equations for particle transport [48].

We can suppose that if there is a PDE, there will be a FDE. The reason is that replacing the integer derivative with fractional derivative and solving the FDE with different numerical methods is not a hard job.

The numerical schemes [49] for these FDEs are listed below:

- finite difference method (FDM) [18, 50, 51],
- finite element method [52–54],
- finite volume method [55–57],
- Adomian decomposition method [58],
- Fourier transform method [59],
- spectral method [60],
- meshless method [61–63],
- exponential difference method [64, 65],
- Monte Carlo method [66].

The Monte Carlo (MC) method, which uses repeated random sampling to obtain numerical results, belongs to undetermined computational methods.

A Hot Topic in Recent Years

Machado et al. [29] collected 20 special issues on fractional calculus. In 2011 and 2012, there are about 7 special issues on this topic. There are more special issues in the nearby four years (2011–2014) than those of 1999 to 2010 [29]. And there are additional 20 special issues in the years of 2013 and 2014. So the researches on fractional calculus can be regarded as a collective revelry.

COMPUTATIONAL CHALLENGE

A Classical Partial Differential Equation (PDE)

Heat Equation/Diffusion Equation

The heat equation is a parabolic PDE which describes the distribution of heat (or variation in temperature) in a given region over time, shown in (1). This equation is also known as the diffusion equation:

$$\frac{\partial u(x,t)}{\partial t} = d(x)\frac{\partial^2 u(x,t)}{\partial x^2} + f(x,t),$$
$$u(x,0) = \phi(x), \quad x \in [x_L, x_R],$$
$$u(x_L,t) = \varphi(t), \quad t \in [0,T],$$
$$u(x_R,t) = \psi(t), \quad t \in [0,T], \tag{1}$$

where the $d(x)$ is the diffusion constant.

Numerical Method

Define $t_n = n\tau, x_i = ih$ for $0 \le n \le N, 0 \le i \le M$, where M and N are positive integer and $\tau = T/N$, $h = (x_R - x_L)/M$ are time step size and space step size, respectively. Define u_i^n, f_i^n, d_i as the numerical approximation to $u(x_i, t_n)$, $f(x_i, t_n)$, and $d(x_i)$. Using a forward difference at time tn and a second-order central difference for the space derivative at position x_i, we get the explicit finite difference approximation for the one-dimensional heat equation:

$$\frac{u_i^{n+1} - u_i^n}{\tau} = d_i\frac{u_{i+1}^n - 2u_i^n + u_{i-1}^n}{h^2} + f_i^n. \tag{2}$$

The u_i^{n+1} can be obtained by this way

$$u_i^{n+1} = a_1 u_{i+1}^n + a_2 u_i^n + a_3 u_{i-1}^n + \tau f_i^n, \tag{3}$$

where $a_1 = a_3 = -d_i\tau/h^2$ and $a_2 = 1 - 2d_i\tau/h^2$.

If we use the backward difference at time t_{n+1} and a second-order central difference for the space derivative at position x_i we get the explicit finite difference approximation for (1):

$$\frac{u_i^{n+1} - u_i^n}{\tau} = d_i\frac{u_{i+1}^{n+1} - 2u_i^{n+1} + u_{i-1}^{n+1}}{h^2} + f_i^{n+1}. \tag{4}$$

The u_i^{n+1} can be obtained by this way:

$$a_1 u_{i+1}^{n+1} + a_2 u_i^{n+1} + a_3 u_{i-1}^{n+1} = u_i^n + \tau f_i^n, \tag{5}$$

where $a_1 = a_3 = -d_i\tau/h^2$ and $a_2 = 1 - 2d_i\tau/h^2$.

The classical PDE is used to compare the fractional equations. For convenience, there are several hypotheses for this paper.

- We just focus on the explicit FDM of (3), because these kinds of comparisons between fractional equations and classical equations are straightforward. The comparison between implicit FDE of (5) and implicit schemes of fractional equations is more complex [67].
- The computational cost of diffusion coefficient di and source f_i^n (or f_i^{n+1}) is ignored, because they only need compute once. And they are different with different equations and make the comparison complicated.

Computational Cost

Each grid point of time step $tn+1$ needs 4 multiplications and 3 additions. There are $M-1$ grid points in each time step. So each time step needs $7(M-1)$ arithmetic logic operations. There are about N time steps. So the total computational cost is about $7(M-1)$. The computational cost will vary linearly along the number of time steps and grid points.

Time Fractional Diffusion Equation

Numerical Method

Liu et al. [63] developed an implicit radial basis function (RBF) meshless approach for time fractional diffusion equations and found that the presented meshless formulation is very effective for modeling and simulation of fractional differential equations. Murillo and Yuste developed an explicit difference method for solving fractional diffusion with Caputo form [68]:

$$\frac{\partial^\alpha u(x,t)}{\partial^\alpha t} = \frac{\partial^2 u(x,t)}{\partial x^2} \quad (0 < \alpha < 1),$$
$$u(x,0) = g(x), \quad x \in (0, x_R),$$
$$u(0,t) = u(x_R,t) = 0 \tag{6}$$

on a finite domain $0<x<x_R$ and $0 \le t \le T$.

The explicit finite difference approximation for (6) is described as follows [69]:

$$\tau^{-\alpha}\sum_{i=0}^{n+1} w_i\left(u_j^{n+1-i} - u_j^0\right) = \frac{1}{h^2}\left(u_{j+1}^n - 2u_j^n + u_{j-1}^n\right), \tag{7}$$

where w_i is the normalized Grunwald weight defined with

$$w_i = (-1)^i\binom{\alpha}{i}. \tag{8}$$

Define $\mu = \tau^\alpha/h^2$, $b_n = \sum_{i=0}^{n-1} w_i$, and $U^n = (u_1^n, u_2^n, \ldots, u_{M-1}^n)^T$; we can get

$$U^{n+1} = b_{n+1}U^0 - \sum_{i=1}^{n+1} w_i U^{n+1-i} + \mu A U^n, \tag{9}$$

where matrix A is a tridiagonal matrix, defined by

$$A_{M-1\times M-1} = \begin{pmatrix} -2 & 1 & & & \\ 1 & -2 & 1 & & \\ & \bullet & \bullet & & \\ & & \bullet & \bullet & 1 \\ & & & 1 & -2 \end{pmatrix}. \tag{10}$$

Computational Cost

In order to get U^{n+1}, the rightsided computation of (9) should be performed. There are mainly one tridiagonal matrix-vector multiplication, many constant-vector multiplications, and many vector-vector additions in the right-sided computation.

(1) The tridiagonal matrix-vector multiplication is AU^n and a new vector $U^{n+1} = AU^n$ is got.

(2) The constant-vector multiplications are $V' = b_{n+1}U^0$, $V'' = \mu V^1, V^i = w_i U^{n+1-i}$.

(3) The vector-vector additions are $U^{n+1} = U^{n+1} + V' + V'' - \sum_{i=1}^{n+1} V^i$.

There are about 5(*M* − 1) operations for tridiagonal matrix-vector multiplication. For time step t_{n+1} needs $(n + 8)(M - 1)$ arithmetic logic operations with $n=1 \rightarrow N$. So the total computational cost for (9) is about

$$8N(M-1) + (1+2+\cdots+N-1)(M-1)$$
$$= 8N(M-1) + \frac{N(N-1)(M-1)}{2}$$
$$= N\left(\frac{N}{2} + 7.5\right)(M-1). \quad (11)$$

The computational cost varies linearly along the number of grid points but squares with the number of time steps.

Space Fractional Diffusion Equation

Numerical Method

A classical numerical scheme for the space fractional diffusion equation is the second-order fractional Crank-Nicolson method proposed by Tadjeran et al. [38, 70], where the Richardson extrapolation technique is used to the first order shift Grünwald formula for space fractional derivative. Tadjeran et al. [70] presented a practical numerical method in time and space to solve a class of initial-boundary value with variable coefficients on a finite domain for

$$\frac{\partial u(x,t)}{\partial t} = d(x)\frac{\partial^\alpha u(x,t)}{\partial x^\alpha} + q(x,t) \quad (12)$$

on a finite domain $xL < x < x_R$ with $1<\alpha<2$ and $0\le t\le T$.

The case of $1<\alpha<2$ models a super-diffusive flow in which a cloud of diffusing particles spreads at a faster rate than the classical diffusion model predictions [71, 72].

The explicit finite difference approximation for (12) is

$$\frac{u_i^{n+1} - u_i^n}{\tau} = \frac{d_i}{h^\alpha}\left(\sum_{k=0}^{i+1} g_{\alpha,k} u_{i-k+1}^n\right) + q_i^n, \quad (13)$$

where $u_i^n = u(x_i, t_n), d_i = d(x_i)$, and $q_i^n = q(x_i, t_n)$. The $g_{\alpha,}$ is the normalized Grunwald weight [¨ 70, 73]:

$$g_{\alpha,k} = \frac{\Gamma(k-\alpha)}{\Gamma(-\alpha)\Gamma(k+1)}. \quad (14)$$

These normalized weights only depend on the order α and the index k. The resulting equation can be explicitly solved for u_i^{n+1} to give

$$u_i^{n+1} = u_i^n + \frac{d_i\tau}{h^\alpha}\left(\sum_{k=0}^{i+1} g_{\alpha,k} u_{i-k+1}^n\right) + \tau q_i^n. \quad (15)$$

Computational Cost

The ith grid point of time step t_{n+1} needs $i+6$ multiplication, addition, and division. There are $M-1$ grid points in each time step. So each time step needs $(M-1)6 + (1+2+\cdots+M-1) = (M-1)((M/2)+6)$ arithmetic logic operations. There are about N time steps. So the total computational cost is about $(M-1)((M/2)+6)$.

Riesz Space Fractional Diffusion Equation

Numerical Method

Shen et al. [74] investigated the Green function and a discrete random walk model for Riesz fractional advection-dispersion equation on infinite domain with an initial condition and also presented implicit and explicit finite differences to this problem on a finite domain. Çelik and Duman [75] applied the Crank-Nicolson method to a fractional diffusion equation which has the Riesz fractional derivative and obtained that the method is unconditionally stable and convergent. The Riesz space fractional reaction-diffusion equation [76, 77] is

$$\frac{\partial u(x,t)}{\partial t} = -u(x,t) + {}_xD_0^\alpha u(x,t) + q(x,t),$$
$$u(x,0) = g(x), \quad x \in (x_L, x_R),$$
$$u(x_L,t) = u(x_R,t) = 0 \quad (16)$$

with $1 < \alpha \le 2$ and $0 \le t \le T$. Both (x, t) and $g(x)$ are real valued and sufficiently well-behaved function. ${}_xD_0^\alpha u(x,t)$ is the Riesz space fractional derivative.

With adopting an Euler approximation in time, the explicit difference approximation can be got:

$$\frac{u_i^{n+1} - u_i^n}{\tau} = -u_i^n - \frac{1}{ch^\alpha} \times \left[\sum_{k=0}^{i+1} g_k u_{i+1-k}^n + \sum_{k=0}^{M-i+1} g_k u_{i-1+k}^n\right] + f_i^n, \quad (17)$$

where $g_0 = 1$, $g_k = (-1)^k \alpha(\alpha-1)\cdots(\alpha-k+1)/k!$, $k = 1, 2, 3, \ldots$ is the normalized Grunwald weight, ¨ $c = 1/2\cos(\alpha\pi/2)$, and $f_i^n = q(x_i, t_n)$.

Equation (17) results in a linear system of equations

$$U^{n+1} = AU^n + Q^n, \quad (18)$$

where $U^n = (u_1^n, u_2^n, \ldots, u_{M-1}^n)^T$, $Q^n = (\tau f_1^n, \tau f_2^n, \ldots, \tau f_{M-1}^n)^T$ with $q_i^n = \tau f_i^n$ $(1 \le i < M-1)$, and $A = (a_{ij})_{(M-1)\times(M-1)}$ is a matrix of coefficient. A is defined by

$$a_{i,j} = \begin{cases} -\frac{\tau}{ch^\alpha} g_{i+1-j}, & \text{for } 1 \le j < i-1, \\ -\frac{\tau}{ch^\alpha}(g_0 + g_2), & \text{for } j = i-1, \\ (1-\tau) - 2\frac{\tau}{ch^\alpha} g_1, & \text{for } j = i, \\ -\frac{\tau}{ch^\alpha}(g_0 + g_2), & \text{for } j = i+1, \\ -\frac{\tau}{ch^\alpha} g_{j-i+1}, & \text{for } i+1 < j < M-1. \end{cases} \quad (19)$$

Computational Cost

From (18), the $M-1$ results are produced by *AUn* for each time step. The inner product of vectors V^1 and V^2 with size m has m multiplications and $m-1$ additions. *AUn* for each time step needs $(M-1)(2M-3)$ operations. Assuming τf_i^n is pre-performed, each time step needs $(M-1)(2M-2)$ arithmetic logic operations. There are about N time steps. So the total computational cost is about $(M-1)(2M-2)$. The computational cost will vary linearly along the number of time steps but square with the number of grid points. From analytical view, the computation of (18) is about four times heavier than that of (15).

Space-Time Riesz-Caputo Fractional Convection-Diffusion Equation

Diffusion Equation. The fractional advection-diffusion (dispersion) equation has been applied to many problems. Fractional advection-dispersion equations are used in groundwater hydrology to model the transport of passive tracers carried out by fluid flow in a porous medium [78]. Shen et al. [79] presented an explicit difference approximation and an implicit difference approximation for the space-time Riesz-Caputo fractional advection-diffusion equation with initial and boundary conditions in a finite domain. They proved that the implicit difference approximation is unconditionally stable and convergent, but the explicit difference approximation is conditionally stable and convergent. Liu et al. [80] proposed an implicit difference method and an explicit difference method to solve the space-time fractional advection-diffusion equation and discussed the stability and convergence of the method.

Numerical Method

We consider the following spacetime Riesz-Caputo fractional advection-diffusion equation (STRCFADE) studied by Shen et al. [79]. This equation is obtained by replacing the space-derivative in the advectiondiffusion equation with a generalized derivative of order β_1, β_2 with $0<\beta_1<1$, $1<\beta_2<2$ and time-derivative with a generalized derivative of order α with $0<\alpha<1$. We consider

$$\begin{aligned} {}_0D_t^{\alpha}u(x,t) &= B_1\frac{\partial^{\beta_1}u(x,t)}{\partial|x|^{\beta_1}} + B_2\frac{\partial^{\beta_2}u(x,t)}{\partial|x|^{\beta_2}} + f(x,t), \\ u(x,0) &= \phi(x), \quad x\in[0,x_R], \\ u(0,t) &= u(x_R,t) = 0, \quad t\in[0,T] \end{aligned} \tag{20}$$

on a finite domain $0\leq x\leq xR$ and $0\leq t\leq T$. The coefficients B_1 and B_2 are both positive constants and represent the diffusion (dispersion) coefficient and the average fluid velocity. The $\partial^{\beta_1}u(x,t)/\partial|x|^{\beta_1}$ and $\partial^{\beta_2}u(x,t)/\partial|x|^{\beta_2}$ are Riesz space fractional derivatives of order β_1 and β_2, respectively. Then we can get the explicit finite differential approximation for (20) [79]:

$$\begin{aligned} u_i^{n+1} &= \sum_{j=0}^{n-1}\left(b_j-b_{j+1}\right)u_i^{n-j} + b_nu_i^0 + B_1\mu_1\left(\sum_{k=-i}^{N-i}\omega_k^{\beta_1}u_{i+k}^n\right) \\ &+ B_2\mu_2\left(\sum_{k=-i}^{N-i}\omega_k^{\beta_2}u_{i+k}^n\right) + \mu_0\varphi_i^n, \quad i=1,\ldots,N-1, \\ u_0^{n+1} &= u_N^{n+1} = 0, \\ u_i^0 &= \phi_i, \end{aligned} \tag{21}$$

where $\mu_0 = \tau^{\alpha}\Gamma(2-\alpha)$, $\mu_1 = \mu_0/h^{\beta_1}$, and $\mu_2 = \mu_0/h^{\beta_2}$. More information can be referred to in [79].

Computational Cost

From Section 3.4.2, we know that the computational cost of $B_1\mu_1(\sum_{k=-i}^{N-i}\omega_k^{\beta_1}u_{i+k}^n) + B_2\mu_2(\sum_{k=-i}^{N-i}\omega_k^{\beta_2}u_{i+k}^n) + \mu_0\varphi_i^n$ of N time steps is about $(M-1)(2M-2)$ operations. From Section 3.2.2, we know that the computational cost of $\sum_{j=0}^{n-1}(b_j-b_{j+1})u_i^{n-j} + b_nu_i^0$ of N time steps with n ranging from 1 to N is about $(N/2)(M-1)$. So the total computational cost is about $(M-1)(2M-2+(N/2))$. The computational cost varies quadratically with the number of time steps or the number of grid points.

For fixed $M = 4097$, the comparison between the computational costs of the numerical solution among classical PDE, time fractional, space fractional, Riesz space fractional, and space-time Riesz-Caputo fractional equations is shown in Figure 1. For fixed $N = 2048$, the computational cost is shown in Figure 2.

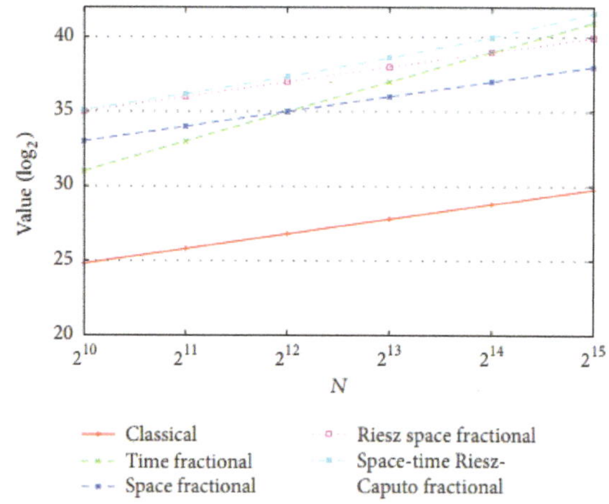

Figure 1: Comparison of the computational cost with different grid points for fixed $M = 4097$ among classical, time fractional, space fractional, Riesz space fractional, and space-time Riesz-Caputo fractional equations.

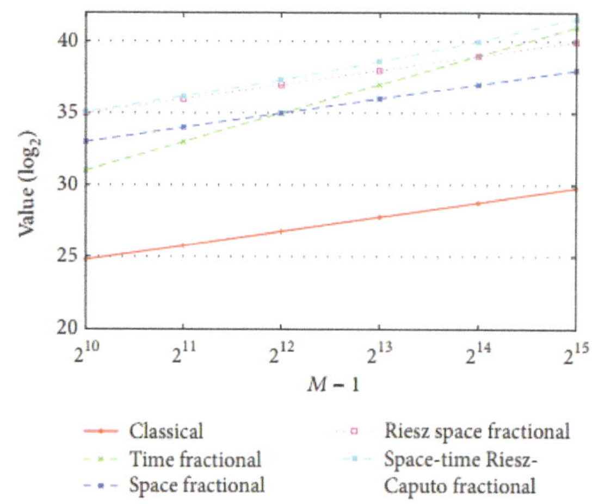

Figure 2: Comparison of the computational cost with different time step for fixed $N = 2048$ among classical, time fractional, space fractional, Riesz space fractional, and space-time Riesz-Caputo fractional equations.

More Challenges

There are more computational challenges listed below:

- high dimensional problems [55, 81],
- implicit schemes [67, 82],
- high order schemes [33, 83],

- variable order problems [84],
- huge memory space requirement.

The high dimensional problems are more computation expensive [55, 81, 85, 86]. For example, the two-dimensional time fractional diffusion equation (2D-TFDE) [67, 87] is

$$
\begin{aligned}
{}_0D_t^{\alpha} u(x,y,t) &= a(x,y,t)\frac{\partial^2 u(x,y,t)}{\partial x^2} \\
&\quad + a(x,y,t)\frac{\partial^2 u(x,y,t)}{\partial y^2} + f(x,y,t), \\
u(x,y,0) &= \phi(x,y), \quad (x,y)\in\Omega, \\
u(x,y,t)|_{\partial\Omega} &= 0, \quad t\in[0,T],
\end{aligned}
\tag{22}
$$

where $\Omega = \{(x, y) \mid 0 \le x \le L_1, 0 \le y \le L_2, a(x, y, t) > 0$, and $b(x, y, t) > 0\}$.

The approximating scheme is [87]

$$
\begin{aligned}
& u_{i,j}^{n+1} - u_{i,j}^{n} + \sum_{s=1}^{n} (b_s)\left(u_{i,j}^{n+1-s} - u_{i,j}^{n-s}\right) \\
&= \mu_1\Gamma(2-\alpha)\, a_{i,j}^{n}\left(u_{i+1,j}^{n} - 2u_{i,j}^{n} + u_{i-1,j}^{n}\right) \\
&\quad + \mu_2\Gamma(2-\alpha)\, b_{i,j}^{n}\left(u_{i,j+1}^{n} - 2u_{i,j}^{n} + u_{i,j-1}^{n}\right) \\
&\quad + \tau^{\alpha}\Gamma(2-\alpha)\, f_{i,j}^{n},
\end{aligned}
\tag{23}
$$

where $\mu_1 = \tau^{\alpha}/h_x^2$ and $\mu_2 = \tau^{\alpha}/h_y^2$. The h_x and h_y are the step size along X and Y directions. The computational complexity is about $(N^2 M^2)$, which is much bigger than the computational complexity of one-dimensional problems when the number of grid points is bigger enough.

The direct Gauss elimination for implicit scheme of FDE is not convenient. Solving unsteady FDE with implicit schemes relies on the iteration method at each time step. The variable order problems [84, 88] have complex coefficients, which need more arithmetic logic operations. The high order schemes [33, 38, 70] need more arithmetic logic operations too.

The memory usage belongs to the computing resources. So the huge memory requirement of FDE is a kind of computational challenge in the broader sense. This is especially true for time fractional problems. Ignoring the memory usage of the coefficients and source terms, the one-dimensional equation (9) needs $8(M-1)$ bytes of memory space and the twodimensional equation (23) needs $8M^2 N$ bytes of memory space. For three-dimensional problems, the memory usage is $8M^3 N$ at least. It needs 15.625 PB (1 PB = 1024^5 bytes) memory space with $M = 10240$, $N = 2048$ for three-dimensional problems. Maybe only the most powerful supercomputer [89] can satisfy the huge memory requirement.

POTENTIAL SOLUTIONS

There are several ways which can be used to overcome the computational challenge of FDEs.

Parallel Computing

Large scale applications and algorithms in science and engineering such as neutron transport [90–92], light transport [93], computational fluid dynamics [94, 95], molecular dynamics [96], and computational finance and different numerical methods [97] rely on parallel computing [98, 99].

Gong et al. [77] present a parallel algorithm for Riesz space fractional diffusion equation based on MPI parallel programming model at the first time. The parallel algorithm is as accurate as the serial algorithm and achieves 79.39% parallel efficiency compared with 8 processes on a distributed memory cluster system. The parallel implicit iterative algorithm was studied for two-dimensional time fractional problem and a task distribution model is shown in Figure 3 [67]. M_x, M_y, P_x, P_y stand for the discrete grid points, parallel processes along X, Y directions.

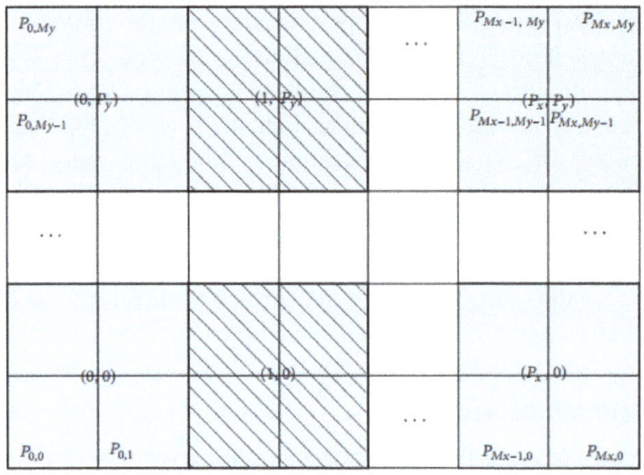

Figure 3: The two-dimensional task distribution model for 2D-TFDE.

Domain decomposition method is regarded as the basic mathematical background for many parallel applications [100–102]. A domain decomposition algorithm for time fractional reaction-diffusion equation with implicit finite difference method was proposed [103]. The domain decomposition algorithm keeps the same parallelism as Jacobi iteration but needs much fewer iterations.

Diethelm [104] implemented the fractional version of the second-order Adams-Bashforth-Moulton method on a parallel computer and discussed the precise nature of the parallelization concept. Parallel computing has already appeared in some studies on FDEs, but until today their power for approximating fractional derivatives and solving FDEs has not been fully recognized.

Memory Access Optimization (Fractional Precomputing Operator)

Memory access optimization is generally regarded as a technology of computer architecture. It is also useful from the view of applications. One feature of the modern computer architecture is multilayer memory. For example, the traditional CPU has fast cache and slow main memory. The new graphics processing unit (GPU) has fast shared memory and slow memory. Reusing the data in shared memory is a key point to improve the performance of GPU applications [105–109]. A very useful optimization is presented for fractional derivative [69, 110]. We can name this fractional precomputing operator, which will be a very basic and useful optimizing technology for the implementation of fractional algorithms and applications. The example of fractional precomputing operator can refer to Algorithms 4 and 5 in reference [69].

On CPU platform, an optimization of the sum of constant vector multiplication is presented and 2-time speedup can be got for both serial and parallel algorithm for the time fractional equation [69]. The key technology is reusing the data in cache through loop unrolling. Zhang et al. [110] presented code optimization for fractional Adams-Bashforth-Moulton method by loop fusion and loop unrolling.

On GPU platform, Liu et al. [111] presented an optimized CUDA kernel for the numerical solution of time fractional equation and 1.2–2.7-time performance improvement is achieved.

Short Memory Principle

The short memory principle [3] means the unknown grid points only rely on the recent past (in time) or near neighbors (in space). This principle has been proved to be an easy and powerful way for various kinds of fractional differential equations [112, 113]. The short memory principle is also called fixed memory principle or logarithmic memory principle. The idea of short memory principle is simple. Taking time fractional equation as an example in Section 3.2.1, the value of w_i becomes smaller while i is increasing. In (9), the accumulation of $\sum_{i=1}^{n+1} w_i U^{n+1-i}$ is replaced with $\sum_{i=\min\{1,n+1-K\}}^{n+1} w_i U^{n+1-i}$. K is a positive integer, which means if n is very big, the computation of the accumulation is fixed.

Based on short memory principle, some principles with better balance of computation speed and computation accuracy are presented. The logarithmic memory principle is developed with a good approximation to the true solution at reasonable computational cost [114]. Another principle is equal-weight memory principle, in which an equal-weight is applied to all past data in history, and the result is reserved instead of being discarded [115]. The equal-weight memory principle is an interesting and useful approximation method to fractional derivative.

FFT Based Solution

Because of the nonlocal property of fractional differential operators, the numerical methods have full coefficient matrices which require computational cost of (M^3) for implicit scheme per time step, where M is the number of grid points. Ford and Simpson [114] developed a faster scheme for the calculation of fractional integrals. A reduction in the amount of computational work can be achieved by using a graded mesh, thereby making the (N^2) method to a $O(N \log N)$ method. The underlying idea is based on the fact that the fractional integral possesses a fundamental scaling property that can be exploited in a natural way [114].

Wang et al. [116, 117] developed a fast finite difference method for fractional diffusion equations, which only requires computational cost of ($N\log_2 N$) while retaining the same accuracy and approximation property as the regular finite difference method. Numerical experiments show that the fast method has a significant reduction of CPU time [86]. The fast method should have a banded coefficient matrix instead of the full matrix. The properties of Toeplitz and circulant matrices, fast Fourier transform (FFT), and inverse FFT are used to reduce the computational cost. The method is also called superfast-preconditioned iterative method for steady-state space fractional diffusion equations [118].

An efficient iteration method for Toeplitz-plus-band triangular systems, which may produced by fractional ordinary differential equations, was developed. Some methods such as matrix splitting, FFT, compress memory storage, and adjustable matrix bandwidth are used in the presented solution. The interesting technologies are the adjustable matrix bandwidth and solving fractional ordinary differential equations with iteration method. The experimental results show that the presented efficient iteration method is 4.25 times faster than the regular solution [10].

Alternating Direction Implicit Method

The alternating direction implicit (ADI) method is a finite difference method for solving traditional PDEs. The approximation methods for fractional equations result in a very complicated set of equations in multiple dimensions, which are hard to solve [67, 81, 85]. So the ADI method is developed for high dimensional problems [33, 117]. The advantage of the fractional ADI method is that the equations that have to be solved in each step have a simpler structure. The time fractional problems can be solved efficiently with the tridiagonal matrix algorithm [33]. The space fractional problems can use the FFT to accelerate the computation [117].

Multigrid Method

The multigrid method is usually exploited for solving ill-conditioned systems. The main idea of multigrid is to accelerate the convergence of a basic iterative method by global correction form, accomplished by solving a coarse problem. Pang and Sun [119] proposed a multigrid method to solve the initial-boundary value problem of a fractional diffusion equation. The experimental results show that the multigrid + FFT method runs hundred times faster than Gaussian elimination method and the conjugate gradient normal residual (CGNR) method. A full V-cycle multigrid method is proposed for the stationary fractional advection dispersion equation [120] and ten-time performance improvement is achieved.

Preconditioning Technology

Preconditioning is typically related to reducing a condition number of the problem with iterative methods. It shows that both the average number of iterations and the CPU time by the PCGNR (preconditioner CGNR) method with circulant preconditioners are much less than those by the CGNR method and less than that by the multigrid method [121]. The circulant preconditioner [121], banded preconditioner [122], fast Poisson preconditioners [123], and preconditioned conjugate gradient squared method plus FFT [118] are developed for different FDEs.

Relationships among These Potential Solutions

The potential solutions for the computational challenge of FDE are investigated above. Many people will be curious about these relationships: can we combine these methods to develop a fastest solution for FDEs? The answer is still unknown. The performance of these solutions varies from different FDE applications. Their relationships are shown in Table 1. The PC, MAO, SMP, FFT, ADI, MGM, and PT stand for parallel computing, memory access optimization, short memory principle, FFT based solution, alternating direction implicit method, multigrid method, and preconditioning technology. The score means the degrees of the two solutions are harmonious. Higher score means using two solutions can achieve better performance.

Table 1: Relationships among the potential solutions for space fractional derivative

	PC	MAO	SMP	FFT	ADI	MGM	FT
PC	—	3	3	2[a]	3	2[a]	2[a]
MAO		—	3	1[b]	3	3	3
SMP			—	1[c]	3	3	3
FFT				—	3	3	3
ADI					—	3	3
MGM						—	2[d]
PT							—

[a] The parallel efficiency of FFT, multigrid, preconditioner is limiting.
[b] It is hard to use MAO within FFT.
[c] Because of the Toeplitz structure, FFT cannot use short memory principle.
[d] The philosophy of multigrid and preconditioning technology are different. But there are some multigrid preconditioners.

For time fractional derivative [124], only memory access optimization [69, 111] and short memory principle [3] are useful. Here, the time fractional derivative is different from time fractional problems. For example, the one- and two-dimensional FDEs are parallelized by Gong et al. [67, 69]. These parallel algorithms are based on the partition of space not time.

FUTURE DIRECTIONS

Fractional Killer Applications

Killer application is a kind of application that is so necessary or desirable that it proves the core value of some larger technology. A killer application is something like Project Apollo in space technology, the IBM 360 in personal computer industry, and the IPhone in the smart phone industry. The fractional research still lacks these kinds of killer applications. It needs fractional applications to solve scientific or engineering problems in physical world, such as the fractional flow/control of hypersonic vehicle, not only the academical problems. The fractional killer application should be proved that it is more useful than the traditional classical application. Solving real problems in physical world will build an economic foundation for fractional researches.

Parallel Computing

The technologies of parallel computing should be regarded as a basic method to overcome the computational challenge for FDEs. There are three potential solutions for the computational challenge of FDEs. The short memory principle is an experimental method, which is useful in real fractional applications. The (N log N) methods [117] used the property of Toeplitz matrices and FFT technology. Parallel computing is a foundational technology for scientific and engineering computation. Fortunately, the short memory principle and (N log N) methods are compatible with parallel computing. So it is interesting to develop algorithms which is faster than (N log N) methods.The numerical methods of space fractional equations with global dependence are much harder to be parallelized than that of the time fractional equations. So the task distribution model, load balance of the parallel algorithm for space fractional equations should be paid attention to.

High Performance Iteration Methods

Different kind of numerical methods is very easily found for FDEs. The direct methods such as Gauss elimination are not suitable for large scale fractional applications. The iterative methods for these numerical methods are not fully studied and very few works can be found [118, 125]. We think that different iterative methods, such as Jacobi method and Gauss-Seidel and Krylov subspace method, are effective for fractional linear systems which are produced from FDEs. Does the coefficient matrix of FDEs have some other special properties or not? The answer is still unknown. The convergence and stability of these iterative methods should be proved as well.

High Order Schemes for Fractional Derivatives

The traditional partial derivatives have many high order schemes. For time fractional equation, the high order schemes for traditional integer derivative are not hard to build. But for fractional derivatives, the high order schemes are under developing [70, 126–128]. High order schemes will be used in the numerical solutions of FDEs where high accuracy is required in the presence of shocks or discontinuities.

Monte Carlo Method

The Monte Carlo method has advantage in solving nonlinear, high dimensional, complex geometry problems. In order to get the approximation of a small domain, the determined methods, such as FDM, must resolve the total definition domain with boundary conditions. The Monte Carlo method only focuses on the small domain. This property is very useful if we are only interested in this small domain. The Monte Carlo method is easy to be parallelized and needs much less memory space than determined methods. The fractional equations are a kind of nonlinear problem and their high dimensional problems are very computation intensive. So Monte Carlo method for FDEs needs to be studied in the future. Because of the high nonlinear and nonlocal property of FDEs, the sampling efficiency will be the key point of Monte Carlo method for FDEs.

CONCLUSIONS

In this paper, we give a comprehensive review of FDEs and its computational challenge. This kind of challenge will become an incoming problem for the computer industry if the real fractional problems need to be approximated. We reviewed a wide range of computational costs that come from different kinds of fractional equations. While we have collected several potential solutions on this challenge, we believe that the long-term legacy of solutions will allow the real world scientific and engineering applications come true.

ACKNOWLEDGMENTS

This research work is supported in part by the National Natural Science Foundation of China under Grants no. 61402039, no. 61303265, and no. 60970033, in part by Specialized Research

Fund for the Doctoral Program of Higher Education under Grant no. 20114307110001, and in part by 973 Program of China under Grants no. 2014CB430205 and no. 61312701001. The authors would like to thank the anonymous reviewers for their helpful comments as well.

REFERENCES

1. R. Klages, G. Radons, and I. Sokolov, Anomalous Transport: Foundations and Applications, Wiley-VCH, Weinheim, Germany, 2008.
2. R. R. Nigmatullin, T. Omay, and D. Baleanu, "On fractional filtering versus conventional filtering in economics," Communications in Nonlinear Science and Numerical Simulation, vol. 15, no. 4, pp. 979–986, 2010.
3. I. Podlubny, Fractional Differential Equations, Academic Press, San Diego, Calif, USA, 1999.
4. G. Maione and A. Punzi, "Combining differential evolution and particle swarm optimization to tune and realize fractional-order controllers," Mathematical and Computer Modelling of Dynamical Systems, vol. 19, no. 3, pp. 277–299, 2013. ·
5. D. Baleanu, A. K. Golmankhaneh, R. Nigmatullin, and A. K. Golmankhaneh, "Fractional Newtonian mechanics," Central European Journal of Physics, vol. 8, no. 1, pp. 120–125, 2010.·
6. C. Farges, M. Moze, and J. Sabatier, "Pseudo-state feedback stabilization of commensurate fractional order systems," Automatica, vol. 46, no. 10, pp. 1730–1734, 2010.
7. Rajeev and M. Kushwaha, "Homotopy perturbation method for a limit case Stefan problem governed by fractional diffusion equation," Applied Mathematical Modelling, vol. 37, no. 5, pp. 3589–3599, 2013.·
8. R. Schumer, M. M. Meerschaert, and B. Baeumer, "Fractional advectiondispersion equations for modeling transport at the Earth surface," Journal of Geophysical Research: Earth Surface, vol. 114, no. 4, Article ID F00A07, 2009.
9. G. Maione, "High-speed digital realizations of fractional operators in the delta domain," IEEE Transactions on Automatic Control, vol. 56, no. 3, pp. 697–702, 2011.
10. C. Gong, W. Bao, G. Tang, C. Min, and J. Liu, "An efficient iteration method for toeplitz -plus-band triangular systems generated from fractional ordinary differential equation," Mathematical Problems in Engineering, vol. 2014, Article ID 194249, 5 pages, 2014. ·
11. J. C. Trigeassou, N. Maamri, J. Sabatier, and A. Oustaloup, "A Lyapunov approach to the stability of fractional differential equations," Signal Processing, vol. 91, no. 3, pp. 437–445, 2011.
12. J. Sabatier, M. Moze, and C. Farges, "LMI stability conditions for fractional order systems," Computers and Mathematics with Applications, vol. 59, no. 5, pp. 1594–1609, 2010.
13. G. Maione, "On the Laguerre rational approximation to fractional discrete derivative and integral operators," IEEE Transactions on Automatic Control, vol. 58, no. 6, pp. 1579–1585, 2013.
14. H. Jiang, F. Liu, I. Turner, and K. Burrage, "Analytical solutions for the multi-term time-fractional diffusion-wave/diffusion equations in a finite domain," Computers and Mathematics with Applications, vol. 64, no. 10, pp. 3377–3388, 2012.
15. M. Alipour and D. Baleanu, "Approximate analytical solution for nonlinear system of fractional differential equations by BPs operational matrices," Advances in Mathematical Physics, vol. 2013, Article ID 954015, 9 pages, 2013.
16. S. Saha Ray, "Analytical solution for the space fractional diffusion equation by two-step adomian decomposition method," Communications in Nonlinear Science and Numerical Simulation, vol. 14, no. 4, pp. 1295–1306, 2009.
17. S. Momani and Z. Odibat, "Comparison between the homotopy perturbation method and the variational iteration method for linear fractional partial differential equations," Computers and Mathematics with Applications, vol. 54, no. 7-8, pp. 910–919, 2007.
18. S. Chen, F. Liu, and V. Anh, "A novel implicit finite difference method for the one-dimensional fractional percolation equation," Numerical Algorithms, vol. 56, no. 4, pp. 517–535, 2011.
19. J. Yan, G.-M. Tan, and N.-H. Sun, "Optimizing parallel Sn sweeps on unstructured grids for multi-core clusters," Journal of Computer Science and Technology, vol. 28, no. 4, pp. 657–670, 2013.
20. H. Yang and X.-C. Cai, "Parallel fully implicit two-grid methods for distributed control of unsteady incompressible flows," International Journal for Numerical Methods in Fluids, vol. 72, no. 1, pp. 1–21, 2013.
21. X. Liu, T. Gu, X. Hang, and Z. Sheng, "A parallel version of QMRCGSTAB method for large linear systems in distributed parallel environments," Applied Mathematics and Computation, vol. 172, no. 2, pp. 744–752, 2006.
22. D. Ming, "A parallel Attainable Region construction method suitable for implementation on a graphics processing unit (GPU)," Computers and Chemical Engineering, vol. 67, pp. 103–120, 2014.
23. X. Liao, L. Xiao, C. Yang, and Y. Lu, "Milkyway-2 supercomputer: system and application," Frontiers of Computer Science, vol. 8, no. 3, pp. 345–356, 2014.
24. W. Xu, Y. Lu, Q. Li et al., "Hybrid hierarchy storage system in MilkyWay-2 supercomputer," Frontiers of Computer Science, vol. 8, no. 3, pp. 367–377, 2014.
25. F. Aquotte and A. F. da Silva, "PSIM: a modular particle system on graphics processing unit," IEEE Latin America Transactions, vol. 12, no. 2, pp. 321–329, 2014.
26. S. J. Pennycook, S. D. Hammond, S. A. Jarvis, and G. R. Mudalige, "Performance analysis of a hybrid MPI/CUDA implementation of the NASLU benchmark," ACM SIGMETRICS Performance Evaluation Review, vol. 38, no. 4, pp. 23–29, 2011.
27. D. Mu, P. Chen, and L. Wang, "Accelerating the discontinuous Galerkin method for seismic wave

propagation simulations using the graphic processing unit (GPU)-single-GPU implementation,"Computers and Geosciences, vol. 51, pp. 282–292, 2013. ·

28. S. Mauger, G. C. de Verdière, L. Bergé, and S. Skupin, "GPU accelerated fully space and time resolved numerical simulations of self-focusing laser beams in SBS-active media," Journal of Computational Physics, vol. 235, pp. 606–625, 2013. ·

29. J. T. Machado, V. Kiryakova, and F. Mainardi, "Recent history of fractional calculus," Communications in Nonlinear Science and Numerical Simulation, vol. 16, no. 3, pp. 1140–1153, 2011.

30. J. A. Tenreiro Machado, V. Kiryakova, and F. Mainardi, "A poster about the recent history of fractional calculus," Fractional Calculus & Applied Analysis, vol. 13, no. 3, pp. 329–334, 2010.

31. A. Loverro, "Fractional calculus: history, definitions and applications for the engineer," Tech. Rep. 46556, Department of Aerospace and Mechanical Engineering, Notre Dame, Ind, USA, 2004.

32. K. Nishimoto, An Essence of Nishimoto's Fractional Calculus (Calculus in the 21st Century): Integrations and Differentiations of Arbitrary Order, Descartes Press Company, 1991.

33. M. Cui, "Compact alternating direction implicit method for two-dimensional time fractional diffusion equation," Journal of Computational Physics, vol. 231, no. 6, pp. 2621–2633, 2012.

34. W. Zhang, X. Cai, and S. Holm, "Time-fractional heat equations and negative absolute temperatures,"Computers and Mathematics with Applications, vol. 67, no. 1, pp. 164–171, 2014.·

35. Q. Yang, F. Liu, and I. Turner, "Numerical methods for fractional partial differential equations with Riesz space fractional derivatives," Applied Mathematical Modelling: Simulation and Computation for Engineering and Environmental Systems, vol. 34, no. 1, pp. 200–218, 2010.

36. J. Zhao, J. Xiao, and Y. Xu, "A finite element method for the multiterm time-space Riesz fractional advection-diffusion equations in finite domain," Abstract and Applied Analysis, vol. 2013, Article ID 868035, 15 pages, 2013.

37. Y. Lin and C. Xu, "Finite difference/spectral approximations for the time-fractional diffusion equation,"Journal of Computational Physics, vol. 225, no. 2, pp. 1533–1552, 2007.

38. C. Tadjeran and M. M. Meerschaert, "A second-order accurate numerical method for the two-dimensional fractional diffusion equation," Journal of Computational Physics, vol. 220, no. 2, pp. 813–823, 2007.

39. N. J. Ford, J. Xiao, and Y. Yan, "Stability of a numerical method for a space-time-fractional telegraph equation," Computational Methods in Applied Mathematics, vol. 12, no. 3, pp. 273–288, 2012.

40. T. Chang, "Boundary integral operator for the fractional laplace equation in a bounded lipschitz domain," Integral Equations and Operator Theory, vol. 72, no. 3, pp. 345–361, 2012.

41. G. Jumarie, "Derivation and solutions of some fractional Black-Scholes equations in coarse-grained space and time. Application to Merton's optimal portfolio," Computers & Mathematics with Applications, vol. 59, no. 3, pp. 1142–1164, 2010.

42. P. Straka, M. M. Meerschaert, R. J. McGough, and Y. Zhou, "Fractional wave equations with attenuation," Fractional Calculus and Applied Analysis, vol. 16, no. 1, pp. 262–272, 2013.

43. W. Deng, "Finite element method for the space and time fractional Fokker-Planck equation," SIAM Journal on Numerical Analysis, vol. 47, no. 1, pp. 204–226, 2008.

44. S. Momani and Z. Odibat, "Analytical solution of a time-fractional Navier-Stokes equation by Adomian decomposition method," Applied Mathematics and Computation, vol. 177, no. 2, pp. 488–494, 2006.·

45. M. A. Herzallah and D. Baleanu, "Fractional Euler-Lagrange equations revisited," Nonlinear Dynamics, vol. 69, no. 3, pp. 977–982, 2012. ·

46. A. I. Saichev and G. M. Zaslavsky, "Fractional kinetic equations: solutions and applications," Chaos, vol. 7, no. 4, pp. 753–764, 1997.

47. T. Wenchang, P. Wenxiao, and X. Mingyu, "A note on unsteady flows of a viscoelastic fluid with the fractional Maxwell model between two parallel plates," International Journal of Non-Linear Mechanics, vol. 38, no. 5, pp. 645–650, 2003.

48. R. A. El-Nabulsi, "The fractional Boltzmann transport equation," Computers and Mathematics with Applications, vol. 62, no. 3, pp. 1568–1575, 2011.

49. K. Diethelm, "An investigation of some nonclassical methods for the numerical approximation of Caputo-type fractional derivatives," Numerical Algorithms, vol. 47, no. 4, pp. 361–390, 2008.

50. K. Diethelm, N. J. Ford, and A. D. Freed, "A predictor-corrector approach for the numerical solution of fractional differential equations," Nonlinear Dynamics, vol. 29, no. 1–4, pp. 3–22, 2002.

51. M. Cui, "Compact finite difference method for the fractional diffusion equation," Journal of Computational Physics, vol. 228, no. 20, pp. 7792–7804, 2009.

52. N. J. Ford, J. Xiao, and Y. Yan, "A finite element method for time fractional partial differential equations," Fractional Calculus and Applied Analysis, vol. 14, no. 3, pp. 454–474, 2011.

53. X. Zhang, J. Liu, J. Wen, B. Tang, and Y. He, "Analysis for one-dimensional time-fractional Tricomi-type equations by LDG methods," Numerical Algorithms, vol. 63, no. 1, pp. 143–164, 2013.

54. K. Mustapha and W. McLean, "Uniform convergence for a discontinuous Galerkin, time-stepping method applied to a fractional diffusion equation," IMA Journal of Numerical Analysis, vol. 32, no. 3, pp. 906–925, 2012.

55. Q. Yang, I. Turner, F. Liu, and M. Ilić, "Novel numerical methods for solving the time-space fractional diffusion equation in two dimensions," SIAM Journal on Scientific Computing, vol. 33, no. 3, pp. 1159–1180, 2011.

56. H. Hejazi, T. Moroney, and F. Liu, "A finite volume method for solving the two-sided time-space fractional advection-dispersion equation," Central European Journal of Physics, vol. 11, no. 10, pp. 1275–1283, 2013.
57. H. Hejazi, T. Moroney, and F. Liu, "Stability and convergence of a finite volume method for the space fractional advection-dispersion equation," Journal of Computational and Applied Mathematics, vol. 255, pp. 684–697, 2014.
58. S. Momani, "An explicit and numerical solutions of the fractional KdV equation," Mathematics and Computers in Simulation, vol. 70, no. 2, pp. 110–118, 2005.·
59. B. Tang, C. Jiang, and H. Zhu, "Fractional fourier transform for confluent hypergeometric beams,"Physics Letters A, vol. 376, no. 38-39, pp. 2627–2631, 2012. ·
60. A. R. Carella and C. A. Dorao, "Least-squares spectral method for the solution of a fractional advection-dispersion equation," Journal of Computational Physics, vol. 232, pp. 33–45, 2013.
61. A. Shirzadi, L. Ling, and S. Abbasbandy, "Meshless simulations of the two-dimensional fractional-time convection-diffusion-reaction equations," Engineering Analysis with Boundary Elements, vol. 36, no. 11, pp. 1522–1527, 2012.
62. Q. Liu, F. Liu, I. Turner, V. Anh, and Y. T. Gu, "A RBF meshless approach for modeling a fractal mobile/immobile transport model," Applied Mathematics and Computation, vol. 226, pp. 336–347, 2014.
63. Q. Liu, Y. T. Gu, P. Zhuang, F. Liu, and Y. F. Nie, "An implicit RBF meshless approach for time fractional diffusion equations," Computational Mechanics, vol. 48, no. 1, pp. 1–12, 2011.
64. R. Garrappa, "A family of Adams exponential integrators for fractional linear systems," Computers and Mathematics with Applications, vol. 66, no. 5, pp. 717–727, 2013.
65. R. Garrappa and M. Popolizio, "Generalized exponential time differencing methods for fractional order problems," Computers & Mathematics with Applications, vol. 62, no. 3, pp. 876–890, 2011.
66. D. Fulger, E. Scalas, and G. Germano, "Monte Carlo simulation of uncoupled continuous-time random walks yielding a stochastic solution of the space-time fractional diffusion equation," Physical Review E, vol. 77, no. 2, Article ID 021122, 2008.
67. C. Gong, W. Bao, G. Tang, Y. Jiang, and J. Liu, "A parallel algorithm for the two-dimensional time fractional diffusion equation with implicit difference method," The Scientific World Journal, vol. 2014, Article ID 219580, 8 pages, 2014.
68. J. Q. Murillo and S. B. Yuste, "An explicit difference method for solving fractional diffusion and diffusion-wave equations in the caputo form," Journal of Computational and Nonlinear Dynamics, vol. 6, no. 2, Article ID 021014, 2011.
69. C. Gong, W. Bao, G. Tang, B. Yang, and J. Liu, "An efficient parallel solution for Caputo fractional reaction-diffusion equation," Journal of Supercomputing, vol. 68, no. 3, pp. 1521–1537, 2014.
70. C. Tadjeran, M. M. Meerschaert, and H. P. Scheffler, "A second-order accurate numerical approximation for the fractional diffusion equation," Journal of Computational Physics, vol. 213, no. 1, pp. 205–213, 2006, http://dx.doi.org/10.1016/j.jcp.2005.08.008.
71. M. M. Meerschaert, D. A. Benson, H.-P. Scheffler, and P. Becker-Kern, "Governing equations and solutions of anomalous random walk limits," Physical Review E, vol. 66, no. 6, Article ID 060102, 2002. ·
72. R. Metzler and J. Klafter, "The restaurant at the end of the random walk: recent developments in the description of anomalous transport by fractional dynamics," Journal of Physics A: Mathematical and General, vol. 37, no. 31, pp. R161–R208, 2004.
73. K. S. Miller and B. Ross, An Introduction to the Fractional Calculus and Fractional Differential Equations, John Wiley & Sons, New York, NY, USA, 1993.
74. S. Shen, F. Liu, V. Anh, and I. Turner, "The fundamental solution and numerical solution of the Riesz fractional advection-dispersion equation," IMA Journal of Applied Mathematics, vol. 73, no. 6, pp. 850–872, 2008.
75. C. Çelik and M. Duman, "Crank-Nicolson method for the fractional diffusion equation with the Riesz fractional derivative," Journal of Computational Physics, vol. 231, no. 4, pp. 1743–1750, 2012.
76. J. Chen and F. Liu, "Analysis of stability and convergence of numerical approximation for the Riesz fractional reaction-dispersion equation," Journal of Xiamen University, vol. 45, no. 4, pp. 466–469, 2006 (Chinese).
77. C. Gong, W. Bao, and G. Tang, "A parallel algorithm for the Riesz fractional reaction-diffusion equation with explicit finite difference method," Fractional Calculus and Applied Analysis, vol. 16, no. 3, pp. 654–669, 2013.
78. A. Yildirim and H. Koçak, "Homotopy perturbation method for solving the space-time fractional advection-dispersion equation," Advances in Water Resources, vol. 32, no. 12, pp. 1711–1716, 2009. ·
79. S. Shen, F. Liu, and V. Anh, "Numerical approximations and solution techniques for the space-time Riesz-Caputo fractional advection-diffusion equation," Numerical Algorithms, vol. 56, no. 3, pp. 383–403, 2011.
80. F. Liu, P. Zhuang, V. Anh, I. Turner, and K. Burrage, "Stability and convergence of the difference methods for the space-time fractional advection-diffusion equation," Applied Mathematics and Computation, vol. 191, no. 1, pp. 12–20, 2007.
81. C.-M. Chen and F. Liu, "A numerical approximation method for solving a three-dimensional space Galilei invariant fractional advection-diffusion equation," Journal of Applied Mathematics and Computing, vol. 30, no. 1-2, pp. 219–236, 2009.
82. K. Mustapha, "An implicit finite-difference time-stepping method for a sub-diffusion equation, with spatial discretization by finite elements," IMA Journal of Numerical Analysis, vol. 31, no. 2, pp. 719–739, 2011.
83. J. Huang, N. Nie, and Y. Tang, "A second order finite difference-spectral method for space fractional diffusion

equations," Science China Mathematics, vol. 57, no. 6, pp. 1303–1317, 2014.·

84. P. Zhuang, F. Liu, V. Anh, and I. Turner, "Numerical methods for the variable-order fractional advection-diffusion equation with a nonlinear source term," SIAM Journal on Numerical Analysis, vol. 47, no. 3, pp. 1760–1781, 2009.

85. M. Cui, "Convergence analysis of high-order compact alternating direction implicit schemes for the two-dimensional time fractional diffusion equation," Numerical Algorithms, vol. 62, no. 3, pp. 383–409, 2013.

86. H. Wang and T. S. Basu, "A fast finite difference method for two-dimensional space-fractional diffusion equations," SIAM Journal on Scientific Computing, vol. 34, no. 5, pp. A2444–A2458, 2012.

87. P. Zhuang and F. Liu, "Finite difference approximation for two-dimensional time fractional diffusion equation," Journal of Algorithms & Computational Technology, vol. 1, no. 1, pp. 1–15, 2007.

88. H. Sun, W. Chen, and Y. Chen, "Variable-order fractional differential operators in anomalous diffusion modeling," Physica A: Statistical Mechanics and Its Applications, vol. 388, no. 21, pp. 4586–4592, 2009. ·

89. X. Liao, "MilkyWay-2: back to the world Top 1," Frontiers of Computer Science, vol. 8, no. 3, pp. 343–344, 2014.

90. S. J. Pennycook, S. D. Hammond, G. R. Mudalige, S. A. Wright, and S. A. Jarvis, "On the acceleration of wavefront applications using distributed many-core architectures," Computer Journal, vol. 55, no. 2, pp. 138–153, 2012.

91. Q. Xu, G.-L. Yu, K. Wang, and J.-L. Sun, "Research on gpu-accelerated algorithm in 3d finite difference neutro n diffusion calculation method," Nuclear Science and Techniques, vol. 25, no. 1, Article ID 010501, 2014.

92. M. Rosa, J. S. Warsa, and M. Perks, "A cellwise block-gauss-seidel iterative method for multigroup $S_N$transport on a hybrid parallel computer architecture," Nuclear Science and Engineering, vol. 174, no. 3, pp. 209–226, 2013.

93. A. K. Jha, M. A. Kupinski, H. H. Barrett, E. Clarkson, and J. H. Hartman, "Three-dimensional Neumann-series approach to model light transport in nonuniform media," Journal of the Optical Society of America A, vol. 29, no. 9, pp. 1885–1899, 2012. ·

94. C. Xu, X. Deng, L. Zhang et al., "Parallelizing a high-order CFD software for 3D, multi-block, structural grids on the TianHe-1A supercomputer," in Supercomputing, vol. 7905 of Lecture Notes in Computer Science, Springer, Berlin, Germany, 2013.

95. Y.-X. Wang, L.-L. Zhang, W. Liu, et al., "Efficient parallel implementation of large scale 3D structured grid CFD applications on the Tianhe-1A supercomputer," Computers & Fluids, vol. 80, no. 1, pp. 244–250, 2013.

96. Q. Wu, C. Yang, T. Tang, and L. Xiao, "Exploiting hierarchy parallelism for molecular dynamics on a petascale heterogeneous system," Journal of Parallel and Distributed Computing, vol. 73, no. 12, pp. 1592–1604, 2013.

97. F. Chen and J. Shen, "A GPU parallelized spectral method for elliptic equations in rectangular domains," Journal of Computational Physics, vol. 250, pp. 555–564, 2013.

98. Z. Mo, A. Zhang, X. Cao et al., "JASMIN: a parallel software infrastructure for scientific computing,"Frontiers of Computer Science in China, vol. 4, no. 4, pp. 480–488, 2010.

99. C. Xu, X. Deng, L. Zhang et al., "Collaborating CPU and GPU for large scale high-order CFD for simulations with complex grids on the tianhe-1A supercom puter," Journal of Computational Physics, vol. 278, pp. 275–297, 2014.

100. R. Chen, Y. Wu, Z. Yan, Y. Zhao, and X.-C. Cai, "A parallel domain decomposition method for 3D unsteady incompressible flows at high reynolds number," Journal of Scientific Computing, vol. 58, no. 2, pp. 275–289, 2014.

101. H. Yang, C. Yang, and X.-C. Cai, "Parallel domain decomposition methods with mixed order discretization for fully implicit solution of tracer transport problems on the cubed-sphere," Journal of Scientific Computing, 2014.

102. C. Yang, J. Cao, and X. C. Cai, "A fully implicit domain decomposition algorithm for shallow water equations on the cubed-sphere," SIAM Journal on Scientific Computing, vol. 32, no. 1, pp. 418–438, 2010.

103. C. Gong, W. Bao, G. Tang, Y. Jiang, and J. Liu, "A domain decomposition method for time fractional reaction-diffusion equation," The Scientific World Journal, vol. 2014, Article ID 681707, 5 pages, 2014. ·

104. K. Diethelm, "An efficient parallel algorithm for the numerical solution of fractional differential equations," Fractional Calculus and Applied Analysis, vol. 14, no. 3, pp. 475–490, 2011.

105. C. Gong, J. Liu, L. Chi, H. Huang, J. Fang, and Z. Gong, "GPU accelerated simulations of 3D deterministic particle transport using discrete ordinates method," Journal of Computational Physics, vol. 230, no. 15, pp. 6010–6022, 2011.

106. C. Gong, J. Liu, Z. Gong, J. Qin, and J. Xie, "Optimizing Sweep3D for graphic processor unit," inAlgorithms and Architectures for Parallel Processing, C.-H. Hsu, L. Yang, J. Park, and S.-S. Yeo, Eds., vol. 6081 of Lecture Notes in Computer Science, pp. 416–426, Springer, Berlin, Germany, 2010.

107. X. Gan, C. Liu, Z. Wang et al., "Accelerating GOR algorithm using CUDA," Applied Mathematics and Information Sciences, vol. 7, no. 2, pp. 563–567, 2013.

108. C. Gong, J. Liu, H. Huang, and Z. Gong, "Particle transport with unstructured grid on GPU," Computer Physics Communications, vol. 183, no. 3, pp. 588–593, 2012.·

109. X. Gan, Z. Wang, L. Shen, and Q. Zhu, "Data layout pruning on GPU," Applied Mathematics & Information Sciences, vol. 5, no. 2, pp. 129–138, 2011.

110. W. Zhang, W. Wei, and X. Cai, "Performance modeling

of serial and parallel implementations of the fractional Adams-Bashforth-Moulton method," Fractional Calculus and Applied Analysis, vol. 17, no. 3, pp. 617–637, 2014.

111. J. Liu, C. Gong, W. Bao, G. Tang, and Y. Jiang, "Solving the Caputo fractional reaction-diffusion equation on GPU," Discrete Dynamics in Nature and Society, vol. 2014, Article ID 820162, 2014.

112. Y. Xu and Z. He, "The short memory principle for solving Abel differential equation of fractional order," Computers and Mathematics with Applications, vol. 62, no. 12, pp. 4796–4805, 2011.

113. W. Deng, "Short memory principle and a predictor-corrector approach for fractional differential equations," Journal of Computational and Applied Mathematics, vol. 206, no. 1, pp. 174–188, 2007.

114. N. J. Ford and A. C. Simpson, "The numerical solution of fractional differential equations: speed versus accuracy," Numerical Algorithms, vol. 26, no. 4, pp. 333–346, 2001.

115. H.-L. Cao, X. Li, Z.-H. Deng, and Y. Qin, "Control-oriented fast numerical approaches of fractional-order models," Control Theory and Applications, vol. 28, no. 5, pp. 715–721, 2011 (Chinese).

116. H. Wang, K. Wang, and T. Sircar, "A direct O(Nlog^{2}N) finite difference method for fractional diffusion equations," Journal of Computational Physics, vol. 229, no. 21, pp. 8095–8104, 2010.

117. H. Wang and K. Wang, "An O(Nlog^{2}N) alternating-direction finite difference method for two-dimensional fractional diffusion equations," Journal of Computational Physics, vol. 230, no. 21, pp. 7830–7839, 2011.

118. H. Wang and N. Du, "A superfast-preconditioned iterative method for steady-state space-fractional diffusion equations," Journal of Computational Physics, vol. 240, pp. 49–57, 2013.

119. H.-K. Pang and H.-W. Sun, "Multigrid method for fractional diffusion equations," Journal of Computational Physics, vol. 231, no. 2, pp. 693–703, 2012.·

120. Z. Zhou and H. Wu, "Finite element multigrid method for the boundary value problem of fractional advection dispersion equation," Journal of Applied Mathematics, vol. 2013, Article ID 385403, 8 pages, 2013.

121. S.-L. Lei and H.-W. Sun, "A circulant preconditioner for fractional diffusion equations," Journal of Computational Physics, vol. 242, pp. 715–725, 2013.

122. T. Moroney and Q. Yang, "A banded preconditioner for the two-sided, nonlinear space-fractional diffusion equation," Computers and Mathematics with Applications, vol. 66, no. 5, pp. 659–667, 2013. ·

123. T. Moroney and Q. Yang, "Efficient solution of two-sided nonlinear space-fractional diffusion equations using fast poisson preconditioners," Journal of Computational Physics, vol. 246, pp. 304–317, 2013.

124. J. A. Tenreiro Machado, "Fractional derivatives: probability interpretation and frequency response of rational approximations," Communications in Nonlinear Science and Numerical Simulation, vol. 14, no. 9-10, pp. 3492–3497, 2009.

125. F.-R. Lin, S.-W. Yang, and X.-Q. Jin, "Preconditioned iterative methods for fractional diffusion equation," Journal of Computational Physics, vol. 256, pp. 109–117, 2014.

126. W. Deng, S. Du, and Y. Wu, "High order finite difference WENO schemes for fractional differential equations," Applied Mathematics Letters, vol. 26, no. 3, pp. 362–366, 2013.

127. H. Zhou, W. Tian, and W. Deng, "Quasi-compact finite difference schemes for space fractional diffusion equations," Journal of Scientific Computing, vol. 56, no. 1, pp. 45–66, 2013.

128. C. Lubich, "Discretized fractional calculus," SIAM Journal on Mathematical Analysis, vol. 17, no. 3, pp. 704–719, 1986.

CHAPTER 10 STATISTICAL ANALYSIS OF TIME SERIES WITH SCALING INDICES

Harald Atmanspacher[1,2], Werner Ehm[1], Herbert Scheingraber[2], and Gerda Wiedenmann [2,3]

[1]Institut ffir Grenzgebiete der Psychologie, Wilhelmstr. 3a, D-79098 Freiburg;

[2]Max-Planck-Institut ffir extraterrestrische Physik, Giessenbachstr., D-85740 Garching;

[3]Nabios GmbH, Donnersberger Str. 41, D-80634 Mnchen

ABSTRACT

Statistical techniques based on scaling indices are applied to detect and investigate patterns in empirically given time series. The key idea is to use the distribution of scaling indices obtained from a delay representation of the empirical time series to distinguish between random and non-random components. Statistical tests for this purpose are designed and applied to specific examples. It is shown that a selection of subseries by scaling indices can significantly enhance the signal-to-noise ratio as compared to that of the total time series.

INTRODUCTION

If the behavior of a system evolving in time shows features that are "irregular" in some sense, the observed data series invites statistical modeling as a stochastic or random process. In such cases it is often useful and possible to conceptually distinguish between some null mode of behavior on one side and deviations from that null mode on the other. The notion of a null mode refers to some knowledge about the basic physical (null) characteristics of the system, which can be understood in terms of random or deterministic mechanisms. If there is no such knowledge, the situation is more difficult insofar as one has to start with assumptions as to model classes that may be appropriate to reproduce the observed data.

There are many approaches that have been developed in this spirit for many different purposes. Their success generally depends on both the nature of the deviations and that of the null mode. Deviations of a pre-conceived sort, such as a shift or an abrupt change in the mean or trend of the process, can be detected efficiently if one uses a correspondingly tailored procedure, and if the actual deviation is of the anticipated sort. On the other hand, if the goal is to detect any deviation, or deviations one has only a vague notion of, then less specific procedures of a wider scope may be more appropriate, even at the risk of losing precision with respect to the distinction between different types of specific deviations.

In many practical cases of pattern detection and pattern recognition, the basic problem is to distinguish a (more or less) faint regular pattern, the deviation, in front of a random background, the null mode. In this framework, the most ambitious situation for modeling purposes is met if neither the type of regularity nor the type of randomness are known. This is the kind of situation for which a data-analytic method called scaling index analysis is particularly helpful. It aims at

Citation: Harald Atmnaspacher, Werner Ehm, Herbert Scheingraber, and Gerda Wiedenmann, "Statistical analysis of time series with scaling indices," Discrete Dynamics in Nature and Society, vol. 5, no. 4, pp. 297-309, 2000. doi:10.1155/S1026022600000595

detecting non-random deviations from a random null mode and is applicable if the random process is (approximately) stationary in the null mode. Non-random contributions can be due to some (weak) regular signal or pattern superimposed on or replacing the null process, or due to increased correlations between successive measurements reducing the local variability of the time series. Using scaling indices, one can study this time variability geometrically by comparing the density gradients in suitably constructed point sets on different distance scales. In physical contexts, scaling indices or "crowding indices" [1] originate from the dimensional analysis of single fractals and multifractals ([2-4], for an overview see [5]). For a mathematically oriented perspective see [6].

Scaling index analysis has primarily been used as a data-analytic tool so far, i.e., as a numerical algorithm extracting potentially interesting features embedded in a random background (see, e.g., [7-11]). The crucial concept in a scaling index analysis is a so-called Ha histogram (see below) whose properties can be investigated and discriminated against the known or expected null mode histogram. This is no problem as long as the deviations from the null behavior are marked enough to be easily visible. If this is not the case, it may be difficult to distinguish systematic but small deviations from deviations due to random fluctuations produced by the null process. Then a statistical test with an appropriate discriminant statistics is required, in which the error of the first kind- to falsely classify a time series as "deviant" although it is in null mode is well controlled. If deviations occur only sporadically, it may also be interesting to single out those time intervals in which "something deviant seems to go on".

The goal of this paper is to propose methods for (i) the construction of statistical tests based on scaling indices, and (ii) the identification of conspicuous parts of the observed time series, selected by particular ranges of scaling indices. In this way, we focus on a precise statistical formulation of scaling index analyses which was not addressed in earlier publications listed above. Section 2.1 indicates the basic definitions and procedures for a scaling index analysis, Section 2.2 describes the test construction, and Section 2.3 gives a detailed example. Section 3 addresses how scaling index analyses can be used to enhance the signal-to-noise-ratio by selecting and investigating those parts of a time series that are responsible for deviations from a random null process. Section 4 discusses and summarizes the main results.

STATISTICAL SCALING INDEX ANALYSIS

Basic Notations and Framework

Consider a (univariate) time series {x(t): 1,... T} of finite length T. This notation implies a discrete notion of a parameter time t, which will subsequently be utilized to indicate the temporal ordering of observations x(t). Using the technique of delay coordinates [12] one can construct an associated d-dimensional time series,

$$z(t) = (x(t), \ldots, x(t+d-1)),$$
$$t = 1, \ldots, T-d+1.$$

For every and pre-defined radii $r_1, r_2 (0 < r_1 < r_2)$ let a scaling index α(t) be defined as

$$\alpha(t) = \frac{\log N_2(z(t)) - \log N_1(z(t))}{\log r_2 - \log r_1}, \tag{1}$$

where $N_{1,2}(z_{\text{ref}}) = \#\{t: \ |z(t) - z_{\text{ref}}| \leq r_{1,2}\}$ denotes the number of all points z(t), t= 1,..., T-d+ 1, whose Euclidean distance to the reference point Z_{re} does not exceed $r_{1,2}$.

Any scaling index analysis is based on the distribution of the scaling indices. This distribution can be represented by a histogram, the socalled Ha histogram. Its integrated version, the (cumulative) empirical distribution function (edf) of the scaling indices (si) is more appropriate for our purposes, because of its improved statistical stability. H(α) will be referred to as the si-edf associated with {x(t)}.

$$H(\alpha) = (T-d+1)^{-1} \#\{t: \alpha(t) \leq \alpha\} \quad (\alpha \geq 0), \tag{2}$$

The basic idea is to compare this si-edf H(c) with an appropriate reference distribution function H_{ref} characterizing the null process. In cases in which a continuous time process can be characterized by a multifractal measure, the limiting H_{ref} for $T \to \infty$, then $r_{1,2}$--+0, increases in the range of c corresponding to the (set of) dimension(s) on which the measure is concentrated. (For single fractals, the increase of H_{ref} reduces to a Heaviside step function corresponding to a δ function type histogram.) If the null process is random, the range of c, over which H_{ref} increases, keeps growing toward larger c with increasing embedding dimension d. By contrast, for regular or chaotic deterministic processes the increase of the reference distribution stays at the same range of α for increasing d, provided that d is sufficiently greater than the "true" (set of) dimension(s) of the process.

In the case of a fixed finite observation segment and fixed radii, H_{ref} is generically broadened. As a consequence, sharp discriminations as in the limits $T \to \infty, r_{1,2} \to 0$ become impossible (even for single fractals). Nevertheless, non-random contributions to a random null process tend to increase the frequency of small scaling indices also in the finite case, such that mass of the si-edf is shifted to smaller values of α. For this reason, discrepancies between the si-edf and H_{ref} in the left wing of the distributions are of particular interest.

Assume for example that the x(t) are independent random variables distributed uniformly on the interval [0,1], and d 3. Up to random fluctuations, {z(t)} then covers the three-dimensional unit cube in a homogeneous manner. The corresponding scaling index distribution function increases over a small range of c centered around a value $d^* < d$ where $(d-d^*)$ depends on T and $r_{1,2}$. Other mechanisms (random, chaotic, or regular) typically produce clusters and voids, resulting in a scaling index distribution whose tails are more pronounced.

The distribution of the scaling indices also provides us with a clue to more refined analyses. For example, it allows to sort out, and study in itself, those parts of the time series corresponding to small scaling indices, which are of special interest as potential carriers of signals or patterns. Properly assessing the statistical significance of effects is particularly important in such a kind of refined analysis.

The main ingredients of the statistical framework adopted here are as follows.

(a) It is assumed that the null mode behavior of the system under study can be described by a stochastic process $\{X_0(t)$: t= 1,..., T} having a certain distribution D_0.

(b) The given time series {x(t)} is interpreted as the realization of another stochastic process {X(t): t= 1,..., T} with distribution D. The null hypothesis H_0 is that {X(t)} is in null mode, that is, has the same distribution as X_0: D D_0.

(c) In addition, there are n calibration time series $\{X_{cal,i}(t)$: t= 1,...,T} (i= 1,...,n). They are assumed to represent a sample of size n from the null process X_0, that is, they are assumed to be independent and identically distributed copies of $\{X_0(t)$: t= 1,... ,T}.

Some remarks: Subsequently, we drop the notational distinction between time series considered as a sequence of measurement data or considered as a stochastic process. Secondly, it should be noted that the null hypothesis does not impose any restriction on the internal structure of the null process. However, our proposals make sense only if the process is stationary (or nearly so at least). Thirdly, *D* denotes the distribution of the whole stochastic process {x(t)}, not the (marginal) distribution of a single random variable x(t) at fixed (and likewise for D_0 and $\{X_{cal,i}(t)\}$). Finally, the "true" null distribution D_0 need not be known, but it is assumed that a reasonable model is available for the null process which allows us to generate a sample of auxiliary time series {xau(t): t- 1,... ,T} (j- 1,..., m) with a distribution close to D_0.

Both calibration data and auxiliary data can be considered as surrogate data [13], though of different type. Usually, surrogate data are generated to simulate the distribution of the test statistics under the null hypothesis. To serve this purpose, calibration data from a real physical system are available in our case. The auxiliary data are generated for a different purpose, namely to construct a test statistics adapted to the null process (see Section 2.2). Furthermore, in our approach the distribution D_0 as a whole should be matched. This is in contrast to the typical use of surrogate data (e.g., based on randomized Fourier phases [14]), where only some characteristics of D_0 are taken into account.

Test Construction

As indicated above the test of the null hypothesis H_0 proposed here will be based on the difference

$$\Delta(\alpha) = H(\alpha) - H_{\text{ref}}(\alpha)$$

of the si-edf $H(\alpha)$ associated with the time series {x(t)} and the reference scaling index distribution function H_{ref}. As $H_{ref\,i}$ we use the mean distribution of the si-edf's Hca,i as obtained from the calibration time series $\{_{Xcal,i}(t)\}$:

$$H_{\text{ref}}(\alpha) = \overline{H_{\text{cal}}}(\alpha) = n^{-1} \sum_{i=1}^{n} H_{\text{cal},i}(\alpha). \tag{3}$$

This mean distribution may be regarded as an estimator of the expected value of $H(\alpha)$ (with respect to D_0). The test depends on the partial maxima

$$M(\alpha) = \max_{\alpha_{\min} \leq \beta \leq \alpha} |\Delta(\beta)|$$

and a function c(a), henceforth referred to as the deviation profile. The null hypothesis H_0 (i.e., {X(t)} is in null mode is rejected if $M(\alpha)$ crosses the deviation profile c(a) somewhere in the interval $[\alpha_{\min}, \alpha_{\max}]$, i.e., if

$$M(\alpha) > c(\alpha) \text{ for some } \alpha \in [\alpha_{\min}, \alpha_{\max}]. \tag{4}$$

The deviation profile $c(\alpha)$ and the interval $[\alpha_{\min}, \alpha_{\max}]$ have to be chosen such that the error of the first kind is (approximately) equal to the desired test level e ε (typical choices are $\varepsilon = 0.05$ and $\varepsilon = 0.01$),

$$P_0(M(\alpha) > c(\alpha) \text{ for some } \alpha \in [\alpha_{\min}, \alpha_{\max}]) = \varepsilon. \tag{5}$$

The notation P_0 indicates that the probability of the event in brackets is computed with respect to the distribution D_0 of the null process.

The deviation profile $c(\alpha)$ has to account for the strong c-dependence of the variance (under $\mathcal{D}_0$ of the random variables $\Delta(\alpha)$. Typically this variance is much larger for a-values in the central part of a scaling index distribution rather than in its tails. If c were chosen as a constant, possible weak systematic deviations in the left wing of $H(\alpha)$ would be concealed by large chance fluctuations in the center. For instance, this would be the case for a classical Kolmogorov-Smirnov type test, which rejects $\mathcal{H}_0$ if $\max_\alpha |\Delta(\alpha)| > c'$ –, or, in terms of the partial maxima, if $M(\alpha) > c'$ for some α.

Using partial maxima $M(\alpha)$ instead of the (sometimes strongly fluctuating) function $\Delta(\alpha)$ has a certain regularizing effect, but the essential features in the left tail of H(a) are retained because $|\Delta(\alpha)|$ tends to increase in that range. Another way to avoid strong fluctuations in $\Delta(\alpha)$ can be achieved by considering only subintervals $[\alpha_{\min}, \alpha_{\max}]$. These intervals have to be adjusted with respect to the parameters T and $r_{1,2}$.

The deviation profile c(a) will be constructed to reflect the local variability of M(a) as expected for the null process. This can be done in different ways. Two of them are described as Versions (A) and (B) below. Both versions use auxiliary time series $\{X_{aux,j}(t)\}$ to obtain preliminary profiles. The final profile has to comply with condition (5), which is achieved by a simple multiplicative correction. For that purpose the calibration time series $\{X_{cal,i}(t)\}$ are used. The null hypothesis is rejected according to (4).

Version (A):

$$c_A(\alpha) = \gamma_A \mu(\alpha),$$

Where

$$\mu(\alpha) = m^{-1} \sum_{j=1}^{m} M_{\text{aux},j}(\alpha)$$
$$= m^{-1} \sum_{j=1}^{m} \max_{\alpha_{\min} \leq \beta \leq \alpha} |\Delta_{\text{aux},j}(\beta)|. \tag{6}$$

The factor $\gamma_A > 0$ is determined (e.g., by trial and error) such that the (empirical) profile crossing probability

$$P_A = n^{-1} \#\{i \leq n : M_{\text{cal},i}(\alpha) > c_A(\alpha) \text{ for some } \alpha \in [\alpha_{\min}, \alpha_{\max}]\} \approx \varepsilon, \tag{7}$$

With

$$M_{\text{cal},i}(\alpha) = \max_{\alpha_{\min} \leq \beta \leq \alpha} |\Delta_{\text{cal},i}(\beta)| \quad (8)$$

calculated from the calibration data. The relative frequency P_A represents a bootstrap estimate of the corresponding error probability in (5). Of course, the number of calibration data and auxiliary data should be large enough to make this a stable estimate.

Version (B):

$$c_B(\alpha) = \mu(\alpha) + \gamma_B \sigma(\alpha),$$

where μ is the same as in (A), and $\sigma(\alpha)$ is computed as the root of the empirical variance

$$\sigma(\alpha)^2 = m^{-1} \sum_{j=1}^{m} M_{\text{aux},j}(\alpha)^2 - \mu(\alpha)^2 \quad (9)$$

from the auxiliary data. The factor γ_B is determined such that the empirical profile crossing probability P_B, defined analogous to P_A, satisfies (7).

Other variants of this approach in addition to these two versions may also be worth considering. For example, one could use the empirical standard deviations $s_{\Delta,\text{aux}}(\alpha) = \sqrt{(1/m) \sum_{j=1}^{m} \Delta_{\text{aux},j}(\alpha)^2}$ to construct the preliminary profile and then correct it by a factor γ_Δ such that one has (with $c_\Delta = \gamma_\Delta s_\Delta$)

$$P_\Delta = n^{-1} \#\{i \leq n : |\Delta_{\text{cal},i}(\alpha)| > c_\Delta(\alpha) \text{ for some } \alpha \in [\alpha_{\min}, \alpha_{\max}]\} \approx \varepsilon.$$

The null hypothesis $\mathcal{H}_0$ is then rejected if $|\Delta(\alpha)| > c_\Delta(\alpha)$ for some $\alpha \in [\alpha_{\min}, \alpha_{\max}]$.

An Example

Details of the proposed test construction for a specific example are illustrated in Figures 1-6. We had n 1320 calibration time series (as described in [9]) at our disposal, each of length T= 10000. As a working hypothesis it is assumed that the $x_{\text{cal},i}(t)(t = 1, \ldots, T;\ i = 1, \ldots, n)$ are independent random variables, identically distributed according to a binomial distribution $B(n_b, \pi_b)$ with n_b--200 trials and a probability of success $\pi_b = 1/2$. A number of $m = 2500$ auxiliary time series (roughly twice as much as the calibration data) were generated according to this "binomial model". The embedding dimension is d= 4, and the radii are $r_1 = 4.6$, $r_2 = 12.7$.

Figure shows H_{ref} together with an individual si-edf $H_{\text{cal},i}$. The a(t)'s can only attain values in a certain finite set determined by T and $r_{1,2}$ and are

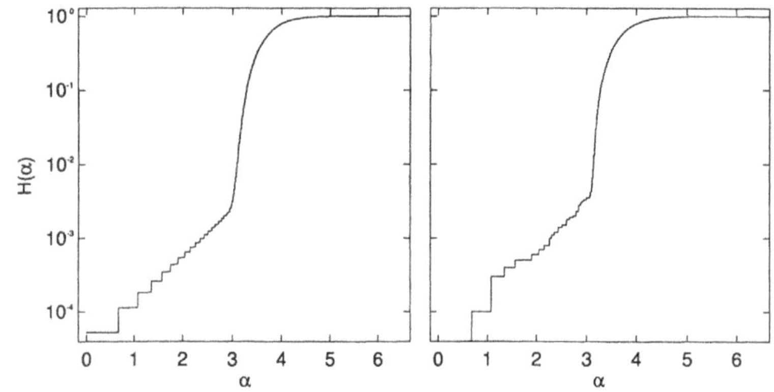

Figure 1: Distribution functions $H(\alpha)$ of scaling indices a. Left: Reference distribution function $H_{\text{ref}}(\alpha) = \overline{H_{\text{cal}}}(\alpha)$ as the empirical mean over 1320 calibration data sets of finite length T= 10000. Right: Distribution function $H_{\text{cal},i}$ of a single calibration data set. Notice the step-like behavior for c < 3 in both distribution functions.

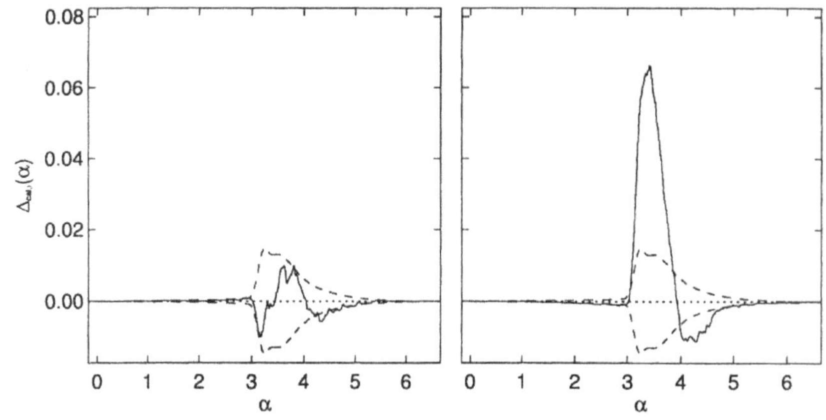

Figure 2: Deviation $\Delta_{\text{cal},i}(\alpha)$of a single distribution function $H_{\text{cal},i}(\alpha)$ from the reference distribution function $H_{\text{ref}}(\alpha)$.. Left: $\Delta_{\text{cal},i}(\alpha)$ for a single calibration time series. The dashed line indicates the lc contour of the calibration data sets used to calculate Hrer(c). Right: Aca,;(c for a time series generated with an i.i.d, random process of length T- 10000 with a binomial distribution B(182,0.55). The dashed line is the same 1σ contour as in the left panel.

therefore generically discrete (*cf.* (1)). In the left tail of H, points with small occupation numbers $N_{1,2}(Z(t))$ produce discrete steps which are clearly visible in Figure 1. The central part of the distribution appears to be continuous, however, since the corresponding occupation numbers are large.

The difference $\Delta(\alpha)$ of an individual si-edf H and H_{rer} is shown in Figure 2. In both cases H is computed from a simulated time series where the x(t) are independent and identically distributed random variables with a binomial distribution $B(n_b, \pi_b)$. The first case corresponds to the binomial model $(n_b = 200,\ \pi_b = 1/2)$, whereas in the second case we set $n_b = 182,\ \pi_b = 0.55$. This leaves the expectation value of the x(t)'s (approximately) unchanged, but it reduces their variance from 50 to 45. The empirical standard error of the Δ's calculated from the calibration data, $s_{\Delta,\mathrm{cal}}(\alpha) = \sqrt{(1/n)\sum_{i=1}^{n} \Delta_{\mathrm{cal},i}(\alpha)^2}$, is also plotted in Figure 2 for comparison. For $B(182, 0.55)$ a prominent deviation from zero can be found within the range $3 < \alpha < 4$, whereas for $\alpha > 4$ Δ is of the same order as $s_{\Delta,\mathrm{cal}}$. The partial maxima $M(0,\alpha)$., with lower with lower limit $\alpha_{\min} = 0$, are shown in Figure 3 for the same data sets. The notation $M(\alpha_{\min},\alpha)$ instead of $M(\alpha)$ indicates the interval over which the maximum is taken. The same notation will be adopted for the empirical error probabilities in (7), *e.g.*, $P_A = P_A(\alpha_{\min},\alpha_{\max})$. Figure 4 exhibits the deviation profiles CA and ca (with the preliminary choice $\gamma_A = \gamma_B = 2$) and, in the lower plot, the (empirical) pointwise profile crossing probabilities QA(CO and Qe(c). They are defined as the relative frequencies with whic

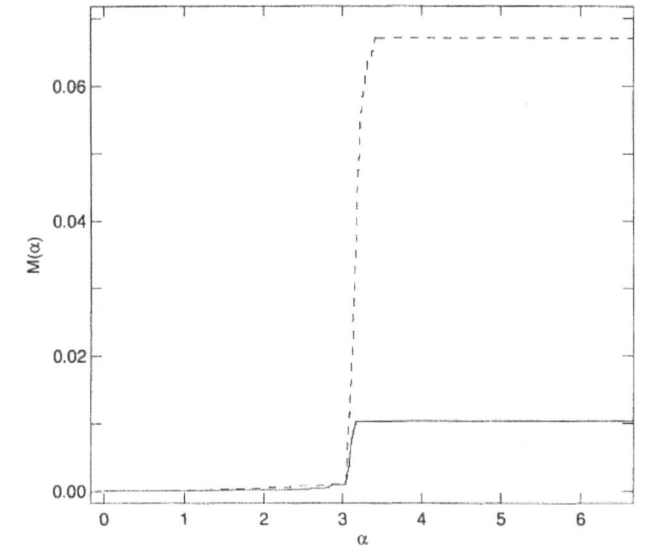

Figure 3: The solid line shows the partial maxima $M_{\mathrm{cal},i}(\alpha)$ for the case shown in the left panel of Figure 2. The dashed line represents the case shown in the right panel of Figure 2.

$M_{\mathrm{cal},i}(0,\alpha)$ exceeds the profile $c_{A,B}(\alpha)$ at a fixed value of c. The rather erratic behavior of these probabilities for small values of c is due to small occupation numbers $N_{1,2}(z(t))$. It prompts us to set $\alpha_{\min} = 3$ in Eq. (5), which approximates the "continuity onset" in Figure 1. "continuity onset" in Figure 1.

Figure 5 shows the (empirical) profile crossing probabilities $P_{A,B}(3, \alpha_{\max})$ as a function of $\alpha_{\max}$, for $\gamma = 2$ and $\gamma = 3$. In all cases $P_{A,B}(3, \alpha_{\max})$ is constant for $\alpha_{\max}$ larger than ≈ 3.5. Therefore $\alpha_{\max}$ is set to the (somewhat arbitrary) value 4. With this choice of $\alpha_{\min}$ and $\alpha_{\max}$, and with an error level of $\varepsilon = 0.05$, the γ's satisfying (7) are found to have the (approximate) values $\gamma_A = 3.42$, $\gamma_B = 2.94$. The deviation profiles C_{AB}, corresponding to these specifications are shown in Figure 6.

Similar considerations will be necessary in any application of the proposed testing procedure. In particular, since the asymptotic distribution of the test statistics (under H_0) is unknown, a sufficiently large pool of calibration time series is required in order to determine the -adjustment of the deviation profiles.

It might be interesting to mention that Ref. [9] discusses a concrete (real-world) example in which a similar, truncated form of Version A is used to detect non-random contributions in a random time series. In contrast to the detailed procedure proposed here, the procedure of [9] includes no adjustment of γ, and the profile $c_A(\alpha)$ is assumed $\mu(\alpha)$ $(\gamma = 1)$.

ENHANCING THE SIGNAL-TO-NOISE RATIO

Let us assume that a random null process is sporadically substituted or superimposed by some faint regular or deterministic signal. Is it possible to identify those subseries of the entire time series which contain the "deviant" non-random contributions? This section deals with the question whether those subseries can be found by selection procedures based on scaling indices. If this can be done, it is an attractive idea to construct tests of

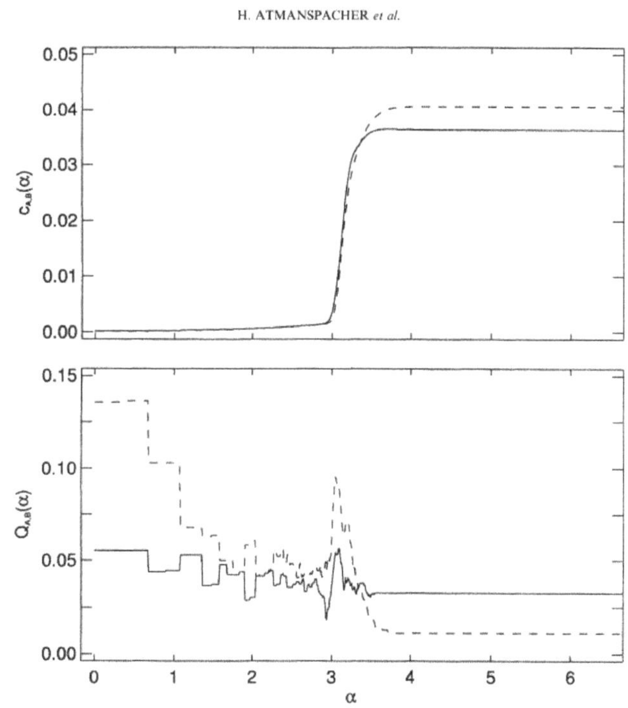

Figure 4: Upper panel: deviation profile $c(\alpha)$ for the two Versions (A) (dashed line) and (B) (solid line) of Section 2.2 with $\gamma = 2$.. Lower panel: the pointwise profile crossing probabilities Q_A (dashed line) and Q_B (solid line) are the relative frequencies with which $M_{\mathrm{cal},i}(\alpha)$ exceeds the deviation profile of the upper panel for a single value c.

the null hypothesis based on the selected subseries and study their statistical characteristics. Some preliminary steps in this direction are included at the end of this section. Details in this respect will be addressed in future work. Obviously there are other conceivable methods to detect deviations from randomness in a time series; e.g., any type of autocorrelation analysis or, equivalently, Fourier analysis. If one focuses on the selection of local subseries containing those deviations rather than a global characterization of them, wavelet techniques might be good candidates for alternative approaches. This, however, would be beyond the scope of the present paper. Our main purpose in this paper is to make a concrete proposal for a selection method based on scaling index distributions and to investigate, by simulation, whether it yields a higher signal-tonoise ratio in the selected subseries than in the original time series. In this context, the signal-to-noise

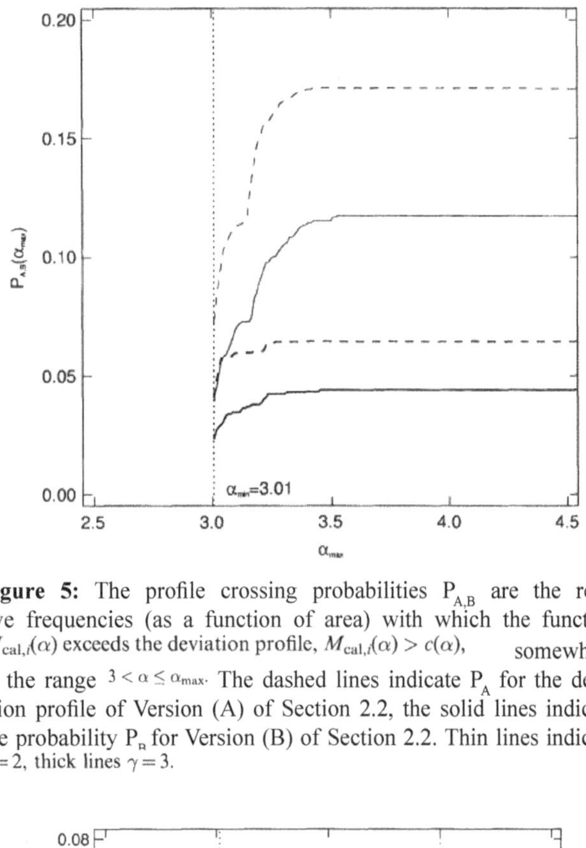

Figure 5: The profile crossing probabilities $P_{A,B}$ are the relative frequencies (as a function of area) with which the function $M_{cal,i}(\alpha)$ exceeds the deviation profile, $M_{cal,i}(\alpha) > c(\alpha)$, somewhere in the range $3 < \alpha \leq \alpha_{max}$. The dashed lines indicate P_A for the deviation profile of Version (A) of Section 2.2, the solid lines indicate the probability P_B for Version (B) of Section 2.2. Thin lines indicate $\gamma = 2$, thick lines $\gamma = 3$.

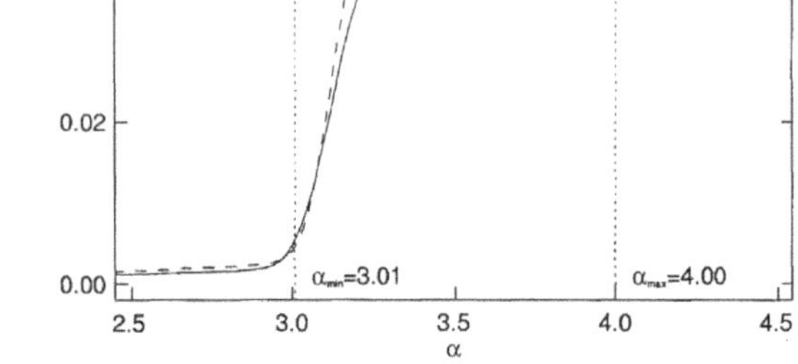

Figure 6: Deviation profiles CA(a) (dashed line) and cB(a) (solid line) according to Versions (A) and (B) of Section 2.2.

ratio is defined as the relative number of data points x(t) due to the non-random signal. Since non-random signals are basically expected to be associated with small scaling indices, the key idea is to select all data points x(t) whose scaling index $\alpha(t)$ falls below some threshold value A_1. In order to avoid the discreteness problems discussed in Section 2.3, a lower threshold value A_0 is required in addition. Since $\alpha(t)$ depends on the dtuple $z(t) = (x(t), \ldots, x(t+d-1))$ rather than $x(t)$, selecting a data point at time in principle implies selecting the subsequent d-1 data points as well. Therefore the selected subseries consists of data points x(t) at instants belonging to a set S which can be formally defined as

$$S = \cup_{k=0}^{d-1} S_k, \text{ where}$$
$$S_0 = \{t: A_0 \leq \alpha(t) \leq A_1\},$$
$$S_k = \{t+k: t \in S_0\}(1 \leq k \leq d-1). \quad (10)$$

Depending on the nature of the non-random contribution to be detected, it may be advantageous to consider only subsets of S. The choice of the threshold values is crucial and not obvious. For our purposes it will be conceived as depending both on H_{ref} and the si-edf H of the time series {x(t)} under study. If the difference $\Delta(\alpha)$ attains its maximum at $\alpha = \alpha_+^*$ then it is expected that most of the a values corresponding to a non-random signal occur at $\alpha < \alpha_+^*$. The following strategy is proposed to fix this range: Define A_0 resp. A_1 as the minimal resp. maximal $\alpha < \alpha_+^*$ at which

$$\Delta(\alpha) = 0.05\Delta(\alpha_+^*) \quad \text{resp.} \quad \Delta(\alpha) = 0.75\Delta(\alpha_+^*).$$

Modifications of this strategy may be appropriate if A_0 falls below the continuity onset of H_{ref} or if A_1 is larger than the median of H_{ref}, say d^*. For the examples to be presented below, the fractions 0.05 and 0.75 have been found to produce the largest signal-to-noise enhancement. To study the performance of the selection procedure, auxiliary time series are generated according to the binomial model of Section 2.3. These auxiliary time series are then perturbed by "signals" in such a way that at randomly selected times $\tau_1 < \cdots < \tau_v$ the segment $x(\tau_j)$, $x(\tau_j+1), \ldots, x(\tau_j+L-1)$ of $\{x(t)\}$ is replaced by some L-tuple $\xi = (\xi_0, \ldots, \xi_{L-1})$ fixed ad hoc (For -$\tau_{i+1} - \tau_i < L$, each segment is overwritten to the extent to which it overlaps with the subsequent segment.) The perturbed data series are then used as the time series {x(t)} under study. Within this setting, the signal-to-noise ratio is defined as #R/T for the full time series, and as #RA S/#S for the subseries {x(t): E S}. Here R denotes the set of all instants for which the original x value has been replaced by a ξ value.

Table I summarizes the results for various tuples ξ of different length and form. Each entry is based on 20 time series generated as described above, with the same embedding dimension d and radii $r_{1,2}$ as in Section 2.3. The largest enhancements of the signal-to-noise ratio, up to a factor of 19, are found when $L \geq d(=4)$ and when the values ξ are close to the expectation value 100 of the B(200,1/2) distribution. This observation may be heuristically explained as follows.

Suppose that L-d, and that $\xi = (\xi_0, \ldots, \xi_{d-1})$ gives rise to a scaling index of

$$\alpha = \frac{\log N_2 - \log N_1}{\log r_2 - \log r_1}, \text{ where}$$

$$N_{1,2} = \#\{t : |z(t) - \xi| \le r_{1,2}\},$$

where the z(t)'s are constructed from the unperturbed time series. Let $\alpha' = \alpha + \delta\alpha$ and $N'_{1,2} = N_{1,2} + \delta N_{1,2}$ denote the corresponding quantities for the perturbed series in which a (small) number $\nu = fT$ of tuples ξ replaces the original z tuples at randomly selected times. It is easy to see that $\delta\alpha \le 0$, , such that the scaling indices always decrease under such replacements. A rough quantitative estimate of that shift can be obtained on noting that a fraction f of the (T-$N_{1,2}$) tuples z(t) outside the ball of radius $r_{1,2}$ around ξ is expected to be replaced by ξ-tuples. This gives the estimate $\delta N_{1,2} \sim f(T - N_{1,2})$, or provided that $[f/(1-f)]T/N_{1,2}$ is sufficiently small. Therefore, the (negative) shift c increases for decreasing N_1. At first sight this seems to contradict the claim that the best enhancement is achieved for ξ values close to 100, where N_1 is large (and $\alpha \approx d^*$). However, the statistical variability of $\Delta(\alpha)$ decreases sharply with decreasing α in the left wing of $H(\alpha)$. On the other hand, in rarefied regions of the embedding space, where N_1 is relatively small, the (expected) c shift is large, so that α' tends to fall below the threshold A_0.

$$\delta\alpha \sim \log \frac{1 - f + fT/N_2}{1 - f + fT/N_1} \Big/ \log \frac{r_2}{r_1}$$
$$\sim -\frac{f}{1-f}\left(\frac{T}{N_1} - \frac{T}{N_2}\right) \Big/ \log \frac{r_2}{r_1}, \quad (11)$$

The perturbed time series have a mean and standard deviation different from that of the unperturbed series. However, the differences are too small to be easily detected by a t-test or a (variance ratio) F-test. What happens if these tests are applied to the selected subseries? Table II shows the number of subseries within the 20 time series of Table I for which the hypothesis is rejected that the mean and the variance are equal to those of the binomial model. These results can be compared to those for subseries of the same length, which are selected randomly (i.e., not by the described procedure) from the respective perturbed time series. While the numbers for those randomly selected subseries for which the null hypothesis is rejected are consistent with the required type I error $\varepsilon = 0.05$, the numbers for the subseries selected by the described procedure significantly exceed this type I error except for the t-test and tuples with values close to the mean of the unperturbed series. It has to be noted, however, that the null distributions of the test statistics for the selected subseries generally are different from the usual ones. To obtain a fair comparison further simulations are required to determine appropriate reference (null) distributions.

Table I: Results of the selection procedure for random time series in which v=25 sequences of x-values have been replaced by the ξ-tuples given in column 1. For each type of ξ-tuple N_{all}=20 independent time series have been generated. N_{test} is the number of time series for which the test rejects H_0, hence indicating non-random contributions. N_{match} is the number of those elements in the selected subseries matching (in both time and amplitude) with elements of the inserted ξ-tuples. The medians and the standard deviations of N_{match} are listed. R_{sn} is the signal-to-noise ratio for the selected subseries and the total time series, respectively. For the selected subseries the medians and the standard deviations are listed as well

L- tuple $\{\xi_0, \xi_1, \ldots, \xi_{L-1}\}$	N_{test} $N_{all} = 20$	N_{match} median ± S.D.	R_{sn} (selected) median ± S.D.	R_{sn} (total)
[100, 100, 100]	13	49 ± 6.3	0.079 ± 0.027	0.0075
[100, 100, 100, 100]	20	86 ± 2.9	0.191 ± 0.033	0.0100
[100, 100, 100, 100, 100]	20	111 ± 2.3	0.240 ± 0.033	0.0125
[107, 107, 107]	2	1 ± 12.3	0.016 ± 0.081	0.0075
[107, 107, 107, 107]	6	79 ± 30.2	0.039 ± 0.236	0.0100
[107, 107, 107, 107, 107]	20	105 ± 5.0	0.135 ± 0.291	0.0125
[101, 99, 98, 96]	16	86 ± 7.6	0.128 ± 0.046	0.0100
[101, 98, 101, 98]	17	83 ± 3.6	0.137 ± 0.030	0.0100
[107, 99, 101, 103]	5	41 ± 27.6	0.032 ± 0.022	0.0100

Tables III and IV show corresponding results for random time series according to the binomial model in which the elements have been reordered in such a way that the same -tuples as used for Tables I and II are created, however without introducing new values of x(t). In contrast to the replacement procedure discussed above, such a reordering keeps the state distribution invariant but may change the distribution of transition probabilities between states considerably. For each type of tuple, 20 independent time series have been generated. The same selection procedure as for Tables I and II has been applied. As in case of replacement, reordering shows that the selection of subseries with small c can lead to an enhancement of the signal-to-noise ratio up to a factor of 21.

Table II: Results of t-tests and F-tests applied to selected subseries. N_{test} is the same as in Table I. P_t is the number of subseries selected by scaling indices for which the hypothesis of no mean shift is rejected (t-test, two-sided, $\varepsilon = 0.05$). PF is the number of subseries selected by scaling indices for which the hypothesis of no variance change is rejected (F-test, two-sided, $\varepsilon = 0.05$). P_t (random) and P_F (random) denote the corresponding numbers for randomly selected subseries

L-tuple $\{\xi_0, \xi_1, \ldots, \xi_{L-1}\}$	N_{test} $N_{all} = 20$	P_t	P_F	P_t (random)	P_F (random)
[100, 100, 100]	13	4	20	1	1
[100, 100, 100, 100]	20	1	20	1	2
[100, 100, 100, 100, 100]	20	0	20	2	2
[107, 107, 107]	2	5	17	1	0
[107, 107, 107, 107]	6	13	20	1	0
[107, 107, 107, 107, 107]	20	15	19	0	0
[101, 99, 98, 96]	16	18	20	1	0
[101, 98, 101, 98]	17	3	20	0	2
[107, 99, 101, 103]	5	11	20	1	0

Table III: Results of the selection procedure for binomial model time series which have been reordered to generate 25 ξ-tuples given in column 1. N_{tes}t, N_{ail}, N_{match}, and R_{sn} as in Table

L-tuple $\{\xi_0, \xi_1, \ldots, \xi_{L-1}\}$	N_{test} $N_{all} = 20$	N_{match} median ± S.D.	R_{sn} (selected) median ± S.D.	R_{sn} (total)
[100, 100, 100]	6	48 ± 13.3	0.086 ± 0.032	0.0075
[100, 100, 100, 100]	19	84 ± 3.9	0.216 ± 0.028	0.0100
[100, 100, 100, 100, 100]	20	109 ± 2.7	0.260 ± 0.027	0.0125
[107, 107, 107]	2	1 ± 16.9	0.004 ± 0.009	0.0075
[107, 107, 107, 107]	6	81 ± 23.3	0.070 ± 0.101	0.0100
[107, 107, 107, 107, 107]	20	106 ± 2.4	0.117 ± 0.187	0.0125
[101, 99, 98, 96]	12	83 ± 4.0	0.131 ± 0.063	0.0100
[101, 98, 101, 98]	15	80 ± 23.0	0.141 ± 0.055	0.0100
[107, 99, 101, 103]	2	43 ± 32.0	0.027 ± 0.042	0.0100

Table IV: Results of runs tests for the reordered time series of Table III. P_{total} ($P_{selected}$) is the number of total (selected) reordered time series for which the independence hypothesis (no temporal order) is rejected ($\varepsilon = 0.05$)

L-tuple $\{\xi_0, \xi_1, \ldots, \xi_{L-1}\}$	N_{test} $N_{all} = 20$	P_{total}	$P_{selected}$
[100, 100, 100]	6	3	9
[100, 100, 100, 100]	19	1	6
[100, 100, 100, 100, 100]	20	1	7
[107, 107, 107]	2	1	9
[107, 107, 107, 107]	6	4	11
[107, 107, 107, 107, 107]	20	8	12
[101, 99, 98, 96]	12	0	9
[101, 98, 101, 98]	15	2	19
[107, 99, 101, 103]	2	1	12

The reordered time series has the same state distribution as the original time series but different transition probabilities. In particular, the elements x(t) are statistically dependent. Therefore, sequential correlations (order) are introduced in the generated time series. These correlations are checked with a runs test (Tab. IV). Comparing P_{total} and $P_{selected}$ in Table IV shows that the runs test is more sensitive when applied to the selected subseries of the reordered time series rather than to the whole reordered series. Of course, the same qualifying remarks as made above concerning t- and F-tests apply with respect to $P_{selected}$. Comparing the whole reordered time series to the original random time series, only tuples of the type [107,107,107, 107,107] lead to a significant difference. For all other types of tuples, P_{total} in Table IV shows no significant difference from the original random time series.

DISCUSSION

There are two ways in which the test proposed in Section 2.2 depends on the null process. (i) It is not distribution free, in the sense that the distribution of the test statistics is in general different for different underlying null distributions D_0 (ii) Even the test statistics itself depends, via the deviation profiles $c(\alpha)$, on the assumed model (for the null process) used for the generation of the auxiliary time series. As a consequence of (i), the γ-adjustments have to be computed anew (on the basis of the given calibration data) if the test is to be applied to another null process. Further massive computation is needed for the construction of the deviation profiles.

The null processes considered in our examples are all of the i.i.d, type. It is expected that qualitatively similar results would be obtained for state (null) distributions different from the binomial distribution B(200,1/2) (our main example), provided they are not too long-tailed. The situation must be more complex with null processes exhibiting statistical dependencies between states, e.g., ARMA processes containing deterministic components.

The power of the test depends on the special type of deviation from the null hypothesis. If the process {x(t)} under study is i.i.d, and only changes of the state distribution of {x(t)} are considered, there are well-known tests which are more efficient than the one proposed here. Since $H(\alpha)$ is invariant under translations of the form $x(t) \rightarrow x(t) +$ constant, the test has no power at all against mean shifts in the state distribution. It does have some power against scale dilations (variance changes), which cannot compete, however, with the power of the (variance ratio) F-test which is especially tailored to deviations of that kind. For instance, for time series generated according to the binomial model of Section 2.3 with B(193, 0.482), corresponding to a reduction of the variance by 3.63%, our test rejects the null hypothesis in about 20% of the data series, whereas the F-test (one-sided, $\varepsilon = 0.05$) has a rejection rate of about 50%.

More interesting situations arise if the time series is not stationary and/or its elements are correlated, particularly when this is the case only sporadically within the observed segment. Corresponding types of deviations can be studied with random time series (of the i.i.d, type) modified by various kinds of perturbations at randomly selected instants (or intervals). For example, tuples of L subsequent x-values may be replaced by some ad hoc fixed L-tuple ξ, or the time series may be reordered in such a way that the ξ's appear at randomly selected instants (or intervals).

As can be seen from Tables I and III, the test proposed in Section 2.2 is the more sensitive the less "complex" the non-random process is. For instance, a deterministic process with a small number of different states around the median of the x(t)'s of the random (null) process with a simple temporal order of the tuples results in a high detection rate. The test works equally well when the empirical distribution of the perturbed x(t)'s is the same as for the unperturbed ones, i.e., when the perturbation consists in a reordering of the time series. If the perturbation consists of a replacement by a fixed L-tuple ξ, the power tends to be the higher the closer the ξ-values are to the median of the x(t)'s. This may be contrasted with the behavior of standard tests which often react sensitively to outliers but draw little information from data points close to the center of the state distribution.

Summing up, the test proposed in this paper is well suited for time series in which (1) states generated by a deterministic process with low complexity are to be separated from random elements, and (2) the deterministic elements are close to the median of the random elements. Within the investigated time series, subseries can be selected for which the signal-to-noise ratio is enhanced compared to the total time series.

REFERENCES

1. Grassberger, P., Badii, R. and Politi, A. (1988). Scaling laws for invariant measures on hyperbolic and nonhyperbolic attractors. J. Stat. Phys., 51, 135-178.
2. Mandelbrot, B. B. (1974). Intermittent turbulence in selfsimilar cascades: divergence of high moments and dimension of the carrier. J. Fluid Mech., 62, 331-358.
3. Frisch, U. and Parisi, G. (1985). On the singularity structure of fully developed turbulence. In: Turbulence and Predictability in Geophysical Fluid Dynamics and Climate Dynamics, Eds. Ghil, M., Benzi, R. and Parisi, G., North Holland, New York, pp. 84-88.
4. Halsey, T. C., Jensen, M. H., Kadanoff, L. P., Procaccia, I. and Shraiman, B. I. (1986). Fractal measures and their singularities: the characterization of strange sets. Phys. Rev. A, 33, 1141 1151.
5. Paladin, G. and Vulpiani, A. (1987). Anomalous scaling laws in multifractal objects. Phys. Rep., 156, 147-225.
6. Falconer, K. (1990). Fractal Geometry, Mathematical Foundations and Applications. Wiley, New York.
7. Atmanspacher, H., Scheingraber, H. and Wiedenmann, G. (1989). Determination off(c0 for a limited random point set. Phys. Rev. A, 40, 3954-3963.
8. Atmanspacher, H., Wiedenmann, G. and Amann, A. (1995). Descartes revisited: the endo/exo distinction and its relevance for the study of complex systems. Complexity, 1(3), 15-21.
9. Atmanspacher, H., B6sch, H., Boller, E., Nelson, R. D. and Scheingraber, H. (1999). Deviations from physical randomness due to human agent intention? Chaos, Solitons, and Fractals, 10, 935-952.
10. Rith, C. and Morrill, G. (1997). Texture detection and texture discrimination with anisotropic scaling indices. J. Opt. Soc. Am. A, 14, 3208-3215.
11. Wiedenmann, G., Scheingraber, H. and Voges, W. (1997). Source detection with the scaling index method. In: Data Analysis in Astronomy V, Eds. di Gesu, V. et al., World Scientific, Singapore, pp. 203-211.
12. Packard, N. H., Crutchfield, J. P., Farmer, J. D. and Shaw, R. S. (1980). Geometry from a time series. Phys. Rev. Lett., 45, 712- 716.
13. Theiler, J., Eubank, S., Longtin, A., Galdrikian, B. and Farmer, J. D. (1992). Testing for nonlinearity in time series: the method of surrogate data. Physica D, 58, 77-94.
14. Theiler, J., Linsay, P. S. and Rubin, D. M. (1993). Detecting nonlinearity in data with long coherence times. In: Time Series Prediction, Eds. Weigend, A. S. and Gershenfeld, N. A. Addison-Wesley, Reading, pp. 429-455.

CHAPTER 11

TIME-DEPENDENT STATISTICAL ANALYSIS OF WIDE-AREA TIME-SYNCHRONIZED DATA

A. R. Messina, P. Esquivel, and F. Lezama

Graduate Studies Program in Electrical Engineering, The Center for Research and Advanced Studies, Avenida Científica 1145, Colonia El Bajío, Guadalajara, 45015 Jalisco, Mexico

ABSTRACT

Characterization of spatial and temporal changes in the dynamic patterns of a nonstationary process is a problem of great theoretical and practical importance. On-line monitoring of large-scale power systems by means of time-synchronized Phasor Measurement Units (PMUs) provides the opportunity to analyze and characterize inter-system oscillations. Wide-area measurement sets, however, are often relatively large, and may contain phenomena with differing temporal scales. Extracting from these measurements the relevant dynamics is a difficult problem. As the number of observations of real events continues to increase, statistical techniques are needed to help identify relevant temporal dynamics from noise or random effects in measured data. In this paper, a statistically based, data-driven framework that integrates the use of wavelet-based EOF analysis and a sliding window-based method is proposed to identify and extract, in near-real-time, dynamically independent spatiotemporal patterns from time synchronized data. The method deals with the information in space and time simultaneously, and allows direct tracking and characterization of the nonstationary time-frequency dynamics of oscillatory processes. The efficiency and accuracy of the developed procedures for extracting localized information of power system behavior from time-synchronized phasor measurements of a real event in Mexico is assessed.

INTRODUCTION

Phenomena observed in power system oscillatory dynamics are diverse and complex. Remotely sensed measured data are known to exhibit noisy, nonstationary fluctuations resulting primarily from small magnitude, random load changes in load, driven by low-scale motions or nonlinear trends originating from control actions or other changes in the system. Extracting from these sets indices that capture significant spatial and temporal dynamics is very challenging [1–4].

Citation: A. R. Messina, P. Esquivel, and F. Lezama, "Time-Dependent Statistical Analysis of Wide-Area Time-Synchronized Data," Mathematical Problems in Engineering, vol. 2010, Article ID 751659, 17 pages, 2010. doi:10.1155/2010/751659

Recent improvements in wide-area monitoring schemes have led to renewed investigation of nonlinear and nonstationary behavior of system oscillations [2, 3]. In the last decade, extensive research has been carried out for developing modal extraction algorithms that can accurately monitor transient response. Multivariate statistical data analysis techniques offer a powerful tool for analyzing power system response from measured data [1]. By seeing the snapshots of system data as a realization of random field generated by some kind of stochastic process, data-driven statistical can be applied to investigate propagating phenomena of different spatial scales and temporal frequencies [5–7]. Existing analysis methods, however, do not take into account the multiscale nature of measured system dynamics arising from events occurring at different locations with different localization in time and frequency [6, 7]. This, in turn, may obscure visualization of transient wide-area phenomena or limit the ability of the method to deal with data measured at different sampling rates or containing missing information.

Analysis and characterization of time-synchronized system measurements requires mathematical tools that are adaptable to the varying system conditions, accurate and fast, while reducing the complexity of the data to make them comprehensible and useful for real-time decisions. This is particularly true in the study of large datasets of dynamic processes whose energy changes with time or frequency.

In this paper, a statistically based, data-driven framework that integrates the use of a wavelet-based empirical orthogonal function (EOF) analysis and the method of snapshots is proposed to identify and extract dynamically independent spatio-temporal patterns from time-synchronized data. Extensions to current approaches to estimating propagating and standing features in near-real-time that can be associated with observed or measured data are discussed and numerical issues are addressed.

The procedure allows identification of the dominant spatial and temporal patterns in a complex dataset and is particularly well suited for the study the temporal evolution of critical modal parameters. It is shown that, in addition to providing spatial and temporal information, the method improves the ability of conventional correlation analysis to capture temporal events and gives a quantitative result for both the amplitude and phase of motion, and modal content, which are essential in the interpretation and characterization of transient processes in power systems.

The efficiency and accuracy of the developed procedures for capturing the temporal evolution of the modal content of data from time-synchronized phasor measurements of a real event in Mexico is assessed. Results show that the proposed method can provide accurate estimation of nonstationary effects, modal frequency, time-varying modes shapes, and time instants of intermittent or irregular transient behavior associated with abrupt changes in system topology or operating conditions in a near-real-time setting.

STATISTICAL CHARACTERIZATION OF MEASURED DATA

Empirical Orthogonal Function Analysis

Time-synchronized phasor measurements collected by PMUs or other dynamic recorders can be interpreted conveniently in terms of statistical models involving both temporal and spatial variability [1–4]. When data is available at multiple locations, a spatio-temporal model is required that represents system behavior. Figure 1shows a conceptual representation of PMU data collected at different spatial locations.

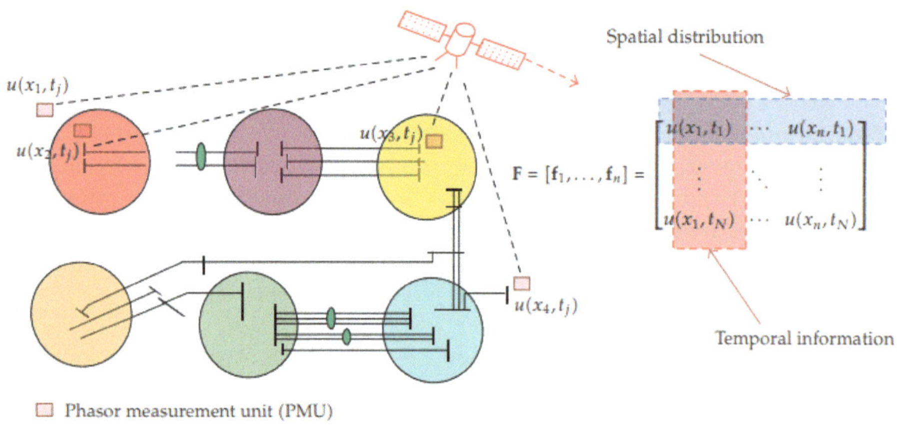

Figure 1: Visualization of PMU data in terms of spatial and temporal information.

Assume, in order to introduce the more general ideas that follow, that measured data is available at n spatial locations measurement locations defined by $x_j, j = 1, \ldots, n,$ at N instants in time, $t_k, k = 1, \ldots, N$. Let $u(x_j, t_k)$. Let $u(x_j, t_k)$ be a space-time scalar field representing a time trace, where x_j, is a set of spatial variables i.e., measurement locations on a space Ω_k, and t_k, is the time at which the observations are made.

Using this notation, the set of data can be represented by an N×n-dimension ensemble observation matrix, F(x, t), of the form

$$\mathbf{F}(\mathbf{x}, t) = [\mathbf{f}_1(\mathbf{x}_1, t) \;\; \mathbf{f}_2(\mathbf{x}_2, t) \;\; \cdots \;\; \mathbf{f}_n(\mathbf{x}_n, t)] = \begin{bmatrix} \overline{u}(x_1, t_1) & \overline{u}(x_2, t_1) & \cdots & \overline{u}(x_n, t_1) \\ \overline{u}(x_1, t_2) & \overline{u}(x_2, t_2) & \cdots & \overline{u}(x_n, t_2) \\ \vdots & \vdots & \ddots & \vdots \\ \overline{u}(x_1, t_N) & \overline{u}(x_2, t_N) & \cdots & \overline{u}(x_n, t_N) \end{bmatrix}. \tag{2.1}$$

In this formulation, each column corresponds to the system response at a specific time, and can represent the system response to a single event or represent an ensemble of time responses to multiple events measured at a single location.

Empirical orthogonal function EOF analysis provides a basis for the modal decomposition of an ensemble of data in terms of the smallest possible number of basic modes or proper orthogonal modes POMs, most energetic global functions [5–8]. This decomposition is of the form [5]

$$\hat{\mathbf{F}}(\mathbf{x}, t) = \sum_{i=1}^{m} \mathbf{a}_i \boldsymbol{\varphi}_i^*(x), \tag{2.2}$$

where a_i are the temporal amplitudes or eigenvectors, $\varphi_i(x)$ are the spatial component maps or eigenfunctions, and m are the statistical modes or POMs, where $\mathbf{a}_i = \mathbf{F}(\mathbf{x}, t)\boldsymbol{\varphi}_i$. Each of these maps represents a standing oscillation, and the temporal coefficients, a_i, represent how this pattern oscillates through time [9–14].

The temporal and spatial components are calculated from the eigenvectors and eigenfunctions of the covariance matrix

$$\mathbf{C} = \frac{1}{N}\mathbf{F}^T(\mathbf{x},t)\mathbf{F}(\mathbf{x},t). \tag{2.3}$$

In standard real-EOF analysis, matrix C is real and symmetric and possesses a set of orthogonal eigenvectors with positive real eigenvalues. The vectors $\varphi_i(x)$ are called empirical orthogonal functions EOFs; the map associated with each eigenvector represents a pattern which is statistically independent of the others and spatially orthogonal to them.

Two important properties of EOFs are that the spatial distributions are orthogonal and their time series are uncorrelated. The method accounts for spatial and temporal changes and can be used to extract dynamic patterns from measured data. Measured data, however, may exhibit quite different dynamics at each system location or exhibit abrupt changes in modal quantities that cannot be captured using existing stationary models [11].

Wavelet-Based EOF Analysis

In real-world applications data are multiscale due to events occurring at different locations with different localization in time and frequency. To address the problem of multiscale modeling in data, a wavelet-based EOF approach has been developed. In this approach, the empirical orthogonal functions of the wavelet coefficients are computed at each scale and then combined the results at relevant scales. The approach is referred to as wavelet-based EOF analysis [15, 16] and involves three main steps:

- computing the wavelet decomposition for each column in the data matrix,
- computing the covariance matrix of wavelet coefficients for each scale of interest, and combining the results at the dominant scales of interest,
- extracting dynamic features from the selected scales

Appendix A briefly summarizes wavelet analysis in the context of the proposed formulation. In what follows we review the theory behind EOF decomposition and present some results and extensions to conventional analysis to treat changes in space and temporal variability.

A complex, near-real-time formulation with the ability to resolve localized information is then proposed.

NEAR-REAL TIME EOF ANALYSIS

As it was highlighted in the previous section, conventional EOF analysis assumes stationarity of the underlying dynamic process and is therefore not suitable for an on-line implementation. In addition, such an approach, can only provide information about standing waves and cannot isolate portions of the phenomena in which dynamic changes take place [1].

In order to overcome the above limitations, a sliding window-based method is used to systematically analyze the observational data in near-real-time. This allows to isolate and extract the portions of data where oscillations are present and improves numerical efficiency and accuracy.

Time-Dependent Covariance Matrix

Assume that $\mathbf{f}_k(x) = [f_k(x_1), f_k(x_2), \ldots, f_k(x_n)]$ denotes a sequence of observations, collected at time instants t_k, to $k = 1,2,\ldots,\infty$, evenly spread throughout the time period, where x_n is set of spatial variables measurement locations.

A sliding window-based approach has been combined with EOF analysis to resolve localized information. In this approach, a sliding window frame of fixed size, say τ, is shifted regularly throughout the data span from the beginning of the record to the end of the data as shown in Figure 2. The analysis window is then slid the same distance repeatedly and the covariance matrix is computed recursively. It should be stressed that τ can range from a single sample to the entire length of the record.

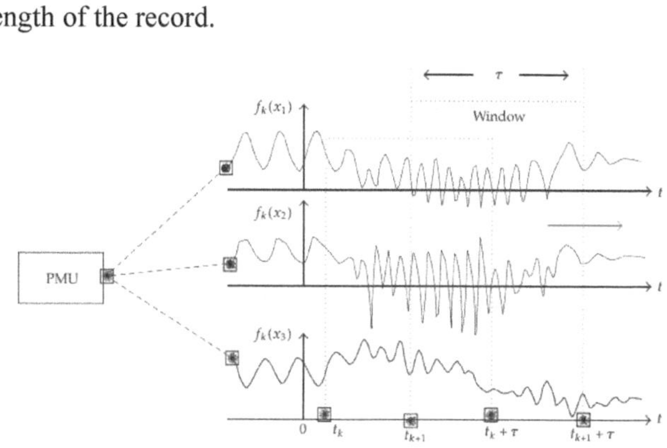

Figure 2: Visualization of PMU data in terms of spatial and temporal information.

Referring to Figure 2, let matrix $C_k(x)$ be the covariance matrix of size $\tau \times n$, where τ is the window size, n is the number of sensors or PMUs, and k indicates the time instant at which the response matrix is computed.

More formally, given a set of available sample time series, the temporal autocorrelation matrix, C_k, of $F_k(x)$ extending over a window length is defined as

$$\mathbf{C}_k \triangleq \frac{\mathbf{F}_k^H(x)\mathbf{F}_k(x)}{k} = \frac{1}{k}\sum_{i=1}^{k}\mathbf{f}_i^H(x)\mathbf{f}_i(x), \tag{3.1a}$$

or, equivalently

$$\mathbf{C}_k \triangleq \frac{\mathbf{F}_k(x)\mathbf{F}_k^H(x)}{k} = \frac{1}{k}\sum_{i=1}^{k}\mathbf{f}_i(x)\mathbf{f}_i(x)^H, \tag{3.1b}$$

where, in the above, the covariance matrix can be real or complex.

In our formulation, matrix C_k, is a positive semidefinite matrix of size n × n, and possesses a set of complex time-dependent orthogonal eigenvectors, $\varphi_i(t),\ i = 1,\ldots,n$, that capture propagating features. Extensions of this approach to consider the case where the autocorrelation matrix is nonintegrable are discussed in [17, 18]. This is, however, not considered here.

An interesting and useful interpretation of the covariance matrix can be obtained by rewriting 3.1a as

$$kC_k = \sum_{i=1}^{k-1} \mathbf{f}_i(x)\mathbf{f}_i^H(x) + \mathbf{f}_k(x)\mathbf{f}_k^H(x). \tag{3.2}$$

Now if we let $C_{k-1} = (1/(k-1)) \sum_{i=1}^{k-1} \mathbf{f}_i(x)\mathbf{f}_i(x)^H$, we can write

$$C_k = \frac{k-1}{k} C_{k-1} + \frac{1}{k} \mathbf{f}_k(x)\mathbf{f}_k^H(x). \tag{3.3}$$

This analysis suggests that the covariance matrix at time step k can be computed recursively using information from both, the previous time step (k – 1) and the current measurement using only elementary operations [19]. The stationarity test for the recursive covariance matrix can be made to demonstrate the stationarity of the dataset [20].

Similar to the previous development, it can be shown that for a fixed window size, τ, (3.1a) and (3.1b) can be rewritten as C_k

$$C_k = \frac{\tau-1}{\tau} C_{k-1} + \frac{1}{\tau} \mathbf{f}_k(x)\mathbf{f}_k^H(x). \tag{3.4}$$

Equation (3.4) provides an efficient method to approximate the time-dependent covariance matrix: since the method is based on local information the technique is wellsuited for real-time applications. The selection of an optimal window size is an important but difficult problem and will be addressed in future research. In the analysis of highly nonstationary signals, large values of τ may obscure the analysis of temporal changes occurring at specific segments of the observed record. As discussed in our numerical simulations, short-width windows provide improved localized information but result in enhanced computational effort. We have found that, the best estimate for the autocorrelation matrix C can be obtained using the averaged two-point correlation function [5].

Complex Formulation

In an effort to extend standard real-EOF analysis to deal with propagating phenomena a complex formulation is adopted. Here, the real part is augmented with an imaginary obtained from the Hilbert transform of each time series. Refer to Esquivel and Messina for more details [11, 21, 22].

Assume then that $F_k = [F_R + jF_I]_k$ is a complex matrix with $j = \sqrt{-1}$, where the subscripts R, I, indicate the real and imaginary vectors. Under these assumptions, the autocorrelation matrix C_k in (3.1a) and (3.1b) [11, 23] becomes

$$\mathbf{F}_k\mathbf{F}_k^H = \left[\mathbf{F}_R\mathbf{F}_R^T + \mathbf{F}_I\mathbf{F}_I^T\right]_k + j\left[\mathbf{F}_I\mathbf{F}_R^T - \mathbf{F}_R\mathbf{F}_I^T\right]_k,$$

$$\mathbf{F}_k^H\mathbf{F}_k = \left[\mathbf{F}_R^T\mathbf{F}_R + \mathbf{F}_I^T\mathbf{F}_I\right]_k + j\left[\mathbf{F}_R^T\mathbf{F}_I - \mathbf{F}_I^T\mathbf{F}_R\right]_k. \tag{3.5}$$

Given a model of the form (3.5), it is straightforward to show that $C_R = C_R^T$ is a symmetrical matrix, and that C_I is an asymmetric matrix or hemisymmetric matrix, that is, $C_I^T = -C_I$. Since the symmetrical matrix is a particular case of the Hermitian matrix, all of its eigenvectors are real; the elements of the asymmetrical matrix are all purely imaginary and its eigenvectors are complex conjugate. Note that the bases for the complex autocorrelation matrix C_k, are now defined as $\varphi_R(x)$ for the real part and $\varphi_I(x)$ for the imaginary part.

Appendix B contains further discussion of this subject.

Propagating Features

Many power system phenomena derive from nonlinear interactions between traveling waves of different spatial scales and temporal frequencies. This section extends the developed model to detect propagating phenomena in nonstationary processes.

Once the spatial eigenvectors associated with the real and imaginary part of C are calculated, the original field can be approximated by a spatio-temporal model [4, 8, 10]. Consider a field f_k composed of standing and traveling components, denoted by f_{swc}, f_{twc} of the form

$$\mathbf{f}_k = [\mathbf{f}_{swc} + \mathbf{f}_{twc}]_k. \tag{3.6}$$

From EOF analysis [11], the complex field can be expressed as the complex expansion

$$[\mathbf{f}_{swc}]_k = \left[\sum_{i=1}^{p} \mathbf{R}_{R(i)}(t)\mathbf{S}_{R(i)}(x)\cos(\omega_{R(i)}t)\right]_k,$$

$$[\mathbf{f}_{twc}]_k = \left[\sum_{i=1}^{q} \mathbf{R}_{I(i)}(t)\mathbf{S}_{I(i)}(x)\cos(\omega_{I(i)}t + \mathbf{K}_{I(i)}x + \pi)\right]_k, \tag{3.7}$$

where R, S are the temporal and spatial amplitude functions, respectively, and ω, K are the frequency functions and wave component to be determined.

Let now the complex field (3.6) be expanded in terms of a truncated EOF basis of p and q modes as [12]

$$\hat{\mathbf{f}}_k = \left[\sum_{i=1}^{p} \mathbf{A}_{R(i)}(t)\boldsymbol{\varphi}_{R(i)}^H(x) + j\sum_{i=1}^{q} \mathbf{A}_{I(i)}(t)\boldsymbol{\varphi}_{I(i)}^H(x)\right]_k, \tag{3.8}$$

where the complex, time-dependent coefficients, $\mathbf{A}_{R(i)}(t)$ and $\mathbf{A}_{I(i)}(t)$ are given by

$$\mathbf{A}_{R(i)} = \left[\mathbf{f}\boldsymbol{\varphi}_{R(i)}(x)\right]_k, \qquad \mathbf{A}_{I(i)} = \left[\mathbf{f}\boldsymbol{\varphi}_{I(i)}(x)\right]_k. \tag{3.9}$$

$$\hat{\mathbf{f}}_k = \left[\sum_{i=1}^{p} \mathbf{R}_{R(i)}(t)\mathbf{S}_{R(i)}(x)e^{j(\boldsymbol{\theta}_{R(i)}+\boldsymbol{\varphi}_{R(i)})}\right]_k + \left[\sum_{i=1}^{q} \mathbf{R}_{I(i)}(t)\mathbf{S}_{I(i)}(x)e^{j(\boldsymbol{\theta}_{I(i)}+\boldsymbol{\varphi}_{I(i)}+\pi)}\right]_k, \tag{3.10}$$

where R(t) and S(x) are the temporal and spatial amplitude functions associated to the wave component of the decomposition, respectively, and θ(t) and ϕ(x) are the temporal and spatial phase functions, respectively, [6, 7]. The original time series can then be reconstructed from the real part of (3.10). The details are omitted. In the d

In the developed models, a criterion for choosing the number of relevant modes is given by the energy percentage contained in the p and q modes:

$$\frac{\sum_{i=1}^{p} [\Delta\boldsymbol{\lambda}_{(i)swc}]_k + \sum_{i=1}^{q} [\Delta\boldsymbol{\lambda}_{(i)twc}]_k}{\|\mathbf{f}_k\|_F^2} = 99\%, \tag{3.11}$$

where $\|\cdot\|_F^2$ denotes the Frobenius norm. From (3.11), $(\Delta\boldsymbol{\lambda}_{swc})_k$ and $(\Delta\boldsymbol{\lambda}_{twc})_k$ are given in difference as

$$(\Delta\boldsymbol{\lambda}_{swc})_k = (\boldsymbol{\lambda}_{swc})_{k+1} - (\boldsymbol{\lambda}_{swc})_k, \qquad (\Delta\boldsymbol{\lambda}_{twc})_k = (\boldsymbol{\lambda}_{twc})_{k+1} - (\boldsymbol{\lambda}_{twc})_k. \tag{3.12}$$

Equations (3.7–3.12) provide a complete characterization of any propagating effects and periodicity in the original data field which might be obscured by normal cross-spectral analysis.

It might be remarked that, in the special case of real analysis, these expressions are simplified to the standard definitions.

RECURSIVE ALGORITHM

A flowchart of the proposed approach is shown in Figure 3. In this plot, dashed boxes indicate the use of instantaneous information from the previous time step (k − 1), and E(·) indicates the expectation value. This approach makes feasible the analysis and characterization of transient processes using real-time information. Variations to these approaches that extend their practical use to the realm of near-real-time stability assessment and control are being investigated. These features will be discussed in future research.

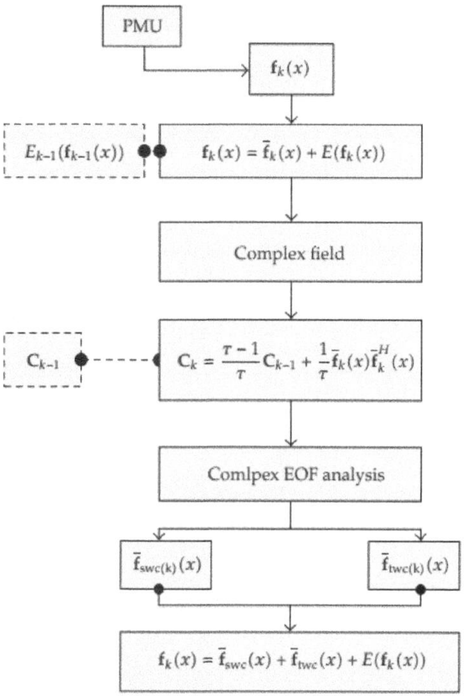

Figure 3: Algorithm for near-real-time computation of standing and propagating features from measured data.

The following sections describe the application of multivariate statistical techniques to measured data including the estimation of instantaneous parameters.

SIMULATIONS

Records of Selected Signals

The data used for this study were recorded by multiple phasor measurement units during a real event in northern Mexico. See [21, 22] for more details about this event.

The main event that originated the oscillations was a failed temporary interconnection of the Northwestern regional system to the Mexican interconnected system through a 230 kV line between Mazatlan Dos and Tres Estrellas substations. As a result of topological changes and load shedding, the observed oscillations exhibit highly complex phenomena including transient motions characterized by changing frequency content and variations in the mode shapes of critical electromechanical modes.

Among the existing PMU locations, frequency measurements at three major substations round the north, northwestern and northeastern systems were selected for study: Hermosillo H, Mazatlan Dos MZD and Tres Estrellas TTE. Figure 4 is an extract from PMU measurements of this event showing the observed oscillations of selected bus frequencies.

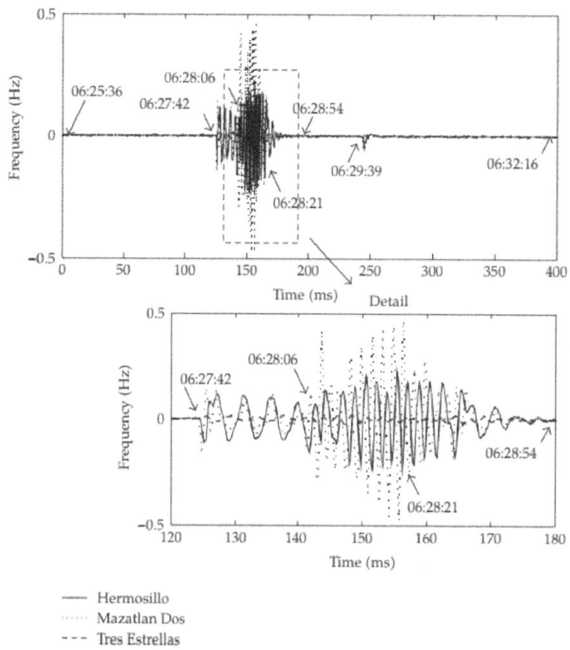

Figure 4: Time traces of recorded bus frequency swings recorded January 1, 2004 and detail of the oscillation buildup.

Measurements were recorded over 400 ms collected at a rate of 0.20 samples per second.

Analysis of Propagating Features

System measurements in this plot demonstrate significant variability suggesting a nonstationary process in both space and time. As observed in these plots, the most prominent variations occur in the interval during which the oscillation starts at 06 : 27 : 42 and the interval in which the operating frequency is restored to the nominal condition (60 Hz) by control actions at about 06 : 28 : 21.

Based on the frequency data collected by PMUs, EOF analysis was applied to reveal spatial and temporal dynamics. As a first step towards the development of an empirical basis, the covariance matrix was formed by the ensembles of the frequency observations at different system locations, that is,

$$F_k = [\mathbf{f}_H(t_k), \mathbf{f}_{MZD}(t_k), \mathbf{f}_{TTE}(t_k)]. \tag{5.1}$$

To visualize the complex temporal and spatial dynamics that takes placed in the system following the failed interconnection, each time series is augmented with an imaginary component using Hilbert analysis and the complex EOF method is employed to approximate the original data. Further, in order to improve the ability of the method to capture temporal behavior, the individual time series are separated into their time-varying mean and fluctuating components; complex-EOF analysis is applied to the fluctuating field to decompose the spatio-temporal data into orthogonal modes associated to the standing and traveling wave components.

Using the proposed approach, two statistical modes describing standing and traveling features were identified. Mode 1, which accounts for 98.5% of the total energy describes the main (standing) feature in the records. The second mode contains approximately 1% of the energy and describes propagating features.

Figure 5 compares the signal reconstructed using conventional EOF and the proposed on-line formulation, whilst Table 1 gives the rms error. A two-sample data analysis window was used in the on-line analysis of system characteristics. For simplicity, only the traveling wave mode is used in the computation. Simulation results clearly show that near-real-time approximations enhance the ability of the method to capture local information.

Table 1: RMS error in the approximation

Signals	Off-line (rms)	On-line (rms)
Hermosillo	0.3591	0.2614
Mazatlan Dos	0.4928	0.4008
Tres Estrellas	0.7536	0.5477

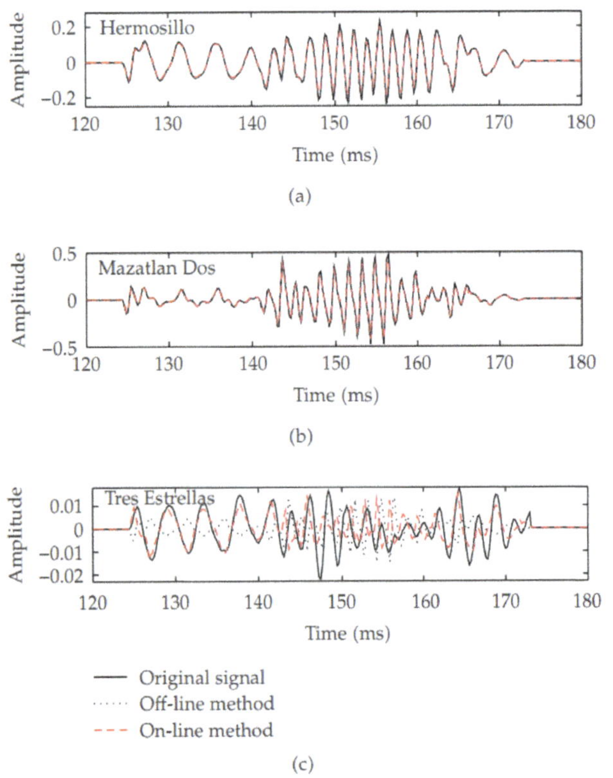

Figure 5: Reconstruction of the original data with the traveling wave mode identified using the off-line and on-line analysis.

Also of interest, Figure 6 compares the amplitude of modal components provided by conventional EOF analysis and that obtained from the proposed formulation. Note that conventional analysis can only provide average information. In sharp contrast with this, the near-real-time implementation enables to single out the times at which sudden changes in system behavior take place. Further, Figure 7 shows the mode shape of dominant electromechanical modes obtained using both approaches.

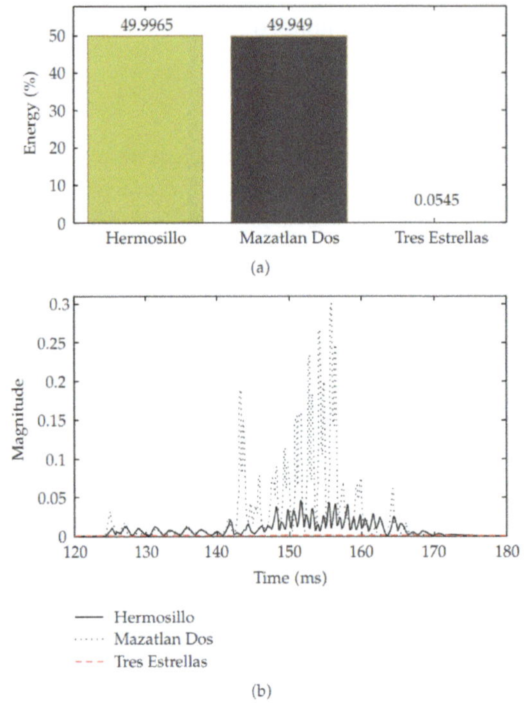

Figure 6: (a) average energy of traveling wave mode using the off-line analysis, and (b) instantaneous energy of traveling wave mode using the on-line analysis.

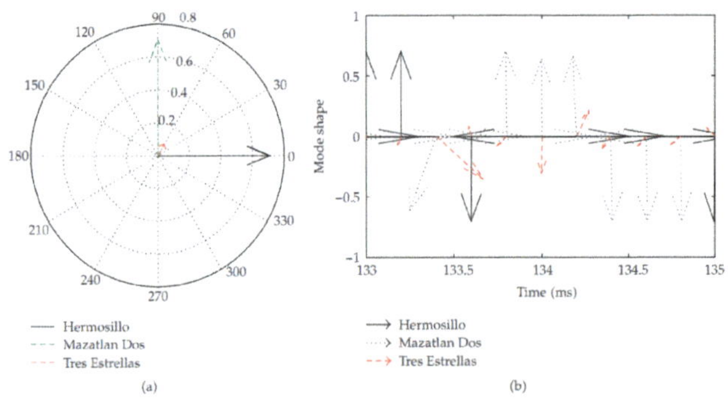

Figure 7: (a) mode shape of traveling wave mode using off-line analysis, and (b) time-varying mode shape of traveling wave mode using the proposed on-line analysis method.

One of the most attractive features of proposed technique is its ability to detect changes in the shape properties of critical modes arising from topology changes [9, 23], and control actions. Changes in the mode shape of electromechanical modes may indicate changes in topology or changes in operating patterns and may be useful for control decisions and the design of special protection systems [1, 22]. In this analysis, complex values are displayed as vectors with the length of the vector proportional to the eigenvector magnitude and the direction equal to the eigenvector phase.

The proposed approach provides an automated way to estimate mode shapes without any prior information of the time intervals of interest. The computational effort for analysis of large blocks of data is directly related to the number of spatial variables and the size of the observation window considered. In our numerical simulations the data analysis window corresponds to on-going that research is being conducted to estimate the appropriate window size for real-time applications.

Finally, Figure 8 shows the time evolution of the dominant travelling wave at different system locations obtained using the wavelet empirical orthogonal function analysis described above. The analysis depicts the fill evolution of temporal dynamics and provides details about the local behavior of multiscale data. Here, the shaded areas in the plot delineate the regions where the energy is significant. This provides detailed information of time instants associated with transient system behavior whose behavior changes over time and frequency. The results stand in contrast with current modeling done at a single scale.

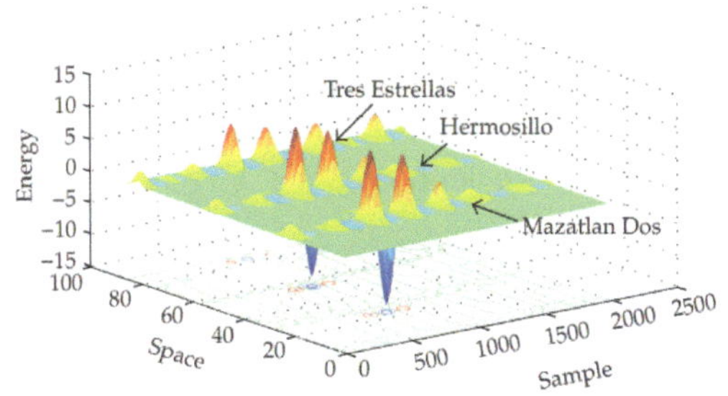

Figure 8: Spatial pattern of the leading mode showing temporal variability.

CONCLUSION

Wide-area, real-time monitoring may prove invaluable in power system dynamic studies by giving a quick assessment of the damping and frequency content of dominant system modes after a critical contingency. In this paper, an alternative technique based on time-dependent complex EOF analysis of measured data is proposed to resolve the localized nature of transient processes and to extract dominant temporal and spatial information. A method of spatially decomposing oscillation patterns in near-real-time into their standing and travelling parts is presented.

By combining a sliding window approach with complex EOF, a novel framework for on-line characterization of temporal behavior is proposed that attempts to consider the influence of both, spatial and temporal variability. Numerical results show that the proposed method provides accurate estimation of nonstationary effects, modal frequency, time-varying mode shapes, and time instants of intermittent transient responses. This information may be important in determining strategies for wide-area control and special protection systems.

It is shown that, in addition to providing spatial and temporal information, the method improves the ability of conventional correlation analysis to capture temporal events and gives a quantitative result for both the amplitude and phase of motions, which are essential in the interpretation and characterization of transient processes in power systems.

Extensions to this approach to determine the optimal locations to place PMUs are underway. Applications to real-time system monitoring, protection and control will be addressed in future work.

APPENDICES

A. Wavelet Transform

Consider a function f(t) belonging to a family of finite energy functions, that is

$$\int_{-\infty}^{\infty} |f(t)|^2 dt < \infty. \tag{A.1}$$

The continuous wavelet transform (WT) of f(t) is defined as [24]

$$W(a,b) = \frac{1}{\sqrt{|a|}} \int_{-\infty}^{\infty} f(t)\psi^*\left(\frac{t-b}{a}\right)dt, \tag{A.2}$$

where $\psi(t)$ is the basis wavelet function or mother wavelet, a is a scale parameter and b is a time parameter. The superscript $*$ denotes complex conjugation. It is assumed that $\psi(t)$ is also a finite energy function satisfying the condition

$$C_\Psi = \int_{-\infty}^{\infty} \frac{|\Psi(\omega)|^2}{|\omega|} d\omega < \infty \tag{A.3}$$

in which $\widehat{\Psi}(\omega)$ is the Fourier transform of $\psi(t)$ defined as Ψ

$$\widehat{\Psi}(\omega) = \frac{1}{\sqrt{2\pi}} \int_{-\infty}^{\infty} \psi(t)e^{-i\omega t}dt. \tag{A.4}$$

The function f(t) can be reconstructed from W(a, b) by using the double integral representation

$$f(t) = \frac{1}{\pi C_\psi} \iint_{-\infty}^{\infty} \frac{1}{a^2} W(a,b)\psi\left(\frac{t-b}{a}\right)\frac{da}{\sqrt{a}}db, \tag{A.5}$$

where the scale parameter a is restricted to positive values only

B. Singular Value Decomposition

This section reviews the singular value decomposition and its features that relevant in the context of the proposed formulation.

Using the SVD decomposition, a complex matrix X can be represented as

$$\begin{aligned} \mathbf{X} &= \|\mathbf{X}\|\left[\cos(\theta_{\mathbf{X}}t) + j\sin(\theta_{\mathbf{X}}t)\right] \\ &= \mathbf{U}_R\Sigma_R\mathbf{V}_R^H + j\mathbf{U}_I\Sigma_I\mathbf{V}_I^H, \end{aligned} \tag{B.1}$$

where $\|\mathbf{X}\|$ and θ_X are the magnitude and phase of X, respectively, U are left singular vectors and Σ are singular values.

Using (B.1), we can rewrite (3.5) as

$$\begin{aligned} \mathbf{X}\mathbf{X}^H &= \|\mathbf{X}\|\left\|\mathbf{X}^T\right\|\{[\cos(\theta_{\mathbf{X}}t)\cos(\theta_{\mathbf{X}^T}t) + \sin(\theta_{\mathbf{X}}t)\sin(\theta_{\mathbf{X}^T}t)] \\ &\quad + j[\sin(\theta_{\mathbf{X}}t)\cos(\theta_{\mathbf{X}^T}t) - \cos(\theta_{\mathbf{X}}t)\sin(\theta_{\mathbf{X}^T}t)]\}, \\ \mathbf{X}^H\mathbf{X} &= \left\|\mathbf{X}^T\right\|\|\mathbf{X}\|\{[\cos(\theta_{\mathbf{X}^T}t)\cos(\theta_{\mathbf{X}_c}t) + \sin(\theta_{\mathbf{X}^T}t)\sin(\theta_{\mathbf{X}}t)] \\ &\quad + j[\cos(\theta_{\mathbf{X}^T}t)\sin(\theta_{\mathbf{X}}t) - \sin(\theta_{\mathbf{X}^T}t)\cos(\theta_{\mathbf{X}}t)]\} \end{aligned} \tag{B.2}$$

or

$$\begin{aligned} \mathbf{X}\mathbf{X}^H &= \left[\mathbf{U}_R\Sigma_R\Sigma_R^T\mathbf{U}_R^T + \mathbf{U}_I\Sigma_I\Sigma_I^T\mathbf{U}_I^T\right] \\ &\quad + j\left[\mathbf{U}_I\Sigma_I\Sigma_R^T\mathbf{U}_R^T - \mathbf{U}_R\Sigma_R\Sigma_I^T\mathbf{U}_I^T\right], \\ \mathbf{X}^H\mathbf{X} &= \left[\mathbf{V}_R^T\Sigma_R^T\Sigma_R\mathbf{V}_R + \mathbf{V}_I^T\Sigma_I^T\Sigma_I\mathbf{V}_I\right] \\ &\quad + j\left[\mathbf{V}_R^T\Sigma_R^T\Sigma_I\mathbf{V}_I - \mathbf{V}_I^T\Sigma_I^T\Sigma_R\mathbf{V}_R\right]. \end{aligned} \tag{B.3}$$

As it is seen from (B.1), the columns of U_R and U_I are the eigenvectors of real and imaginary parts of XX^H, and the columns of V_R and V_I are the eigenvectors of real and imaginary parts of X^HX, respectively, [10, 11]. The n singular values on the diagonal of Σ_R and Σ_I are the square roots of the nonzero eigenvalues of the real and imaginary parts of both XX^H and X^HX divided by the number of samples N.

From the decomposition given in (B.2), it can be seen that the imaginary part is zero when time is in phase with the extremum of the cosine or sine, that is, the sum of the two components is zero, for this instant both are symmetrical matrixes.

The imaginary part measures the grade of asymmetries when the sum of both matrixes is different from zero; this is used to define the existence of traveling wave components.

REFERENCES

1. A. R. Messina, Inter-area Oscillations In Power Systems: A Nonlinear and Nonstationary Perspective, Springer, Berlin, Germany, 2009.
2. J. F. Hauer, W. A. Mittelstadt, R. Adapa, M. K. Donelly, and W. H. Litzenberger, "Power system dynamics and stability—section 8: direct analysis of wide-area dynamics," in CRC Electric Power Engineering Handbook, chapter 11, CRC Press, Cleveland, Ohio, USA, 2000.
3. J. F. Hauer and J. G. DeSteese, "A tutorial on detection and characterization of special behavior in large electric power systems," Tech. Rep. PNL-14655, Pacific Northwest National Laboratory, Cambridge, Mass, USA, July 2004.
4. J.-P. Chilès and P. Delfiner, Geostatistics: Modeling Spatial Uncertainty, Wiley Series in Probability and Statistics: Applied Probability and Statistics, John Wiley & Sons, New York, NY, USA, 1999.
5. P. Holmes, J. L. Lumley, and G. Berkooz, Turbulence, Coherent Structures, Dynamical Systems and Symmetry, Cambridge Monographs on Mechanics, Cambridge University Press, Cambridge, Mass, USA, 1996.
6. T. P. Barnett, "Interaction of the monsoon and Pacific trade wind system at interannual time scales. Part I: the equatorial zone," Monthly Weather Review, vol. 111, no. 4, pp. 756–773, 1983.
7. R. D. Susanto, Q. Zheng, and X. H. Yan, "Complex singular value decomposition analysis of equatorial waves in the pacific observed by TOPEX/Poseidon altimeter," American Meteorological Society, vol. 15, pp. 764–774, 1997.
8. N. Aubry, R. Guyonnet, and R. Lima, "Spatiotemporal analysis of complex signals: theory and applications," Journal of Statistical Physics, vol. 64, no. 3-4, pp. 683–739, 1991.
9. C. Wolter, M. A. Trindade, and R. Sampaio, "Obtaining mode shape through the Karhunen-Loeve expansion for distributed-parameter linear systems," Vibrations and Acoustic, vol. 10, pp. 444–452, 2001.
10. H. Dankowicz, P. Holmes, G. Berkooz, and J. Elezgaray, "Local models of spatio-temporally complex fields," Physica D, vol. 90, no. 4, pp. 387–407, 1996.
11. P. Esquivel and A. R. Messina, "Complex empirical orthogonal function analysis of wide-area system dynamics," in Proceedings of IEEE Power and Energy Society General Meeting (PES '08), July 2008.
12. G. Kerschen, J.-C. Golinval, A. F. Vakakis, and L. A. Bergman, "The method of proper orthogonal decomposition for dynamical characterization and order reduction of mechanical systems: an overview," Nonlinear Dynamics, vol. 41, no. 1–3, pp. 147–169, 2005.
13. A. Hannachi, I. T. Jolliffe, and D. B. Stephenson, "Empirical orthogonal functions and related techniques in atmospheric science: a review," International Journal of Climatology, vol. 27, no. 9, pp. 1119–1152, 2007.
14. J. Terradas, R. Oliver, and J. L. Ballester, "Application of statistical techniques to the analysis of solar coronal oscillations," Astrophysical Journal, vol. 614, no. 1, pp. 435–447, 2004.
15. D. Mwale, T. Y. Gan, K. Devito, C. Mendoza, and U. Silins, "Precipitation variability and its relationship to hydrologic variability in Alberta," Hydrological Processes, vol. 23, pp. 3040–3056, 2009.
16. S. Uhlig, "On the complexity of Internet traffic dynamics on its topology," Telecommunication Systems, vol. 43, no. 3-4, pp. 167–180, 2010.
17. M. Li and S. C. Lim, "Modeling network traffic using generalized Cauchy process," Physica A, vol. 387, no. 11, pp. 2584–2594, 2008.
18. M. Li, "Generation of teletraffic of generalized Cauchy type," Physica Scripta, vol. 81, no. 2, pp. 1–10, 2010.
19. J. G. Proakis and D. G. Manolakis, Digital Treatment of Signals, Pearson Education, Delhi, India, 2007.
20. M. Li, W.-S. Chen, and L. Han, "Correlation matching method of the weak stationarity test of LRD traffic," Telecommunication Systems, vol. 43, no. 3-4, pp. 181–195, 2010.
21. A. R. Messina and V. Vittal, "Extraction of dynamic patterns from wide-area measurements using empirical orthogonal functions," IEEE Transactions on Power Systems, vol. 22, no. 2, pp. 682–692, 2007.
22. A. R. Messina, V. Vittal, D. Ruiz-Vega, and G. Enríquez-Harper, "Interpretation and visualization of wide-area PMU measurements using Hilbert analysis," IEEE Transactions on Power Systems, vol. 21, no. 4, pp. 1763–1771, 2006.
23. B. F. Feeny, "A complex orthogonal decomposition for wave motion analysis," Journal of Sound and Vibration, vol. 310, no. 1-2, pp. 77–90, 2008.
24. C. Torrence and G. P. Compo, "A practical guide to wavelet analysis," Bulletin of the American Meteorological Society, vol. 79, no. 1, pp. 61–78, 1998.

CHAPTER 12

STATISTICAL EVALUATION OF A FULLY AUTOMATED MAMMOGRAPHIC BREAST DENSITY ALGORITHM

Mohamed Abdolell,[1,2,3] Kaitlyn Tsuruda,[2] Gerry Schaller,[1,2], and Judy Caines[1,2,4]

[1]Department of Diagnostic Radiology, Dalhousie University, Halifax, NS, Canada B3H 2Y9

[2]Department of Diagnostic Imaging, Capital District Health Authority, Halifax, NS, Canada B3H 2Y9

[3]Division of Medical Education/Informatics, Dalhousie University, Halifax, NS, Canada B3H 2Y9

[4]Nova Scotia Breast Screening Program, Halifax, NS, Canada B3H 2Y9

ABSTRACT

Visual assessments of mammographic breast density by radiologists are used in clinical practice; however, these assessments have shown weaker associations with breast cancer risk than area-based, quantitative methods. The purpose of this study is to present a statistical evaluation of a fully automated, area-based mammographic density measurement algorithm. Five radiologists estimated density in 5% increments for 138 "For Presentation" single MLO views; the median of the radiologists' estimates was used as the reference standard. Agreement amongst radiologists was excellent, ICC=0.884, 95% CI (0.854, 0.910). Similarly, the agreement between the algorithm and the reference standard was excellent, ICC=0.862, falling within the 95% CI of the radiologists' estimates. The Bland-Altman plot showed that the reference standard was slightly positively biased (+1.86%) compared to the algorithm-generated densities. A scatter plot showed that the algorithm moderately overestimated low densities and underestimated high densities. A box plot showed that 95% of the algorithm-generated assessments fell within one BI-RADS category of the reference standard. This study demonstrates the effective use of several statistical techniques that collectively produce a comprehensive evaluation of the algorithm and its potential to provide mammographic density measures that can be used to inform clinical practice.

INTRODUCTION

Breast density refers to fibroglandular tissue in the breast and is one of the top major risk factors for breast cancer. Women with extremely dense breasts (75% or greater mammographic density) have a four- to sixfold increase in the risk of developing breast cancer compared to those with fatty breasts (less than 25% density) [1–3].

Citation: Mohamed Abdolell, Kaitlyn Tsuruda, Gerry Schaller, and Judy Caines, "Statistical Evaluation of a Fully Automated Mammographic Breast Density Algorithm," Computational and Mathematical Methods in Medicine, vol. 2013, Article ID 651091, 6 pages, 2013. doi:10.1155/2013/651091

Traditionally, visual assessment by radiologists has been used to characterize and quantify mammographic density (and a woman's risk for breast cancer) using Wolfe Grades, Tabar Patterns, Boyd Scales, or the American College of Radiologists' (ACR) Breast Imaging Reporting and Data System (BI-RADS) density lexicon [4–7]. Despite good reproducibility, methods used to characterize mammographic density have shown weaker associations with breast cancer risk compared to methods quantifying mammographic density [2, 3, 8] and suffer from inter- and intraobserver variability.

The ACR has stated that radiologists' visual assessments of percent breast density using the BI-RADS lexicon are "not reliably reproducible" [9]. This fundamental lack of reproducibility has led to the development of various semi- and fully automated algorithms to quantify percent breast density as a means to overcome inter- and intraobserver variability. It is therefore important to apply rigorous statistical methods to evaluate the performance of these algorithms.

State of the Art

Area-based methods used to quantify mammographic density have produced reliable and standardized mammographic density measurements on a continuous scale. The de facto standard of such methods is the Cumulus software [10, 11]. Using Cumulus, a digitized film-screen mammogram is displayed and a trained user selects a threshold value to separate the breast area from the background (i.e., the region of interest). A second threshold is then selected to identify regions of dense breast tissue, and the percent breast density is calculated as the area of dense tissue divided by the area of the region of interest. Despite being a proven predictor of breast cancer risk, the semiautomated nature of Cumulus' breast density assessments is susceptible to inter- and intraobserver variability and could be improved by a fully automated method. Additionally, this software is intended for use with digitized film-screen mammograms. As 90% of certified mammography units in the USA are now full-field digital [12], a software for use with full-field digital mammograms (FFDMs) is needed.

Volume-based methods theoretically yield accurate estimates of mammographic density and so it is simply assumed that volume-based density estimates are associated with breast cancer risk, as has been demonstrated to be the case for area-based estimates (both visually and algorithmically assessed) [13, 14]. Volumetric methods use "For Processing" FFDMs and DICOM header information to calculate density. Yet, volume-based estimates have not been shown to demonstrate a similarly strong association with breast cancer risk [11, 15, 16]. Additionally, the underlying distribution of mammographic density estimates from volumetric methods is significantly more left-skewed than that of area-based methods (typical range 0–40% versus 0–100%) [17], making them difficult to interpret by radiologists, who are not simply able to visualize mammographic density as a volumetric construct [11, 15].

The assessment of the agreement between percent breast density algorithms and an expert radiologist should necessarily quantify the consistency or reproducibility of measurements made by these two "raters" on the same set of digital mammograms. The intraclass correlation coefficient (ICC) provides such a measure of agreement [18]. The BlandAltman plot is another way to assess agreement between raters. Scatter and box plots can also yield insights into the level of agreement between raters. Yet, much of the literature validating emerging density measurement algorithms relies on the use of the Pearson correlation coefficient, ρ, which is a measure of the linear dependence between two raters and can be quite high despite the agreement being poor [18, 19]. Overall percent agreement is another statistic that is used to assess agreement but is also flawed as it does not factor in any inherent inter- and intrarater variability [19]. Reporting of a single numerical measure of agreement alone is one-dimensional and does not present a comprehensive perspective on algorithm performance.

This paper presents several statistical methods that collectively provide a more comprehensive evaluation of the performance of a fully automated area-based image analysis algorithm that generates percent breast density measures from FFDMs.

MATERIALS AND METHODS

138"For Presentation" FFDMs collected from the Capital District Health Authority in Nova Scotia were retrospectively analyzed. Images were acquired on Siemens full-field digital mammography machines and automatically postprocessed by the manufacture's proprietary software at the time of acquisition. This early stage work has focused on the mediolateral oblique views and excluded craniocaudal views as it has been shown in the literature that mammographic density estimates from only one view are sufficient to indicate breast cancer risk [20]. In addition, the ACRs' National Mammography Database breast density element definition stipulates that "if left and right breasts differ, use the higher density" [21].

Percent Density Analysis

Percent mammographic density was measured by a fully automated research-based algorithm that uses "For Presentation" FFDMs to calculate an area-based measure of density as a percentage on a continuous scale (Figure 1, Panels 1(a) through 1(d)). Using view position and image laterality information from the DICOM header (elements (0018, 5101) and (0020, 0062), resp.) the software creates and applies a mask to identify the breast envelope (region of interest) by removing the pectoral muscle, subcutaneous fat, and overlay text (Panel 1(b)). A variation of the MaxEntropy and Moments thresholding methods is applied to determine a threshold for dense tissue in the breast [22, 23]. The area of the dense tissue (i.e., the number of pixels of dense tissue) is then calculated (Panel 1(c)), as is the area of the region of interest (i.e., the number of pixels in the breast area, Panel 1(d)), and the final density estimate is calculated as the ratio of dense tissue area to the region of interest. In this manner, the software uniquely generates a reproducible, fully automated, area-based estimate of mammographic density using "For Presentation" FFDM images.

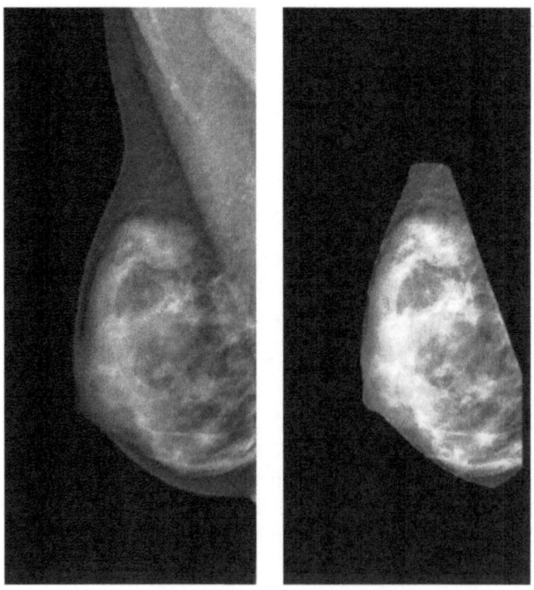

(a) Source (b) Mask

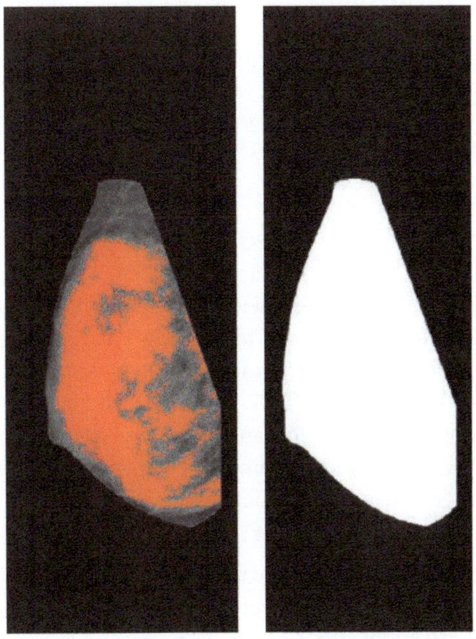

(c) Density (d) ROI

Figure 1: A sequence of processed images generated at various steps of the algorithm for estimating area-based mammographic density: (a) a "For Presentation" mammogram from our sample; (b) the image after a mask has been applied to identify the breast envelope; (c) the area of dense tissue (red pixels); and (d) the region of interest as a binary map of the breast envelope. The algorithm calculates percent breast density as the number of red pixels in Panel (c) divided by the number of white pixels in Panel (d).

To evaluate the agreement between the algorithm and an expert mammographer, percent mammographic density was visually assessed by five radiologists in 5% density increments (0%, 5%, . . . , 95%, 100%) using five megapixel Barco Screens supported by the Syngo MammoReport Software (VB24D, Siemens AS). Visual assessments were performed by two senior mammographers, one junior mammographer, one senior resident, and one fellow. This 21-point scale was used as a proxy for a continuous measure.

Statistical Analysis

To quantify the reliability of estimates performed by the radiologists' visual assessments, Intraclass Correlation Coefficients (ICCs) were used to measure interobserver agreement. Although the interpretation of ICCs can vary depending on the context, the ICC is equivalent to a quadratically weighted Kappa, and a widely referenced scale for interpretation of Kappa values can be used as a general guide [24, 25]. Specifically, ICC values of 0.00–0.20, 0.21–0.40, 0.41–0.60, 0.61–0.80, and 0.81–1.00 were used to indicate poor, fair, moderate, substantial, and excellent to perfect agreement, respectively.

It has repeatedly been shown that radiologists' visual assessments of mammographic density are associated with breast cancer risk [1, 3, 4, 10, 26]. As such, the median of the visual assessments performed by the five participating radiologists was considered to be the reference standard for this analysis. The algorithm was considered promising in informing clinical practice if the agreement between the algorithm and the reference standard fell within the 95% CI of the ICC of the radiologists.

The ICC was used to quantify the level of agreement between the algorithm and the reference standard, and a scatterplot was used to demonstrate the relationship between the two. A Bland-Altman difference plot was used to analyze the agreement between the algorithm and the reference standard and to quantify the amount and direction of bias as well as the upper and lower limits of agreement (bias $\pm 1.96\sigma$ of the difference) [27]. Lastly, a box-and-whisker plot was used to visualize the results in terms of the BI-RADS density lexicon (0–24%, 25–49%, 50–74%, and 75–100%) [7].

RESULTS

Five radiologists visually assessed 138 images to estimate mammographic density, and the algorithm was applied to those same 138 images to generate a fully automated density assessment for each of the images.

The radiologists' visual assessments were in excellent agreement with an ICC = 0.884, 95% CI (0.854, 0.910). The algorithm demonstrated excellent agreement with the reference standard with an ICC = 0.862, which fell within the 95% CI of the agreement between the radiologists' visual assessments. The algorithm is validated well on an external set of 261 mammograms, ICC = 0.841.

The Pearson correlation coefficient between the algorithm and the reference standard assessments was $\rho = 0.889$.

The algorithm slightly overestimated low densities and underestimated high densities compared to the reference standard (Figure 2). Overall, there was a small, positive bias in the reference standard assessments compared to the algorithm assessments, as measured by the mean difference between the reference standard and the algorithm assessments (bias = 1.86%) (Figure 3). Additionally, the upper and lower agreement levels were both less than 25%, and thus approximately 95% of the data classified by the algorithm was within one BI-RADS category of the reference standard classification (Figure 3).

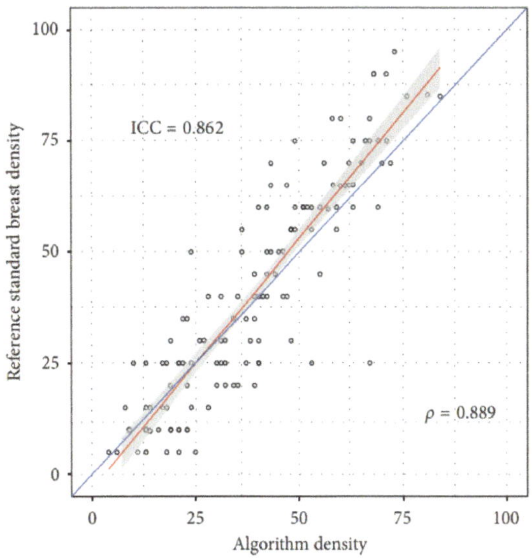

Figure 2: Scatter plot showing the relationship between the mammographic density estimates produced by the algorithm (x-axis) and the reference standard (y-axis). The blue line indicates perfect agree-

ment between the algorithm and the reference standard, in which case all points would fall exactly on the line of agreement. The red line is the line of the best fit determined by linear least squares regression analysis and shows that the algorithm tends to slightly overestimate density compared to the reference standard for lower densities and slightly underestimate density compared to the reference standard for higher densities.

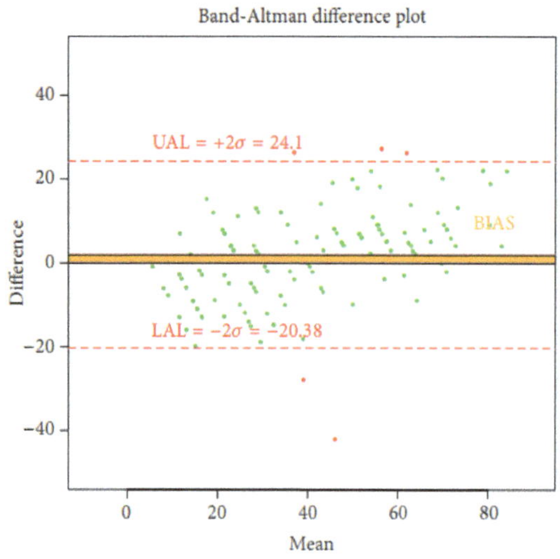

Figure 3: Bland-Altman difference plot showing agreement between the algorithm and the reference standard measures of mammographic density. The difference refers to the reference standard minus the algorithm assessment. The absolute values of the upper and lower agreement limits are <25%, which is the span of a single category in the 4-level BI-RADS density classification scheme. A bias of +1.86%, as indicated by the orange band above the horizontal zero difference line, shows that the reference standard density is on average only slightly higher than the density generated by the algorithm.

When the algorithm and reference standard estimates were classified using the BI-RADS density lexicon, the box-and-whisker plots showed good agreement within categories (Figure 4). Each box was contained in the accordant colour bar, and, as expected from the Bland-Altman difference plot, the tails on the graphs did not exceed the adjacent BI-RADS categories.

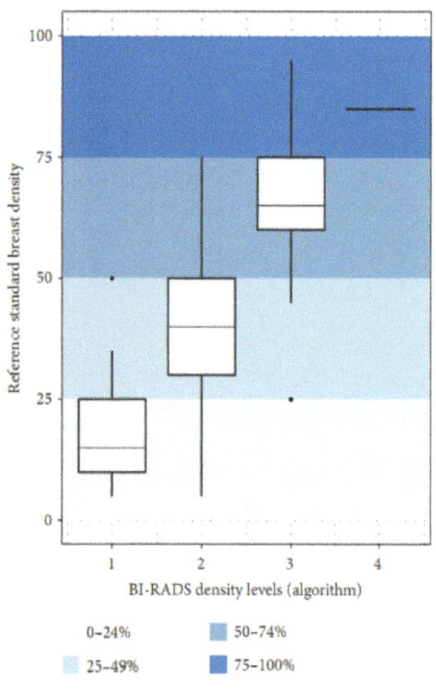

Figure 4: Box-and-whisker plot displaying the distribution of reference standard mammographic density assessments falling into the algorithm-derived classifications designated by the standard 4-level BI-RADS density lexicon. Ideally, each of the boxes and their whiskers should be entirely contained in their respective BI-RADS levels. The reference standard mammographic density assessments in the lowest and the highest BI-RADS levels are well classified, while the middle two levels overlap in both directions into adjacent BI-RADS levels.

DISCUSSION

The algorithm demonstrates excellent agreement with radiologists' visual assessments of mammographic density. Critically, the observed magnitude of this agreement falls within the 95% CI of agreement observed between radiologists. This algorithm is unique in that it generates fully automated mammographic density measurements that can be straightforwardly compared with visually determined radiologists' estimates, which are well accepted as being associated with breast cancer risk.

The sole use of the Pearson correlation coefficient (ρ) provides a one-dimensional and overinflated impression of the level of agreement.

The statistical evaluation presented in this paper used ICCs and Bland-Altman, scatter, and box plots to quantify agreement and bias in breast density assessment between a fully automated algorithm and radiologists' assessments. This multifaceted methodology can be employed to comprehensively evaluate the performance of any breast density measurement algorithm and provides an alternative to the often reported Pearson correlation coefficient and percent agreement statistics which do not consider random chance agreement and cannot quantify bias between different raters.

As breast density legislation gains momentum in the USA and mammography providers are required to disclose breast density in the lay report, there will be an increasing need for automated solutions that provide reliable and accurate measurements of breast density. A woman's breast density will be used to determine her optimal followup, and thus the performance of these algorithms must be evaluated using robust statistical methodologies.

CONCLUSION

Further work is needed to extend the applicability of the breast density algorithm to FFDMs from other manufacturers as each manufacturer has their own proprietary image processing algorithms that generate "For Presentation" images. Additionally, as radiologists use both mediolateral and craniocaudal views to assess breast density in a clinical setting, the present algorithm must also be extended to accommodate the analysis of craniocaudal views.

The present algorithm is an effective research tool and shows promise in its ability to provide automated mammographic density measurements that can be used to inform clinical practice. The Pearson correlation coefficient (ρ) provides an inadequate, inflated, and overoptimistic measure of the level of agreement. The statistical methods employed provide a comprehensive evaluation of the level of agreement between the algorithm and the reference standard and confirm that the algorithm has an excellent level of agreement with the reference standard. Agreement between raters can only be adequately assessed using multiple statistical methods.

CONFLICT OF INTERESTS

Mohamed Abdolell is the founder of Densitas Inc. and is a shareholder in the company. Kaitlyn Tsuruda is an employee at the company.

ACKNOWLEDGMENTS

The authors would like to thank Dr. Melanie McQuaid, Dr. Ieva Klavina, and Dr. Chris Lightfoot for providing visually assessed mammographic density measurements used in this study. This research was supported by the Department of Diagnostic Radiology, Dalhousie University and Capital District Health Authority, and the Canadian Breast Cancer Foundation (Atlantic Region). The study sponsors had no involvement in the study design; in the collection, analysis, and interpretation of data; in the writing of the paper; nor in the decision to submit the paper for publication.

REFERENCES

1. N. F. Boyd, H. Guo, L. J. Martin et al., "Mammographic density and the risk and detection of breast cancer," New England Journal of Medicine, vol. 356, no. 3, pp. 227–236, 2007.
2. J. Brisson, C. Diorio, and B. Mâsse, "Wolfe's parenchymal pattern and percentage of the breast with mammographic densities: redundant or complementary classifications?" Cancer Epidemiology Biomarkers and Prevention, vol. 12, no. 8, pp. 728–732, 2003.
3. V. A. McCormack and I. dos Santos Silva, "Breast density and parenchymal patterns as markers of breast cancer risk: a meta-analysis," Cancer Epidemiology Biomarkers and Prevention, vol. 15, no. 6, pp. 1159–1169, 2006.
4. J. N. Wolfe, "Risk for breast cancer development determined by mammographic parenchymal pattern,"Cancer, vol. 37, no. 5, pp. 2486–2492, 1976.
5. I. T. Gram, E. Funkhouser, and L. Tabár, "The Tabar classification of mammographic parenchymal patterns," European Journal of Radiology, vol. 24, no. 2, pp. 131–136, 1997.
6. N. F. Boyd, H. M. Jensen, G. Cooke, and H. L. Han, "Relationship between mammographic and histological risk factors for breast cancer," Journal of the National Cancer Institute, vol. 84, no. 15, pp. 1170–1179, 1992.
7. Breast Imaging Reporting and Data Systems (BIRADS), American College of Radiology, Reston, Va, USA, 1993.
8. M. Garrido-Estepa, F. Ruiz-Perales, J. Miranda et al., "Evaluation of mammographic density patterns: reproducibility and concordance among scales," BMC cancer, vol. 10, supplement 485, 2010.
9. American College of Radiology, "ACR Statement on Reporting Breast Density in Mammography Reports and Patient Summaries," 2012, http://www.acr.org/About-Us/Media-Center/Position-Statements.
10. N. F. Boyd, J. W. Byng, R. A. Jong et al., "Quantitative classification of mammographic densities and breast cancer risk: results from the Canadian National Breast Screening Study," Journal of the National Cancer Institute, vol. 87, no. 9, pp. 670–675, 1995.
11. N. Boyd, L. Martin, A. Gunasekara et al., "Mammographic density and breast cancer risk: evaluation of a novel method of measuring breast tissue volumes," Cancer Epidemiology Biomarkers and Prevention, vol. 18, no. 6, pp. 1754–1762, 2009.
12. FDA, "MQSA National Statistics," 2013, http://www.fda.gov/Radiation-EmittingProducts/MammographyQualityStandardsActandProgram/FacilityScorecard/ucm113858.htm.
13. O. Alonzo-Proulx, N. Packard, J. M. Boone et al., "Validation of a method for measuring the volumetric breast density from digital mammograms," Physics in Medicine and Biology, vol. 55, no. 11, pp. 3027–3044, 2010.
14. M. J. Yaffe, "Mammographic density. Measurement of mammographic density," Breast Cancer Research, vol. 10, no. 3, article 209, 2008.
15. D. Kontos, P. R. Bakic, R. J. Acciavatti, E. F. Conant, and A. D. A. Maidment, "A comparative study of volumetric and area-based breast density estimation in digital mammography: results from a screening population," in Digital Mammography, vol. 6136 of Lecture Notes in Computer Science, pp. 378–385, 2010.
16. J. Ding, R. Warren, I. Warsi et al., "Evaluating the effectiveness of using standard mammogram form to predict breast cancer risk: case-control study," Cancer Epidemiology Biomarkers and Prevention, vol. 17, no. 5, pp. 1074–1081, 2008.
17. R. Highnam, S. Brady, M. Yaffe, N. Karssemeijer, and J. Harvey, "Robust breast composition measurement-volpara TM," in Proceedings of the 10th International Conference on Digital Mammography (IWDM '10), vol. 6136 of Lecture Notes in Computer Science, pp. 342–349, 2010.
18. J. M. Bland and D. G. Altman, "Statistical methods for assessing agreement between two methods of clinical measurement," The Lancet, vol. 1, no. 8476, pp. 307–310, 1986.
19. R. J. Hunt, "Percent agreement, Pearson's correlation, and kappa as measures of inter-examiner reliability," Journal of Dental Research, vol. 65, no. 2, pp. 128–130, 1986.
20. J. Stone, J. Ding, R. M. L. Warren, and S. W. Duffy, "Predicting breast cancer risk using mammographic density measurements from both mammogram sides and views," Breast Cancer Research and Treatment, vol. 124, no. 2, pp. 551–554, 2010.
21. American College of Radiology, "National mammography database data elements," version 2.0, 2009, https://nrdr.acr.org/Portal/HELP/NMD/nmd_data_elements.pdf.
22. J. N. Kapur, P. K. Sahoo, and A. K. C. Wong, "A new method for gray-level picture thresholding using the entropy of the histogram," Computer Vision, Graphics, & Image Processing, vol. 29, no. 3, pp. 273–285, 1985.
23. W. H. Tsai, "Moment-preserving thresholding: a new approach," Computer Vision, Graphics, & Image Processing, vol. 29, no. 3, pp. 377–393, 1985.

24. J. L. Fleiss and J. Cohen, "The equivalence of weighted kappa and the intraclass correlation coefficient as measures of reliability," Educational and Psychological Measurement, vol. 33, pp. 613–619, 1973.

25. J. R. Landis and G. G. Koch, "The measurement of observer agreement for categorical data," Biometrics, vol. 33, no. 1, pp. 159–174, 1977.

26. J. A. Harvey and V. E. Bovbjerg, "Quantitative assessment of mammographic breast density: relationship with breast cancer risk," Radiology, vol. 230, no. 1, pp. 29–41, 2004.·

27. J. M. Bland and D. G. Altman, "Statistical methods for assessing agreement between two methods of clinical measurement," The Lancet, vol. 1, no. 8476, pp. 307–310, 1986.

CHAPTER 13 COMPUTATIONAL PERFORMANCE OPTIMISATION FOR STATISTICAL ANALYSIS OF THE EFFECT OF NANO-CMOS VARIABILITY ON INTEGRATED CIRCUITS

Zheng Xie and Doug Edwards

School of Computer Science, The University of Manchester, Manchester M13 9PL, UK

ABSTRACT

The intrinsic variability of nanoscale VLSI technology must be taken into account when analyzing circuit designs to predict likely yield. Monte-Carlo- (MC-) and quasi-MC- (QMC-) based statistical techniques do this by analysing many randomised or quasirandomised copies of circuits. The randomisation must model forms of variability that occur in nano-CMOS technology, including "atomistic" effects without intradie correlation and effects with intradie correlation between neighbouring devices. A major problem is the computational cost of carrying out sufficient analyses to produce statistically reliable results. The use of principal components analysis, behavioural modeling, and an implementation of "Statistical Blockade" (SB) is shown to be capable of achieving significant reduction in the computational costs. A computation time reduction of 98.7% was achieved for a commonly used asynchronous circuit element. Replacing MC by QMC analysis can achieve further computation reduction, and this is illustrated for more complex circuits, with the results being compared with those of transistor-level simulations. The "yield prediction" analysis of SRAM arrays is taken as a case study, where the arrays contain up to 1536 transistors modelled using parameters appropriate to 35 nm technology. It is reported that savings of up to 99.85% in computation time were obtained.

INTRODUCTION

Anticipating the impact of device variability on performance is a critical aspect of design procedures for integrated circuits. With nanoscale technology, "intradie" variability, causing behavioural variation from device to device within each die, is an important consideration [1]. With some dimensions approaching atomic scales, intrinsic atomic scale variations such as line edge roughness and dopant granularity have become the main sources of such variation [2, 3]. These "atomistic" variabilities are random in nature and result in "within-die" fluctuation which cannot be disregarded. Traditional variability analysis, based on "worst case" corner models [4] and guard bands for parameter variations, is likely to be very pessimistic in its estimations of the effects of the variability. Consequently, new circuit analysis techniques are needed which adopt a statistical treatment of the intradie variability of device performances. This has led to much interest in statistical analysis which can take into account parameter variation in all parts of a design in a single comprehensive computational procedure, allowing the impact on yield to be efficiently estimated.

Citation: Zheng Xie and Doug Edwards, "Computational Performance Optimisation for Statistical Analysis of the Effect of Nano-CMOS Variability on Integrated Circuits," VLSI Design, vol. 2013, Article ID 984376, 22 pages, 2013. doi:10.1155/2013/984376

Because of the high dimensionality of the parameter space, it is very difficult to derive analytical models of large-scale ICs for analysis. Sets of equations describing specific circuit performance parameters, like timing or yield, in terms of the huge number of parameters would be very difficult to derive analytically. Therefore, the use of conventional statistical methods, based on the analysis of such equations, has restricted applicability for the variability analysis of nanoscale ICs. With Monte Carlo (MC) analysis methods, the integrated circuits are simulated directly, and there is no need to derive differential equations that describe the dependency of the properties of interest on circuit parameters. The only requirement is that the circuit properties to be modeled are capable of being described by probability density functions (pdfs) that are dependent on the pdfs of circuit parameters and input variables. Monte Carlo analysis proceeds by generating a random sample of the value of each circuit parameter and each input variable, based on their known statistical properties. It then simulates the circuit thus obtained, using a finite difference analysis package, to compute a random sample of the circuit property of interest. The process is repeated many times to obtain a sequence of samples of the property of interest from which statistical models can be derived.

In nanoscale technology, "atomistic" variabilities are random and generally uncorrelated from device to device. According to Srivastava et al. [4], a critical form of variability is gate-length variability which occurs "interdie" due to variation in exposure time and "intradie" because of other lithography effects [5]. Device threshold voltages will be dependent on gate lengths and channel doping concentration, and variation in these parameters will cause comparable amounts of independent interdie variability and spatially correlated intradie variability. Intradie variations will have therefore both spatially correlated and uncorrelated contributions. The effect of the correlation in "intradie" variation must be given consideration.

MC analyses are particularly suitable for nanoscale IC statistical simulation to achieve statistical estimates of properties of interest. General conclusions drawn from the analysis of many randomised samples of a circuit can be made representative of the effects of variability. To quantify these conclusions, statistical averages are produced. The statistical reliability of the conclusions generally improves as the number of circuit increases, though the rate of improvement can often be increased by carefully choosing the samples. MC techniques are especially useful for predicting the "yield" from many copies of the circuit when these are manufactured with typical accuracy and parameter variations.

A major problem is the computation required for carrying out sufficient analyses to produce statistically reliable averages. The introduction of intradie correlation into circuit models increases the computational complexity considerably. To simplify the computation, a form of Extreme Value Theory known as statistical blockade (SB) [6, 7] may be employed to identify "rare event" circuits whose responses fall in the "tails" of their pdfs and are therefore worth analyzing. These circuits are needed for circuit yield failure predictions. Circuits in the "body" of the distributions are not analysed. The use of "quasi-Monte Carlo (QMC)" analysis with "low-discrepancy sequences" achieves further computation reduction [8–10]. The use of "statistical behavioural circuit blocks (SBCB)" and "Principal Component Analysis (PCA)" to reduce the dimensionality of the analyses [8] also reduces computational complexity. PCA allows the effects of correlation within the parameters of each device and from device to device to be partitioned thus reducing the sizes of the matrices which characterize the correlation and making them easier to process. Despite these economies, the statistical analysis of large and complicated ICs requires computational resources that can only be provided by parallel and/or distributed computing, for example, by the Condor framework [11, 12].

This paper contains seven sections. The first is an introduction, and Section 2 deals with the use of MC techniques for the statistical analysis of nanoscale technology with the introduction of correlation due to the intradie proximity of components. Section 3 discusses two methods of reducing the dimensionality of the input parameter space to achieve computational efficiency in MC simulations, PCA and SBCB. Section 4introduces the concept of Extreme Value Theory (EVT) and explores the algorithm known as "statistical blockade" (SB) [11]. The potential for using this technique to achieve major computational savings is explored and illustrated by examples. Section 5 investigates the use of quasi-Monte Carlo (QMC) techniques and "low-discrepancy" sampling to achieve further efficiency improvements, over what was achieved in earlier sections with Monte Carlo circuit simulation. The effect of using a "Sobol" low-discrepancy sequence generator to replace the uniformly distributed pseudorandom number generator previously used to produce the required Gaussian variation is discussed and illustrated by example. Section 6 evaluates the results obtained with VLSI SRAM circuits, and Section 7 presents conclusions. The use of parallel processing for efficiently undertaking the intensive computation required will be discussed, taking into account the intrinsically parallel nature of massive MC simulations.

MC SIMULATION FOR THE DESIGN OF NANOSCALE VLSI CIRCUITS

Monte Carlo Methods

Monte Carlo methods use repeated pseudorandom sampling of the behaviour of mathematical equations, or real or simulated systems, to solve mathematical problems or to determine the properties of systems [13]. In this work, the systems are integrated circuits simulated using a finite difference circuit analysis technique, that is, the public licensed version of SPICE, NGSPICE [14]. The transient behaviour of sets of highly complex multidimensional equations describing integrated circuits may thus be analysed by repeated random sampling to produce observations to which statistical inference can be applied to obtain information about the equations or systems. Monte Carlo methods use pseudorandom processes implemented in software. The simulation is not required to be numerically identical to the true physical process since the aim is to produce statistical results such as averages, expectations, and distributions rather than deterministic numerical measurements. The derivation of such results requires a "sampling" of the population of all possible modes of behaviour of the system.

One of the most often quoted applications of Monte Carlo methods is the evaluation of multidimensional integrals [15] such as that in

$$I = \int_{a_1}^{b_1} \int_{a_2}^{b_2} \int_{a_3}^{b_3} \cdots \int_{a_K}^{b_K} f(x_1, x_2, x_3, \ldots, x_K) \times dx_K dx_{K-1} \ldots dx_2 dx_1 \quad \text{written as} \int_V f(\underline{x})\, d\underline{x}. \tag{1}$$

Here, x is the vector $(x_1, x_2, x_3, \ldots, _K)$, f is some function of the K variables of $\underline{x}$, and V denotes the region of integration. $(\underline{x})$ may be evaluated at regularly spaced points or uniformly distributed random points in K-dimensional space as a means of evaluating the integral. The problem with regularly spaced points is that the number of them, say N, must increase exponentially with the dimension K if the error is not to increase exponentially with K. The error with regular spacing and a fixed value of N is known to increase as the Kth root of the order of magnitude [16]. The error for one-dimensional "trapezoidal rule" integration with N regularly spaced points can be shown to be proportional to $1/N^2$, whereas the error for the K-dimensional equivalent of the trapezoidal rule has an error proportional to $1/N^{2/K}$. This is "the curse of dimensionality" [17]. With regular sampling and fixed N, as K increases, each dimension must be sampled more and more sparsely and less and less efficiently, since more and more points will have the same value in a given dimension.

Monte Carlo sampling avoids the inefficiency of the rectangular grids created by regular sampling by using a purely random set of N points uniformly distributed over the K-dimensional region V. The advantages of the Monte Carlo method with randomly distributed points now become apparent. The Monte Carlo error has the property that, for high dimensions K, its error is proportional to $1/(\sqrt{N})$, which means that, to reduce the error by a factor of 10, the sample size N must be increased by a factor of 100. This effect is independent of the order of magnitude K when the input variables are statistically independent which means that there is no correlation between them. It can be simply illustrated by comparing the performances of regular sampling and Monte Carlo integration for the following integral:

$$I = \int_0^{\pi} \int_0^{\pi} \int_0^{\pi} \cdots \int_0^{\pi} \sin(x_1 + x_2 + x_3 + \cdots + x_K) \times dx_K dx_{K-1} \cdots dx_2 dx_1. \tag{2}$$

Figures 1(a), 1(b), and 1(c) show the error for K=3, 4, and 5, respectively, for both regular sampling and uniformly distributed random sampling for a range of values of N. The random sampling has zero correlation from dimension to dimension and from sample to sample. The increasing advantage of independent random sampling over regular sampling as K increases is clear.

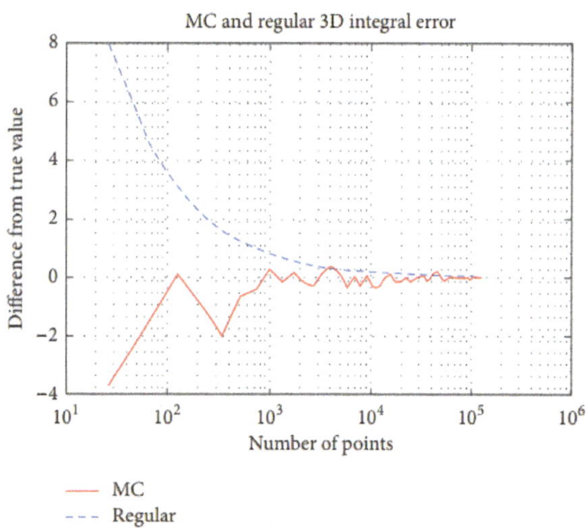

(a)

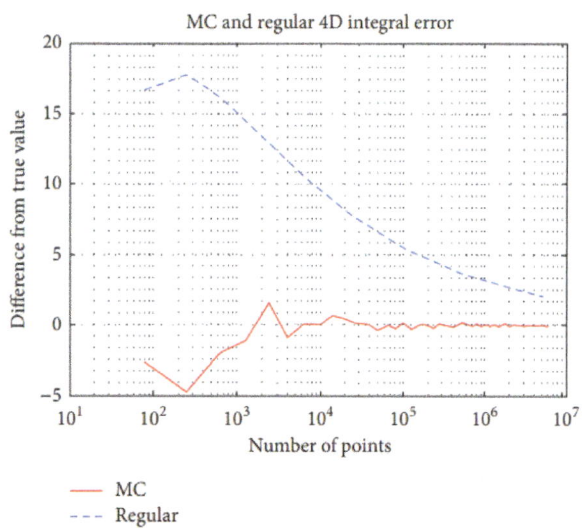

(b)

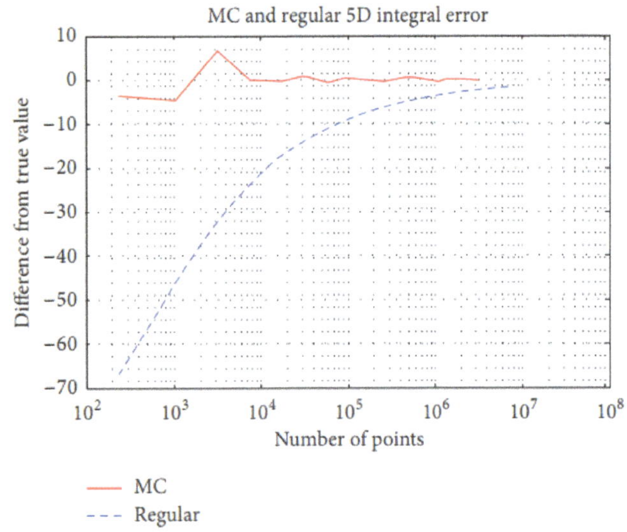

(c)

Figure 1: Convergence of MC and regular integration for (a) 3D integral, (b) 4D integral, and (c) 5D integral.

Much research has been devoted to finding ways of decreasing the Monte Carlo error even further to make the technique still more efficient. One approach has been to use variance reduction techniques [18] which are able to reduce the variance of f by transforming it to another function whose integral is the same. Another approach is to use "quasirandom" or "low-discrepancy" sampling of the space V. The use of such quasirandom sampling for numerical integration is referred to as "quasi-Monte Carlo" integration. Quasirandom sampling based on "scrambled nets" [18–22] has the property that, for "well-behaved" functions, the error becomes proportional to $N^{-3/2} \log^{K/2N}$, which is much less than the $1/(\sqrt{N})$ for traditional Monte Carlo integration.

Section 5 will discuss quasi-Monte Carlo methods. Other approaches use "recursive stratified sampling" [23] which breaks down a Monte Carlo calculation into a series of Monte Carlo subcalculations with feedback from each stage to decide how to best continue the series. Thus, the calculation is adapted to the application. In the case of integration, the region of integration is progressively divided up into subvolumes to concentrate the sampling into regions where the variance of the function is largest or of the most interest. This makes the sampling more efficient. In the example of the multidimensional sin function considered above, there would be a higher probability of samples occurring at the edges of the function, where the rate of change is greater than in the central part. The well-known "MISER" algorithm of Press and Farrar [24] is based on this approach.

The "Vegas" Monte Carlo approach of Lepage [25] is based on "importance sampling." The idea, when used for integration, is to use the pdf of the function to determine how sampling points can be concentrated in subspaces that produce values of the function that contribute most to the integral. Vegas has been amended to incorporate stratified sampling as well as importance sampling, and it also uses a form of variance reduction in subspaces where importance sampling is inappropriate because the sampling turns out to be too sparse [26]. From these well-known references and many others on Monte Carlo integration, it is clear that much improvement in efficiency can be gained over the original Monte Carlo approach.

The ideas proposed for integration have inspired similar ideas for efficiency improvement when Monte Carlo techniques are used for simulation, and these prove to be especially valuable for VLSI circuit simulation where the dimensionality and complexity are very high.

Monte Carlo Simulation

Monte Carlo simulation is the application of Monte Carlo methods to study properties of systems having stochastic components. It uses repeated pseudorandom sampling of input variables to determine the behaviour of some physical system as characterized by a computer model. In this work, the physical system is an integrated circuit modelled by SPICE, the input variables are component values which are variable due to the uncontrollability of manufacturing effects referred to in the introduction, and the behaviour we are interested in may be viability, or otherwise, of the circuit. With repeated sampling used to simulate the fabrication of batches of nominally identical integrated circuits with the specified component variation, the estimation of the probability of a circuit being viable, that is, that it works, can be considered an estimate of the expected "yield," that is, the percentage of working circuits within a batch. The criteria that determine viability are many, including correct logical operation, the power consumption, and the propagation delay in the whole circuit or parts of it.

As argued in [18], Monte Carlo simulation can be formulated in terms of integration. The direct simulation approach provides an intuitive way of defining the problem, while transforming it into an integration formulation can be useful when studying theoretical properties of the estimators obtained, especially when variance reduction or quasi-Monte Carlo techniques are used. A comparison of the direct view of simulation versus an integration formulation can be summarised as follows.

The direct simulation approach samples observations of the random vector, $\underline{X}$, of inputs to and parameters of the simulated system and for each vector calculates the outputs that are of interest. We thus obtain a random distribution of each output measurement, say $(\underline{X})$, which is of interest.

The integration formulation of simulation samples the "source of randomness" $\underline{U}$ as a vector of independent uniformly distributed random numbers. This is transformed into a vector of observations $\underline{X}$ with the appropriate multivariate distribution (e.g., Gaussian) and covariance matrix C by calculating

$$\underline{X} = Ag(\underline{U}), \tag{3}$$

where g is the appropriate "inverse cumulative distribution function" (ICDF) and A is a matrix such that

$$A^T A = C. \tag{4}$$

The covariance matrix C expresses the interdependency that exists between different elements of $\underline{X}$ and may be derived from assumptions about the effects of proximity as explained in chapter 2 of [4]. There are many ways of deriving A for a given covariance matrix C, the best known and fastest being

Cholesky decomposition. The required matrix A is not unique, and an alternative is to calculate

$$A = \left[\sqrt{\lambda_1}\underline{v}_1 \;\; \sqrt{\lambda_2}\underline{v}_2 \;\; \sqrt{\lambda_3}\underline{v}_3 \;\; \cdots \;\; \sqrt{\lambda_N}\underline{v}_N\right] = V\Lambda^{1/2}, \tag{5}$$

where $\lambda_1\lambda_2 \cdots \lambda_N$ are the eigenvalues and $\underline{v}_1, \underline{v}_2, \ldots, \underline{v}_N$ are the corresponding eigenvectors of C. C must be positive semidefinite to be a covariance matrix. V is the matrix of eigenvectors and Λ is the diagonal matrix of eigenvalues as supplied by the MATLAB function:

$$[V\Lambda] = \mathrm{eig}(C). \tag{6}$$

In comparison to the Cholesky decomposition, the eigenvalue/eigenvector method is more intuitive, and a recent paper by Keiner and Waterhouse [27] gives a more efficient way of performing the same transformation.

Calculating the distribution, between limits, of $(Ag(\underline{U}))= h(\underline{U})$ for an output measurement of interest, say f, can now be seen as a process of integration over the range of the multidimensional vector $\underline{U}$. The integration formulation simply reexpresses the simulation in terms of input vectors, $\underline{U}$, of uncorrelated uniformly distributed pseudorandom elements which are transformed into input vectors $\underline{X}$ intended to be representative of the observations expected of true inputs and parameters. This approach has the immediate advantage of being able to model correlation between elements such as that may occur intradie on integrated circuit devices or interdie from sample to sample within a batch of integrated circuits.

The direct approach is clearly applicable when actual component or parameter measurements are available, or when they have been synthesised as for the transistor set provided by RandomSPICE [28]. The randomisation is then achieved by selecting randomly from the sets of parameters provided. Although a pseudorandom modelling process of physical effects was used to generate the RandomSPICE parameters, they could have been obtained by direct measurement of real devices. Then a model of the parameter variation is not needed since the true natural physical variation, with its inherent distribution and correlation, will be fed directly into the series of simulations.

However, even when real sets of parameters are available, instead of using them directly, it may be advantageous to produce a model of them as the transformation of a smaller set of independent uniformly distributed random variables. Then the integration formulation may be adopted, based on models derived from real data. The models may be derived by employing Principal Components Analysis (PCA) to extract a smaller set of statistically independent parameters that may be transformed back to the complete set with little distortion. The dimensionality may thus be reduced, and each of the independent parameters may be modelled as the transformation of a uniformly distributed random variable. If the independent variables may be considered Gaussian, it is straightforward to model each of them as a transformed uniform random variable. The transformation to Gaussian is achieved by the Gaussian ICDF function. Transformations to independent random variables with distributions other than Gaussian may be achieved by different ICDFs. Multivariate versions of these functions allow correlation to be introduced. With the different distributions, essentially the same methodology with respect to statistical delay estimation as used with Gaussian, Pareto, and low-discrepancy sequences in this work can remain valid.

Apart from the likely reduction in dimensionality, this transformation of a direct simulation approach to an integration-like formulation allows a much larger set of randomised devices to be generated than are available in the original set. Hence more simulations may be run with different sets of parameters based on parameters obtained by measuring real devices.

Viewed in either formulation, Monte Carlo simulation samples the probability distribution of all the input variables and system parameters to produce many repeated versions of the system. These are in turn analysed to determine how certain key output measurements vary due to the input variability. A histogram of each key output measurement gives an estimate of its likely distribution, the estimate becoming more and more reliable as the number of simulations increases. Since the number of simulations must be restricted for practical reasons, the accuracy of these results is also limited by practicality

Where valid assumptions can be made about the shape of the distribution, for example, that it is Gaussian or Chisquared, a maximum likelihood fit to the histogram can be made on such assumptions. Such a fit would produce a value of mean and variance thus allowing a pdf as shown in Figure 2 to be drawn. Assuming the measurement to be a delay that is required to be less than D for viability and a Gaussian distribution, the yield of the circuit can now be estimated as the area under the pdf "tail" from D to infinity which may be derived from the "complementary error function" evaluated at D.

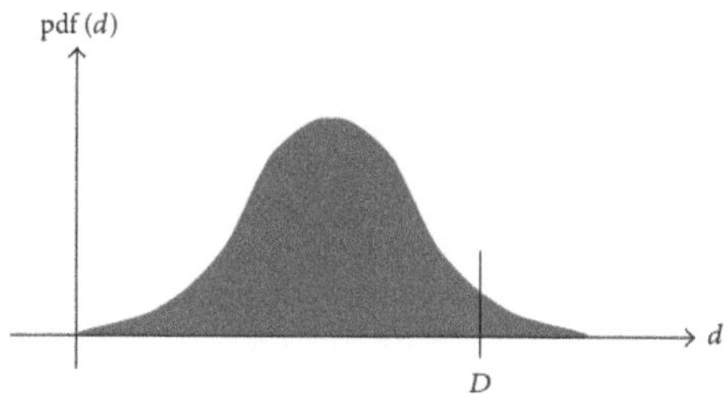

Figure 2: Gaussian probability density function of a circuit propagation delay and delay threshold D.

The accuracy of this estimation will depend on the number of simulations which must be limited. Unfortunately, the effect of the limitation will be most serious over the tails of the distribution, which is the part we are most interested in. For example, for a Gaussian pdf, the probability of being more than three standard deviations greater than the mean is $(3) = 0.5 \times \mathrm{erfc}(3/\sqrt{2})$, where erfc is the traditional Gaussian "complementary error function." $Q(3)$ is about 0.0013 meaning that, if 1000 circuits are simulated, we can only expect to find one value of the key output in this region. There would be a need to have many more than one value to have a chance of reasonable accuracy. This illustrates the need for complexity reduction techniques when applying Monte Carlo simulation to integrated circuit variability, and such techniques will be considered in the next sections.

In general, Monte Carlo methods proceed as follows.

- The characteristics of the input vectors are determined.
- Random vectors are generated with appropriate

distributions and intercorrelation either directly or by transforming independent uniformly distributed random vectors.

- A deterministic computation is performed to simulate the behaviour of the system for each of the randomized input vectors.
- For each key output measurement, its pdf is estimated in the best way possible, given the inevitable limitations in the amount of data available.
- Deductions about the probability of certain events are made from the estimated pdf.

The procedure of an IC's Monte Carlo simulation is described as follows.

- Find the statistical distribution for each parameter.
- Sample the statistical process to produce a value for each parameter.
- Parameterize one circuit and simulate it.
- Repeat for many copies of circuit and obtain the statistical distribution of a specific measurement.

Introducing Intradie Correlation

Correlation between device parameters may be due to the intradie proximity of components, or other causes. The device parameters may be direct physical quantities, for example, resistance or capacitance, or they may be coefficients of principal component vectors which are ultimately transformed back to physical quantities. Define a matrix X_{mat} of "column" vectors $\underline{X}_j$, each containing M parameters:

$$X_{mat} = [\underline{X}_1\ \underline{X}_2\ \underline{X}_3\ \cdots\ \underline{X}_R]. \qquad (7)$$

Each column vector, $\underline{X}_j$, of parameters is for a different randomised circuit copy. Within X_{mat}, there is a row-to-row correlation due to interdependencies between devices or the parameters of individual devices. To model intradie correlation between parameters due to proximity, let parameter i be defined for a point $P_i = (a_i, b_i)$ on the chip. Many models of intradie correlation due to proximity have been proposed, including the widely known Pelgrom model [4] and two simpler approaches: "the exponential model" and the "Matern model," as analysed and compared by Hargreaves et al. [5]. The "exponential model" represents the correlation (i, m) between parameters i and m as

$$k(i,m) = e^{-\lambda d(P_i,P_m)}, \qquad (8)$$

where $d(P_i, P_m)$ is the Euclidean distance between any two points P_i and P_m, in units of nanometers. This is assumed to be the Pearson correlation coefficient defined as

$$k(i,m) = \frac{\text{cov}(\text{row}_i, \text{row}_m)}{\sigma_i \sigma_m}, \qquad (9)$$

where σ_i and σ_m are standard deviations of parameters i and m, respectively, "cov" means covariance, and the rows are those of X_{mat}. A value for λ may be calculated from measurements of actual device parameters, or manufacturer's data. Clearly $(i, i) = 1$, and if it may be assumed that at a distance of μ nm the correlation reduces to some small value, say α,

$$\exp(-\lambda \cdot \mu) = \alpha, \qquad (10)$$

it follows that

$$\lambda = -\frac{1}{\mu}\ln(\alpha). \qquad (11)$$

Assuming $\alpha = 0.01$ and $\mu = 200$, we find that $\lambda = 0.023$. Therefore, if we have a location $P_i = (a_i, b_i)$ on the chip for each element i, a value of correlation (i, m) between rows i and m may be modelled. Hence, we obtain a "row-to-row" (parameter-to-parameter) correlation matrix:

$$K = \begin{bmatrix} 1 & k(1,2) & \cdots & k(1,R) \\ k(2,1) & 1 & \cdots & k(2,R) \\ \vdots & \vdots & \ddots & \vdots \\ k(R,1) & k(R,2) & \cdots & 1 \end{bmatrix}. \qquad (12)$$

A similar matrix may be constructed for the more complex Matern model which was found [1] to be more accurate. To provide an example for the simpler model, assume that there are four devices at P_1, P_2, P_3, and P_4, each with a parameter whose mean and standard deviation are m_1, m_2, m_3, m_4 and s_1, s_2, s_3, s_4, respectively. Let

$$\underline{m} = \begin{bmatrix} m_1 \\ m_2 \\ m_3 \\ m_4 \end{bmatrix}, \quad \underline{s} = \begin{bmatrix} s_1 \\ s_2 \\ s_3 \\ s_4 \end{bmatrix}. \qquad (13)$$

We need to generate, for each Monte Carlo randomised circuit j, random variables $(1, j)$, $x(2, j)$, $x(3, j)$, and $x(4, j)$ as the values of the four parameters to obtain a parameter vector $\underline{X}_j$. To generate a pseudorandom variable for each device with the right amount of intradie correlation, we first need to deduce, from K, an appropriate row-to-row covariance matrix, which is as follows:

$$C = [c(i,m)], \quad \text{where } c(i,m) = k(i,m) \times s_i \times s_m. \qquad (14)$$

Then find matrix A such that $A^T \cdot A = C$ using the "Cholesky Decomposition" or the "eigenvector-eigenvalue method" [27], which calculates A with (5).

Finally, generate a multivariate (4-element) correctly correlated random vector as follows:

$$\underline{X}_j = \underline{m} + A \cdot \underline{r}, \qquad (15)$$

where $\underline{r}$ is a 4 by 1 vector of independent random or pseudorandom variables. This is generated from a vector $\underline{u}$ of uniformly distributed random or pseudorandom variables in the range 0 to 1 as follows:

$$\underline{r} = \phi^{-1}(\underline{u}), \qquad (16)$$

where ϕ^{-1} is the ICDF corresponding to the required pdf for the elements of $\underline{r}$. We can do this repeatedly for each randomised circuit j, producing many column vectors $\underline{X}_j$.

Introducing intradie variability into the multiple parameters of transistor devices is possible using the same approach as used for component values. In such applications, it is useful to partition a large correlation matrix into a number of smaller ones, each catering for one type of parameter or principal component. This is possible when there can be assumed no correlation between the different types or principal components. This is guaranteed for principal components. Clearly, a different value of λ can be used for each partition.

The example below demonstrates the effect of correlation on statistical performance analysis of a binary full adder with behavioural models of NAND gates. Consider the binary full adder shown in Figure 3, whose on-chip layout is assumed to be as shown in Figure 4.

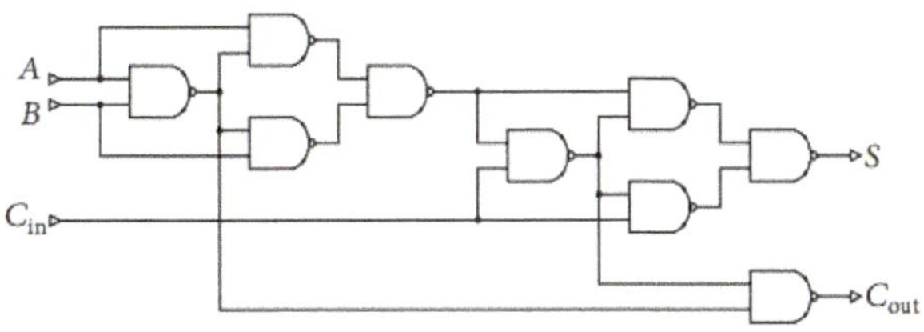

Figure 3: Binary full adder (BFA) circuit.

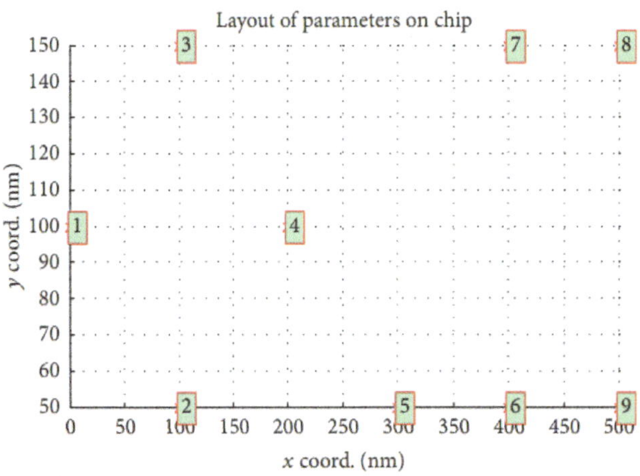

Figure 4: On-chip layout assumed for BFA circuit.

With one delay parameter for each behavioural NAND gate [8, 9], as will be described in Section 3, there are nine parameters in total. Hence, there are just nine statistically varying parameters. Assuming the exponential model of intradie correlation with $\lambda = 0.007$, the parameter-parameter correlation matrix K is found to be as in (17).

Knowing the standard deviations of the parameters allows K to be converted to a parameter-to-parameter covariance matrix C using (14). Matrix A may be computed such that $A^T \cdot A = C$, and finally the vectors $\underline{X}_j$ of 500 random circuits may be generated and analysed using NGSPICE [14] to produce the histogram shown in Figure 5.The mean is 8.64 and the standard deviation is 0.345 picoseconds (ps).

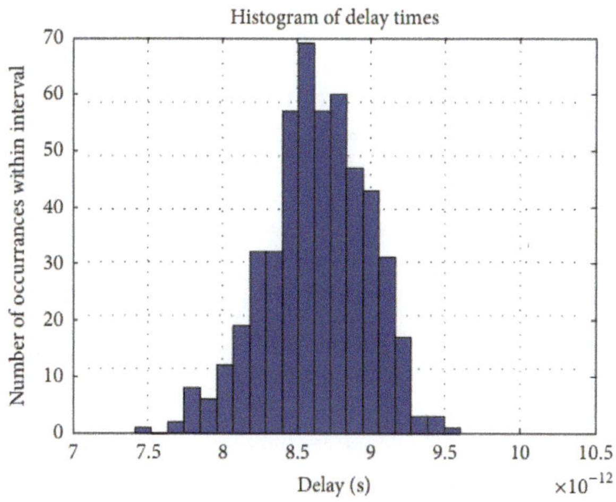

Figure 5: Histogram of delay times for 500 BFA circuits (($\lambda = 0.007$).

Consider

$$K = \begin{bmatrix} 1 & 0.46 & 0.46 & 0.25 & 0.12 & 0.06 & 0.06 & 0.03 & 0.03 \\ 0.46 & 1 & 0.5 & 0.46 & 0.25 & 0.12 & 0.11 & 0.06 & 0.06 \\ 0.46 & 0.5 & 1 & 0.46 & 0.21 & 0.11 & 0.12 & 0.06 & 0.06 \\ 0.25 & 0.46 & 0.46 & 1 & 0.46 & 0.24 & 0.24 & 0.12 & 0.12 \\ 0.12 & 0.25 & 0.21 & 0.46 & 1 & 0.5 & 0.37 & 0.21 & 0.25 \\ 0.06 & 0.12 & 0.11 & 0.24 & 0.5 & 1 & 0.5 & 0.37 & 0.5 \\ 0.06 & 0.11 & 0.12 & 0.24 & 0.37 & 0.5 & 1 & 0.5 & 0.37 \\ 0.03 & 0.06 & 0.06 & 0.12 & 0.21 & 0.37 & 0.5 & 1 & 0.5 \\ 0.03 & 0.06 & 0.06 & 0.12 & 0.25 & 0.5 & 0.37 & 0.5 & 1 \end{bmatrix}$$

Repeating the same procedure with $\lambda = 10$ (very low correlation) and 500 training circuits produces the histogram shown in Figure 6, whose mean is 8.647 ps and standard deviation is 0.318 ps. In comparison to the correlated case where $\lambda = 0.007$, the mean remains approximately the same, but the standard deviation reduces from 0.345 ps to 0.318 ps, that is, by about 7.8%.

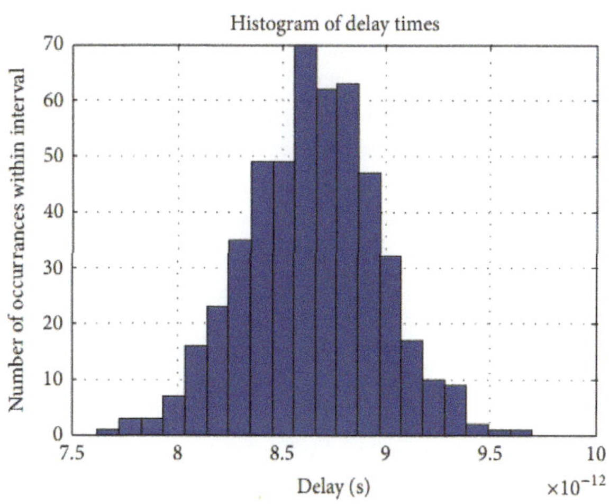

Figure 6: Histogram of delay times for 500 BFA circuits ($\lambda = 10$).

DIMENSION REDUCTION OF MC CIRCUIT SIMULATION

The assertion that the error resulting from MC analyses is proportional only to the square root of the sample size does not mean that the same sample size is appropriate to any circuit no matter how complicated it is. There are clear advantages in reducing the dimensionality of analysis problems including the simplification of the computational complexity of the analyses. This chapter deals with two methods of reducing the dimensionality of Monte Carlo analysis. The first is Principal Components Analysis (PCA) which transforms the random variables required to characterize a circuit to a reduced number of statistically independent variables. PCA is also useful as a means of introducing intradie and interdie correlations. The second is the use of statistical behavioural circuit blocks (SBCB) which substitute functional but computationally simpler circuit models for device-level analogue subcircuits. The aim of this research is to apply them in new ways which may be suitable for inclusion in the ongoing NGSPICE open-source project [14].

Principal Component Analysis (PCA)

PCA is a technique for transforming samples of M variables into samples of a smaller number of variables by exploiting interdependency or correlation among the M variables. Referring to a set of R parameter vectors ("feature vectors") in an M dimensional vector space, the transformation converts each parameter vector to a lower dimensional vector in such a way that no information, or little information, is lost. This means that the original vectors, $\underline{X}_i$ for $i = 1, \ldots, R$, can be reconstructed from the transformed vectors either exactly or with a small error. The elements of the transformed (reduced dimensional) vectors are the coefficients (or "loadings") of "principal component" (PC) vectors. PC vectors are eigenvectors of the $M \times M$ covariance matrix C which are normalized and statistically independent.

Performing the Analysis

Taking the summed squared differences between the elements of an original component ("feature") vector and a reconstructed one as a measure or the error or loss of information incurred by PCA, of all possible linear transformations to a lower dimensional space, PCA is optimal in minimising this error over all vectors. Further, the PC vectors are conveniently ordered in the sense that the first one has the highest variance and accounts for as much variability as possible. Each succeeding PC vector has lower variance, and therefore less importance, but has the highest variance possible while being uncorrelated to all the previous ones.

PCA may be carried out by eigenvalue/eigenvector decomposition of the M by M covariance matrix of the original vectors data matrix which is defined as

$$C = \left[c_{ij}\right], \quad \text{where } c_{ij} = \frac{1}{R-1}\sum_{k=1}^{R}\left(x_{ik} - m_i\right)\left(x_{jk} - m_j\right). \tag{18}$$

In this expression, x_{ik} is the ith element of vector Xk with mi denoting the mean of x_{ik} for each variable i over all R vectors, that is, the mean of row i of matrix $[x_{ik}]$ for $k = 1, 2, \ldots, R$. Therefore, C is the covariance matrix of variations from the mean of each parameter and is unaffected by the means themselves. The means of columns are not subtracted from columns. If the eigenvectors of C are $\underline{u}_1, \underline{u}_2, \ldots, \underline{u}_M$, with corresponding eigenvalues $\lambda_1, \lambda_2, \ldots, \lambda_M$, these are easily calculated by the MATLAB statement "[U, D] = eig(C)." This statement produces the matrix

$$U = \left[\underline{u}_1\ \underline{u}_2 \cdots\ \underline{u}_M\right] \tag{19}$$

composed of all the eigenvectors as columns and matrix D whose diagonal elements are $\lambda_1, \lambda_2, \ldots, \lambda_M$ with all other elements being zero. It follows from the definitions of eigenvectors and eigenvalues ($C\underline{u}_k = \lambda_k \underline{u}_k$ for all k) that

$$CU = UD \ \therefore\ U^T CU = D, \tag{20}$$

since eigenvectors are all orthogonal to each other and normal (i.e., of unit length) meaning that U^T is always the inverse of U. Therefore, $C = UDU^T$, meaning that

$$C = \lambda_1\left(\underline{u}_1\underline{u}_1^T\right) + \lambda_2\left(\underline{u}_2\underline{u}_2^T\right) + \cdots + \lambda_M\left(\underline{u}_M\underline{u}_M^T\right). \tag{21}$$

If matrix X is transformed to Y as follows:

$$Y = U^T \cdot X, \tag{22}$$

then

$$X = U \cdot Y. \tag{23}$$

If any of the eigenvalues $\lambda_1, \lambda_2, \ldots, \lambda_M$ are zero and we remove their corresponding eigenvectors and corresponding rows of Y in (22), the remaining eigenvectors are principal components which can represent all the original data, without any loss of accuracy. Equation (23) will reconstruct the original vector exactly from the nonsquare matrix Y of reduced dimensional PC coefficient (loading) vectors. Taking this idea further, we can remove elements of Y with their eigenvectors when the corresponding eigenvalues are small on the grounds that, if they do not significantly affect C, they should not significantly affect Xeither. It may be shown that$C$ will always be a positive semidefinite symmetric matrix (i.e., positive definite or singular); therefore, all eigenvalues will be real and positive or zero.

The previous outline of PCA hides the obvious difficulty of deciding what error is incurred by removing components with nonzero eigenvalues which are considered small and how small an eigenvalue must be to be considered negligible. Such considerations of PCA are application specific and best related to the specific objective and how the error is to be quantified.

Application of PCA for Modelling Statistical Variation

Assume that we have a database of sets of randomised device parameters which have been published by a manufacturer or generated on the basis of theoretical modelling. Taking the RandomSPICE [28] Toshiba NMOS database as an example, for each device there is a set of 201 randomised parameter lists each with 300 parameters. Many of the parameters are zero or fixed, but in general they need not be. We compute the 300 by 300 element covariance matrix C for the parameter sets after subtracting the mean for each parameter. The 300 eigenvectors and eigenvalues of C are calculated and then the original mean-subtracted data is transformed by projecting each vector onto the set of 300 eigenvectors. The first ten ordered eigenvalues are plotted in Figure 7 and are seen to fall off rapidly in magnitude after number six. It is therefore reasonable to delete all but the first six eigenvalues and eigenvectors to obtain the required reduced dimensional PC coefficient vectors. Figure 8 shows how the mean squared difference between original (mean subtracted) data and reconstructed data varies with the number of eigenvectors. This shows how the approximation improves with the number of eigenvectors and that the mean squared error falls to around 10^{-20} when this number reaches about six. The modelling technique used by Glasgow University [29] explains this result. Similar results and graphs were obtained for the PMOS data provided by RandomSPICE. PCA analysis often needs some consideration of numerical stability because of the wide variation of parameter values.

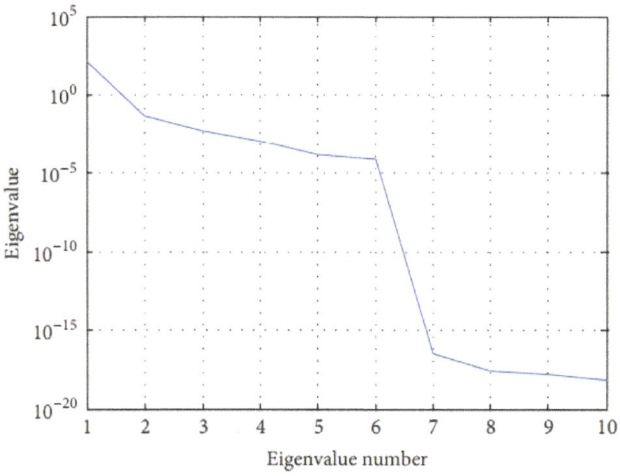

Figure 7: Values of first ten ordered eigenvalues for Toshiba NMOS data.

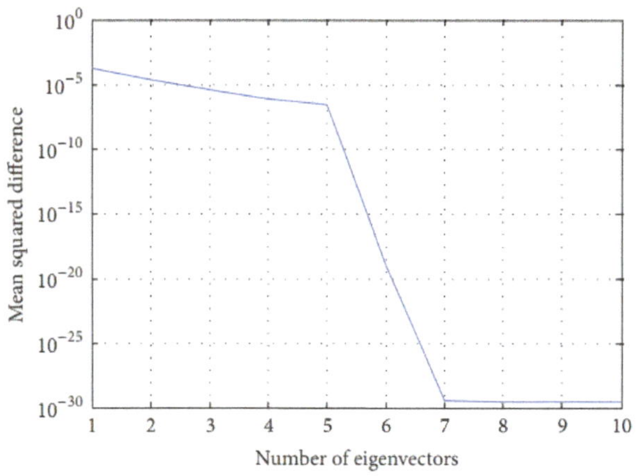

Figure 8: Mean square difference between original (mean-subtracted) data and PCA approximated data as the number of eigenvectors increases.

Application of PCA to Reduce Dimensionality in MC Simulation

PCA clearly has value in reducing the dimensionality of the randomisation required for MC analysis. It is now possible to randomize the principal component coefficient vectors rather than the complete list of device parameters, and then transform these back to a set of parameters for each device. An independent randomisation may clearly be performed for each device, where the effects of interdie or intradie correlations are not required to be modeled.

However, the modelling of intradie variability is afforded in a convenient way by the use of PC coefficient vectors, and the correlation introduced by proximity on the die can be conveniently applied to these. Interdie variability can also be introduced in this way. The approach is to determine a set of PCs for each device model and then to introduce correlation into the corresponding PC coefficient vectors for each device within a circuit or subcircuit, according to the exponential model outlined previously. The correlation matrix should be partitioned into a number of smaller ones, each catering for one principal component which will be independent of all the others. If the device model has N PCs, there will be N partitions, one for each PC. A different value of λ can be used for each partition.

Statistical Behavioural Circuit Blocks (SBCB)

A statistical behavioural circuit block (SBCB) is a behavioural model of a device such as a transistor, or a circuit building block such as a gate or an adder. Such a block may be based on a combination of a look-up table and a simplified passive circuit. Its purpose is to model the most important aspects of the device's or circuit building block's behaviour, to an acceptable accuracy, with a relatively small number of parameters. An SBCB may be defined as a dependent voltage or current source combined with a linear time-invariant "tau" circuit. Such a combination can be optimised to match a required delay and switching waveshape, and this approach has been found to eliminate difficulties with the time-step adjustment algorithm that is sometimes encountered when using MC analysis with versions of SPICE.

Look-Up Tables and Tau Modelling

SPICE provides versatile dependent voltage and current sources [30] which can model switching behaviour which is a linear or nonlinear function of controlling-node voltages, branch currents, or time. These elements have many possible functions including "behavioural" voltage or current sources [30] and ideal delay elements. Ideal delay elements could be very useful in behavioural simulation, but their use for MC analysis raises problems which will be discussed later. A 2-input NAND gate ($X=A$ NAND B) using an "e-element" look-up table to model ideal switching behaviour is represented by the SPICE netlist in Table 1. Figure 9 shows the response of this NAND gate to a voltage pulse with finite (10 ns) rise time and fall time.

Table 1: Netlist for 2-input NAND gate using e-element

e *X* 0 NAND (2) *A* 0 *B* 0	
+0.0	5.0 v
+0.5	4.8 v
+1.0	4.5 v
+4.0	0.5 v
+5.0	0.0 v

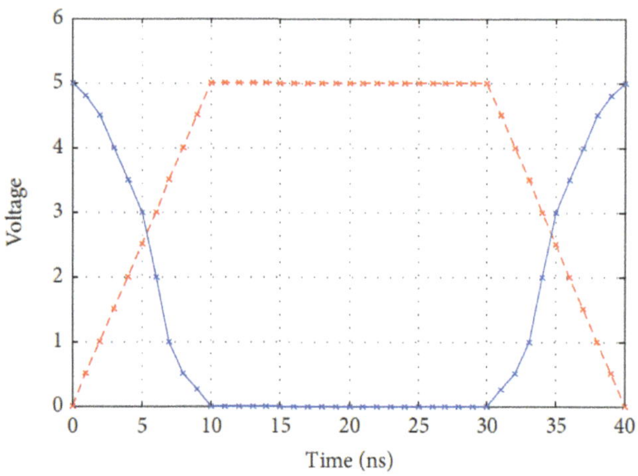

Figure 9: Response of 2-input NAND as defined in Table 1.

The use of such ideal voltage-dependent elements provides a good way to build up behavioural models suitable for augmenting with delay modelling for statistical timing analysis. It is also useful to employ voltage-controlled resistors to implement a switch-level MOSFET.

The tau model of a transistor has long been used as a simple behavioural model in many transistor optimisation tools for designing integrated circuits, such as TILOS [31], COP [32], and EPOXY [33]. It is commonly used for both synchronous and asynchronous circuits [34]. In its simplest form, each transistor is modelled as an ideal switch with appropriate on/off resistance and source, gate, and drain capacitance introduced by discrete capacitors each being determined from the gate dimensions. The gate delays between inputs *A* and *B* and the output *X* of a CMOS 2-input "pull-down" circuit may be modelled [34] by the *RC* circuit in Figure 10.

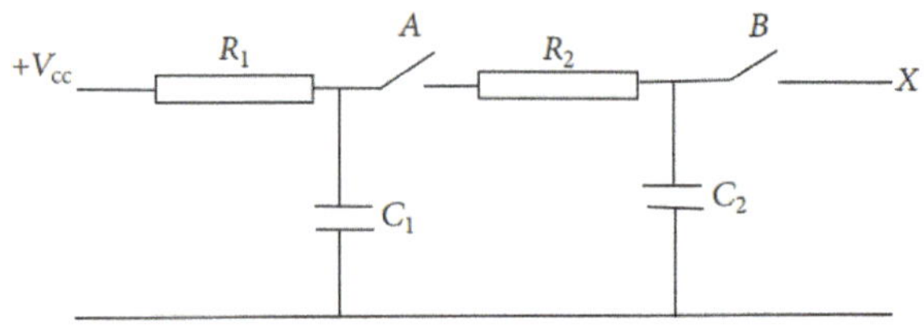

Figure 10: Tau model for CMOS "pull down" sub-circuit.

The following expressions are obtained for $\alpha_{\uparrow AX}$ and $\alpha_{\uparrow BX}$ which are the time constants in the response to rising *A* and *B* transitions, respectively:

$$\alpha_{\uparrow AX} = R_1 C_1 + (R_1 + R_2) C_2,$$

$$\alpha_{\uparrow BX} = (R_1 + R_2) C_2. \quad (24)$$

Look-up tables, as exemplified in Table 1, and "tau models" as in Figure 10 are very simple but individually have limitations. Look-up tables can model limiting and nonlinear "slew rates" but not delay, whereas tau models are either restrictive if simple versions are used or complicated with more accurate ones. Time constants are achieved with characteristic exponentially rising or falling waveforms that may not be close to the true switching waveforms. However, combining these two techniques produces better behavioural models that are still quite simple. The tau model is used to produce the required delay, and the look-up table then modifies the waveshape with appropriately chosen entries.

If the output of a tau model is applied to the look-up table-defined e-element in Table 1, the result will be an output waveform affected both by delay and waveshaping according to the look-up table.

A curve fitting procedure can optimize the tau-model elements and the look-up table for the true waveshape produced by the device for which a behavioural model is required.

This "tau and delay" SBCB model may be used for statistical static timing analysis. In some ways, it is similar to the "composite current source" (CCS) modelling technique produced by Synopsys [35] and the "effective current source model" (ECSM) provided by CADENCE Design Systems Ltd [36]. CCS and ECSM use similar modelling techniques and are supported by comprehensive libraries of cell models and interconnect models [37], which are based on industry-supplied data. Some details of these models are commercial and not openly available. Similar approaches are the "blade and razor" model [38] and a patent by Cadence Design Systems [39]. There have been many other publications inspired by the original idea of using controlled current sources with passive delay circuits to model the behaviour of interconnection and cells with respect to their timing delay, noise generation, power consumption, and statistical variability characteristics [40–43].

The "tau and delay" modelling approach proposed previously uses voltage-controlled voltage sources (VCVS) rather than voltage- or time-dependent current sources. The choice was made arbitrarily since we did utilise any existing libraries, though the dominance of interconnection delay in submicron technologies offers some justification for our approach. It is argued [42] that nonlinearised Thevenin or voltage-source-based driver cell models cannot easily be adapted to accurately modelling the effect of loads with highly nonlinear characteristics. Current source modelling has therefore been generally preferred for modelling the nonlinear aspects of the input-output relationships of cells and their interconnections. However, it is often pointed out (e.g., [35]) that VCCS-based models can easily be converted to VCVS-based models and vice versa.

Our SBCS modelling approach was used to produce a single model of each cell type. Each SBCS is characterised by parameters which may be randomised to simulate the effect of statistical circuit variation. The statistical characteristics of the randomisation (distribution, mean, and standard deviation) were derived from transistor-level simulations of true devices. In principal, a different look-up table is needed for each value of delay, but the required adjustments were found to be very small.

Behavioural Models for MC Simulation

SPICE offers a large number of different ways of defining and randomising behavioural models, and we have suggested yet another alternative. The most sophisticated version of SPICE, HSPICE, does not often specify how certain features are implemented, and the open-sourced NGSPICE, though based on the same long-established analysis engine, does not have many of these features. All dependent sources in HSPICE have "ideal" delay as an option, which is trivial to achieve in digital circuits but unachievable exactly in analogue circuits. Modelling ideal delay in analogue circuits can cause difficulties with MC analysis since randomising such delays can cause SPICE to make increasingly slow progress and eventually to "hang." Investigations revealed that, when this happened, it was not the models, but the step-size selection that was to blame. If ideal delays are specified with high numerical precision, the relative timing of events on a single chip can appear to vary almost continuously. Coincident switching events when randomised may become different but very close together. The time-step adaptation algorithm will try to model the very small timing differences and thus generate exceedingly small time steps. Quantizing the Monte Carlo variation eliminates this problem which means that the randomisation should ideally be done with reference to the anticipated time-step size. However, the effect on the results of the statistical analysis must then be investigated.

The modified tau-modelling approach has been adopted for the statistical behavioural circuit blocks to be described in the next subsection. Matching MC randomisation of behavioural model parameters to the step-adaptation algorithm of SPICE is a matter deserving further investigation as there may be great economies and insights to be gained.

Building Up SBCBs

SBCBs are used to replace true or accurately modelled subblocks to reduce the dimensionality and therefore the complexity of the analysis. By analysing a representative and random sample of fabricated gates, a delay distribution may be obtained whose statistical properties (pdf, mean, variance, etc.) can be used to define the SBCB.

COMPUTATION REDUCTION BY EXTREME VALUE THEORY

Extreme value theory (EVT) [44] is a branch of statistics concerned with the estimation of probabilities which are "extreme" in the sense that the range of values of interest is many standard deviations from the mean of an assumed probability distribution. An algorithm known as "statistical blockade" (SB) [6, 7] applies EVT to circuit analysis by eliminating or "blocking out" randomised parameter vectors that are considered unlikely to produce circuits that fall in the low-probability tails. The intention is that only the ones likely to produce "rare events" are analysed. In our application, the rare events are the circuit yield failure predictions which are extreme in the sense that they are on the "tails" of Gaussian-like probability distributions for circuit quantities such as overall delay. Because they are designed to be rare, reliable estimates of these failures by conventional MC techniques require very large numbers of randomised input vectors.

The idea of SB is to try to concentrate on parameter vectors that are likely to generate the "rare events" of failing circuits and block out or disregard the ones that are unlikely to produce such failing circuits. Many input vectors are generated, but only the ones likely to produce "rare events" are simulated. This partial sampling of the performance distributions is the basis of EVT. The computational complexity involved in introducing the bias and compensating for it is much less expensive than performing many uninteresting circuit simulations. The "blockade filter" is a standard classifier used in machine learning and data mining. It is trained by simulating a relatively small "training set" of randomized circuits and is further refined as more and more simulations are carried out. Statistical blockade with this recursive updating is intended to make estimation of rare event statistics computationally feasible.

The implementation of SB is initiated by a "seed" netlist which specifies the basic circuit with its SBCB blocks. This netlist also specifies which parameters are to be randomized and the statistics (mean, standard deviation, etc.) of the required randomisation. It can be divided into four parts.(i)The training of an estimator for predicting circuit performance with minimal computation. This requires a sufficiently large training set of randomized circuits to be generated and analysed by SPICE. In our work, the coefficients of a linear estimator are calculated using the "pseudoinverse" approach, and there must be many more randomized circuits than parameters. The coefficients are computed to make the estimator minimise the sum of the squared differences between the estimated circuit output measurements and the "true" circuit output measurement, as obtained from SPICE, over the whole set of training circuits. (ii)The generation of a much larger set of randomized versions of the circuit, and the use of a classifier to "block" the versions that are not likely to be within the tail. The classifier consists of the "linear estimator" followed by a "threshold" comparison with a "start of tail" parameter. Only the circuit copies which are estimated to fall within the tail will be unblocked and submitted for analysis by simulation.(iii)The "recursive" refinements of the linear estimator as more and more simulations are carried out. When a sufficient number of nonblocked "tail" circuits have been analysed, a second estimator is calculated using the "pseudoinverse" technique. The second estimator is more accurate than the original estimator for the tail and may be used for more accurate blocking. The use of recursion can move the defined "start of tail" parameter further away from the mean: typically from two to 3 or 4 standard deviations. Through recursion, we can thus get more accuracy in more extreme parts of the tail.(iv)The fitting of a Pareto Distribution (PD) to the measurements obtained from the nonblocked ("statistical tail") versions of the circuit. This is necessary because, with SB, the non-tail circuits are blocked (not analysed) so we can no longer use Gaussian statistics. Also, very few measurements will occur in the "far tail" even when large numbers of circuits are generated. The use of PD fitting to the rarely occurring "tail circuits" allows the prediction of likely yield without the very large number of circuit simulations that would be required with traditional MC analysis.

To illustrate the computation time savings that may be achieved when synchronous and asynchronous circuits employing SBCB blocks are statistically analysed by MC techniques with SB, a frequently used handshaking component in the asynchronous control circuits produced by the BALSA design package [45], that is, a C-element [46], was considered. The intention was to compare the speed and accuracy achievable with that of straightforward MC analysis. A binary full adder, using NAND gates as building blocks, and a 4-Phase Bundled Data Muller pipeline and a Muller "ring," each using the C-element as building blocks, were also used as test circuits. The use of SB to analyse the switching delay of the output of a single C-element was found to reduce the computation time by about 98.5%, when the start of the distribution tail was defined to be two standard deviations (2σ) from the mean.

The accuracy of the linear estimator obtained with the start of tail defined 2σ from the mean is illustrated by the scatter graph in Figure 11. It was obtained by applying SB to 1000 copies of the binary full adder circuit. The blue points represent the measurements which are in the tail and not blocked.

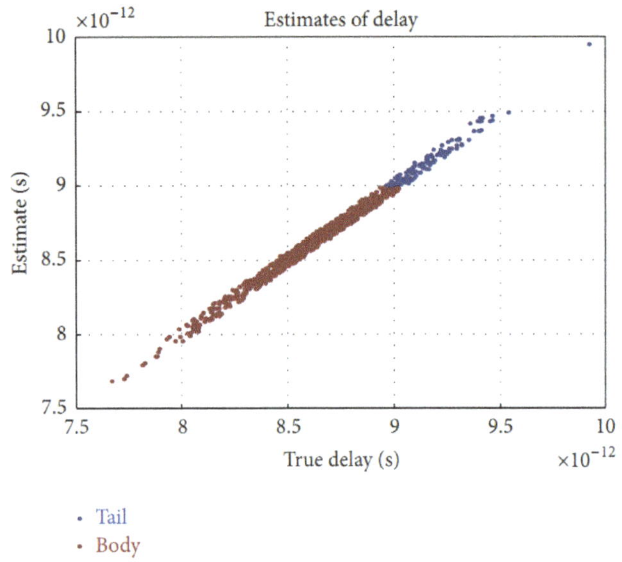

Figure 11: Accuracy of linear estimator. Tail defined to start at $9e-12s$. Classification errors out of 1000: wrong to block: 4, wrong not to block: 2.

To obtain accurate predictions of behaviour further from the mean, recursion was employed to refine the accuracy of the original estimator using the results of nonblocked simulations. Figure 12(b) shows the effect of recalculating the estimator from the tail points, shown in Figure 12(a), as identified by the original 2σ estimator. The experiment is applying recursion to the tail points obtained from blocking 1000 copies of the 4-Phase Bundled Data Muller pipeline circuit shown in Figure 13.

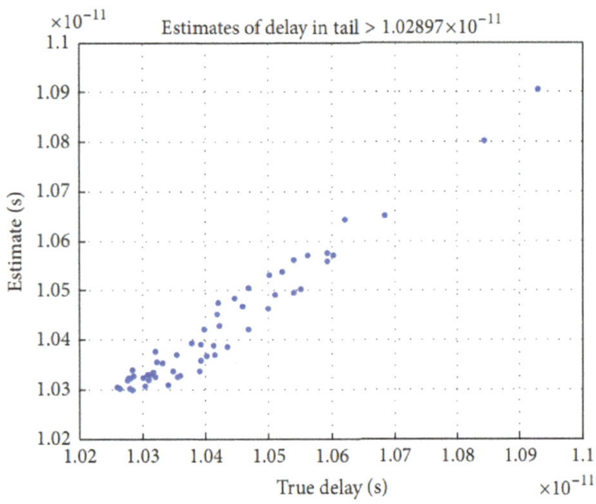

(a) Original

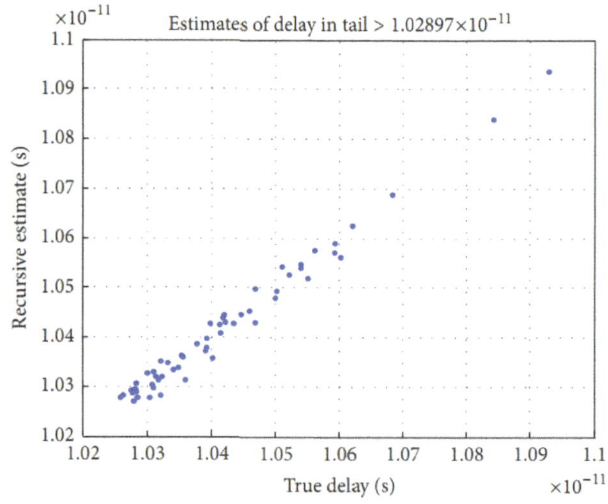

(b) Refined

Figure 12: Refining linear estimator by recursion.

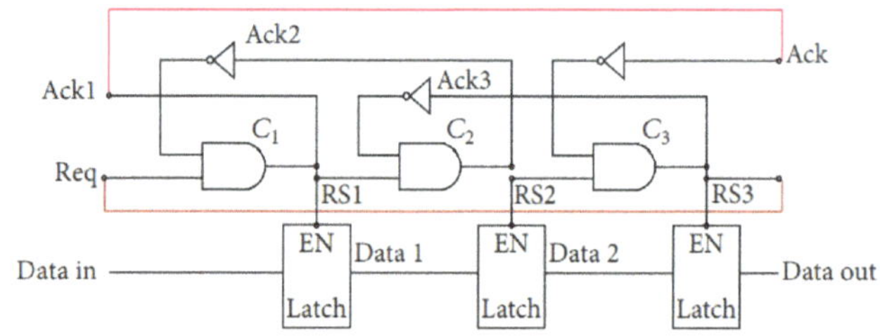

Figure 13: 4-Phase 3-stage Bundled Data Muller pipeline "ring."

The estimated failure probability distributions shown in Figures 16(a) and 16(b) were obtained for the behavioural model of a single C-element, as shown in Figure 14, with parameters for each behavioural gate model extracted from transistor-level simulations referred to in Section 3.2.3. Figure 15(a) was obtained by traditional MC analysis and plots the yield failure probability against yield threshold, showing how the failure probability reduces as the permissible delay increases. The threshold value is measured in seconds relative to a reference delay 200 ps from the start of the analysis where the trigger occurs at 100 picoseconds from the start. The graphs show the distribution tails only, which are assumed to start at two standard deviations (i.e., 2×0.657 ps) from the mean which is 29.7 ps relative to 200 ps. Therefore, the graphs show a time scale from 31 ps (relative to 200 ps) and extending over 5 standard deviations. The graph shown in Figure 15(b) was obtained from MC analysis with SB and a Pareto fit to the tail assumed to start at two standard deviations from the mean, which was set to 31 ps. Figure 15(b) may be seen to be close to Figure 15(a) as obtained from traditional MC analysis with much greater computation. To assess the quality of fit, the two graphs are shown on the same axes in Figure 15(c).

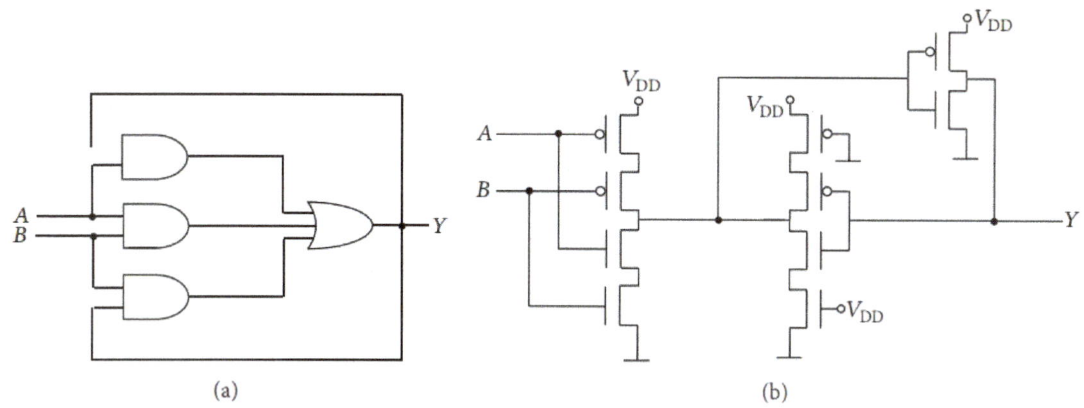

Figure 14: Muller C-element: (a) gate level, (b) transistor level.

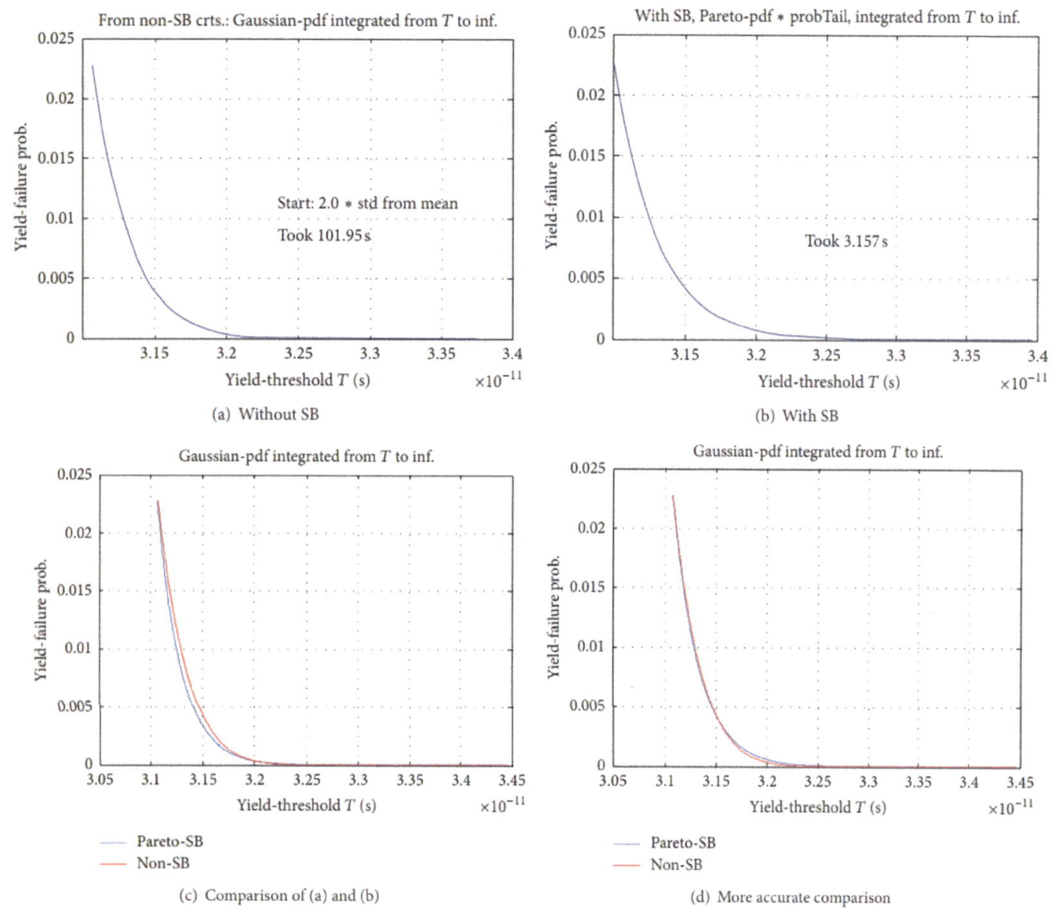

Figure 15: Failure probability for a "C-element" realisation from 500 versions: (a) without SB, (b) with SB (2σ from mean), (c) comparison of (a) and (b), and (d) comparison with more accurate estimates of mean and standard deviation used for Pareto-SB.

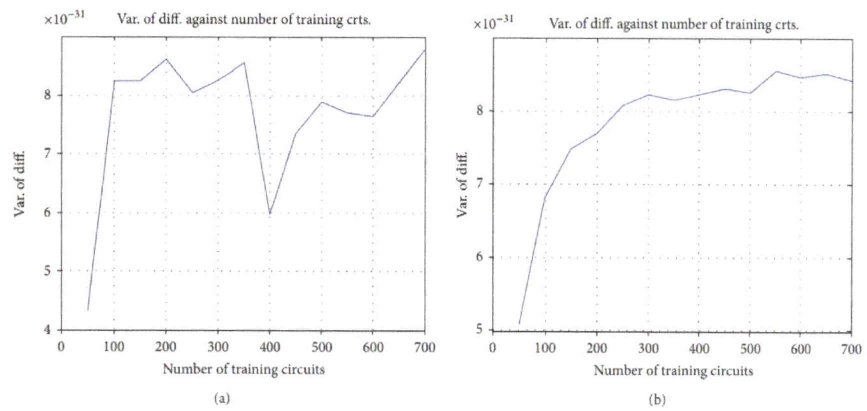

Figure 16: Error analysis of linear estimators in RandomLA training phase: (a) MC simulation and (b) QMC simulation.

It may be seen that the maximum difference in yield threshold delay between the two graphs for any yield failure probability is about 0.06ps seconds, which is about 0.1 standard deviations. A more useful measure of difference is the maximum difference in yield failure probability. This cannot accurately be deduced from the graphs, but a resampling of the data plotted in one of the two graphs (since the sampling instants are different) revealed that this maximum difference occurred at a yield threshold of 31.23ps and is equal to a probability difference of 0.002. This represents a discrepancy of approximately 14.2% from the probability 0.0129 predicted by the non-SB Monte Carlo simulation being used as a reference. Thus the maximum discrepancy in the yield failure probability is 14.2% which occurs when the yield threshold delay is 0.1 standard deviations.

Since a possible source of this discrepancy is the quality and suitability of the Pareto fit, some investigations were carried out. It was observed that one source of the discrepancy was the difference in mean and standard deviation of the Gaussian fits to the delay measurements produced on one hand by the non-SB MC simulations ("meanNB" and "sigmaNB") and on the other hand by the training procedure ("meanTR" and "sigmaTR"). These are used to determine the "start of tail" parameter at two standard deviations from the mean. The more accurate estimations "meanNB" and "sigmaNB" are available for producing the comparisons since a computationally expensive non-SB will have been carried out for test purposes. But in reality, only the less accurate "meanTR" and "sigmaTR" estimates (based on far fewer randomised circuits) will be available to the SB version and were therefore used in the comparison.

As a test, "meanTR" and "sigmaTR" were replaced by "meanNB" and "sigmaNB," thus eliminating two sources of discrepancy and allowing the suitability of the Pareto fit to be seen more clearly in Figure 15(d). It was found that the two graphs did indeed become closer, the maximum discrepancy being 0.00061 in a non-SB yield probability measurement of 0.0136, that is, a 4.5% discrepancy. A conclusion from this investigation is that the Pareto fit is capable of giving a reasonable approximation to a Gaussian tail, incurring error likely to be less than that resulting from other statistical estimates. Also, we concluded that there is scope for increased accuracy in the SB estimations, for example, by updating the estimates of mean and standard deviation as statistical analysis proceeds.

With a more accurate estimator, the "start of tail" parameter may then be redefined as two or even three standard deviations from the mean to obtain even greater time saving since even fewer circuits need to be analysed. This increases the possibility of finding measurements yet further from the mean, that is, "rarer events," in reasonable computational time and allows a yet more accurate estimation of the statistics of the "far tail."

Table 2 summarises the computation time savings that were obtained by applying SB to the statistical variability analysis of three of the circuits mentioned above. The computation was carried out on a standard desktop PC with a dual core 2.8GHz Intel processor. A MATLAB program that harnesses an implementation of SPICE carried out the randomisation, implementation of SB, and statistical analysis. It may be seen that the most significant computation time saving, 98.7%, was achieved for a 4-Phase 3-stage Bundled Data Muller pipeline "ring," with the start of the tail defined at two standard deviations from the mean.

Table 2: Time saving illustrated by comparing simulations with SB to simulations without SB.

Circuit	Binary full adder 9 parameters		C-element 12 parameters		Muller pipeline ring 21 parameters	
Start of tail	1.5σ	2σ	1.5σ	2σ	1.5σ	2σ
1000 circuit without SB	215.99 s	221.34 s	250.05 s	288.51 s	949.59 s	1003.9 s
1000 circuit with SB	6.75 s	3.96 s	7.63 s	4.24 s	27.17 s	13.15 s
Time saving	96.9%	98.2%	96.94%	98.5%	97.1%	98.7%

COMPUTATION REDUCTION BY QUASI-MONTE CARLO TECHNIQUES

This section investigates the use of "low-discrepancy" sampling to achieve further efficiency improvements, over what was achieved in earlier sections, with Monte Carlo circuit simulation. Low-discrepancy sampling is the basis of "quasi-Monte Carlo" (QMC) techniques as often applied to multidimensional integration; therefore, this approach to circuit simulation may be referred to as "quasi-Monte Carlo" simulation. QMC methods are modified Monte Carlo methods where the input vectors are not totally random but are to a degree deterministic in that they conform to "low-discrepancy sequences" [47, 48]. A low-discrepancy sequence is a sequence of N-dimensional vectors which covers a finite space more uniformly than is achieved by Ndimensional vectors of independent uniformly distributed random elements. The discrepancy of a sequence of vectors is a measure of how the number of points they define in a multidimensional cube varies with the position and size of the cube. If the discrepancy is low, the same-sized cube will always contain approximately the same number of points wherever it is located, and the number of points will be proportional to the volume of the cube. A sequence of vectors of independent uniformly distributed random elements does not give low discrepancy when the dimensionality is high. It is known that the use of low-discrepancy vector sequences can achieve significant speed gains over standard Monte Carlo integration techniques by reducing the number of input vectors needed for a given accuracy [49]. Similar gains are anticipated when QMC is used for statistical circuit simulation.

As mentioned in Section 2.1, traditional Monte Carlo methods with statistically independent input vectors are argued to have a convergence rate proportional to $R^{-1/2}$ which is independent of dimensionality N. Quasi-Monte Carlo (QMC) methods are claimed to have a much better rate of convergence approaching proportionality with R^{-1} in optimal cases [50]. A theoretical upper bound for the convergence rates of multivariate low-discrepancy sequences is reported to be proportional to $(\ln R)/R$ [5], where N is the number of dimensions. QMC performance therefore decreases with the dimensionality N.

Uniformly distributed numbers in the interval (0, 1) can be generated as pseudorandom numbers or quasirandom numbers, and the variables for all other distributions may be derived from these by means of the appropriate cumulative distribution function inversion. In practice the range must be restricted from (0, 1) to $(\alpha, 1-\alpha)$ for small positive α; otherwise, Gaussian variables very far from the mean may occur with QMC and cause numerical instability. Examining a Gaussian pdf graph reveals that taking $\alpha = 10^{-6}$ or 10^{-11} restricts the transformed variables between 5 or 7 standard deviations, respectively, from the mean.

The MATLAB functions "Haltonset" and "Sobolset" are provided for constructing initial sequences of N-dimensional quasirandom vectors with the required properties. To avoid the undesirable effects of any correlations, especially in the initial segments, the random sequence obtained can be required to skip, leap over, or scramble values in the sequence as generated. Scrambling reduces correlations while also improving uniformity. These sequences use different prime bases to form successively finer uniform partitions of the unit interval in each dimension. Latin hyper-cube sequences, as used by SPICE, are generated by the "lhsdesig" function. Strictly, these are not LD sequences, but they nevertheless produce uniform samples of a sort.

As suggested in this work, the idea is to use a lowdiscrepancy sequence generator to replace the uniform random number generator as the source of randomisation in both the training and the recursive SB phases of RandomLA, the developed MATLAB software in the research. The choice of LDS will be "Sobol." First, we present an example that compares the effect of using QMC rather than MC for training the linear estimator. Then we investigate the effectiveness of QMC for MC simulation with and without Statistical Blockade.

To provide comparison for training, an SRAM32×1 array circuit was taken as an example that is described in more detail in Section 6. The convergence of the linear estimator training using MC and QMC was analysed and compared.

As shown in Figure 16, the QMC training converges more quickly and smoothly to an estimator producing the minimum "variance of difference" attainable, approximately 9×10^{-31}, than MC training with pseudorandom vectors, which is shown in Figure 16(a). The measure is just the variance of the prediction error. With QMC training, the variance becomes close to optimum with about 300 training circuits, whereas the number needed for MC is about 700 training circuits. The reason for this improved training is probably the more reliable coverage of QMC, for a given number of circuits (sample size) across the whole domain of parameters which gives us more "tail" circuits, even without the advantages of Statistical Blockade.

Figure 17 shows the yield predictions obtained by MC and QMC analysis with and without Statistical Blockade and Pareto fitting for the "binary full adder" circuit in Figure 3. There are 36 transistors, and each was randomized based on two PCA components giving 72 parameters for the "transistor-level" statistical analysis. The nonblockade analysis was carried out, with MC randomisation only, on 3000 circuits which took 3497.1 seconds. The results were taken as a benchmark for comparison with both MC-SB and QMC-SB, though a benchmark close to this could have been obtained with about 700 fewer circuits using nonblockade QMC.

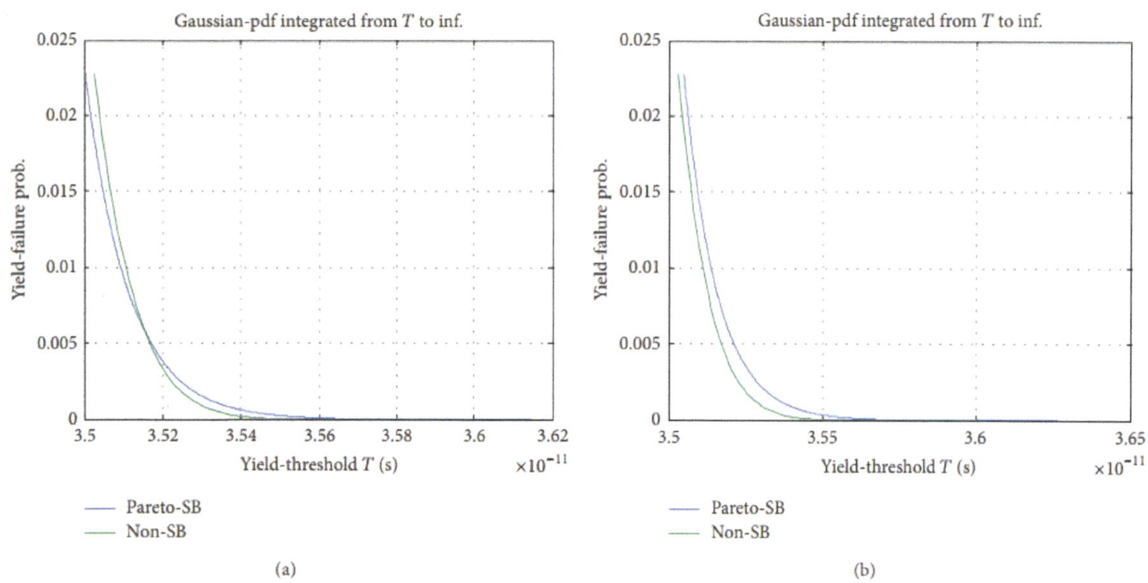

Figure 17: (a) MC-SB compared to MC-non-SB for BFA (3000 circuits), (b) QMC-SB compared to MC-non-SB for BFA (3000 circuits).

Both MC and QMC Statistical Blockades were applied using 300 training circuits in both cases. The estimator order, as always, was equal to the number of parameters, that is, 72 in this case. The analysis time for recursive SB with MC and QMC was 146.6 s and 120.6 s, respectively, achieving close to 99% savings in each case with statistical variation from run to run, depending on how many circuits are blocked; it is not uncommon for QMC-SB to take longer than MCSB when the same number of circuits is specified. Where the criterion is accuracy and reliability, QMC reduces the required sample size. For a given sample size, the advantages of QMC with SB over "non-SB" are not as striking as those of MC-SB over MC without SB. More analysis is needed on this matter. As in Section 5, the effects of the difference in mean and standard deviation produced by the non-SB simulations and the training procedure can be seen in Figure 17. If better estimates were available, the graphs would be closer. For QMC, the maximum discrepancy in yield failure estimates between SB and non-SB is a probability difference of about 0.003 or 0.3%. For MC the discrepancy was less, that is, about 0.1%.

RESULTS AND EVALUATION WITH SRAM ARRAYS

Effect of Correlation on Failure Yield Analysis of an SRAM8 × 1 Array

The 8×1 SRAM array shown in Figure 18 was analysed to predict its yield, subject to a maximum delay constraint. All "Bitlines" were set to "1," the "bit" nodes were initialised to "0," and the "Wordline" inputs switched from "0" to "1" at a fixed point in time, causing the "bit" outputs to switch to "1" with random delay. A SPICE harness in MATLAB randomised the device parameters and made repeated calls to SPICE to analyse the effect of these parameter variations on the delays at the "bit" nodes.

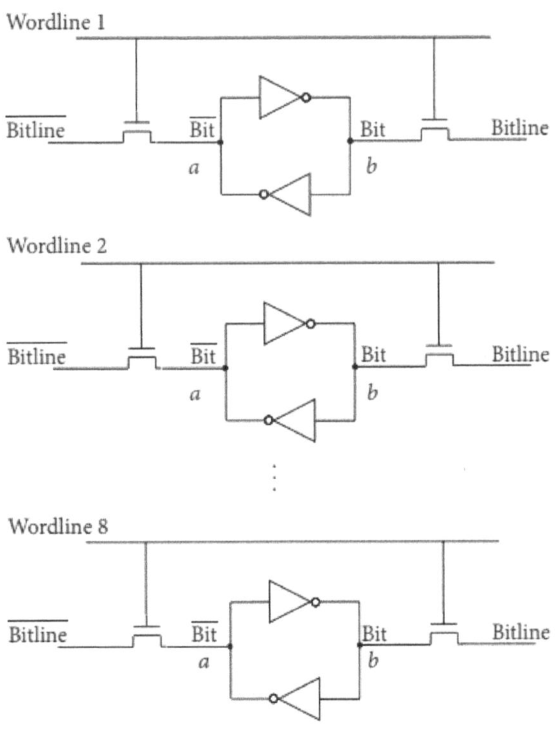

Figure 18: SRAM array circuit.

There are 48 transistors within the circuit. Transistorlevel simulations of the array were carried out to estimate the yield failure probability for different values of yield threshold when statistical variability is included in the model for each transistor. This was obtained by connecting the eight outputs from the array, all initialised to zero, to a behaviourally modelled NAND gate whose output switching delay was compared to the threshold. The statistics for the parameter variation were derived from analyses of the 35 nm transistor model data set provided by RandomSPICE. Two extreme cases were considered: firstly where there is assumed to be strong intradie cell-to-cell correlation between randomised device parameters of a particular type and secondly where there is no intradie correlation between devices from cell to cell. A graph obtained for yield failure probability against allowable delay threshold for the strong correction case is shown in Figure 19. The "vth0" parameters of all six devices within each of the eight cells were parameterised with $\lambda = 0.007$.

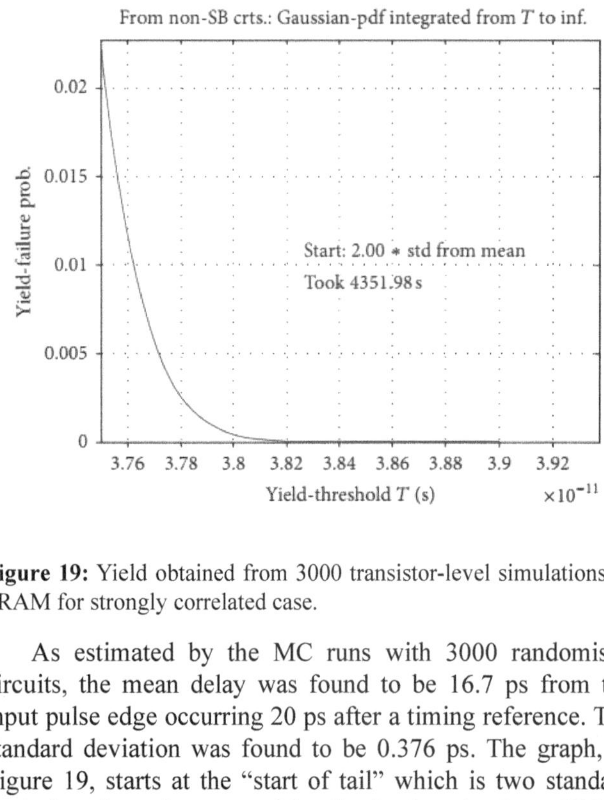

Figure 19: Yield obtained from 3000 transistor-level simulations of SRAM for strongly correlated case.

As estimated by the MC runs with 3000 randomised circuits, the mean delay was found to be 16.7 ps from the input pulse edge occurring 20 ps after a timing reference. The standard deviation was found to be 0.376 ps. The graph, in Figure 19, starts at the "start of tail" which is two standard deviations from the mean of the distribution, that is, at 37.5 ps from the timing reference.

The results obtained from the noncorrelation case are presented in Figure 20. The eight cells were randomised by independent variables with negligible correlation ($\lambda = 10$). The mean was observed to be 40.1 ps from the timing reference (i.e., 20 ps from the edge), and the standard deviation was 0.263 ps. There is a reduction in standard deviation from 0.376 ps for the strongly correlated case to 0.263 ps, which is a factor of 0.69. With independent Gaussian parameter variations, the distribution of worst case cell delay which determines the yield failure probability is no longer Gaussian. It becomes a type of "Gumbel" distribution [51]. The results indicate that the standard deviation reduces by a factor of 0.69, and the mean increases by 1.436 standard deviations. Comparing the strongly correlated case (Figure 19) with the noncorrelated case (Figure 20), it can be seen that the intradie correlation can have a significant effect on predictions of yield failure probability

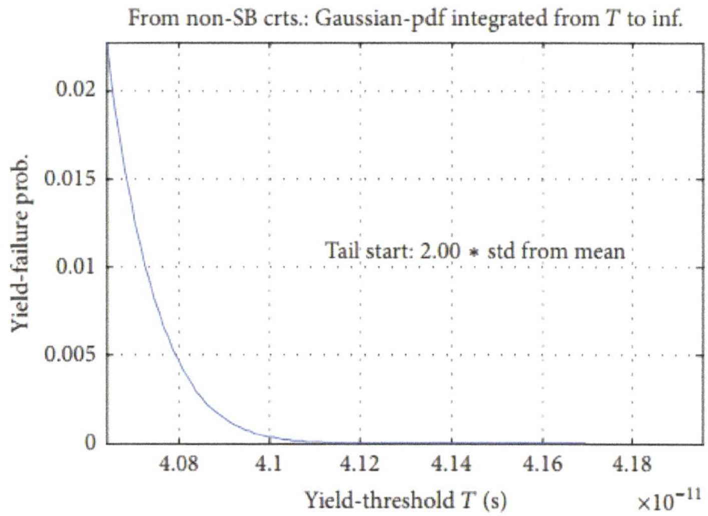

Figure 20: Yield obtained from 3000 transistor-level simulations of SRAM for noncorrelated case.

Evaluation with an SRAM Array

Thirty-two copies of Figure 18 were cascaded to construct the 32×8 array shown as Figure 21. There are 1536 transistors within the circuit. The SBCB model of this array is established from the single cell model and connected together. The simulations were undertaken for the strong correlation case only.

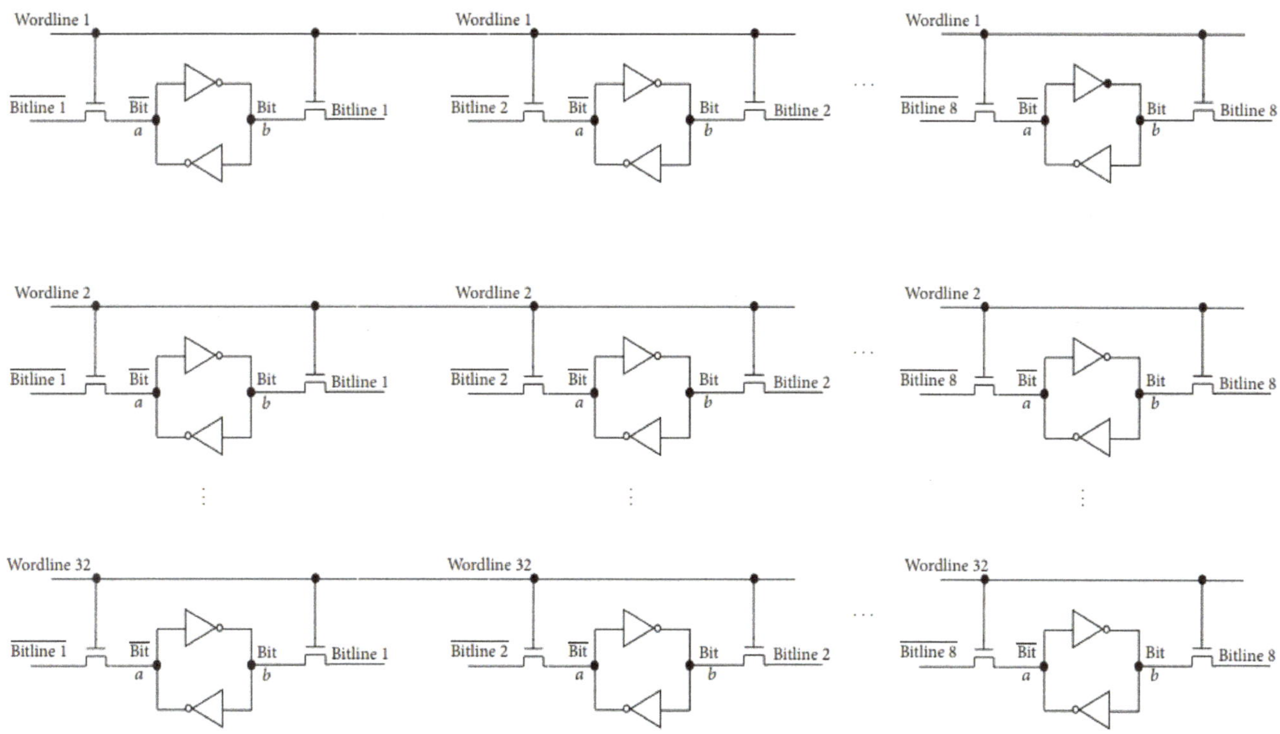

Figure 21: SRAM array circuit.

Figures 22 and 23 present the graphs obtained from the simulations; the run times are given in Table 3. The observed delay mean and standard deviation are very close to the ones in Figure 19 for the SRAM8×1 array, which is as expected for the strongly correlated case with all cells in parallel.

Table 3: Run times and time savings for MC/QMC simulations of the SRAM32 × 8 array (strongly correlated)

	Transistor model: ngSRAM32 × 8.seed				SBCB model: ngswSRAM32 × 8.seed			
	MC		QMC		MC		QMC	
	Non-SB	SB	Non-SB	SB	Non-SB	SB	Non-SB	SB
CPU time/s	47263.96	1481.69 $W = 13$	39373.99	1183.59 $W = 0$	2376.14	63.70 $W = 6$	2148.03	69.84 $W = 0$
Time saving	96.87%		96.99%		97.32%		96.75%	
Overall time saving = (47263.96 − 69.84)/47263.96 = 99.85%								

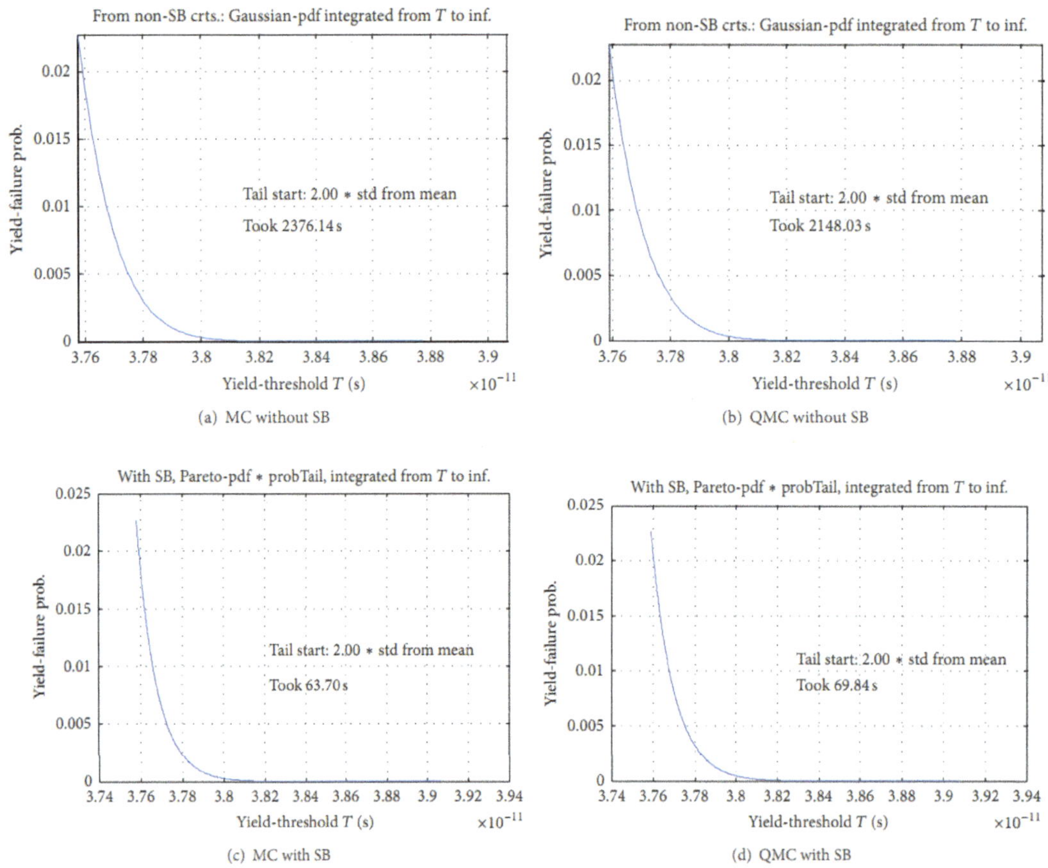

Figure 22: Yield obtained from 3000 behavioural-level simulations of SRAM for strongly correlated case, (a) MC without SB, (b) QMC without SB, (c) MC with SB, and (d) QMC with SB.

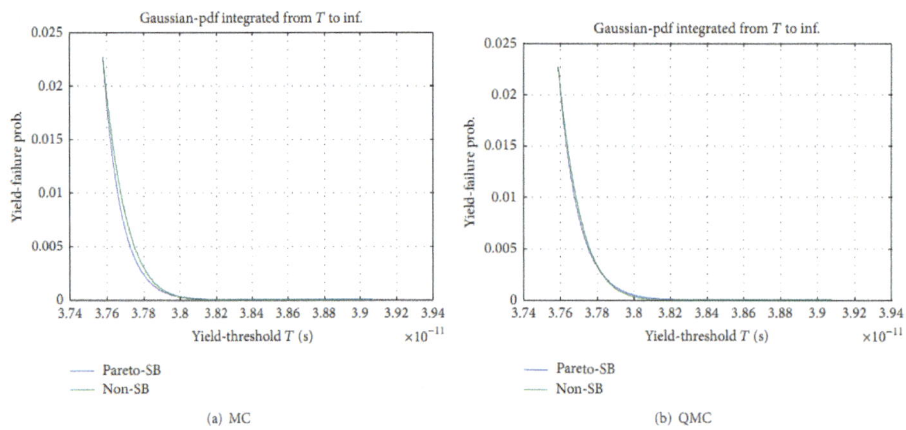

Figure 23: Comparison of yield analysis results of SB and non-SB for behavioural-level SRAM simulations for strongly correlated case, (a) MC and (b) QMC.

Analysis of the results revealed the following.

- SB with Pareto fitting version is reasonably accurate and much faster in comparison to the "nonblockade" version.
- For the SB simulations with strong correlation, the number of wrong decisions not to block "W" was always close to zero for QMC with Sobol points, while the number for MC fluctuated between zero and about 20 when there were 3000 circuits being analysed. This is an indication of the accuracy of the linear estimator which was found to be better for "Sobol" vector training with under 200 training circuits than for MC with pseudorandom parameter vectors. The results also demonstrate that QMC with Sobol vectors can make nonblockade simulation more efficient, reaching a given accuracy with fewer runs than are required with MC.
- For the noncorrelation examples, the estimator was much less accurate for both MC and QMC training. This caused many more wrong decisions not to block. The results of these wrong decisions are discarded for the Pareto tail fitting procedure with some loss of efficiency. The behaviour of the linear estimator when adapting to the maximum delay criterion explains this loss of efficiency.
- The use of QMC with "Sobol" vectors makes nonblockade more efficient than with MC in that a given accuracy is achieved with fewer runs.
- QMC with SB compared with QMC alone offers further savings, but these remain to be fully analysed.
- When comparing overall time savings for MC with SB and QMC with SB, both the training and the analysis times must be taken into account. A lower number of training circuits were required for QMC simulations than for MC to reach a given estimator accuracy.

From the Gaussian distribution, it may be deduced that, if the delay distribution is Gaussian and the tail is assumed to start at two standard deviations from the mean, the percentage of unblocked circuits may be expected to be about 2.1%. Therefore, out of 3000 randomly generated circuits, about 63 unblocked circuits should be observed. Out of the first 500 circuits, about ten unblocked circuits should occur, and this observation suggests a simple adaptation mechanism for countering inaccuracy in the estimator. After a certain number of random circuits, say 500, have been generated, if the number of unblocked circuits is significantly different from what is expected, say 10, the tail threshold can be decreased or increased accordingly. The decision can be revisited later in the run, say after 1000 circuits, 2000 circuits, and so on. This adaptation was found to be useful in the noncorrelated examples presented in this chapter where the accuracy of the estimator was found to be lower than for the strongly correlated examples. Decreasing the threshold does not greatly affect the computation run time if the intention is to base the tail estimation on a specific number of circuits, say 2.1% of the total. This approach appears even more advantageous when higher deviations from the mean are to be examined, say three or more standard deviations. Instead of specifying a fixed number of randomised circuits, the simulations could be allowed to continue until a suitable number of unblocked circuits have been produced to allow a reliable estimation of the tail distribution.

The timing results quoted in this section are for single-core nondistributed computation. The RandomLA SPICE harness has been developed in such a way that it may be run on multicore machines and distributed frameworks such as Condor. Using parallel or distributed computing facilities can achieve great time savings. For example, rerunning the simulations in this chapter on a dual-core PC achieves a time saving which is very close to 50%, that is, a factor of two reductions in runtime. Using Condor, the run time of the transistor-level simulations of SRAM reduced from 47263.96 s (13.13 hours) to 720 s (12 minutes).

CONCLUSIONS

Monte Carlo (MC) analysis with analogue simulation is an effective tool for the statistical variability analysis of nanoscale IC designs, taking into account the effects of intradie correlation as modelled by well-known techniques. Computational complexity is a major problem, though a variety of adaptations to the standard MC approach can greatly reduce this complexity as demonstrated by examples based on the simple "exponential" model of correlation due to proximity. These examples indicate that disregarding the effects of intradie correlation may give pessimistic estimates of yield. The results obtained from the simulations of SRAM arrays demonstrate the potential of RandomLA to achieve computation reduction for yield analysis with a delay specification. The RandomLA software is highly suitable for parallel and distributed implementations, which have already been shown to achieve great computation time savings.

CONFLICT OF INTERESTS

The software packages mentioned in this paper, such as Cadence, Synopsys, and MATLAB, were purely used for research under the licenses of the University of Manchester. The authors of this paper do not have a direct financial relationship with the owners of those software packages. RandomLA is the software developed by the authors, intending to contribute to "gEDA" project [14] for developing a full GNU public licensed suit of EDA tools.

ACKNOWLEDGMENTS

This research was sponsored by the Engineering and Physical Sciences Research Council (EPSRC) under Grant no. EP/E001947/1. The authors acknowledge the financial support from EPSRC and the collaboration among the people of the Nano-CMOS pilot project, Meeting the Design Challenges of Nano-CMOS Electronics.

REFERENCES

1. H. Onodera, "Variability: modeling and its impact on design," IEICE Transactions on Electronics, vol. E89-C, no. 3, pp. 342–348, 2006.
2. A. Asenov, A. R. Brown, J. H. Davies, S. Kaya, and G. Slavcheva, "Simulation of intrinsic parameter fluctuations in decananometer and nanometer-scale MOSFETs," IEEE Transactions on Electron Devices, vol. 50, no. 9, pp. 1837–1852, 2003.

3. G. Roy, A. R. Brown, F. Adamu-Lema, S. Roy, and A. Asenov, "Simulation study of individual and combined sources of intrinsic parameter fluctuations in conventional nano-MOSFETs," IEEE Transactions on Electron Devices, vol. 53, no. 12, pp. 3063–3069, 2006.
4. A. Srivastava, D. Sylvester, and D. Blaauw, Statistical Analysis and Optimization for VLSI: Timing and Power, Springer, Berlin, Germany, 2005.
5. B. Hargreaves, H. Hult, and S. Reda, "Within-die process variations: How accurately can they be statistically modeled?" in Proceedings of Asia and South Pacific Design Automation Conference (ASP-DAC '08), pp. 524–530, March 2008.
6. A. Singhee and R. A. Rutenbar, "Statistical blockade: a novel method for very fast Monte Carlo simulation of rare circuit events, and its application," in Proceedings of Design, Automation and Test in Europe Conference and Exhibition, pp. 1379–1384, April 2007.
7. A. Singhee, J. Wang, B. H. Calhoun, and R. A. Rutenbar, "Recursive statistical blockade: an enhanced technique for rare event simulation with application to SRAM circuit design," in Proceedings of the 21st International Conference on VLSI Design, pp. 131–136, January 2008.
8. Z. Xie, Computation reduction for statistical analysis of the effect of nano-CMOS variability on integrated circuits [Ph.D. thesis], The University of Manchester, Manchester, UK, 2012.
9. Z. Xie and D. Edwards, "Computation reduction for statistical analysis of the effect of nano-CMOS variability on asynchronous circuits," in Proceedings of the 13th IEEE International Symposium on Design and Diagnostics of Electronic Circuits and Systems (DDECS '10), pp. 161–166, Vienna, Austria, April 2010.
10. E. J. Gumbel, Statistical Theory of Extreme Values and Some Practical Applications, vol. 33 of Applied Mathematical, US Department of Commerce, National Bureau of Standards, Washington, DC, USA, 1954.
11. D. Thain, T. Tannenbaun, and M. Livny, "Distributed computing in practice: the condor experience,"Concurrency and Computation, vol. 17, no. 2–4, pp. 323–356, 2005.
12. "High Throughput Computing Using Condor at Manchester," October 2011, http://condor.eps.manchester.ac.uk/.
13. N. Metropolis and S. Ulam, "The Monte Carlo method," Journal of the American Statistical Association, vol. 44, no. 247, pp. 335–341, 1949. ·
14. "NGSPICE release 23," June 2011, http://www.sourceforge.net,.
15. G. Peter Lepage, "A new algorithm for adaptive multidimensional integration," Journal of Computational Physics, vol. 27, no. 2, pp. 192–203, 1978. ·
16. H. Niederreiter, " Random Number Generation and Quasi-Monte Carlo Methods, vol. 63 of Regional Conference Series in Applied Mathematics, SIAM, Philadelphia, Pa, USA, 1992.
17. R. Bellman, Adaptive Control Processes: A Guided Tour, Princeton University Press, Princeton, NJ, USA, 1961.
18. C. Lemieux, Monte Carlo and Quasi-Monte Carlo Sampling, Springer Series in Statistics, Springer, New York, NY, USA, 2009.
19. H. Niederreiter, "Quasi-Monte Carlo methods and pseudo-random numbers," Bulletin of the American Mathematical Society, 1978.
20. S. K. Chaudhary, Acceleration of Monte Carlo methods using low discrepancy sequences [Ph.D. thesis], UCLA, Los Angeles, Calif, USA, 2004.
21. D. I. Asotsky, E. E. Myshetskaya, and I. M. Sobol', "The average dimension of a multidimensional function for quasi-Monte Carlo estimates of an integral," Computational Mathematics and Mathematical Physics, vol. 46, no. 12, pp. 2061–2067, 2006. · ·
22. A. B. Owen, "Scrambled net variance for integrals of smooth functions," Annals of Statistics, vol. 25, no. 4, pp. 1541–1562, 1997. ·
23. W. H. Press and G. R. Farrar, "Recursive stratified sampling for multidimensional Monte Carlo integration," Computers in Physics, vol. 4, pp. 190–195, 1990.
24. R. Schürer, "Adaptive Quasi-Monte Carlo integration based on MISER and VEGAS," in Monte Carlo and Quasi-Monte Carlo Methods, pp. 393–406, Springer, Berlin, Germany, 2002.
25. G. P. Lepage, "A new algorithm for adaptive multidimensional integration," Journal of Computational Physics, vol. 27, pp. 192–203, 1978.
26. G. P. Lepage, "VEGAS: an adaptive multi-dimensional integration program," Cornell preprint CLNS 80-447, March 1980.
27. J. Keiner and U. Waterhouse, "Fast principal components analysis method for finance problems with unequal time steps," in Monte Carlo and Quasi-Monte Carlo Methods 2008, P. L'Ecuyer and A. B. Owen, Eds., Springer, New York, NY, USA, 2010.
28. "RandomSPICE"-info@GoldStandardSimulations.comhttp://www.GoldStandardSimulations.com/services/circuit-simulation/random-spice/, 2013.
29. B. Bindu, B. Cheng, G. Roy, X. Wang, S. Roy, and A. Asenov, "Parameter set and data sampling strategy for accurate yet efficient statistical MOSFET compact model extraction," Solid-State Electronics, vol. 54, no. 3, pp. 307–315, 2010.
30. HSPICE User Guide: Simulation and Analysis, Version A-2007, Synopsys, Mountain View, Calif, USA, 2007.
31. J. P. Fishburn and A. E. Dunlop, "TILOS: a polynomial programming approach to transistor sizing," inProceedings of IEEE International Conference on Computer-Aided Design (ICCAD '85), pp. 326–328, November 1985.
32. D. P. Marple and A. El Gamal, "Optimal selection of transistor sizes in digital VLSI," in Proceedings of the Stanford Conference on Advanced Research in VLSI, pp. 151–172, MIT Press, 1987.
33. W. Obermeier, An open architecture for improving VLSI circuit performance [Ph.D. thesis], University of

California, Berkekey, Calif, USA, 1989.

34. S. M. Burns, Performance analysis and optimization of Asynchronous Circuits [Ph.D. thesis], California Institute of Technology, Pasadena, Calif, USA, 1990.
35. G. Mekhtarian, Composite Current Source (CCS) Modeling Technology Backgrounder, Synopsys, Mountain View, Calif, USA, 2005, . 11/05.KF.WO .05-13816.
36. R. Goyal and N. Kumar, Current Based Delay Models: A Must for Nanometer Timing, Cadence Design Systems, Noida, India, 2005.
37. Synopsys, "Liberty Library Modeling," July 2012, http://www.synopsys.com/community/interoperability/pages/libertylibmodel.aspx.
38. J. F. Croix and D. F. Wong, "Blade and Razor: cell and interconnect delay analysis using current-based models," in Proceedings of the 40th Design Automation Conference, pp. 386–389, June 2003.
39. J. Li, H. Zhao, and H.-Y. Chiu, "Accuracy Timing Models for Integrated Circuit Verification," U.S. patent number 6721929, April 2004.
40. D. Dasx, W. Scotty, S. Nazariany, and H. Zhoux, "An efficient current-based logic cell model for crosstalk delay analysis," in Proceedings of the 10th International Symposium on Quality Electronic Design (ISQED '09), pp. 627–633, March 2009.
41. M. Rewieński and J. White, "A trajectory piecewise-linear approach to model order reduction and fast simulation of nonlinear circuits and micromachined devices," IEEE Transactions on Computer-Aided Design of Integrated Circuits and Systems, vol. 22, no. 2, pp. 155–170, 2003.
42. P. Li, Z. Feng, and E. Acar, "Characterizing multistage nonlinear drivers and variability for accurate timing and noise analysis," IEEE Transactions on Very Large Scale Integration (VLSI) Systems, vol. 15, no. 11, pp. 1205–1214, 2007.
43. C. Visweswariah, K. Ravindran, K. Kalafala et al., "First-order incremental block-based statistical timing analysis," IEEE Transactions on Computer-Aided Design of Integrated Circuits and Systems, vol. 25, no. 10, pp. 2170–2179, 2006.
44. S. I. Resnick, Extreme Values, Regular Variation and Point Processes, Springer, New York, Ny, USA, 1987.
45. D. Edwards, A. Bardsley, L. Janin, and W. Toms, Balsa: A Tutorial Guide, School of Computer Science, University of Manchester, Manchester, UK, 2008, http://apt.cs.man.ac.uk/projects/tools/balsa/.
46. J. Sparsø and S. Furber, Principles of Asynchronous Circuit Design, Kluwer Academic Publishers, Norwell, Mass, USA, 2005.
47. A. Singhee, Novel Algorithms for Fast Statistical Analysis of Scaled Circuits [Ph.D. thesis], Carnegie Mellon University, Pittsburgh, Pa, USA, 2007.
48. R. E. Caflisch, "Monte Carlo and quasi-Monte Carlo methods," Acta Numerica, vol. 7, pp. 1–49, 1998.
49. L. Kuipers and H. Niederreiter, Uniform Distribution of Sequences, Dover Publications, Dover, UK, 2005.
50. J. Spanier, "Quasi-Monte Carlo methods for particle transport problems," in Monte Carlo and Quasi-Monte Carlo Methods in Scientific Computing, H. Niederreiter and P. J. -S. Shiue, Eds., pp. 121–148, Springer, New York, NY, USA, 1995.
51. E. J. Gumbel, "Statistical Theory of Extreme Values and Some Practical Applications, vol. 33 of Applied Mathematical, Series, US Department of Commerce, National Bureau of Standards, Washington, DC, USA, 1954.

CHAPTER 14

AN INTEGRATED PROCEDURE FOR BAYESIAN RELIABILITY INFERENCE USING MCMC

Jing Lin[1,2]

[1]Division of Operation and Maintenance Engineering, Luleå University of Technology, 97187 Luleå, Sweden

[2]Luleå Railway Research Centre (JVTC), 97187 Luleå, Sweden

ABSTRACT

The recent proliferation of Markov chain Monte Carlo (MCMC) approaches has led to the use of the Bayesian inference in a wide variety of fields. To facilitate MCMC applications, this paper proposes an integrated procedure for Bayesian inference using MCMC methods, from a reliability perspective. The goal is to build a framework for related academic research and engineering applications to implement modern computational-based Bayesian approaches, especially for reliability inferences. The procedure developed here is a continuous improvement process with four stages (Plan, Do, Study, and Action) and 11 steps, including: (1) data preparation; (2) prior inspection and integration; (3) prior selection; (4) model selection; (5) posterior sampling; (6) MCMC convergence diagnostic; (7) Monte Carlo error diagnostic; (8) model improvement; (9) model comparison; (10) inference making; (11) data updating and inference improvement. The paper illustrates the proposed procedure using a case study.

INTRODUCTION

The recent proliferation of Markov Chain Monte Carlo (MCMC) approaches has led to the use of the Bayesian inference in a wide variety of fields, including behavioural science, finance, human health, process control, ecological risk assessment, and risk assessment of engineered systems [1]. Discussions of MCMC-related methodologies and their applications in Bayesian Statistics now appear throughout the literature [2,3]. For the most part, studies in reliability analysis focus on the following topics and their cross-applications: (1) hierarchical reliability models [4–7]; (2) complex system reliability analysis [8–10]; (3) faulty tree analysis [11, 12]; (4) accelerated failure models [13–17]; (5) reliability growth models [18, 19]; (6) masked system reliability [20]; (7) software reliability engineering [21, 22]; (8) reliability benchmark problems [23, 24]. However, most of the literature emphasizes the model's development; no studies offer a full framework to accommodate academic research and engineering applications seeking to implement modern computational-based Bayesian approaches, especially in the area of reliability.

To fill the gap and to facilitate MCMC applications from a reliability perspective, this paper proposes an integrated procedure for the Bayesian inference. The remainder of the paper is organized as follows. Section 2outlines the integrated procedure; this comprises a continuous improvement

Citation: Jing Lin, "An Integrated Procedure for Bayesian Reliability Inference Using MCMC," Journal of Quality and Reliability Engineering, vol. 2014, Article ID 264920, 16 pages, 2014. doi:10.1155/2014/264920

process including four stages and 11 sequential steps. Sections 3 to 8 discuss the procedure, focusing on (1) prior elicitation; (2) model construction; (3) posterior sampling; (4) MCMC convergence diagnostic; (5) Monte Carlo error diagnostic; (6) model comparison. Section 9 gives examples and discusses how to use the procedure. Finally, Section 10offers conclusions.

DESCRIPTION OF PROCEDURE

The proposed procedure uses the Bayesian reliability inference to determine system (or unit) reliability and failure distribution, to support the optimisation of maintenance strategies, and so forth.

The general procedure begins with the collection of reliability data (see Figure 1). These are the observed values of a physical process, such as various "lifetime data." The data may be subject to uncertainties, such as imprecise measurement, censoring, truncated information, and interpretation errors. Reliability data are found in the "current data set"; they contain original data and include the evaluation, manipulation, and/or organisation of data samples. At a higher level in the collection of data, a wide variety of "historical information" can be obtained, including the results of inspecting and integrating this "information," thereby adding to "prior knowledge." The final level is reliability inference, which is the process of making a conclusion based on "posterior results."

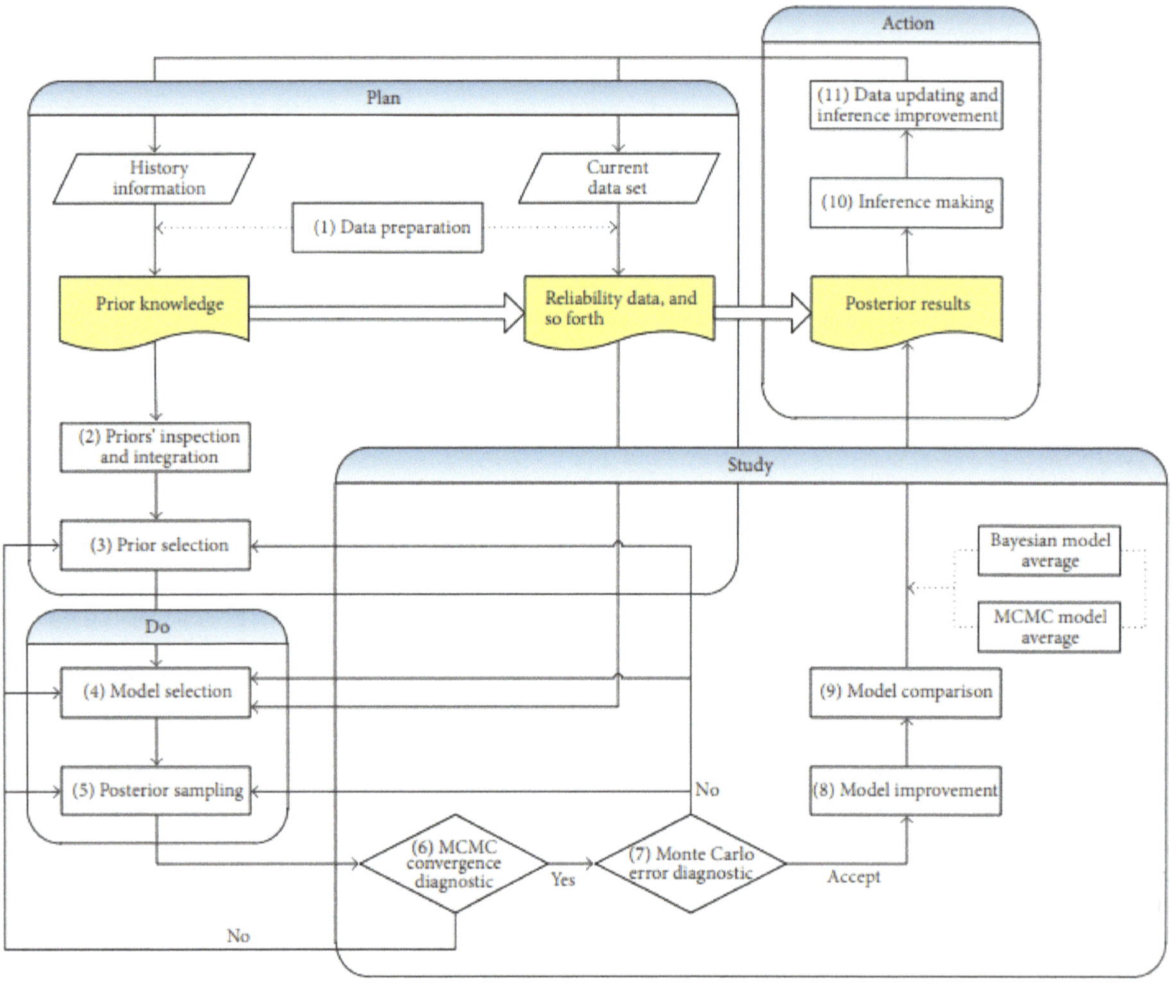

Figure 1: An integrated procedure for Bayesian reliability inference via MCMC.

Using the definitions shown in Figure 1, we propose an integrated procedure which constructs a full framework for the standardized process of Bayesian reliability inference. As shown in Figure 1, the procedure is composed of a continuous improvement process including four stages (Plan, Do, Study, and Action) which will be discussed later in this section and 11 sequential steps: (1) data preparation; (2) prior inspection and integration; (3) prior selection; (4) model selection; (5) posterior sampling; (6) MCMC convergence diagnostic; (7) Monte Carlo error diagnostic; (8) model improvement; (9) model comparison; (10) inference making; (11) data updating and inference improvement.

Step 1 (data preparation). The original data sets for "history information" and "current data" related to reliability studies need to be acquired, evaluated, and merged. In this way, "history information" can be transferred to "prior knowledge," and "current data" can become "reliability data" in later steps.

Step 2 (prior inspection and integration). During this step, "prior knowledge" receives a second and more extensive treatment, including a reliability consistency check, a credence test, and a multisource integration. This step improves prior reliability data.

Step 3 (prior selection). This step uses the results achieved in Step 2 to determine the model's form and parameters, for instance, selecting informative or noninformative priors, or unknown parameters and their distributed forms.

Step 4 (model selection). This step determines a reliability model (parametric or nonparametric), selecting from n. candidates for the studied system/units. It considers both "reliability data" and the inspection, integration, and selection of priors to implement the *i*th ($i = 1, \ldots, i + 1, \ldots, n$).

Step 5 (posterior sampling). In this step, we determine a sampling method (e.g., Gibbs sampling, Metropolis-Hastings sampling, etc.) to implement MCMC simulation for the model's posterior calculations.

Step 6 (MCMC convergence diagnostic). In this step, we check whether the Markov chains have reached convergence. If they have, we move on to the next step; if they have not, we return to Step 5 and redetermine the iteration times of posterior sampling or rechoose the sampling methods; if the results still cannot be satisfied, we return to Steps 3 and 4 and redetermine the prior selection and model selection.

Step 7 (Monte Carlo error diagnostic). We need to decide if the Monte Carlo error is small enough to be accepted in this step. As discussed in Step 6, if it is accepted, we go on to the next step; if it is not, we return to Step 5 and redecide the iteration times of the posterior sampling or rechoose the sampling methods; if the results still cannot be accepted, we go back to Steps 3 and 4 and recalculate the prior selection and model selection.

Step 8 (model improvement). Here, we choose the *i+1th* candidate model and restart from Step 4.

Step 9 (model comparison). After implementing candidate models, we need to (1) compare the posterior results to determine the most suitable model or (2) adopt the average posterior estimations (using the Bayesian model average or the MCMC model average) as the final results.

Step 10 (inference making). After achieving the posterior results in Step 9, we can perform Bayesian reliability inference to determine system (or unit) reliability, find the failure distribution, optimise maintenance strategies, and so forth.

Step 11 (data updating and inference improvement). Along with the passage of time, new "current data" can be obtained, relegating "previous" inference results to "historical data." By updating "reliability data" and "prior knowledge," and restarting at Step 1, we can improve the reliability inference.

In summary, by using this step-by-step method, we can create a continuous improvement process for the Bayesian reliability inference.

Note that Steps 1, 2, and 3 are assigned to the "Plan" stage when data for MCMC implementation are prepared. In addition, a part of Steps 1, 2, and 3 refers to the elicitation of prior knowledge. Steps 4 and 5 are both assigned to the "Do" stage, where the MCMC sampling is carried out. Steps 6 to 9 are treated as the "Study" stage; in these steps, the sampling results are checked and compared; in addition, knowledge is accumulated and improved upon by implementing various candidate reliability models. The "Action" stage consists of Steps 10 and 11; at this point, a continuously improved loop can be obtained. In other words, by implementing the step-by-step procedure, we can accumulate and gradually update prior knowledge. Equally, posterior results will be improved upon and become increasingly robust, thereby improving the accuracy of the inference results.

Also note that this paper will focus on six steps and their relationship to MCMC inference implementation: (1) prior elicitation; (2) model construction; (3) posterior sampling; (4) MCMC convergence diagnostic; (5) Monte Carlo error diagnostic; (6) model comparison.

ELICITATION OF PRIOR KNOWLEDGE

In the proposed procedure, the elicitation of prior knowledge plays a crucial role. It is related to Steps 1, 2, and 3 and is part of the Plan Stage, as shown in Figure 1.

In practice, prior information is derived from a variety of data sources and is also considered "historical data" (or "experience data"). Those data taking various forms require various processing methods. Although in the first step, "historical information" can be transferred to "prior knowledge," this is not enough. Credible prior information and proper forms of these data are necessary to compute the model's posterior probabilities, especially in the case of a small sample set. Meanwhile, either noncredible or improper prior data may cause instability in the estimation of the model's probabilities or lead to convergence problems in MCMC implementation. This section will discuss some relevant prior elicitation problems in Bayesian reliability inference, namely, including acquiring priors, performing a consistency check and credence test, fusing multisource priors, and selecting which priors to use in MCMC implementation.

Acquisition of Prior Knowledge

In Bayesian reliability analysis, prior knowledge comes from a wide range of historical information. As shown in Figure 2, data sources include (1) engineering design data; (2) component test data; (3) system test data; (4) operational data from similar systems; (5) field data in various environments; (6) computer simulations; (7) related standards and operation manuals; (8) experience data from similar systems; (9) expert judgment and personal experience. Of these, the first seven yield objective prior data, and the last two provide subjective prior data.

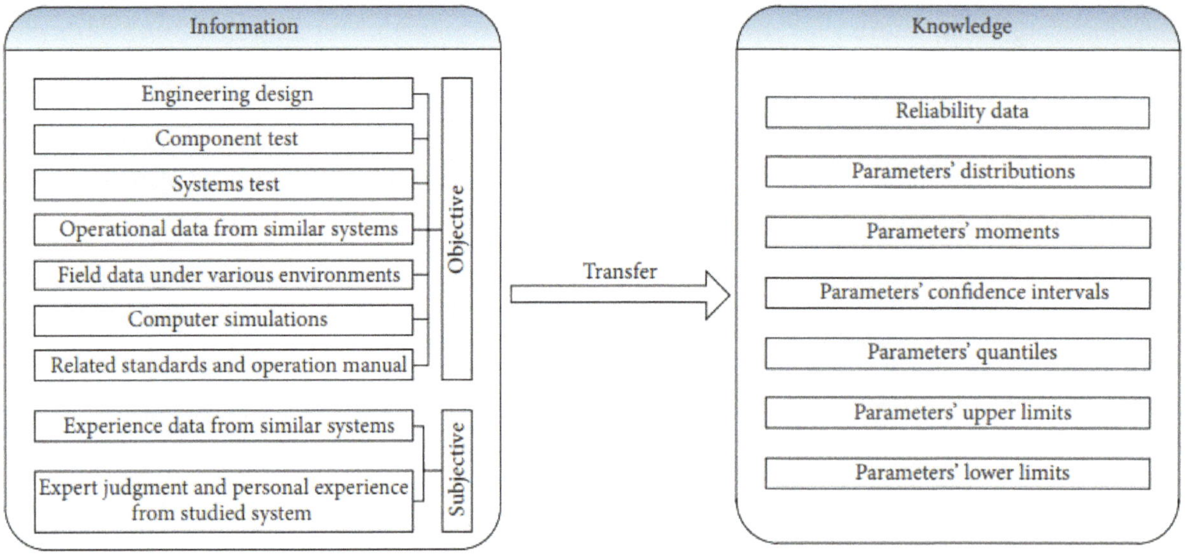

Figure 2: Data source: transfer from historical to prior knowledge.

Prior data also take a variety of forms, including reliability data, the distribution of reliability parameters, moments, confidence intervals, quantiles, and upper and lower limits.

Inspection of Priors

In Bayesian analysis, different prior information will lead to similar results when the data sample is sufficiently large. While the selection of priors and their form has little influence on posterior inferences, in practice, particularly with a small data sample, we know that some prior information is associated with the current observed reliability data. However, we are not sure whether the prior distributions are the same as the posterior distributions. In other words, we cannot confirm that all posterior distributions converge and are consistent (a consistency check issue). Even if they pass a consistency check, we can only say that they are consistent under a certain specified confidence interval. Therefore, an important prerequisite for applying any prior information is to confirm its credibility by performing a consistency check and credence test.

As noted by Li [25], the consistency check of prior and posterior distributions was first studied from a statistical viewpoint by Walker [26]. Under specified conditions, posterior distributions are not only consistent with those of the priors, but they have an asymptotic normality which could simplify their calculation. Li [25] also notes that studies on the consistency check of priors have focused on checking the moments and confidence intervals of reliability parameters, as well as historical data. A number of checking methodologies have been developed, including robustness analysis, significance test, Smirnov test, rank-sum test, and mood test. More studies have been reviewed by Ghosal [27] and Choi et al. [28].

The credibility of prior information can be viewed as the probability that it and the collected data come from the same population. Li [25] lists the following methods to perform a credence test: frequency method, bootstrap method, rank-sum text, and so forth. However, in the case of a small sample or simulated data, the above methods are not suitable because even if data pass the credence test, selecting different priors will lead to different results. We therefore suggest a comprehensive use of the above methods to ensure the superiority of Bayesian inference.

Fusion of Prior Information

Due to the complexity of the system, not to mention the diversification of test equipment and methodologies, prior information can come from many sources. As all priors can pass a consistency check, an integrated fusion estimation based on the smoothness of credibility is sometimes necessary. In such situations, a common choice is parallel fusion estimation or serial fusion estimation, achieved by determining the reliability parameters' weighted credibility [25]. However, as the credibility computation can be difficult, other methods to fuse the priors may be called for. In the area of reliability, related research studies include the following. Savchuk and Martz [29] develop Bayes estimators for the true binomial survival probability when there are multiple sources of prior information; Ren et al. [30] adopt Kullback information as the distance measure between different prior information and fusion distributions, minimizing the sum to get the combined prior distribution; looking at aerospace propulsion as a case study, Liu et al. [31] discuss a similar fusion problem in a complex system and suggest [32] a fusion approach based on expert experience with the analytic hierarchy process (AHP); Fang [33] proposes using multisource information fusion techniques with Fuzzy-Bayesian for reliability assessment; Zhou et al. [34] propose a Bayes fusion approach for assessment of spaceflight products, integrating degradation data and field lifetime data with Fisher information and the Weiner process. In general, the most important thing for multisource integration is to determine the weights of the different priors.

Selection of Priors Based on MCMC

In Bayesian reliability inference, two kinds of priors are very useful: the conjugate prior and the noninformative prior. To apply MCMC methods, however, the "log-concave prior" is recommended.

The conjugate prior family is very popular because it is convenient for mathematical calculation. The concept, along with the term "conjugate prior," was introduced by Howard and Robert [35] in their work on Bayesian decision theory. If the posterior distributions are in the same family as the prior distributions, the prior and posterior distributions are called conjugate distributions, and the prior is called a conjugate prior. For instance, the Gaussian family is a conjugate of itself (or a self-conjugate) with respect to a Gaussian likelihood function: if the likelihood function is Gaussian, choosing a Gaussian prior distribution over the mean distribution will ensure that the posterior distribution is also Gaussian. This means that the Gaussian distribution is a conjugate prior for the likelihood function which is also Gaussian. Other examples include the following: the conjugate distribution of a normal distribution is a normal or inverse-normal distribution; the Poisson and the exponential distribution's conjugate both have a Gamma distribution, while the Gamma distribution is a self-conjugate; the binomial and the negative binomial distribution's conjugate both have a Beta distribution; the polynomial distribution's conjugate is a Dirichlet distribution.

Noninformative prior refers to a prior for which we only know certain parameters' value ranges or their importance; for example, there may be a uniform distribution. A noninformative prior can also be called a vague prior, flat prior, diffuse prior, ignorance prior, and so forth. There are many different ways to determine the distribution of a noninformative prior, including Bayes hypothesis, Jeffrey's rule, reference prior, inverse reference prior, probability-matching prior, maximum entropy prior, relative likelihood approach, cumulative distribution function, Monte Carlo method, bootstrap method, random weighting simulation method, Haar invariant measurement, Laplace prior, Lindley rule, generalized maximum entropy principle, and the use of marginal distributions. From another perspective, the types of prior distribution also include informative prior, hierarchical prior, Power prior, and nonparameter prior processes.

At this point, there are no set rules for selecting prior distributions. Regardless of the manner used to determine a prior's distribution, the selected prior should be both reasonable and convenient for calculation. Of the above, the conjugate prior is a common choice. To facilitate the calculation of MCMC, especially for adaptive rejection sampling and Gibbs sampling, a popular choice is log-concave prior distribution. Log-concave prior distribution refers to a prior distribution in which the natural logarithm is concave; that is, the second derivative is nonpositive. Common logarithmic concavity prior distributions include the normal distribution family, logistic distribution, Student's-*t* distribution, the exponential distribution family, the uniform distribution on a finite interval greater than the gamma distribution with a shape parameter greater than 1, and Beta distribution with a value interval (0, 1). As logarithmic concavity prior distributions are very flexible, this paper recommends their use in reliability studies.

MODEL CONSTRUCTION

To apply MCMC methods, we divide the reliability models into four categories: parametric, semiparametric, frailty, and other nontraditional reliability models.

Parametric modelling offers straightforward modelling and analysis techniques. Common choices include Bayesian exponential model, Bayesian Weibull model, Bayesian extreme value model, Bayesian log-normal model, and Gamma model. Lin et al. [36] present a reliability study using the Bayesian parametric framework to explore the impact of a railway train wheel's installed position on its service lifetime and to predict its reliability characteristics. They apply a MCMC computational scheme to obtain the parameters' posterior distributions. Besides the hierarchical reliability models mentioned above, other parametric models include Bayesian accelerated failure models (AFM), Bayesian reliability growth models, and Bayesian faulty tree analysis (FTA).

Semiparametric reliability models have become quite common and are well accepted in practice, since they offer a more general modelling strategy with fewer assumptions. In these models, the failure rate is described in a semiparametric form, or the priors are developed by a stochastic process. With respect to the semiparametric failure rate, Lin and Asplund [37] adopt the piecewise constant hazard model to analyze the distribution of the locomotive wheels' lifetime. The applied hazard function is sometimes called a piecewise exponential model; it is convenient because it can accommodate various shapes of the baseline hazard over a number of intervals. In a study of the processes of priors, Ibrahim et al. [38] examine the gamma process, beta process, correlated prior processes, and the Dirichlet process separately, using an MCMC computational scheme. By introducing the gamma process of the prior's increment, Lin et al. [39] propose its reliability when applied to the Gibbs sampling scheme.

In reliability inference, most studies are implemented under the assumption that individual lifetimes are independent and identically distributed (i.i.d.). However, Cox proportional hazard (CPH) models can sometimes not be used because of the dependence of data within a group. Take train wheels as an example because they have the same operating conditions, the wheels mounted on a particular locomotive may be dependent. In a different context, some data may come from multiple records of wheels installed in the same position but on other locomotives. Modelling dependence has received considerable attention, especially in cases where the datasets may come from related subjects of the same group [40, 41]. A key development in modelling such data is to build frailty models in which the data are conditionally independent. When frailties are considered, the dependence within subgroups can be considered an unknown and unobservable risk factor (or explanatory variable) of the hazard function. In a recent reliability study, Lin and Asplund [37] consider a gamma shared frailty to explore the unobserved covariates' influence on the wheels on the same locomotive.

Some nontraditional Bayesian reliability models are both interesting and helpful. For instance, Lin et al. [10] point out that in traditional methods of reliability analysis, a complex system is often considered to be composed of several subsystems in series. The failure of any subsystem is usually considered to lead to the failure of the entire system. However, some subsystems' lifetimes are long enough or they never fail during the life cycle of the entire system. In addition, such subsystems' lifetimes will not be influenced equally under different circumstances. For example, the lifetimes of some screws will far exceed the lifetime of the compressor in which they are placed. However, the failure of the compressor's gears may directly lead to its failure. In practice, such interferences will affect the model's accuracy, but are seldom considered in traditional analysis. To address these shortcomings, Lin et al. [10] present a new approach to reliability analysis for complex systems, in which a certain fraction of subsystems is defined as a "cure fraction" based on the consideration that such subsystems' lifetimes are long enough or they never fail during the life cycle of the entire system; this is called the cure rate model.

POSTERIOR SAMPLING

To implement MCMC calculations, Markov chains require a stationary distribution. There are many ways to construct these chains. During the last decade, the following Monte Carlo (MC) based sampling methods for evaluating high-dimensional posterior integrals have been developed: MC importance sampling, Metropolis-Hastings sampling, Gibbs sampling, and other hybrid algorithms. In this section, we introduce two common samplings: (1) Metropolis-Hastings sampling, the best known MCMC sampling algorithm, and (2) Gibbs sampling, the most popular MCMC sampling algorithm in the Bayesian computation literature, which is actually a special case of Metropolis-Hastings sampling.

Metropolis-Hastings Sampling

Metropolis-Hastings sampling is a well-known MCMC sampling algorithm, which comes from importance sampling. It was first developed by Metropolis et al. [42] and later generalized by Hastings [43]. Tierney [44] gives a comprehensive theoretical exposition of the algorithm; Chib and Greenberg [45] provide an excellent tutorial on it.

Suppose that we need to create a sample using the probability density function (θ). Let K be a regular constant; this is a complicated calculation (e.g., a regular factor in Bayesian analysis) and is normally an unknown parameter. Then, let $(\theta) = h(\theta)/K$. Metropolis sampling from (θ) can be described as follows.

Step 1. Choose an arbitrary starting point θ_0, and set $h(\theta_0) > 0$.

Step 2. Generate a proposal distribution (θ_1, θ_2), which represents the probability for θ_2 to be the next transfer value as the current value is $\theta 1$. The distribution (θ_1, θ_2) is named as the candidate generating distribution. This candidate generating distribution is symmetric, which means that $(\theta_1, \theta_2) = q(\theta_2, \theta_1)$. Now based on the current θ, generate a candidate point θ^* from (θ_1, θ_2).

Step 3. For the specified candidate point $\theta*$, calculate the density ratio α with $\theta^*$and the current value θ_{t-1} as follows:

$$\alpha(\theta_{t-1}, \theta^*) = \frac{p(\theta^*)}{p(\theta_{t-1})} = \frac{h(\theta^*)}{h(\theta_{t-1})}. \tag{1}$$

The ratio α refers to the probability to accept θ^*, where the constant K can be neglected.

Step 4. If θ^* increases the probability density, so that $\alpha>1$, then accept θ^* and let $\theta_t = \theta^*$. Otherwise, if $\alpha<1$, then let $\theta_t = \theta_{t-1}$ and go to Step 2.

The acceptance probability α can be written as

$$\alpha(\theta_{t-1}, \theta^*) = \min\left(1, \frac{h(\theta^*)}{h(\theta_{t-1})}\right). \tag{2}$$

Following the above steps, generate a Markov chain with the sampling points $\theta_0, \theta_1, \ldots, \theta_k, \ldots$. The transfer probability from θ_t to θ_{t+1} is related to θ_t but not related to $\theta_0, \theta_1, \ldots, \theta_{t-1}$. After experiencing a sufficiently long burn-in period, the Markov chain reaches a steady state and the sampling points $\theta_{t+1}, \ldots, \theta_{t+n}$ from $p(\theta)$ are obtained.

Metropolis-Hastings sampling was promoted by Hastings [43]. The candidate generating distribution can adopt any form and does not need to be symmetric. In MetropolisHastings sampling, the acceptance probability α can be written as

$$\alpha(\theta_{t-1}, \theta^*) = \min\left(1, \frac{h(\theta^*)\, q(\theta^*, \theta_{t-1})}{h(\theta_{t-1})\, q(\theta_{t-1}, \theta^*)}\right). \tag{3}$$

In the above equation, as $q(\theta^*, \theta_{t-1}) = q(\theta_{t-1}, \theta^*)$, and Metropolis-Hastings sampling becomes Metropolis sampling. The Markov transfer probability function can therefore be

$$p(\theta, \theta^*) = \begin{cases} q(\theta_{t-1}, \theta^*) & h(\theta^*) > h(\theta_{t-1}) \\ q(\theta_{t-1}, \theta^*)\dfrac{h(\theta^*)}{h(\theta_{t-1})} & h(\theta^*) < h(\theta_{t-1}). \end{cases} \tag{4}$$

From another perspective, when using Metropolis-Hastings sampling, say we need to generate the candidate point θ^*. In this case, generate an arbitrary μ from a uniform distribution (0, 1). Set $\theta_t = \theta^*$ if $\mu \le \alpha(\theta_{t-1}, \theta^*)$ and $\theta_t = \theta_{t-1}$ otherwise.

Gibbs Sampling

Metropolis-Hastings sampling is convenient for lower-dimensional numerical computation. However, if θ has a higher dimension, it is not easy to choose an appropriate candidate generating distribution. By using Gibbs sampling, we only need to know the full conditional distribution. Therefore, it is more advantageous in high-dimensional numerical computation. Gibbs sampling is essentially a special case of Metropolis-Hastings sampling, as the acceptance probability equals one. It is currently the most popular MCMC sampling algorithm in the Bayesian reliability inference literature. Gibbs sampling is based on the ideas of Grenander [46], but the formal term comes from S. Geman and D. Geman [47] to analyze lattice in image processing. A landmark work for Gibbs sampling in problems of Bayesian inference is Gelfand and Smith [48]. Gibbs sampling is also called heat bath algorithm in statistical physics. A similar idea, data augmentation, is introduced by Tanner and Wong [49].

Gibbs sampling belongs to the Markov update mechanism and adopts the ideology of "divide and conquer." It supposes that all other parameters are fixed and known, inferring a set of parameters. Let θ_i be a random parameter or several parameters in the same group. For the jth group, the conditional distribution is (θ_j). To carry out Gibbs sampling, the basic scheme is as follows.

Step 1. Choose an arbitrary starting point $\theta^{(0)} = (\theta_1^{(0)}, \ldots, \theta_k^{(0)})$.

Step 2. Generate $\theta_1^{(1)}$ from the conditional distribution $f(\theta_1 \mid \theta_2^{(0)},\ldots,\theta_k^{(0)})$ and generate $\theta_2^{(1)}$ from the conditional distribution $f(\theta_2 \mid \theta_1^{(1)},\theta_3^{(0)},\ldots,\theta_k^{(0)})$.

Step 3. Generate $\theta_j^{(1)}$ from $f(\theta_j \mid \theta_1^{(1)},\ldots,\theta_{j-1}^{(1)},\theta_{j+1}^{(0)},\ldots,\theta_k^{(0)})$.

Step 4. Generate $\theta_k^{(1)}$ from $f(\theta_k \mid \theta_1^{(1)},\theta_2^{(1)},\ldots,\theta_{k-1}^{(1)})$.

As shown above, one-step transitions from $\theta^{(0)}$ to $\theta^{(1)} = (\theta_1^{(1)},\ldots,\theta_k^{(1)})$, where $\theta^{(1)}$ can be viewed as a one-time accomplishment of the Markov chain.

Step 5. Go back to Step 2.

After t iterations, $\theta^{(t)} = (\theta_1^{(t)},\ldots,\theta_k^{(t)})$ can be obtained, and each component $\theta^{(1)},\theta^{(2)},\theta^{(3)},\ldots$ will be achieved. The Markov transition probability function is

$$p(\theta,\theta^*) = f(\theta_1 \mid \theta_2,\ldots,\theta_k)\, f(\theta_2 \mid \theta_1^*,\theta_3,\ldots,\theta_k)\cdots f(\theta_k \mid \theta_1^*,\ldots,\theta_{k-1}^*). \quad (5)$$

Starting from different $^{(0)}$, as $t\rightarrow\infty$, the marginal distribution of $\theta^{(t)}$ can be viewed as a stationary distribution based on the theory of the ergodic average. In this case, the Markov chain is seen as converging and the sampling points are seen as observations of the sample.

For both methods, it is not necessary to choose the candidate generating distribution, but it is necessary to do sampling from the conditional distribution. There are many other ways to do sampling from the conditional distribution, including sample-importance resampling, rejection sampling, and adaptive rejection sampling (ARS).

MARKOV CHAIN MONTE CARLO CONVERGENCE DIAGNOSTIC

Because of the Markov chain's ergodic property, all statistics inferences are implemented under the assumption that the Markov chain converges. Therefore, the Markov Chain Monte Carlo convergence diagnostic is very important. When applying MCMC for reliability inference, if the iteration times are too small, the Markov chain will not "forget" the influence of the initial values; if the iteration times are simply increased to a large number, there will be insufficient scientific evidence to support the results, causing a waste of resources.

Markov chain Monte Carlo convergence diagnostic is a hot topic for Bayesian researchers. Efforts to determine MCMC convergence have been concentrated in two areas. The first is theoretical, and the second is practical. For the former, the Markov transition kernel of the chain is analyzed in an attempt to predetermine a number of iterations that will insure convergence in a total variation distance within a specified tolerance of the true stationary distribution. Related studies include Polson [50], Roberts and Rosenthal [51], and Mengersen and Tweedie [52]. While approaches like these are promising, they typically involve sophisticated mathematics, as well as laborious calculations that must be repeated for every model under consideration. As for practical studies, most research is focused on developing diagnostic tools, including Gelman and Rubin [53], Raftery and Lewis [54], Garren and Smith [55], and Roberts and Rosenthal [56]. When these tools are used, sometimes the bounds obtained are quite loose; even so, they are considered both reasonable and feasible.

At this point, more than 15 MCMC convergence diagnostic tools have been developed. In addition to a basic tool which provides intuitive judgments by tracing a time series plot of the Markov chain, other examples include tools developed by Gelman and Rubin [53], Raftery and Lewis [54], Garren and Smith [55], Brooks and Gelman [57], Geweke [58], Johnson [59], Mykland et al. [60], Ritter and Tanner [61], Roberts [62], Yu [63], Yu and Mykland [64], Zellner and Min [65], Heidelberger and Welch [66], and Liu et al. [67].

We can divide diagnostic tools into categories depending on the following: (1) if the target distribution needs to be monitored; (2) if the target distribution needs to calculate a single Markov chain or multiple chains; (3) if the diagnostic results depend on the output of the Monte Carlo algorithm, not on other information from the target distribution.

It is not wise to rely on one convergence diagnostic technique, and researchers suggest a more comprehensive use of different diagnostic techniques. Some suggestions include (1) simultaneously diagnosing the convergence of a set of parallel Markov chains; (2) monitoring the parameters' autocorrelations and cross-correlations; (3) changing the parameters of the model or the sampling methods; (4) using different diagnostic methods and choosing the largest preiteration times as the formal iteration times; (5) combining the results obtained from the diagnostic indicators' graphs.

Six tools have been achieved by computer programs. The most widely used are the convergence diagnostic tools proposed by Gelman and Rubin [53] and Raftery and Lewis [54]; the latter is an extension of the former. Both are based on the theory of analysis of variance (ANOVA); both use multiple Markov chains and both use the output to perform the diagnostic.

Gelman-Rubin Diagnostic

In traditional literature on iterative simulations, many researchers suggest that to guarantee the Markov chain's diagnostic ability, multiple parallel chains should be used simultaneously to do the iterative simulation for one target distribution. In this case, after running the simulation for a certain period, it is necessary to determine whether the chains have "forgotten" the initial value and if they converge. Gelman and Rubin [53] point out that lack of convergence can sometimes be determined from multiple independent sequences but cannot be diagnosed using simulation output from any single sequence. They also find that more information can be obtained during one single Markov chain's replication process than in multiple chains' iterations. Moreover, if the initial values are more dispersed, the status of nonconvergence is more easily found. Therefore, they propose a method using multiple replications of the chain to decide whether it becomes stationary in the second half of each sample path. The idea behind this is an implicit assumption that convergence will be achieved within the first half of each sample path; the validity of this assumption is tested by the Gelman-Rubin diagnostic or the variance ratio method.

Based on normal theory approximations to exact Bayesian posterior inference, Gelman-Rubin diagnostic involves two steps. In Step 1, for a target scalar summary φ, select an overdispersed starting point from its target distribution (φ). Then, generate m Markov chains for (φ), where each chain has $2n$ times iterations. Delete the first n times iterations and use the second n times iterations for analysis. In Step 2, apply the between-sequence variance B/n and the within-sequence variance W to compare the corrected scale reduction factor (CSRF). CSRF is calculated by m Markov chains and the formed mn values in the sequences which stem from (φ). By comparing the CSRF value, the convergence diagnostic can be implemented. In addition,

$$\frac{B}{n} = \frac{1}{m-1}\sum_{j=1}^{m}\left(\bar{\varphi}_{j.} - \bar{\varphi}_{..}\right)^2,$$

$$\bar{\varphi}_{j.} = \frac{1}{n}\sum_{t=1}^{n}\varphi_{jt}, \qquad \bar{\varphi}_{..} = \frac{1}{m}\sum_{j=1}^{m}\bar{\varphi}_{j.},$$

$$W = \frac{1}{m(n-1)}\sum_{j=1}^{m}\sum_{t=1}^{n}\left(\varphi_{jt} - \bar{\varphi}_{j.}\right)^2, \tag{6}$$

where φ^{jt} denotes the tth of the n iterations of φ in chain j and $j = 1, \ldots, m$, $t = 1, \ldots, n$. Let φ be a random variable of (φ), with mean μ and variance σ^2 under the target distribution. Suppose that μ□ has some unbiased estimator $\hat{V}$. To explain the variability between $\hat{\mu}$ and $\hat{V}$, Gelman and Rubin construct Student's t-distribution with a mean μ□ and variance V□ as follows:

$$\hat{\mu} = \bar{\varphi}_{..}, \qquad \hat{V} = \frac{n-1}{n}W + \left(1 + \frac{1}{m}\right)\frac{B}{n}, \tag{7}$$

where $\hat{V}$ is a weighted average of W and B. The above estimation will be unbiased if the starting points of the sequences are drawn from the target distribution. However, it will be overestimated if the starting distribution is overdispersed. Therefore, $\hat{V}$ is also called a "conservative" estimate. Meanwhile, because the iteration number n is limited, the within-sequence variance W can be too low, leading to falsely diagnosing convergence. As $n\rightarrow\infty$, both $\hat{V}$ and W should be close to σ^2 . In other words, the scale of current distribution of φ should be decreasing as n is increasing.

Denote $\sqrt{\hat{R}_s} = \sqrt{\hat{V}/\sigma^2}$ as the scale reduction factor (SRF). By applying W, $\sqrt{\hat{R}_p} = \sqrt{\hat{V}/W}$ becomes the potential scale reduction factor (PSRF). By applying a correct factor df/(df–2) for PSRF, a correct scale reduction factor (CSRF) can be obtained as follows:

$$\sqrt{\hat{R}_c} = \sqrt{\left(\frac{\hat{V}}{W}\right)\frac{df}{df-2}} = \sqrt{\left(\frac{n-1}{n} + \frac{m+1}{mn}\frac{B}{W}\right)\frac{df}{df-2}}, \tag{8}$$

where df represents the degree of freedom in Student's t-distribution. Following Fisher [68], $df \approx 2\hat{V}/\mathrm{Var}(\hat{V})$. The diagnostic based on CSRF can be implemented as follows: if $\hat{R}_c > 1$, it indicates that the iteration number n is too small. When n is increasing, $\hat{V}$ will become smaller and W will become larger. If $\hat{R}_c$ is close to 1 (e.g., $\hat{R}_c < 1.2$), we can conclude that each of the m sets of n simulated observations is close to the target distribution, and the Markov chain can be viewed as converging.

Brooks-Gelman Diagnostic

Although the Gelman-Rubin diagnostic is very popular, its theory has several defects. Therefore, Brooks and Gelman [57] extend the method in the following way.

First, in the above equation, df/(df − 2) represents the ratio of the variance between the Student t-distribution and the normal distribution. Brooks and Gelman [57] point out some obvious defects in the equation. For instance, if the convergence speed is slow, or df < 2, CSRF could be infinite and may even be negative. Therefore, they set up a new and correct factor for PSRF; the new CSRF becomes

$$\sqrt{\hat{R}_c^*} = \sqrt{\left(\frac{n-1}{n} + \frac{m+1}{mn}\frac{B}{W}\right)\frac{df+3}{df+1}}. \tag{9}$$

Second, Brooks and Gelman [57] propose a new and more easily implemented way to calculate PSRF. The first step is similar to Gelman-Rubin's diagnostic. Using m chains' second n iterations, obtain an empirical interval 100(1 − %) after each chain's second n iteration. Then, m empirical intervals can be achieved within a sequence, denoted by l. In the second step, determine the total empirical intervals for sequences from mn estimates of m chains, denoted by L. Finally, calculate the PSRF as follows:

$$\sqrt{\hat{R}_p^*} = \sqrt{\frac{l}{L}}. \tag{10}$$

The basic theory behind the Gelman-Rubin and BrooksGelman diagnostics is the same. The difference is that we compare the variance in the former and the interval length in the latter.

Third, Brooks and Gelman [57] point out that the value of CSRF being close to one is a necessary but not sufficient condition for MCMC convergence. Additional condition is that both W and $\hat{V}$ should stabilize as a function of n. That is to say, if W and $\hat{V}$ have not reached the steady state, CSRF could still be one. In other words, before convergence, $W < \hat{V}$ and both should be close to one. Therefore, as an alternative, Brooks and Gelman [57] propose a graphical approach to monitoring convergence. Divide the$m$sequences into batches of length b.Then calculate $\hat{V}(k)$, $W(k)$, and $\hat{R}_c(k)$ based upon the latter half of the observations of a sequence of length $2kb$, for $k = 1, \ldots, n/b$. Plot $\sqrt{\hat{V}(k)}$, $\sqrt{W(k)}$,, and $\hat{R}_c(k)$ as a function of k on the same plot. Approximate convergence is attained if $\hat{R}_c(k)$ is close to one and at the same time, both $\hat{V}(k)$ and (k) stabilize at one.

Fourth and finally, Brooks and Gelman [57] discuss the multivariate situation. Let φ denote the parameter vector and calculate the following:

$$\frac{B}{n} = \frac{1}{m-1}\sum_{j=1}^{m}\left(\bar{\varphi}_{j.} - \bar{\varphi}_{..}\right)\left(\bar{\varphi}_{j.} - \bar{\varphi}_{..}\right)',$$

$$W = \frac{1}{m(n-1)}\sum_{j=1}^{m}\sum_{t=1}^{n}\left(\varphi_{jt} - \bar{\varphi}_{j.}\right)\left(\varphi_{jt} - \bar{\varphi}_{j.}\right)'. \tag{11}$$

Let λ^1 be maximum characteristic root of $W^{-1}B/n$; then, the PSRF can be expressed as

$$\sqrt{R_p} = \sqrt{\frac{n-1}{n} + \frac{m+1}{m}\lambda_1}. \tag{12}$$

MONTE CARLO ERROR DIAGNOSTIC

When implementing the MCMC method, besides determining the Markov chains' convergence diagnostic, we must check two uncertainties related to the Monte Carlo point estimation: statistical uncertainty and Monte Carlo uncertainty.

Statistical uncertainty is determined by the sample data and the adopted model. Once the data are given and the models are selected, the statistical uncertainty is fixed. For maximum likelihood estimation (MLE), statistical uncertainty can be calculated by the inverse square root of the Fisher information. For Bayesian inference, statistical uncertainty is measured by the parameters' posterior standard deviation.

Monte Carlo uncertainty stems from the approximation of the model's characteristics, which can be measured by a suitable standard error (SE). Monte Carlo standard error of the mean, also called Monte Carlo error (MC error), is a well-known diagnostic tool. In this case, define MC error as the ratio of the sample's standard deviation and the square root of the sample volume, which can be written as

$$\mathrm{SE}\left[\hat{I}(y)\right] = \frac{\mathrm{SD}\left[\hat{I}(y)\right]}{\sqrt{n}} = \left[\frac{1}{n}\left(\frac{1}{n-1}\sum_{i=1}^{n}(h(y \mid x_i)) - \hat{I}(y)\right)^2\right]^{1/2}. \tag{13}$$

Obviously, as n becomes larger, MC error will be smaller. Meanwhile, the average of the sample data will be closer to the average of the population.

As in the MCMC algorithm, we cannot guarantee that all the sampled points are independent and identically distributed (i.i.d.); we must correct the sequence's correlation. To this end, we introduce the autocorrelation function and sample size inflation factor (SSIF).

Following the sampling methods introduced in Section 5, define a sampling sequence $\theta_1,\ldots,_n$ with length n. Suppose there are autocorrelations which exist among the adjacent sampling points; this means that $(\theta_i, \theta_{i+1}) \neq 0$. Furthermore,

$(\theta_i, \theta_{i+k}) \neq 0$. Then, the autocorrelation coefficient ρ_k can be calculated by

$$\hat{\rho}_k = \frac{\mathrm{Cov}(\theta_t, \theta_{t+k})}{\mathrm{Var}(\theta_t)} = \frac{\sum_{t=1}^{n-k}(\theta_t - \bar{\theta})(\theta_{t-k} - \bar{\theta})}{\sum_{t=1}^{n-k}(\theta_t - \bar{\theta})^2}, \tag{14}$$

where $\bar{\theta} = 1/n\sum_{t=1}^{n}\theta_t$. Following the above discussion, the MC error with consideration of autocorrelations in MCMC implementation can be written as

$$\mathrm{SE}(\bar{\theta}) = \frac{\mathrm{SD}}{\sqrt{n}}\sqrt{\frac{1+\rho}{1-\rho}}. \tag{15}$$

In the above equation, $\mathrm{SD}/\sqrt{n}$ represents the MC error shown in $\mathrm{SE}[\hat{I}(y)]$. Meanwhile, $\sqrt{(1+\rho)/(1-\rho)}$ represents the SSIF. $\mathrm{SD}/\sqrt{n}$ is helpful to determine whether the sample volume n is sufficient, and SSIF reveals the influence of the autocorrelations on the sample data's standard deviation. Therefore, by following each parameter's MC error, we can evaluate the accuracy of its posterior.

The core idea of the Monte Carlo method is to view the integration of some function (x) as an expectation of the random variable; therefore, the sampling methods implemented on the random variable are very important. If the sampling distribution is closer to (x), the MC error will be smaller. In other words, by increasing the sample volume or improving the adopted models, the statistical uncertainty could be reduced; the improved sampling methods could also reduce the Monte Carlo uncertainty.

MODEL COMPARISON

In Step 8, we might have several candidate models which could pass the MCMC convergence diagnostic and the MC error diagnostic. Thus, model comparison is a crucial part of reliability inference. Broadly speaking, discussions of the comparison of Bayesian models focus on Bayes factors, model diagnostic statistics, measure of fit, and so forth. In a more narrow sense, the concept of model comparison refers to selecting a better model after comparing several candidate models. The purpose of doing model comparison is not to determine the model's correctness. Rather, it is to find out why some models are better than others (e.g., which parametric model or non-parametric model; which prior distribution; which covariates; which family of parameters for application, etc.) or to obtain an average estimation based on the weighted estimate of the model parameters and stemming from the posterior probability of model comparison (e.g., model average).

In Bayesian reliability inference, the model comparison methods can be divided into three categories:

- separate estimation [69–82] including posterior predictive distribution, Bayes factors (BF) and its approximate estimation-Bayesian information criterion (BIC), deviance information criterion (DIC), pseudoBayes factor (PBF), and conditional predictive ordinate (CPO). It also includes some estimations based on the likelihood theory, using the same as BF but offering more flexibility, for instance, harmonic mean estimator, importance sampling, reciprocal importance estimator, bridge sampling, candidate estimator, Laplace-Metropolis estimator, data augmentation estimator, and so forth;
- comparative estimation including different distance measures [83–87]: entropy distance, Kullback-Leibler divergence (KLD), *L*-measure, and weighted *L*-measure;
- simultaneous estimation [49, 88–92] including reversible Jump MCMC (RJMCMC), birth-and-death MCMC (BDMCMC), and fusion MCMC (FMCMC).

Related reference reviews are given by Kass and Raftery [70], Tatiana et al. [91], and Chen and Huang [93].

This section introduces three popular comparison methods used in Bayesian reliability studies: BF, BIC, and DIC. BF is the most traditional method, BIC is BF's approximate estimation, and DIC improves BIC by dealing with the problem of the parameters' degree of freedom.

Bayes Factors (BF)

Suppose that M represents k models which need to be compared. The data set D stems from M_i ($i = 1, \ldots, k$), and $M_1,\ldots,M_k$ are called competing models. Let $(D \mid \theta_i, M_i) = L(\theta_i$

$| D, M_i)$ denote the distribution of D, with consideration of the ith model and its unknown parameter vector θ of dimension p_i, also called the likelihood function of D with a specified model. Under prior distribution $(\theta_i \mid M_i)$ and $\sum_{i=1}^{k} \pi(\theta_i \mid M_i) = 1$, the marginal distributions of D are found by integrating out the parameters as follows:

$$p(D \mid M_i) = \int_{\Theta_i} f(D \mid \theta_i, M_i) \pi(\theta_i \mid M_i) d\theta_i, \quad (16)$$

where Θ_i represents the parameter data set for the ith mode. As in the data likelihood function, the quantity $(D \mid M_i) = L(D \mid M_i)$ is called model likelihood. Suppose we have some preliminary knowledge about model probabilities (M_i); after considering the given observed data set D, the posterior probability of ith model being the best model is determined as

$$\begin{aligned} p(M_i \mid D) &= \frac{p(D \mid M_i) \pi(M_i)}{p(D)} \\ &= \frac{\pi(M_i) \int f(D \mid \theta_i, M_i) \pi(\theta_i \mid M_i) d\theta_i}{\sum_{j=1}^{k} \left[\pi(M_j) \int f(D \mid \theta_j, M_j) \pi(\theta_j \mid M_j) d\theta_j\right]}. \end{aligned} \quad (17)$$

The integration part of the above equation is also called the prior predictive density or marginal likelihood, where (D) is a nonconditional marginal likelihood of D.

Suppose there are two models, M_1 and M_2. Let BF_{12} denote the Bayes factors, equal to the ratio of the posterior odds of the models to the prior odds:

$$BF_{12} = \frac{p(M_1 \mid D)}{p(M_2 \mid D)} \times \frac{\pi(M_2)}{\pi(M_1)} = \frac{p(D \mid M_1)}{p(D \mid M_2)}. \quad (18)$$

The above equation shows that BF_{12} equals the ratio of the model likelihoods for the two models. Thus, it can be written as

$$\frac{p(M_1 \mid D)}{p(M_2 \mid D)} = \frac{p(D \mid M_1)}{p(D \mid M_2)} \times \frac{\pi(M_1)}{\pi(M_2)}. \quad (19)$$

We can also say that BF_{12} shows the ratio of posterior odds of the model M_1 and the prior odds of M_1. In this way, the collection of model likelihoods $(D \mid M_i)$ is equivalent to the model probabilities themselves (since the prior probabilities $\pi(M_i)$ are known in advance) and, hence, could be considered as the key quantities needed for Bayesian model choice.

Jeffreys [94] recommends a scale of evidence for interpreting Bayes factors. Kass and Raftery [70] provide a similar scale, along with a complete review of Bayes factors, including their interpretation, computation or approximation, and robustness to the model-specific prior distributions and applications in a variety of scientific problems.

Bayesian Information Criterion (BIC)

Under some situations, it is difficult to calculate BF, especially for those models which consider different random effects, or adopt diffusion priors or a large number of unknown and informative priors. Therefore, we need to calculate BF's approximate estimation. The Bayesian information criterion (BIC) is also called the Schwarz information criterion (SIC) and is the most important method to get BF's approximate estimation. The key point of BIC is to obtain the approximate estimation of $(D \mid M_i)$. It is proved by Volinsky and Raftery [72] that

$$\ln p(D \mid M_i) \approx \ln f\left(D \mid \hat{\theta}_i, M_i\right) - \frac{p_i}{2} \ln(n). \quad (20)$$

Then, we get SIC as follows:

$$\begin{aligned} \ln BF_{12} &= \ln p(D \mid M_1) - \ln p(D \mid M_2) \\ &= \ln f\left(D \mid \hat{\theta}_1, M_1\right) - \ln f\left(D \mid \hat{\theta}_2, M_2\right) - \frac{p_1 - p_2}{2} \ln(n). \end{aligned} \quad (21)$$

As discussed above, considering two models, M_1 and M_2, BIC_{12} represents the likelihood ratio test statistic with model sample size n and the model's complexity as penalty. It can be written as

$$\begin{aligned} BIC_{12} &= -2 \ln BF_{12} \\ &= -2 \ln\left(\frac{f\left(D \mid \hat{\theta}_1, M_1\right)}{f\left(D \mid \hat{\theta}_2, M_2\right)}\right) + (p_1 - p_2) \ln(n), \end{aligned} \quad (22)$$

where p_i is proportional to the model's sample size and complexity.

Kass and Raftery [70] discuss BIC's calculation program. Kass and Wasserman [73] show how to decide n. Volinsky and Raftery [72] discuss the way to choose n if the data are censored. If n is large enough, BF's approximate estimation can be written as

$$BF_{12} \approx \exp\left(-0.5 BIC_{12}\right). \quad (23)$$

Obviously, if the BIC is smaller, we should consider model M_1; otherwise, M_2 should be considered.

Deviance Information Criterion (DIC)

Traditional methods for model comparison consider two main aspects: the model's measure of fit and the model's complexity. Normally, the model's measure of fit can be increased by increasing the model's complexity. For this reason, most model comparison methods are committed balancing both two points. To utilize BIC, the number p of free parameters of the model must be calculated. However, for complex Bayesian hierarchical models, it is very difficult to get p's exact number. Therefore, Spiegelhalter et al. [74] propose the deviance information criterion (DIC) to compare Bayesian models. Celeux et al. [95] discuss DIC issues for a censored data set; this paper and other researchers' discussion of it are representative literature in the DIC field in recent years.

DIC utilizes deviance to evaluate the model's measure of fit, and it utilizes the number of parameters to evaluate its complexity. Note that it is consistent with the Akaike information criterion (AIC), which is used to compare classical models [96].

Let (θ) denote the Bayesian deviance, and

$$D(\theta) = -2 \log(p(D \mid \theta)). \quad (24)$$

Let p_d denote the model's effective number of parameters, and

$$\begin{aligned} p_d &= \overline{D}(\theta) - D(\overline{\theta}) \\ &= -\int 2 \ln(p(D \mid \theta)) d\theta - \left(-2 \ln\left(p\left(D \mid \overline{\theta}\right)\right)\right). \end{aligned} \quad (25)$$

Then,

$$DIC = D\left(\overline{\theta}\right) + 2p_d = \overline{D}(\theta) + p_d. \quad (26)$$

Select the model with a lower DIC value. As DIC < 5, the difference between models can be ignored.

DISCUSSIONS WITH A CASE STUDY

In this section, we discuss a case study for a locomotive wheel's degradation data to illustrate the proposed procedure. The case was first discussed by Lin et al. [36].

Background

The service life of a railway wheel can be significantly reduced due to failure or damage, leading to excessive cost and accelerated deterioration. This case study focuses on the wheels of the locomotive of a cargo train. While two types of locomotives with the same type of wheels are used in cargo trains, we consider only one.

There are two bogies for each locomotive and three axels for each bogie (Figure 3). The installed position of the wheels on a particular locomotive is specified by a bogie number (I, II—number of bogies on the locomotive), an axel number (1, 2, 3—number of axels for each bogie) and the side of the wheel on the alxe (right or left) where each wheel is mounted.

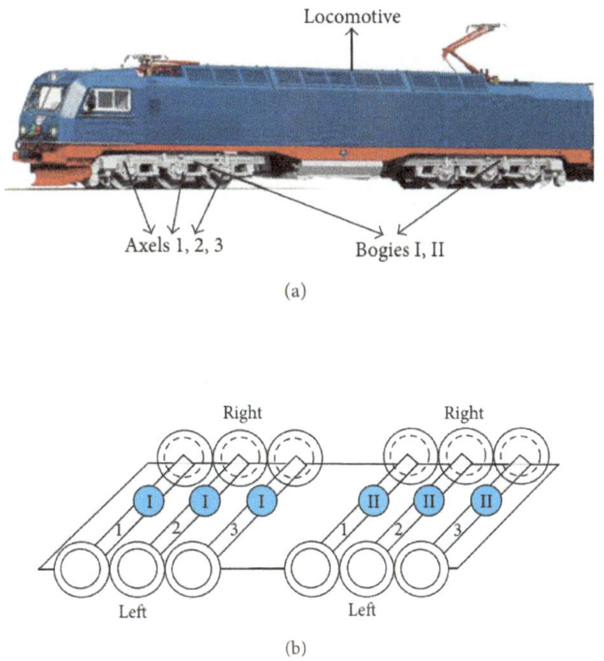

Figure 3: Locomotive wheels' installation positions.

The diameter of a new locomotive wheel in the studied railway company is 1250 mm. In the company's current maintenance strategy, a wheel's diameter is measured after running a certain distance. If it is reduced to 1150 mm, the wheel is replaced by a new one. Otherwise, it is reprofiled or other maintenance strategies are implemented. A threshold level for failure is defined as 100 mm (= 1250 mm – 1150 mm). The wheel's failure condition is assumed to be reached if the diameter reaches 100 mm.

The company's complete database also includes the diameters of all locomotive wheels at a given observation time, the total running distances corresponding to their "time to be maintained," and the wheels' bill of material (BOM) data, from which we can determine their positions.

Two assumptions are made: (1) for each censored datum it is supposed that the wheel is replaced; (2) degradation is linear. Only one locomotive is considered in this example to ensure that (1) all wheel's maintenance strategies are the same; (2) the alxe load and running speed are obviously constant; and (3) the operational environments including routes, climates, and exposure are common for all wheels.

The data set contains 46 datum points (n = 46) of a single locomotive throughout the period November 2010 to January 2012.We take the following steps to obtain locomotive wheels' lifetime data (see Figure 4).

(i) Establish a threshold level L_s, where L_s = 100 mm (1250 mm – 1150 mm).

(ii) Transfer observed 90 records of wheel diameters at reported time t degradation data; this equals to 1250 mm minus the corresponding observed diameter.

(iii) Assume a liner degradation path and construct a degradation line L_i (e.g., L_1, L_2) using the origin point and the degradation data (e.g., B_1, B_2).

(iv) Set $L_s = L_i$, get the point of intersection and the corresponding lifetimes data (e.g., D_1, D_2).

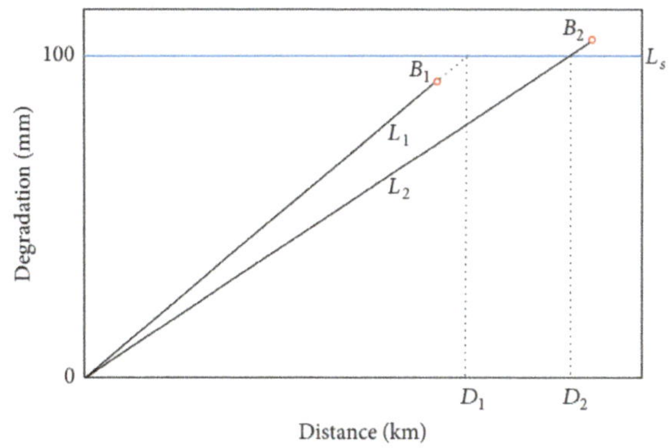

Figure 4: Plot of the wheel degradation data: one example.

To explore the impact of a locomotive wheel's installed position on its service lifetime and to predict its reliability characteristics, the Bayesian exponential regression model, Bayesian Weibull regression model, and Bayesian log-normal regression model are used to establish the wheel's lifetime using degradation data and taking into account the position of the wheel. For each reported datum, a wheel's installation position is documented, and as mentioned above, positioning is used in this study as a covariate. The wheel's position (bogie, axel, and side) or covariate X is denoted by x_1 (bogie I: $x_1 = 1$, bogie II: $x_1 = 2$), x_2 (axel 1: $x_2 = 1$, axel 2: $x_2 = 2$, and axel 3, $x_2 = 3$), and x_3 (right: $x_3 = 1$, left: $x_3 = 2$). Correspondingly, the covariates' coefficients are represented by β_1, β_2, and β_3. In addition, β_0 is defined as random effect. The goal is to determine reliability, failure distribution, and optimal maintenance strategies for the wheel.

Plan

During the Plan Stage, we first collect the "current data," as mentioned in Section 9.1, including the diameter measurements of the locomotive wheel, total distances corresponding to the "time to maintenance," and the wheel's bill of material (BOM) data. Then, see Figure 4, we note the installed position and transfer the diameter into degradation data, which becomes "reliability data" during the "data preparation" process.

We consider the noninformative prior for the constructed models and select the vague prior with log-concave form, which has been determined to be a suitable choice as a noninformative prior selection. For exponential regression: $\beta \sim (0, 0.0001)$; for Weibull regression: $\alpha \sim G(0.2, 0.2)$, $\beta \sim N(0, 0.0001)$; for lognormal regression: $\tau \sim G(1, 0.01)$, $\beta \sim N(0, 0.0001)$.

Do

In the Do Stage, we set up the three models noted above for the degradation analysis: Bayesian exponential regression model, Bayesian Weibull regression model, and Bayesian log-normal regression model. For our calculations, we implement Gibbs sampling.

The joint likelihood function for the exponential regression model, Weibull regression model, and log-normal regression model is given as follows (Lin et al. [36]):

(i) exponential regression model:

$$L(\beta \mid D) = \prod_{i=1}^{n} \left[\exp(\mathbf{x}_i'\beta) \exp(-\exp(\mathbf{x}_i'\beta) t_i)\right]^{\upsilon_i} \times \left[\exp(-\exp(\mathbf{x}_i'\beta) t_i)\right]^{1-\upsilon_i} = \exp\left[\sum_{i=1}^{n} \upsilon_i \mathbf{x}_i'\beta\right] \exp\left[-\sum_{i=1}^{n} \exp(\mathbf{x}_i'\beta) t_i\right]; \quad (27)$$

(ii) Weibull regression model:

$$L(\alpha, \beta \mid D) = \alpha^{\sum_{i=1}^{n} \upsilon_i} \exp\left\{\sum_{i=1}^{n} \upsilon_i \left[\mathbf{x}_i'\beta + \upsilon_i (\alpha - 1) \ln(t_i) - \exp(\mathbf{x}_i'\beta) t_i^{\alpha}\right]\right\}; \quad (28)$$

(iii) log-normal regression model:

$$L(\beta, \tau \mid D) = (2\pi\tau^{-1})^{-(1/2)\sum_{i=1}^{n} \upsilon_i} \exp\left\{-\frac{\tau}{2} \sum_{i=1}^{n} \upsilon_i \left[(\ln(t_i) - \mathbf{x}_i'\beta)\right]^2\right\} \times \prod_{i=1}^{n} t_i^{-\upsilon_i} \left\{1 - \Phi\left[\frac{\ln(t_i) - \mathbf{x}_i'\beta}{\tau^{-1/2}}\right]\right\}^{1-\upsilon_i}. \quad (29)$$

Study

After checking the MCMC convergence diagnostic and accepting the Monte Carlo error diagnostic for all three models, in the Study Stage, we compare the model with the three DIC values. After comparing the DIC values, we select the Bayesian log-normal regression model as the most suitable one (see Table 1).

Table 1: DIC summaries.

Model	$\overline{D}(\theta)$	$D(\overline{\theta})$	p_d	DIC
Exponential	648.98	645.03	3.95	652.93
Weibull	472.22	467.39	4.83	477.05
Log-normal	442.03	436.87	5.16	447.19

Accordingly, the locomotive wheels' reliability functions are achieved:

(i) exponential regression model:

$$R(t_i \mid \mathbf{X}) = \exp\left[-\exp(-5.862 - 0.072x_1 - 0.032x_2 - 0.012x_3) \times t_i\right]; \quad (30)$$

(ii) Weibull regression model:

$$R(t_i \mid \mathbf{X}) = \exp\left[-\exp(-60.47 - 0.078x_1 - 0.146x_2 - 0.050x_3) \times t_i^{10.08}\right]; \quad (31)$$

(iii) log-normal regression model:

$$R(t_i \mid \mathbf{X}) = 1 - \Phi\left[\frac{\ln(t_i) - (5.864 + 0.067x_1 + 0.02x_2 + 0.001x_3)}{(187.5)^{-1/2}}\right]. \quad (32)$$

Action

With the chosen model's posterior results, in the Action Stage, we make our maintenance predictions (Table2) and apply them to the proposed maintenance inspection level. This, in turn, allows us to evaluate and optimise the wheel's replacement and maintenance strategies (including the reprofiling interval, inspection interval, and lubrication interval).

Table 2: MTTF statistics based on Bayesian log-normal regression model.

Bogie	Axel	Side	μ_i	MTTF ($\times 10^3$ km)
I ($x_1 = 1$)	1 ($x_2 = 1$)	Right ($x_3 = 1$)	5.9532	387.03
		Left ($x_3 = 2$)	5.9543	387.46
	2 ($x_2 = 2$)	Right ($x_3 = 1$)	5.9740	395.16
		Left ($x_3 = 2$)	5.9751	395.60
	3 ($x_2 = 3$)	Right ($x_3 = 1$)	5.9947	403.43
		Left ($x_3 = 2$)	5.9958	403.87
II ($x_1 = 2$)	1 ($x_2 = 1$)	Right ($x_3 = 1$)	6.0205	413.97
		Left ($x_3 = 2$)	6.0216	414.43
	2 ($x_2 = 2$)	Right ($x_3 = 1$)	6.0413	422.67
		Left ($x_3 = 2$)	6.0424	423.14
	3 ($x_2 = 3$)	Right ($x_3 = 1$)	6.0621	431.56
		Left ($x_3 = 2$)	6.0632	432.03

As more data are collected in the future, the old "current data set" will be replaced by new "current data"; meanwhile, the results achieved in this case will become "history information," which will be transferred to be "prior knowledge" and a new cycle will start. With this step-by-step method, we can create a continuous improvement process for the locomotive wheel's reliability inference.

CONCLUSIONS

This paper has proposed an integrated procedure for Bayesian reliability inference using Markov chain Monte Carlo methods. The goal is to build a full framework for related academic research and engineering applications to implement modern computational-based Bayesian approaches, especially for reliability inference. The suggested procedure is a continuous improvement process with four stages (Plan, Do, Study, and

Action) and 11 sequential steps including (1) data preparation; (2) priors' inspection and integration; (3) prior selection; (4) model selection; (5) posterior sampling; (6) MCMC convergence diagnostic; (7) Monte Carlo error diagnostic; (8) model improvement; (9) model comparison; (10) inference making; (11) data updating and inference improvement.

The paper illustrates the proposed procedure using a case study. It concludes that the procedure can be used to perform Bayesian reliability inference to determine system (or unit) reliability, failure distribution and to support maintenance strategies optimization, and so forth.

ACKNOWLEDGMENTS

The author would like to thank Luleå Railway Research Centre (Järnvägstekniskt Centrum, Sweden) for initiating the research study and Swedish Transport Administration (Trafikverket) for providing financial support.

REFERENCES

1. D. L. Kelly and C. L. Smith, "Bayesian inference in probabilistic risk assessment—the current state of the art," Reliability Engineering and System Safety, vol. 94, no. 2, pp. 628–643, 2009.·
2. P. Congdon, Bayesian Statistical Modeling, John Wiley & Sons, Chichester, UK, 2001.
3. P. Congdon, Applied Bayesian Modeling, John Wiley & Sons, Chichester, UK, 2003.
4. D. G. Robinson, "A hierarchical bayes approach to system reliability analysis," Tech. Rep. Sandia 2001-3513, Sandia National Laboratories, 2001.
5. V. E. Johnson, "A hierarchical model for estimating the reliability of complex systems," in Bayesian Statistics 7, J. M. Bernardo, Ed., Oxford University Press, Oxford, UK, 2003.
6. A. G. Wilson, "Hierarchical Markov Chain Monte Carlo (MCMC) for bayesian system reliability,"Encyclopedia of Statistics in Quality and Reliability, 2008.
7. J. Lin, M. Asplund, and A. Parida, "Bayesian parametric analysis for reliability study of locomotive wheels," in Proceedings of the 59th Annual Reliability and Maintainability Symposium (RAMS '13), Orlando, Fla, USA, 2013.
8. G. Tonţ, L. Vlădăreanu, M. S. Munteanu, and D. G. Tonţ, "Hierarchical Bayesian reliability analysis of complex dynamical systems," in Proceedings of the 9th WSEAS International Conference on Applications of Electrical Engineering (AEE '10), pp. 181–186, March 2010.
9. J. Lin, "A two-stage failure model for Bayesian change point analysis," IEEE Transactions on Reliability, vol. 57, no. 2, pp. 388–393, 2008.
10. J. Lin, M. L. Nordenvaad, and H. Zhu, "Bayesian survival analysis in reliability for complex system with a cure fraction," International Journal of Performability Engineering, vol. 7, no. 2, pp. 109–120, 2011.
11. M. Hamada, H. F. Martz, C. S. Reese, T. Graves, V. Johnson, and A. G. Wilson, "A fully Bayesian approach for combining multilevel failure information in fault tree quantification and optimal follow-on resource allocation," Reliability Engineering and System Safety, vol. 86, no. 3, pp. 297–305, 2004. ·
12. T. L. Graves, M. S. Hamada, R. Klamann, A. Koehler, and H. F. Martz, "A fully Bayesian approach for combining multi-level information in multi-state fault tree quantification," Reliability Engineering and System Safety, vol. 92, no. 10, pp. 1476–1483, 2007.
13. L. Kuo and B. Mallick, "Bayesian semiparametric inference for the accelerated failure-time model," The Canadian Journal of Statistics, vol. 25, no. 4, pp. 457–472, 1997.
14. S. Walker and B. K. Mallick, "A Bayesian semiparametric accelerated failure time model," Biometrics, vol. 55, no. 2, pp. 477–483, 1999.
15. T. Hanson and W. O. Johnson, "A Bayesian semiparametric AFT model for interval-censored data,"Journal of Computational and Graphical Statistics, vol. 13, no. 2, pp. 341–361, 2004.·
16. S. K. Ghosh and S. Ghosal, "Semiparametric accelerated failure time models for censored data," inBayesian Statistics and Its Applications, S. K. Upadhyay, Ed., Anamaya Publishers, New Delhi, India, 2006.
17. A. Komárek and E. Lesaffre, "The regression analysis of correlated interval-censored data: illustration using accelerated failure time models with flexible distributional assumptions," Statistical Modelling, vol. 9, no. 4, pp. 299–319, 2009.
18. G. Y. Li, Q. G. Wu, and Y. H. Zhao, "On bayesian analysis of binomial reliability growth," The Japan Statistical Society, vol. 32, no. 1, pp. 1–14, 2002.
19. J. Y. Tao, Z. M. Ming, and X. Chen, "The bayesian reliability growth models based on a new dirichlet prior distribution," in Reliability, Risk and Safety, C. G. Soares, Ed., Chapter 237, CRC Press, 2009.
20. L. Kuo and T. Y. Yang, "Bayesian reliability modeling for masked system lifetime data," Statistics and Probability Letters, vol. 47, no. 3, pp. 229–241, 2000.
21. K. Ilkka, "Methods and problems of software reliability estimation," Tech. Rep. VTT Working Papers 1459-7683, VTT Technical Research Centre of Finland, 2006.
22. Y. Tamura, H. Takehara, and S. Yamada, "Component-oriented reliability analysis based on hierarchical bayesian model for an open source software," American Journal of Operations Research, vol. 1, pp. 25–32, 2011.
23. G. I. Schuëller and H. J. Pradlwarter, "Benchmark study on reliability estimation in higher dimensions of structural systems—an overview," Structural Safety, vol. 29, no. 3, pp. 167–182, 2007.
24. S. K. Au, J. Ching, and J. L. Beck, "Application of subset simulation methods to reliability benchmark problems," Structural Safety, vol. 29, no. 3, pp. 183–193, 2007.
25. R. Li, Bayes reliability studies for complex system [Doctor thesis], National University of Defense Technology, 1999, Chinese.
26. A. M. Walker, "On the asymptotic behavior of posterior distributions," Journal of Royal Statistics Society B, vol. 31, no. 1, pp. 80–88, 1969.

27. S. Ghosal, "A review of consistency and convergence of posterior distribution. Technical report," inProceedings of National Conference in Bayesian Analysis, Benaras Hindu University, Varanashi, India, 2000.

28. T. Choi, R. V. B. C. Ramamoorthi, and S. Ghosal, Eds., Pushing the Limits of Contemporary Statistics: Contributions in Honor of Jayanta K. Ghosh, Institute of Mathematical Statistics, Beachwood, Ohio, USA, 2008.

29. V. P. Savchuk and H. F. Martz, "Bayes reliability estimation using multiple sources of prior information: binomial sampling," IEEE Transactions on Reliability, vol. 43, no. 1, pp. 138–144, 1994.

30. K. J. Ren, M. D. Wu, and Q. Liu, "The combination of prior distributions based on kullback information," Journal of the Academy of Equipment of Command & Technology, vol. 13, no. 4, pp. 90–92, 2002.

31. Q. Liu, J. Feng, and J.-L. Zhou, "Application of similar system reliability information to complex system Bayesian reliability evaluation," Journal of Aerospace Power, vol. 19, no. 1, pp. 7–10, 2004.

32. Q. Liu, J. Feng, and J. Zhou, "The fusion method for prior distribution based on expert's information,"Chinese Space Science and Technology, vol. 24, no. 3, pp. 68–71, 2004.

33. G. H. Fang, Research on the multi-source information fusion techniques in the process of reliability assessment [Doctor thesis], Hefei University of Technology, China, 2006.

34. Z. B. Zhou, H. T. Li, X. M. Liu, G. Jin, and J. L. Zhou, "A bayes information fusion approach for reliability modeling and assessment of spaceflight long life product," Journal of Systems Engineering, vol. 32, no. 11, pp. 2517–2522, 2012.

35. R. Howard and S. Robert, Applied Statistical Decision Theory, Division of Research, Graduate School of Business Administration, Harvard University, 1961.

36. J. Lin, M. Asplund, and A. Parida, "Reliability analysis for degradation of locomotive wheels using parametric bayesian approach," Quality and Reliability Engineering International, 2013.

37. J. Lin and M. Asplund, "Bayesian semi-parametric analysis for locomotive wheel degradation using gamma frailties," Journal of Rail and Rapid Transit, 2013.

38. J. G. Ibrahim, M. H. Chen, and D. Sinha, Bayesian Survival Analysis, 2001.

39. J. Lin, Y.-Q. Han, and H.-M. Zhu, "A semi-parametric proportional hazards regression model based on gamma process priors and its application in reliability," Chinese Journal of System Simulation, vol. 22, pp. 5099–5102, 2007.

40. S. K. Sahu, D. K. Dey, H. Aslanidou, and D. Sinha, "A weibull regression model with gamma frailties for multivariate survival data," Lifetime Data Analysis, vol. 3, no. 2, pp. 123–137, 1997.

41. H. Aslanidou, D. K. Dey, and D. Sinha, "Bayesian analysis of multivariate survival data using Monte Carlo methods," Canadian Journal of Statistics, vol. 26, no. 1, pp. 33–48, 1998. ·

42. N. Metropolis, A. W. Rosenbluth, M. N. Rosenbluth, A. H. Teller, and E. Teller, "Equation of state calculations by fast computing machines," The Journal of Chemical Physics, vol. 21, no. 6, pp. 1087–1092, 1953.

43. W. K. Hastings, "Monte carlo sampling methods using Markov chains and their applications,"Biometrika, vol. 57, no. 1, pp. 97–109, 1970.

44. L. Tierney, "Markov chains for exploring posterior distributions," The Annals of Statistics, vol. 22, no. 4, pp. 1701–1762, 1994.

45. S. Chib and E. Greenberg, "Understanding the metropolis-hastings algorithm," Journal of American Statistician, vol. 49, pp. 327–335, 1995.

46. U. Grenander, Tutorial in Pattern Theory, Division of Applied Mathematics, Brow University, Providence, RI, USA, 1983.

47. S. Geman and D. Geman, "Stochastic relaxation, Gibbs distributions and the Bayesian restoration of images," IEEE Transactions on Pattern Analysis and Machine Intelligence, vol. 6, no. 6, pp. 721–741, 1984.

48. A. E. Gelfand and A. F. M. Smith, "Sampling-based approaches to calculation marginal densities,"Journal of American Asscioation, vol. 85, pp. 398–409, 1990.

49. M. A. Tanner and W. H. Wong, "The calculation of posterior distributions by data augmentation (with discussion)," Journal of American Statistical Association, vol. 82, pp. 805–811, 1987.

50. N. G. Polson, "Convergence of markov chain conte carlo algorithms," in Bayesian Statistics 5, Oxford University Press, Oxford, UK, 1996.

51. G. O. Roberts and J. S. Rosenthal, "Markov-chain Monte Carlo: some practical implications of theoretical results," Canadian Journal of Statistics, vol. 26, no. 1, pp. 4–31, 1997.

52. K. L. Mengersen and R. L. Tweedie, "Rates of convergence of the Hastings and Metropolis algorithms,"The Annals of Statistics, vol. 24, no. 1, pp. 101–121, 1996.

53. A. Gelman and D. B. Rubin, "Inference from iterative simulation using multiple sequences (with discussion)," Statistical Science, vol. 7, pp. 457–511, 1992.

54. A. E. Raftery and S. Lewis, "How many iterations in the gibbs sampler," in Bayesian Statistics 4, pp. 763–773, Oxford University Press, Oxford, UK, 1992.

55. S. T. Garren and R. L. Smith, Convergence Diagnostics for Markov Chain Samplers, Department of Statistics, University of North Carolina, 1993.

56. G. O. Roberts and J. S. Rosenthal, "Markov-chain Monte Carlo: some practical implications of theoretical results," Canadian Journal of Statistics, vol. 26, no. 1, pp. 5–31, 1998.

57. S. P. Brooks and A. Gelman, "General methods for monitoring convergence of iterative simulations,"Journal of Computational and Graphical Statistics, vol. 7, no. 4, pp. 434–455, 1998.

58. J. Geweke, "Evaluating the accuracy of sampling-based approaches to the calculation of posterior moments,"

in Bayesian Statistics 4, J. M. Bernardo, J. Berger, A. P. Dawid, and A. F. M. Smith, Eds., pp. 169–193, Oxford University Press, Oxford, UK, 1992.

59. V. E. Johnson, "Studying convergence of markov chain monte carlo algorithms using coupled sampling paths," Tech. Rep., Institute for Statistics and Decision Sciences, Duke University, 1994.

60. P. Mykland, L. Tierney, and B. Yu, "Regeneration in markov chain samplers," Journal of the American Statistical Association, no. 90, pp. 233–241, 1995.

61. C. Ritter and M. A. Tanner, "Facilitating the gibbs sampler: the gibbs stopper and the griddy gibbs sampler," Journal of the American Statistical Association, vol. 87, pp. 861–868, 1992.

62. G. O. Roberts, "Convergence diagnostics of the gibbs sampler," in Bayesian Statistics 4, pp. 775–782, Oxford University Press, Oxford, UK, 1992.

63. B. Yu, Monitoring the Convergence of Markov Samplers Based on Estimated L1 Error, Department of Statistics, University of California, Berkeley, Calif, USA, 1994.

64. B. Yu and P. Mykland, Looking at Markov Samplers through Cusum Path Plots: A Simple Diagnostic Idea, Department of Statistics, University of California, Berkeley, Calif, USA, 1994.

65. A. Zellner and C. K. Min, "Gibbs sampler convergence criteria," Journal of the American Statistical Association, vol. 90, pp. 921–927, 1995.

66. P. Heidelberger and P. D. Welch, "Simulation run length control in the presence of an initial transient,"Operations Research, vol. 31, no. 6, pp. 1109–1144, 1983.

67. C. Liu, J. Liu, and D. B. Rubin, "A variational control variable for assessing the convergence of the gibbs sampler," in Proceedings of the American Statistical Association, Statistical Computing Section, pp. 74–78, 1992.

68. J. F. Lawless, Statistical Models and Method for Lifetime Data, John Wiley & Sons, New York, NY, USA, 1982.

69. A. Gelman, J. B. Carlin, H. S. Stern, and D. B. Rubin, Bayesian Data Analysis, Chapman and Hall/CRC Press, New York, NY, USA, 2004.

70. R. A. Kass and A. E. Raftery, "Bayes factor," Journal of American Stattistical Association, vol. 90, pp. 773–795, 1995.

71. A. Gelfand and D. Dey, "Bayesian model choice: asymptotic and exact calculations," Journal of Royal Statistical Society B, vol. 56, pp. 501–514, 1994.

72. C. T. Volinsky and A. E. Raftery, "Bayesian information criterion for censored survival models,"Biometrics, vol. 56, no. 1, pp. 256–262, 2000.

73. R. E. Kass and L. Wasserman, "A reference bayesian test for nested hypotheses and its relationship to the schwarz criterion," Journal of American Statistical Association, vol. 90, pp. 928–934, 1995.

74. D. J. Spiegelhalter, N. G. Best, B. P. Carlin, and A. van der Linde, "Bayesian measures of model complexity and fit," Journal of the Royal Statistical Society B, vol. 64, no. 4, pp. 583–639, 2002.

75. S. Geisser and W. Eddy, "A predictive approach to model selection," Journal of American Statistical Association, vol. 74, pp. 153–160, 1979.

76. A. E. Gelfand, D. K. Dey, and H. Chang, "Model determinating using predictive distributions with implementation via sampling-based methods (with discussion)," in Bayesian Statistics 4, Oxford University Press, Oxford, UK, 1992.

77. M. Newton and A. Raftery, "Approximate bayesian inference by the weighted likelihood bootstrap,"Journal of Royal Statistical Society B, vol. 56, pp. 1–48, 1994.

78. P. J. Lenk and W. S. Desarbo, "Bayesian inference for finite mixtures of generalized linear models with random effects," Psychometrika, vol. 65, no. 1, pp. 93–119, 2000.

79. X.-L. Meng and W. H. Wong, "Simulating ratios of normalizing constants via a simple identity: a theoretical exploration," Statistica Sinica, vol. 6, no. 4, pp. 831–860, 1996. ·

80. S. Chib, "Marginal likelihood from the Gibbs output," Journal of the American Statistical Association, vol. 90, pp. 1313–1321, 1995.

81. S. Chib and I. Jeliazkov, "Marginal likelihood from the metropolis-hastings output," Journal of the American Statistical Association, vol. 96, no. 453, pp. 270–281, 2001.

82. S. M. Lewis and A. E. Raftery, "Estimating Bayes factors via posterior simulation with the Laplace-Metropolis estimator," Journal of the American Statistical Association, vol. 92, no. 438, pp. 648–655, 1997.

83. S. K. Sahu and R. C. H. Cheng, "A fast distance-based approach for determining the number of components in mixtures," Canadian Journal of Statistics, vol. 31, no. 1, pp. 3–22, 2003.

84. K. Mengersen and C. P. Robert, "Testing for mixtures: a bayesian entropic approach," in Bayesian Statistics 5, Oxford University Press, Oxford, UK, 1996.

85. J. G. Ibrahim and P. W. Laud, "A predictive approach to the analysis of designed experiments," Journal of the American Statistical Association, vol. 89, pp. 309–319, 1994.

86. A. E. Gelfand and S. K. Ghosh, "Model choice: a minimum posterior predictive loss approach,"Biometrika, vol. 85, no. 1, pp. 1–11, 1998.

87. M.-H. Chen, D. K. Dey, and J. G. Ibrahim, "Bayesian criterion based model assessment for categorical data," Biometrika, vol. 91, no. 1, pp. 45–63, 2004.

88. P. J. Green, "Reversible jump Markov chain monte carlo computation and Bayesian model determination," Biometrika, vol. 82, no. 4, pp. 711–732, 1995.

89. C. Robert and G. Casella, Monte Carlo Statistical Methods, Springer, New York, NY, USA, 2004.

90. M. Stephens, "Bayesian analysis of mixture models with an unknown number of components—an alternative to reversible jump methods," Annals of Statistics, vol. 28, no. 1, pp. 40–74, 2000.

91. M. Tatiana, F. S. Sylvia, and D. A. Georg, Comparison of Bayesian Model Selection Based on MCMC with an Application to GARCH-Type Models, Vienna University of Economics and Business Administration, 2003.

92. P. C. Gregory, "Extra-solar planets via Bayesian fusion MCMC," in Astrostatistical Challenges for the New Astronomy, J. M. Hilbe, Ed., Springer Series in Astrostatistics, Chapter 7, Springer, New York, NY, USA, 2012.

93. H. Chen and S. Huang, "A comparative study on model selection and multiple model fusion," inProceedings of the 7th International Conference on Information Fusion (FUSION '05), pp. 820–826, July 2005.

94. H. Jeffreys, Theory of Probability, Oxford Univiersity Press, Oxford, UK, 1961.

95. G. Celeux, F. Forbes, C. P. Robert, and D. M. Titterington, "Deviance information criteria for missing data models," Bayesian Analysis, vol. 1, no. 4, pp. 651–674, 2006.

96. H. Akaike, "Information theory and an extension of the maximum likelihood principle," in Proceedings of the 2nd International Symposium on Information Theory, Tsahkadsor, 1971.

CHAPTER 15

NON-STATIONARY RANDOM RESPONSE OF MDOF DUFFING SYSTEMS

J.H. Lin[1], J. Wang[2], and Y.H. Zhang[1]

[1]State Key Laboratory of Structural Analysis of Industrial Equipment, Dalian University of Technology, Dalian 116023, China

[2]Department of Civil Engineering, SUNY at Buffalo, 109 Red Jacket Quard., Buffalo, NY 14261, USA

ABSTRACT

This paper presents a method to solve non-stationary random responses of nonlinear multi-degrees-of-freedom (MDOF) Duffing systems subjected to evolutionary random excitations. Specific phase-lags between the excitations can also be taken into account. The power spectral density (PSD) of the input excitations is not confined to simple white noise or filtered white noise, in fact it can also take more complicated forms. The MDOF nonlinear random differential equations are iteratively solved by means of the Equivalent Linearization Method (ELM) combined with the Pseudo Excitation Method (PEM). This combined method is easy and efficient. Two examples are given in which this method is well justified by the Monte-Carlo numerical simulations. Although only a Duffing model is dealt with in this paper for computational simplicity, the proposed method is in fact quite general, e.g. it can also deal with nonlinear hysteretic structures that will be dealt with in a separate paper.

INTRODUCTION

The response of many real structural systems subjected to external random excitations can be described by nonlinear random differential equations. In general, approximation methods have to be used to solve such nonlinear equations. Only in very few cases can an exact solution for stationary response be found in closed form. Although the non-stationary random response analysis of MDOF nonlinear systems is much more difficult than such problems, some pioneering work has laid a good foundation in this field [1–11].

Citation: J.H. Lin, J. Wang, and Y.H. Zhang, "Non-Stationary Random Response of MDOF Duffing Systems," Shock and Vibration, vol. 11, no. 5-6, pp. 615-624, 2004. doi:10.1155/2004/675683

One of the most popular methods used in the study and engineering applications of nonlinear random vibration problems is equivalent linearization, particularly if the random excitations are stationary. For nonlinear systems subjected to non-stationary random excitations, however, the equivalent linear systems are time-dependant, its solution is still not so easy. In particular, if the excitations are not uniform, i.e. phase lags exist between the excitations, the solution will become more difficult.

It is well known that for an arbitrary nonlinear system subjected to stationary random excitations, an equivalent time-independent linear system can be found readily based on the least-quadratic criterion. If the nonlinear system is instead subjected to non-stationary random excitations, then at any time t, an equivalent linear system can be found similarly based on the least quadratic criterion. And based on this idea, a nonlinear SDOF (Single Degree of Freedom) system subjected to a non-stationary random excitation is solved iteratively [11], wherein the analytical solution of the time-dependent mean-square response for the linear time-independent system must be available. Therefore its application field is limited.

In this paper, the pseudo excitation method (PEM) [12–16] is extended to solve the non-stationary random responses of MDOF Duffing systems subjected to evolutionary random excitations. It is not necessary to know the analytical expressions of the time-dependent mean-square responses for the linear MDOF time-independent system, therefore the proposed method is not confined to structures subjected to white-noise or filtered white-noise excitations. In addition, phase-lags (or time-lags) are permitted between the excitations.

Two examples are given in which the Monte-Carlo simulation is used to justify the proposed method

LINEAR SYSTEMS SUBJECTED TO EVOLUTIONARY MULTI-PHASE RANDOM EXCITATIONS

Consider a linear structure subjected to an evolutionary random excitation

$$[M]\{\ddot{y}\} + [C]\{\dot{y}\} + [K]\{y\} = \{P\}f(t) \tag{1}$$

in which

$$f(t) = g(t)x(t) \tag{2}$$

g(t) is a given slowly varying modulation function, while x(t) is a zero-mean-valued stationary random process of which the auto-PSD $S_{xx}(\omega)$ is also known. The PSD curve of f(t) has constant shape, however its amplitude varies with g(t). In other words, a stationary random process x(t) is modulated by a deterministic function g(t). In order to compute the PSD matrices of two arbitrary response vectors {y(t)} and {z(t)}, the following pseudo excitation should be used [13,15]

$$\tilde{f}(t) = g(t)\sqrt{S_{xx}(\omega)}e^{i\omega t} \tag{3}$$

Under the action of this deterministic loading, the equations of motion Eq. (1) of the linear structure are

$$[M]\{\ddot{y}\} + [C]\{\dot{y}\} + [K]\{y\} = \{p\}g(t)\sqrt{S_{xx}(\omega)}e^{i\omega t} \tag{4}$$

in which [M], [C] and [K] are time independent mass, damping and stiffness matrices, {p} is a given constant vector. For seismic problems, the structure is initially at rest, namely, {y 0} = {y˙0} = {0} when t = 0. Thus the time-histories of two arbitrary responses of interest, denoted as y(ω, t) and z(ω, t), can be computed in terms of the Newmark, Wilson-θ schemes or the precise integration method [15] with ω regarded as a parameter. It has been verified that [13] the auto- and cross-PSD functions of these responses can be accurately computed by using the following equations

$$S_{yy}(\omega) = y(\omega,t)^* y(\omega,t) = |y(\omega,t)|^2 \tag{5}$$

$$S_{yz} = y(\omega,t)^* z(\omega,t) \tag{6}$$

If the interested responses are two vectors, denoted as {y(t)} and {z(t)}, the corresponding time history {y(ω, t)} and {z(ω, t)} should be solved from Eq. (3) before the following equations are used to give their accurate auto- and cross-PSD matrices [13]

$$[S_{yy}(\omega)] = \{y(\omega,t)\}^*\{y(\omega,t)\}^T \tag{7}$$

$$[S_{yz}(\omega)] = \{y(\omega,t)\}^*\{z(\omega,t)\}^T \tag{8}$$

It has also been verified that if the precise integration method [15,17] is used in solving Eq. (4), the efficiency would be much higher than using Newmark method.

If the random excitation *f*(t) in Eq. (2) is a vector, specific time-lags exist between all its components, then

$$\{f(t)\} = \begin{Bmatrix} F_1(t) \\ F_2(t) \\ \vdots \\ F_n(t) \end{Bmatrix} = \begin{Bmatrix} a_1 g(t-t_1)F(t-t_1) \\ a_2 g(t-t_2)F(t-t_2) \\ \vdots \\ a_n g(t-t_n)F(t-t_n) \end{Bmatrix}$$
$$= [G(t)]\{F(t)\} = \begin{bmatrix} a_1 g(t-t_1) & & & \\ & a_2 g(t-t_2) & & \\ & & \ddots & \\ & & & a_n g(t-t_n) \end{bmatrix} \begin{Bmatrix} F(t-t_1) \\ F(t-t_2) \\ \vdots \\ F(t-t_n) \end{Bmatrix} \tag{9}$$

in which a_j (j = 1, 2,...,n) are given non-negative real numbers, t_1, t_2,...,t_n represent the time lags between the forces applying on different points of the structure. $a_k = 0$ means no load applies on the k-th DOF. F(t) is a stationary random process, its auto-PSD $S_{FF}(\omega)$ is known. Using Wiener-Khintchine formula and denoting $\tau = \tau_l - \tau_k$ gives

$$E[\{F(\tau_k)\}\{F(\tau_l)\}^T] = E\begin{bmatrix} F(\tau_k-t_1)F(\tau_l-t_1) & F(\tau_k-t_1)F(\tau_l-t_2) & \dots & F(\tau_k-t_1)F(\tau_l-t_n) \\ F(\tau_k-t_2)F(\tau_l-t_1) & F(\tau_k-t_2)F(\tau_l-t_2) & \dots & F(\tau_k-t_2)F(\tau_l-t_n) \\ \vdots & \vdots & \ddots & \vdots \\ F(\tau_k-t_n)F(\tau_l-t_1) & F(\tau_k-t_n)F(\tau_l-t_2) & \dots & F(\tau_k-t_n)F(\tau_l-t_n) \end{bmatrix}$$
$$= \int_{-\infty}^{\infty} \begin{bmatrix} 1 & e^{i\omega(t_1-t_2)} & \dots & e^{i\omega(t_1-t_n)} \\ e^{i\omega(t_2-t_1)} & 1 & \dots & e^{i\omega(t_2-t_n)} \\ \vdots & \vdots & \ddots & \vdots \\ e^{i\omega(t_n-t_1)} & e^{i\omega(t_n-t_2)} & \dots & 1 \end{bmatrix} e^{i\omega\tau} S_{FF}(\omega)d\omega$$
$$= \int_{-\infty}^{\infty} [V]^*[R_0][V]^T e^{i\omega\tau} S_{FF}(\omega)d\omega \tag{10}$$

in which

$$[V] = \mathrm{diag}[e^{-i\omega t_1}, e^{-i\omega t_2}, \dots, e^{-i\omega t_n}] \tag{11}$$

$$[R_0] = \{q_0\}\{q_0\}^T = \begin{bmatrix} 1\,1 \dots 1 \\ 1\,1 \dots 1 \\ \vdots\ \vdots\ \ddots \dots \\ 1\,1 \dots 1 \end{bmatrix} \tag{12}$$

herein $[R_0]$ and $\{q_0\}$ are matrix and vector with all elements be unity.

Assume that {y(t)} is an arbitrary response vector due to the excitation {*f*(t)}, then

$$\{y(t)\} = \int_0^t [h(t-\tau)]\{f(\tau)\}d\tau = \int_0^t [h(t-\tau)][G(\tau)]\{F(\tau)\}d\tau \tag{13}$$

If $\{y_k(t_k)\}$ and $\{y_l t_l)\}$ are two kinds of response vectors, then their cross-correlation matrix would be

$$[R_{y_k y_l}(t_k, t_l] = E[\{y_k(t_k)\}\{y_l(t_l)\}^T] = \int_0^t \int_0^t [h_k(t_k - \tau_k)][G(\tau_k)]E[\{F(\tau_k)\}\{F(\tau_l)\}^T] [G(\tau_l)]^T [h_l(t_l - \tau_l)]^T d\tau_k d\tau_l \tag{14}$$

Substituting Eqs (10), (11) and (12) into Eq. (14) gives

$$[R_{y_k y_l}(t_k, t_l)] = \int_{-\infty}^{\infty} \{I_k\}^* \{I_l\}^T S_{FF}(\omega) d\omega \tag{15}$$

in which

$$I_k(\omega, t_k) = \int_0^{t_k} [h_k(t_k - \tau_k)][G(\tau_k)][V]\{q_0\} e^{i\omega\tau_k} d\tau_k \tag{16}$$

It is known from Eq. (15) that when $t_k = t_l = t$, the cross-PSD matrix of $\{y_k\}$ and $\{y_l\}$ is

$$[S_{y_k y_l}(\omega, t)] = \{I_k(\omega, t)\}^* \{I_l(\omega, t)\}^T S_{FF}(\omega) \tag{17}$$

It is also known from Eq. (16), that $I_k(\omega, t)$ is the transient response due to the deterministic excitation $[G(t)][V]\{q0\}e^{i\omega t}$. Therefore by using the following pseudo excitation

$$\{\tilde{f}(t)\} = [G(t)][V]\{q_0\}\sqrt{S_{FF}(\omega)} e^{i\omega t} = \begin{Bmatrix} g(t - t_1) a_1 e^{-i\omega t_1} \\ g(t - t_2) a_2 e^{-i\omega t_2} \\ \vdots \\ g(t - t_n) a_n e^{-i\omega t_n} \end{Bmatrix} e^{i\omega t} \sqrt{S_{FF}(\omega)} \tag{18}$$

the resulted response must be

$$\{y_k(\omega, t_k)\} = \{I_k(\omega, t)\}\sqrt{S_{FF}(\omega)} \tag{19}$$

Therefore, according to Eq. (17), one obtains

$$[S_{y_k y_l}(\omega, t)] = \{y_k(\omega, t)\}^* \{y_l(\omega, t)\}^T \tag{20}$$

Let k = l, Eq. (20), gives the auto-PSD matrix of $\{y_k\}$.

$$[S_{y_k y_k}(\omega, t)] = \{y_k(\omega, t)\}^* \{y_k(\omega, t)\}^T \tag{21}$$

By neglecting the subscript k, Eq. (7) is obtained. For two responses $\{y(t)\}$ and $\{z(t)\}$, just follow the above process, Eq. (8) can also be derived.

DUFFING SYSTEMS SUBJECTED TO EVOLUTIONARY MULTI-PHASE RANDOM EXCITATIONS

The nonlinear equations of motion can be written as

$$[M]\{\ddot{Y}\} + [C]\{\dot{Y}\} + [K]\{Y\} + \{g\} = \{f(t)\} \tag{22}$$

in which $\{g\}$ represents the nonlinear property of the structure. For the MDOF Duffing system as shown in Fig. 1, $\{g\}$ has the following form

$$\{g\} = \begin{Bmatrix} \mu_1 k_1 x_1^3 - \mu_2 k_2 x_2^3 \\ \mu_2 k_2 x_2^3 - \mu_3 k_3 x_3^3 \\ \vdots \\ \mu_{n-1} k_{n-1} x_{n-1}^3 - \mu_n k_n x_n^3 \\ \mu_n k_n x_n^3 \end{Bmatrix} \tag{23}$$

$$\{x\} = \begin{Bmatrix} x_1 \\ x_2 \\ \vdots \\ x_n \end{Bmatrix} = \begin{Bmatrix} y_1 \\ y_2 - y_1 \\ \vdots \\ y_n - y_{n-1} \end{Bmatrix}, \qquad \{\mu\} = \{\mu_1, \mu_2, \ldots, \mu_n\}^T \tag{24}$$

$\{x\}$ is the story drift vector, $\{\mu\}$ is the vector which characterizes the intensity of system non-linearity, $\{f(t)\}$ is a zero-mean-valued evolutionary random process.

According to the least quadratic criterion [7–9], the nonlinear $\{g\}$ term can be linearized as

$$\{g\} = [K_\mu(t)]\{Y\} \tag{25}$$

where $[K_\mu(t)]$ is a time-variant tri-diagonal symmetric matrix which relies on the time-variant structural responses:

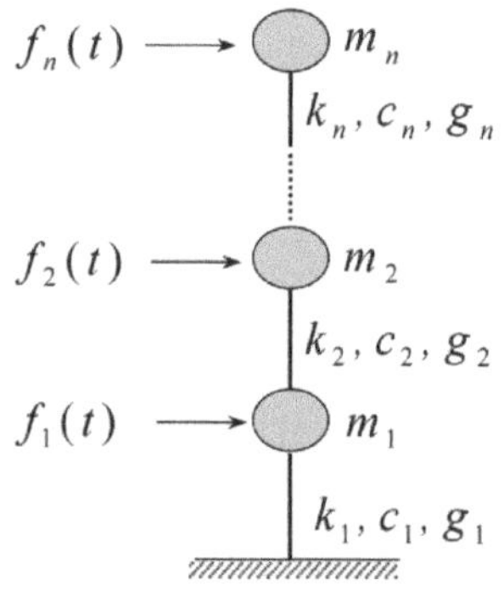

Figure 1: Shear type MDOF Duffing system.

$$[K_\mu(t)] = 3 \begin{bmatrix} \mu_1 k_1 E[x_1^2(t)] + \mu_2 k_2 E[x_2^2(t)] & -\mu_2 k_2 E[x_2^2(t)] & & 0 \\ & \mu_2 k_2 E[x_2^2(t)] + \mu_3 k_3 E[x_3^2(t)] & -\mu_3 k_3 E[x_3^2(t)] & \\ & \ddots & \ddots & \\ Sym & & \mu_{n-1} k_{n-1} E[x_{n-1}^2(t)] + \mu_n k_n E[x_n^2(t)] & -\mu_n k_n E[x_n^2(t)] \\ & & & \mu_n k_n E[x_n^2(t)] \end{bmatrix} \tag{26}$$

At any time t,

$$E[x_i^2(t)] = \int_{-\infty}^{\infty} S_{x_i}(\omega, t) d\omega \quad (i = 1, 2, \ldots, n) \tag{27}$$

It can be computed conveniently according to PEM:

$$E[x_1^2(t)] = 2\int_0^\infty |x_1(\omega, t)|^2 d\omega = 2\int_0^\infty |y_1(\omega, t)|^2 d\omega$$
$$E[x_i^2(t)] = 2\int_0^\infty |x_i(\omega, t)|^2 d\omega = 2\int_0^\infty |y_i(\omega, t) - y_{i-1}(\omega, t)|^2 d\omega \quad i = 2, 3, \ldots, n \tag{28}$$

Equations (22), (25), (26) and (28) constitute a closed iteration ring from which the non-stationary solution at time t of the equivalent linear system can be computed. When the displacement variance at time t_j, $\{E[y^2(t_j]\}$, has been obtained, this response at the next time t_{j+1}, $\{E[y^2(t_{j+1})]\}$, can be computed by means of the following steps:

(1) Take $t = t_{j+1}$ in Eq. (18);

(2) Let $\{g\} = 0$ in Eq. (22), compute $\{y(\omega, t_{j+1})\}$ over a series of significant frequencies using a time-history method such as Newmark method;

(3) Compute the mean-square value of $\{x(t_{j+1})\}$ by using Eq. (28);

(4) Compute $[K\mu(t_{j+1})]$ according to Eq. (26), which will be assembled into the stiffness matrix [K] of Eq. (22)

(5) Solve Eq. (22) for $\{y(\omega, t_{j+1})\}$ over a series of significant frequencies, repeat steps (3) ~ (5) until $\{y(\omega, t_{j+1})\}$ converges;

(6) Compute the PSD vector $\{S_{yy}(\omega, t_{j+1})\}$ and mean square value vector $\{E[y^2(t_{j+1})]\}$ from $\{y(\omega, t_{j+1})\}$ at time t_{j+1}.

Clearly, in the above steps, the analytical expressions of the time-dependent mean-square response for the equivalent linear MDOF time-independent system need not be known, therefore this method applies not only to structures subjected to simple white-noise or filtered white-noise excitations, but also to structures subjected to more complicated random excitations. It can also be seen from Eq. (9) or Eq. (11) that the proposed method permits phase-lags (or time-lags) existing between the excitations.

MONTE-CARLO SIMULATION

Sample time history curves

A uniformly modulated evolutionary random process with the form of f(t) in Eq. (2) can be simulated by the following expression [16,18,19]

$$f_{ns}(t) = g(t)\sum_{k=1}^{N} A_k \cos(\omega_k t + \varphi_k) \tag{29}$$

in which

$$\Delta\omega = (\omega_u - \omega_l)/N,\quad A_k^2 = 4S_{ff}(\omega_k)\cdot\Delta\omega$$

$$\omega_k = \omega_l + (k - \frac{1}{2})\Delta\omega,\quad k = 1, 2, \ldots, N \tag{30}$$

ω_l and ω_u are the lower and upper bounds of the frequency region, φ_k is a random real number uniformly distributed in the region $[0, 2\pi]$.

For m fully coherent evolutionary random excitations $f^{(i)}(t)(i = 1, 2,...,m)$, if specific phase-lags exist between all its components, then these excitations can be simulated by the following expression [16]

$$f_{ns}^{(i)}(t) = g(t)\sum_{k=1}^{N} A_k \cos(\omega_k t + \omega_k t_i + \varphi_k) \tag{31}$$

When N is sufficiently large, $f_{ns}^{(i)}(t)(i = 1, 2, \ldots, m)$ simulates the fully coherent random process $f^{(i)}(t)$ with invariant time-phases t [16].

Numerical simulation for nonlinear systems

Provided the equations of motion of a nonlinear dynamic system is

$$M\ddot{Y} + G(\dot{Y}, Y) = F(t) \tag{32}$$

in which $G(\dot{Y}, Y)$ is the nonlinear term.

The simulation process for the nonlinear system is as follows:

(1) Substitute an excitation according to Eq. (29) into the right hand side of Eq. (32), compute the displacement vectors {Y } at a series of time points by means of a time history method; For the displacement values corresponding to each element in the vector {Y } at a series of discrete time points, the Fast Fourier Transformation (FFT) scheme is used to obtain the PSD values at a series of frequencies which

(2) will then be used to compute the PSD vector $\{_{SYY}(\omega)\}$ of the displacement vector at these frequencies.

(3) Integrate the PSD vector $\{S_{YY}(\omega)\}$ in the effective frequency region to obtain the corresponding response variances $\{\sigma_Y^2\}$.

(4) The above steps (1)~(3) are repeated for a large amount of excitation samples to generate corresponding $\{\sigma_Y^2\}$ samples, and the statistics.

For nonlinear equations, iterations must be executed at each time step. The statistics of the responses at any arbitrary time will then be computed by means of the assemble average of a great deal of response samples.

It is noted that the time step size must be small enough to ensure the integration precision [18,19].

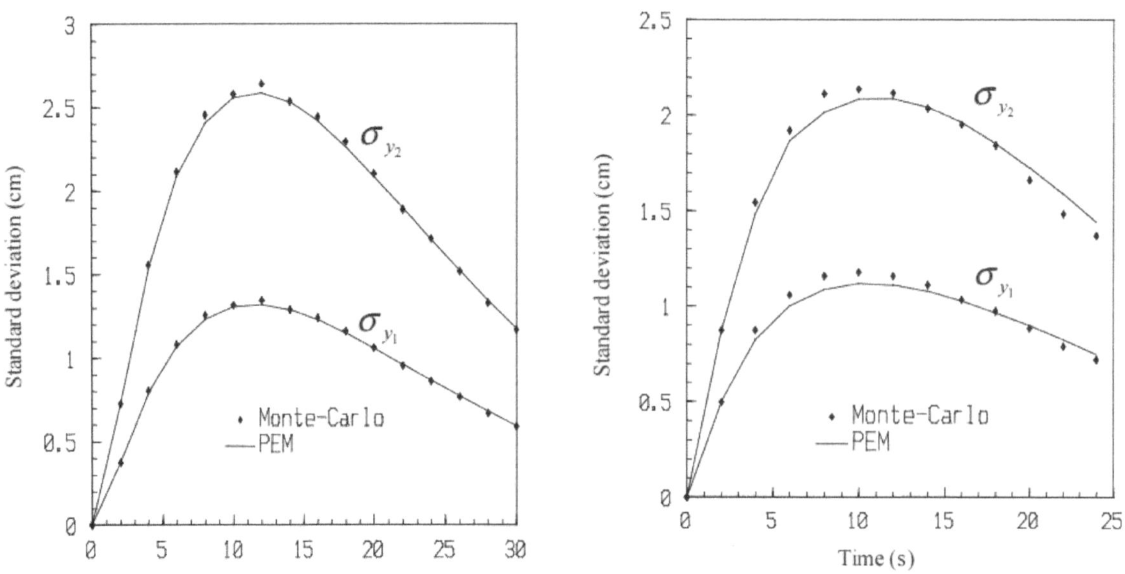

(a) T=0 (b) T=1.0

Figure 2: Displacement standard deviation comparison using PEM and Monte-Carlo method.

NUMERICAL EXAMPLES

Example 1. Two DOF Duffing system

Consider a 2 DOF shear-type Duffing system, with $m_1 = m_2 = 1000$ kg, $k_1 = 150$ kN/m, $k_2 = 100$ kN/m and $[C] = \begin{bmatrix} 440 & -120 \\ -120 & 260 \end{bmatrix}$ see Fig. 1, which is subjected to the following evolutionary random excitations

$$\{f(t)\} = \begin{Bmatrix} f_1(t) \\ f_2(t) \end{Bmatrix} = \begin{Bmatrix} g(t)x(t) \\ g(t+T)x(t+T) \end{Bmatrix} \tag{33}$$

in which T is the time-lag between $f_1(t)$ and $f_2(t)$. The PSD functions of $f_1(t)$ and $f_2(t)$ are equal to each other, and both will simultaneously take one of the following forms:

$$1)\ S_{x1}(\omega) = S_0 = 2.5 \times 10^{-3}\ (\mathrm{KN^2s});\ \text{or} \tag{34}$$

$$2)\ S_{x2}(\omega) = \frac{C}{\pi} \cdot \frac{4ab\omega^2}{(\omega_0^2 - \omega^2)^2 + 4a^2\omega^2} = \frac{0.03927}{3.14} \cdot \frac{80\omega^2}{(50 - \omega^2)^2 + 40\omega^2}\ (\mathrm{kN^2s}) \tag{35}$$

The modulation function has the form

$$g(t) = d(e^{-p_1 t} - e^{-p_2 t}) = 4.0(e^{-0.0995t} - e^{-0.199t}) \tag{36}$$

When the excitation PSD is a white noise expressed by Eq. (34) and for T = 0.0 or T = 1.0, without or with timelags between the excitations, the displacement standard deviations computed by PEM are shown in Figs 2(a)–(b). Such standard deviations are also computed using Monte-Carlo simulation method, with 4000 samples, $\omega_l = 0.0$, $\omega_u = 100.0$, N = 2000; and the results are also shown in Figs 2(a)–(b). Clearly, these two methods give quite close results. When T = 0.0, the maximum difference is less than 3.0%, and when T = 1.0 the errors are mostly within 5.0%, the maximum is 7.0%. As the PEM is an accurate method for linear systems, the errors come from the linearization of the nonlinear system.

When using Eq. (34) as the PSD of both excitations, Fig. 3 gives the comparison of the two methods for T = 0.4, 1.0 and 1.6. It is shown that for all cases, the two methods give quite close results; it is also shown that the non-stationary responses of the nonlinear system rely heavily on the time lag T .

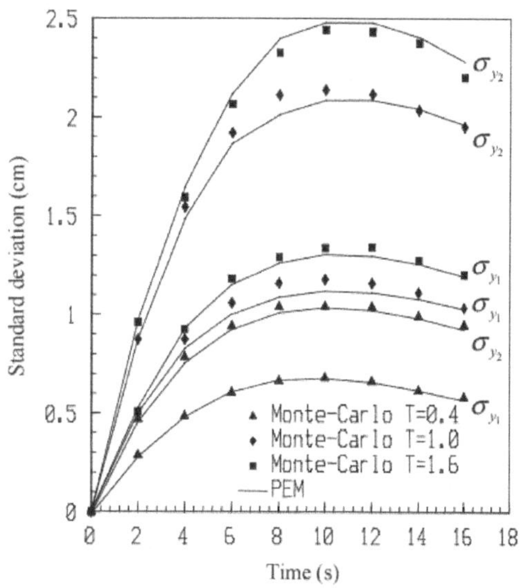

Figure 3: Displacement standard deviation comparison for different time lags

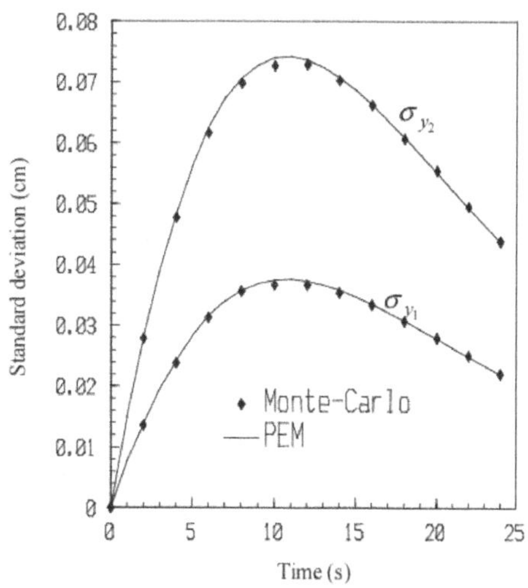

Figure 4: Displacement standard deviation for non white spectrum and time lag T = 1.6 s.

The PSD form of Eq. (35) is somewhat similar to a wind-gust spectrum. Under this excitation and with T = 1.6, the responses due to the two methods still meet quite well, as shown in Fig. 4.

For this example, $\mu 1 = \mu 2 = 0.05$ represents rather strong non-linearity. In fact, for the corresponding linear system, i.e. for $\mu 1 = \mu 2 = 0.0$, the eigenvalues of the system are $(\omega_1^2, \omega_2^2) = (50.0, 300.0) 1/s^{-2}$ for $\mu_1 = \mu_2 = 0.05$ and with stationary excitations, the eigenvalues of the equivalent linear system are $(\omega_1^2, \omega_2^2) = (61.4, 368.7)$, the increments are both about 23%.

*Example 2. **Five DOF Duffing System***

Consider a 5 DOF shear type Duffing system as shown in Fig. 1, subjected to seismic evolutionary random excitations, Its parameters are $m_1 = m_2 = 3000.0$ kg, $m_3 = m_4 = 2000.0$ kg, $m_5 = 1500$ kg, $k_1 = k_2 = 500.0$ kN/m, $k_3 = k_4 = 400.0$ kN/m, $k_5 = 300.0$ kN/m, $\mu_i = 0.15 (i = 1, 2, 3, 4, 5)$; [C]=0.014[K]s. The ground acceleration PSD takes the following Kanai-Tajimi filtered white noise spectrum

$$S_f(\omega) = \frac{\omega_g^4 + 4\zeta_g^2 \omega_g^2 \omega^2}{(\omega_g^2 - \omega^2)^2 + 4\zeta_g^2 \omega_g^2 \omega^2} S_0 \tag{37}$$

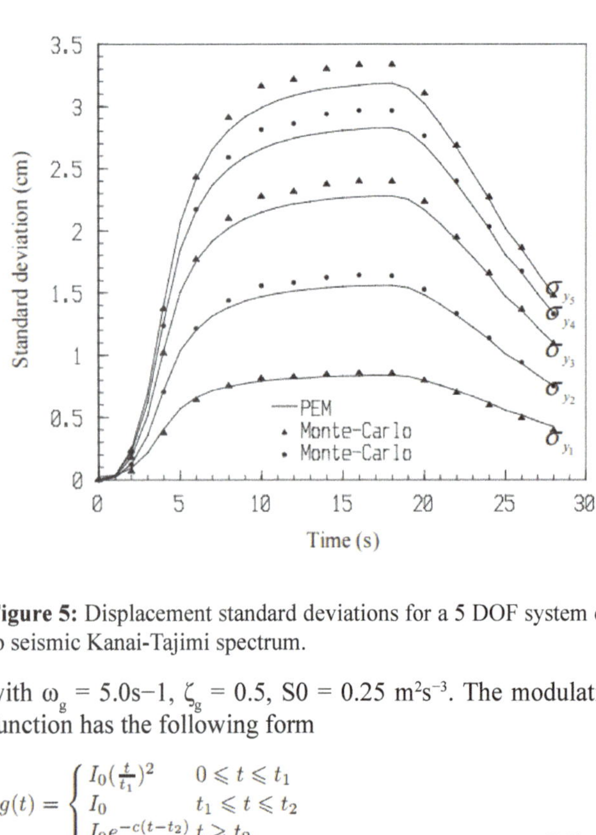

Figure 5: Displacement standard deviations for a 5 DOF system due to seismic Kanai-Tajimi spectrum.

with $\omega_g = 5.0s{-}1$, $\zeta_g = 0.5$, S0 = 0.25 m^2s^{-3}. The modulation function has the following form

$$g(t) = \begin{cases} I_0(\frac{t}{t_1})^2 & 0 \leqslant t \leqslant t_1 \\ I_0 & t_1 \leqslant t \leqslant t_2 \\ I_0 e^{-c(t-t_2)} & t \geqslant t_2 \end{cases} \tag{38}$$

with $I_0 = 1.0$, $t_1 = 4.0$s, $t_2 = 18.0$ s, c = 0.18.

The standard deviation curves of the non-stationary displacement responses are computed using PEM and MonteCarlo method with 1000 samples, $\omega_l = 0.0$, $\omega_u = 50.0$, N = 2000, respectively. And the results are both shown in Fig. 5. Once again, It is found that the results from PEM agree well with those from Monte-Carlo simulation. The differences are all within 6%. The first eigenvalue of the structure is 19.11 (for $\mu_i = 0$) and 23.79 (for $\mu_i = 0.15$) respectively, the difference is 11%, which also signifies a rather strong nonlinear characteristics. Figure 5 also shows that the maximum difference, about 6%, takes place in the strong excitation region. This phenomenon shows that stronger excitations will lead to stronger non-linearity, and so more severe errors will take place due to the equivalent linearization. It should be noted that in essence the proposed method does not apply to problems with strong non-linearity.

CONCLUSIONS

The pseudo excitation method [12–15] is extended to the analysis of non-stationary random responses of nonlinear structures. Duffing models are used in the given examples for computational simplicity. In fact, the proposed method is quite general, for instance it can also deal with structures with nonlinear hysteretic damping [16]. This method not only has good precision, but also has high computational efficiency, especially for structures with many degrees of freedom. Its implementation is also rather convenient.

ACKNOWLEDGEMENTS

This work has been supported by the NSFC(No. 10072015) and NKBRSF (No. G1999032805).

REFERENCES

1. W.D. Iwan and L.D. Lutes, Response of the bilinear hysteretic system to stationary random excitation, J. Acoust. Soc. Am. 43 (1968), 545–552.
2. T.K. Caughey, Random excitation of a system with bilinear hysteresis, J. Appli. Mech. 27 (1960), 649–652.
3. R.L. Grossmayer, Stochastic analysis of elasto-plastic systems, J. Eng. Mech. Div. ASCE107 (1981), 97–116.
4. J.B. Roberts and P.D. Spanos, Random Vibration and Statistical Linearization, Chichester: Wiley, 1990.
5. R.N. Iyengar and P.K. Dash, Study of the random vibration of nonlinear systems by the gaussian closure technique, J. Appl. Mech. 45 (1978), 393–399.
6. K. She and T. Shen, Cumulant-Neglect Closure for random vibration of hysteretic system, Vibration and Shock 2 (1989), 1–11.
7. Y.K. Lin and G.Q. Cai, Probabilistic Structural Dynamics, Advanced Theory and Applications, New York: McGraw-Hill, 1995.
8. P.D. Spanos, Stochastic linearization in structural dynamics, ASME Appl Mech Rev 34 (1981), 1–8.
9. F. Kozin, The method of statistical linearization for non-linear stochastic vibration, Nonlinear Stochastic Dynamic Engineering Systems, F. Ziegler and G.I. Schuller, eds, Berlin: Springer, 1987, pp. 45–56.
10. P. Bernard, Stochastic linearization: the theory, J Appl Prob 35 (1998), 718–730.
11. K. Kimura and M. Sakata, Nonstationary response analysis of nonsymmetric nonlinear multi-degree of freedom system to nonwhite random excitations, JSME Series III 31 (1998), 690–697.
12. J.H. Lin, W.S. Zhang and F.W. Williams, Pseudo-excitation algorithm for nonstationary random seismic

responses, Engineering Structures 16 (1994), 270–276.

13. J.H. Lin, J.J. Li, W.S. Zhang and F.W. Williams, Random Seismic Responses of Multi-support Structures in Evolutionary Inhomogeneous Random Fields, Earthquake Engineering and Structural Dynamics 26 (1997), 135–145.
14. J.H. Lin, D.K. Sun, Y. Sun and F.W. Williams, Structural Responses to Non-uniformly Modulated Evolutionary Random Seismic Excitations, Communications in Numerical Methods in Engineering 13 (1997), 605–616.
15. J.H. Lin, W.P. Shen and F.W. Williams, Accurate High-speed Computation of Non-stationary Random Structural Response, Engineering Structures 19 (1997), 586–593.
16. J. Wang, Pseudo excitation analysis of non-linear structures subjected to multi-phase random excitations, M.E. Deg. Dissertation, Dalian Univ. of Technology, 1999.
17. W.X. Zhong, Review of a high-efficiency algorithm series for structural random responses, Progress in Natural Science 6 (1996), 257–268.
18. M. Hoshiya, Probabilistic method in vibration analysis (Chinese version), Beijing: Earthquake Engineering Press, 1977.
19. M. Shinozuka and G. Deodatis, Simulation of stochastic processes by special representation, Appl. Mech. Rev. 44 (1991), 191–203.

CHAPTER 16

A REVIEW ON THE USE OF GRID-BASED BOLTZMANN EQUATION SOLVERS FOR DOSE CALCULATION IN EXTERNAL PHOTON BEAM TREATMENT PLANNING

Monica W. K. Kan,[1,2] Peter K. N. Yu,[2], and Lucullus H. T. Leung[1]

[1]Department of Oncology, Princess Margaret Hospital, Hong Kong

[2]Department of Physics and Materials Science, City University of Hong Kong, Tat Chee Avenue, Kowloon Tong, Hong Kong

ABSTRACT

Deterministic linear Boltzmann transport equation (D-LBTE) solvers have recently been developed, and one of the latest available software codes, Acuros XB, has been implemented in a commercial treatment planning system for radiotherapy photon beam dose calculation. One of the major limitations of most commercially available model-based algorithms for photon dose calculation is the ability to account for the effect of electron transport. This induces some errors in patient dose calculations, especially near heterogeneous interfaces between low and high density media such as tissue/lung interfaces. D-LBTE solvers have a high potential of producing accurate dose distributions in and near heterogeneous media in the human body. Extensive previous investigations have proved that D-LBTE solvers were able to produce comparable dose calculation accuracy as Monte Carlo methods with a reasonable speed good enough for clinical use. The current paper reviews the dosimetric evaluations of D-LBTE solvers for external beam photon radiotherapy. This content summarizes and discusses dosimetric validations for D-LBTE solvers in both homogeneous and heterogeneous media under different circumstances and also the clinical impact on various diseases due to the conversion of dose calculation from a conventional convolution/superposition algorithm to a recently released D-LBTE solver.

INTRODUCTION

Highly conformal photon dose distributions in various treatment sites can be achieved using different techniques of multileaf collimator-based intensity modulated radiotherapy, including static intensity modulated radiotherapy (IMRT) and volumetric modulated arc therapy (VMAT). Radiotherapy using intensity modulated techniques improves the possibility to escalate the target dose and minimize doses to critical organs when compared to three-dimensional conformal radiotherapy [1–11]. The use of IMRT or VMAT in patients usually involves many small field segments, some of which might pass through regions of low and high density media such as lung, air, and bone, depending on the location of the tumor and the surrounding normal tissues. One issue that affects the dose calculation accuracy in highly conformal planning is the ability of the algorithm to correctly account for the effects of radiation transport with the presence of heterogeneous medium.

Correction-based algorithms implemented in commercially available clinical treatment planning system include the pencil beam algorithm (PBC), collapsed cone convolution algorithm (CCC), and the analytical anisotropic algorithm (AAA). For PBC, it assumes that any collimated

Citation: Monica W. K. Kan, Peter K. N. Yu, and Lucullus H. T. Leung, "A Review on the Use of Grid-Based Boltzmann Equation Solvers for Dose Calculation in External Photon Beam Treatment Planning," BioMed Research International, vol. 2013, Article ID 692874, 10 pages, 2013. doi:10.1155/2013/692874

photon beam incident on the patient is composed of a large number of infinitely narrow pencil beams of photons. The total dose is calculated by superposition of pencil beam dose kernels at each point in space around the incident beam derived from Monte Carlo simulations. The effects of tissue variations and patient contour are usually modeled based on equivalent path length methods or the modified Batho correction method [12–14]. More advanced superposition/convolution methods such as AAA and CCC are able to incorporate electron and secondary photon transport in an approximate way for dose calculations in a heterogeneous medium. These methods use the superposition of the Monte Carlo derived dose kernels of both primary and scatter components to obtain doses in voxels of the irradiated volume. To account for the presence of inhomogeneities, simple density scaling of the kernels is applied so that the secondary electron transport is only modeled macroscopically. Both AAA and CCC were proved to produce inaccurate dose distribution in media with complex heterogeneities in certain circumstances [14–18].

The Monte Carlo (MC) methods have been considered the most accurate methods for radiotherapy treatment planning dose calculation. They are statistical simulation methods based on random sampling. They solve the radiation transport problem stochastically by simulating the tracks of a sufficiently large number of individual particles using the random number generated probability distribution governing the individual physical processes. They are therefore capable of accurately computing the radiation dose in media under almost all circumstances [19, 20]. However, the computation time required may still limit the use of MC methods for complex intensity modulated techniques in the clinical environment.

The desire to develop a fast alternative dose calculation method with comparable accuracy to MC methods has led to the exploration of deterministic solutions to the coupled system of linear Boltzmann transport equations (LBTE) [21–26]. It was first demonstrated using the prototype software, Attila, which was a general purpose grid-based Boltzmann solver code. It was followed by Acuros developed by Transpire, Inc. (Gig Harbor, WA, USA), specially designed for radiotherapy dose calculations. Recently, a version of deterministic LBTE solver, namely, Acuros XB (AXB), has been developed and implemented in the Eclipse treatment planning system (Varian Medical Systems, Palo Alto, CA, USA). The LBTE is the governing equation that describes the macroscopic behavior of ionizing particles as they travel through and interact with matter. The electron angular fluence is first obtained by solving the LBTE, and then the dose can be generated by using the macroscopic electron energy deposition cross-sections and the density of the materials. With sufficient refinement without using any approximation, that is, if an MC algorithm simulates an infinite number of particles and a deterministic LBTE (D-LBTE) solver discretizes the variables such as space and energy into infinitely small grids, both approaches will converge on the same solution. The achievable accuracy of both approaches is equivalent and is limited only by uncertainties in the particle interaction data and uncertainties related to the transported radiation fields. Extensive efforts have been made by several investigators to validate the accuracy of D-LBTE solvers in different circumstances by comparison against MC and by experimental verification against measurements. Performed validations ranged from using a simple geometric phantom with simple fields to a complex humanoid phantom with multiple intensity modulated fields. Most studies reported that D-LBTE solvers were capable of producing comparable accuracy as MC methods and either equivalent or better accuracy than superposition/convolution algorithms [22–35]. Dosimetric impact on different media of various clinical sites due to the conversion of the currently used model-based algorithms to the newly implemented D-LBTE solvers was also investigated by several authors [32, 36–38]. This paper summarizes and discusses the findings of the most recent dosimetric evaluation for D-LBTE solvers in various treatment sites.

THE DETERMINISTIC LBTE SOLVERS

More detailed description of the D-LBTE solvers can be found in the literature [21–26]. Only a summary is reported here.

The time-independent three-dimensional (3D) system of the coupled LBTE is solved to determine the energy deposition of photon and electron transport:

$$\widehat{\Omega}\cdot\vec{\nabla}\Phi^{\gamma}+\sigma^{\gamma}\Phi^{\gamma}=q^{\gamma\gamma}+q^{\gamma}, \tag{1}$$

$$\widehat{\Omega}\cdot\vec{\nabla}\Phi^{e}+\sigma^{e}\Phi^{e}-\frac{\partial}{\partial E}(S_R\Phi^{e})=q^{ee}+q^{\gamma e}+q^{e},$$
$$\vec{r}\in V,\ \widehat{\Omega}\in 4\pi,\ E>0, \tag{2}$$

where Φ^{γ} and Φ^{e} are the photon and electron angular fluence, respectively, σ^{γ} and σe are the macroscopic photon and electron total interaction cross-sections for all materials in volume V and energies, respectively, $q^{\gamma\gamma}$, $q^{\gamma e}$, and qee represent the photon scattering source generated from photon interaction, electron scattering source generated from photon interaction, and electron scattering source generated from electron interactions everywhere in V for all angles and energies, respectively, q^{γ} and q^{e} represent the external photon and electron source from the treatment head, respectively, $\vec{r}$ is the spatial position vector, E is the energy, $\widehat{\Omega}$ is the unit vector denoting particle direction, and $\vec{\nabla}$ is referred to as the "streaming operator" which may be interpreted as the number of particles flowing into a volume dV, minus the number of particles flowing out of dV for particles travelling in a direction $d\Omega$ about Ω with energy E about dE. The second terms on the left-hand side of (1) and (2) are the "collision operators," which may be thought of as the number of particles removed from the volume by absorption or scattering. Equation (2) is the Boltzmann Fokker-Plank transport equation, which is solved for the electron transport. The third term on the left-hand side of (2) represents the continuous slowing down operator, where S_R is the restricted plus collisional radiative stopping power. Equations (1) and (2) are usually solved through discretization in space, angle, and energy. Energy discretization is achieved with the standard multigroup method. Space discretization can be achieved with a variably sized Cartesian adaptive mesh refinement technique (used by AXB) or by using a high-order Galerkin-based linear discontinuous finite-element method to solve the multigroup discrete ordinates equations on fully unstructured tetrahedral elements (used by Attila). For the former technique, the mesh is limited to refinement in factors of 2 or smaller in any direction. This allows for the use of finer resolution in higher dose and high dose gradient regions. Angle discretization for fluences and scattering sources is achieved with the standard ordinates method, where the quadrature order is adaptive by the energy group. The photon angular fluence of (1) is the summation of uncollided (primary photon without interaction with matter) and collided fluence components (photons produced or scattered by photon interactions in the patient), where the latter is discretized using a linear discontinuous finite-element method, providing a linear solution variation throughout each element, with discontinuities permitted across element faces. After solving the electron angular fluence, the dose in any grid voxel, i, is calculated as follows:

$$D_i = \int_0^1 dE \int_{4\pi} \frac{d\hat{\Omega}\left(\sigma_{\mathrm{ED}}^{e}\left(\vec{r}, E\right)\right)}{\rho\left(\vec{r}\right)} \Phi^{e}\left(\vec{r}, E, \hat{\Omega}\right), \tag{3}$$

where σ_{ED}^{e} is the macroscopic energy deposition cross-section and ρ is the material density of the local voxel.

Similar to the MC methods, D-LBTE solvers also use energy cut-offs for electrons and photons. A particle is assumed to deposit all of its energy locally below the cut-off energy. For example, AXB uses an electron cut-off energy of 500 keV and a photon cut-off energy of 10 keV. Assumptions similar to those used in some MC methods are also applied to (1) and (2) of D-LBTE solvers. It is assumed that both secondary charged particles produced by pair production are electrons, not one electron plus one positron. It is also assumed that photons produce electrons, but electrons do not produce photons. The energy from photons produced by the electrons is assumed to be deposited locally. For (2), it is assumed that the Fokker-Planck operator is used for "soft" interactions leading to small-energy losses. Catastrophic interactions leading to large energy losses are represented with the standard Boltzmann scattering.

Both MC methods and D-LBTE solvers produce errors. MC methods produce stochastic errors when an insufficient number of particle histories is followed. LBTE solvers produce systematic errors due to finite discretization resolution in space, angle, and energy. Better accuracy always requires longer computation time. In addition, the achievable accuracy of MC and D-LBTE solver is limited by uncertainties in particle interaction data, patient geometry, and composition of the radiation field being modeled.

Similar to some MC methods, two options of dose reporting modes, that is, dose-to-water, D_w, and dose-tomedium, D_m, are usually provided in D-LBTE solvers. Both options calculate dose considering the elemental composition of each material in which particles are transported. The difference between them is mainly in the postprocessing step, in which D_w is obtained by rescaling D_m using the stopping power ratio of water to medium.

VALIDATION IN HOMOGENEOUS WATER

It is important to validate a new dose calculation algorithm in basic geometrical conditions such as that in homogeneous water before going ahead for more complicated ones. The information regarding the accuracy in simple cases is important to identify the sources of errors or uncertainties in more complicated geometries. Fogliata et al. performed a comprehensive assessment of AXB in Eclipse to model photon beams of low and high energy in homogeneous water with simple geometries [26]. They also included "flattening filter free" (FFF) beams from the Varian TrueBeam machine. The use of an FFF beam significantly increases the dose rate and therefore reduces the delivery time of a treatment machine. Due to the removal of flattening filter, the physical aspects of FFF beams are different from those of conventional flattened ones, including forward peaked intensity profiles in the middle instead of uniform flat profiles across the fields, steeper dose fall-off of percentage depth doses in the exponential region, less variation of off-axis beam hardening, lower mean energy, less photon head scatter, and higher surface dose. For conventional flattened beams, the performance of AXB was determined by comparison of calculated data against measured data in water for open and wedged fields. For FFF beams, the verification tests were performed for open fields only. The overall accuracy was found to be within 1% for open beams and 2% for mechanical wedges.

Testing the performance of AXB using open fields in homogeneous water was also performed by several other investigators [27, 28, 32]. Doses calculated using AXB were compared to measured/golden beam data, data calculated using AAA and CCC, as well as MC simulated data using different field sizes for different energy beams. Output factors, percentage depth doses (PDD), and lateral dose profiles at various depths were examined. In general, the agreement between the calculated data generated by the various models and the measured/golden beam data were found to be better than or close to 2%, with slightly larger discrepancies found in the build-up and penumbra regions. The calculated penumbral widths were usually found to be slightly smaller than the measured ones.

In homogeneous water, comparable performance was found between AXB and AAA/CCC. This was expected as most commercially available correction-based algorithms, and radiation transport algorithms were capable of accurately predicting the photon beam dose distribution in homogenous water. The discrepancies between calculated data and measured data were mostly limited by the precision and spatial resolution of the beam measurement devices used, especially in regions of high dose gradient. For example, the use of ion chamber with finite size for measuring dose profiles would broaden the penumbra width.

VERIFICATION WITH INHOMOGENEOUS SIMPLE GEOMETRIC PHANTOM USING SINGLE OPEN FIELDS

Several investigations have been performed to examine the accuracy of several different D-LBTE solvers for predicting the dose distribution in heterogeneous simple geometric phantoms using single fields of different photon energies [22, 25, 27–31]. The media of interest included soft tissue, normal lung, light lung, air, bone, aluminium, stainless steel, and titanium alloy. Most of the verifications were performed by benchmarking against the dose distributions calculated by MC methods. Table 1 summarizes the methods, phantom geometries, beam configurations, and comparison results between MC and D-LBTE solvers of some previous investigations. In general, good agreement was found between D-LBTE solvers and MC, with discrepancies of better than or equal to 2% in most cases. Verification using AXB of version 10 showed that there were slightly larger discrepancies of up to about 4 to 6% found in the presence of very low density media such as light lung or air, especially at/near the interface in the secondary build-up region when small fields were used [27, 30]. The accuracy of D-LBTE solvers depends on the material assignment and the level of sampling the structure voxels to the calculation grid. Fogliata et al. showed that the version 11 of AXB gave better agreement with MC when predicting doses in the presence of air than the version 10.0 of AXB, which was due to the inclusion of air material assignment (air material was not included in version 10.0) and the provision of better resampling process of the structure voxels to the calculation grid [29].

Table 1: A summary describing information of some previous investigations for the accuracy of D-LBTE solvers in predicting the doses in heterogeneous simple geometric phantoms using single open fields

Published investigations	Gifford et al. 2006 [22]	Vassiliev et al. 2010 [25]	Bush et al. 2011 [27]	Han et al. 2011 [28]	Kan et al. 2012 [30]	Lloyd and Ansbacher 2013 [31]
Beam energy	18 MV	6 and 18 MV	6 and 18 MV	6 and 18 MV	6 MV	6 and 18 MV
Field sizes	$1.5 \times 1.5\ cm^2$	$2.5 \times 2.5\ cm^2$ $5.0 \times 5.0\ cm^2$ $10.0 \times 10.0\ cm^2$	$4.0 \times 4.0\ cm^2$ $10.0 \times 10.0\ cm^2$ $15.0 \times 10.0\ cm^2$	$2.5 \times 2.5\ cm^2$ $5.0 \times 5.0\ cm^2$ $10.0 \times 10.0\ cm^2$	$2.0 \times 2.0\ cm^2$ $3.0 \times 3.0\ cm^2$ $5.0 \times 5.0\ cm^2$	$10.0 \times 10.0\ cm^2$
Phantom(s) geometry	One multilayer phantom: water (0–3 cm), aluminium, Al (3–5 cm), lung (5–12 cm), water (12–30 cm)	One multilayer phantom: water (0–3 cm), bone (3–5 cm), lung (5–12 cm), water (12–30 cm)	Two phantoms: (i) one with a single insert of normal lung, light lung, or air in water, (ii) a bone/lung phantom with several disk-shaped bony structures	One multilayer phantom: water (0–3 cm), bone (3–5 cm), lung (5–12 cm), water (12–30 cm)	$30.0 \times 30.0 \times 30.0\ cm^3$ of water containing $5.0 \times 5.0 \times 30.0\ cm^3$ of air	$20.0 \times 20.0 \times 20.0\ cm^3$ of muscle cube containing $2.0 \times 2.0 \times 18.0\ cm^3$ of stainless steel or titanium alloy
Monte carlo simulation	EGS4/Presta, 0.3% statistical uncertainty, resolution: $0.5 \times 0.5 \times 0.2\ cm^3$ voxels	DOSXYZnrc, <0.1% statistical uncertainty, resolution: $0.2 \times 0.2 \times 0.2\ cm^3$ voxels, 0.1 cm laterally in penumbra region	DOSXYZnrc ~1% statistical uncertainty in media except up to 4.5% in air, resolution: $0.25 \times 0.25 \times 0.25\ cm^3$ voxels	DOSXYZnrc, <1% statistical uncertainty, resolution: $0.2 \times 0.2 \times 0.2\ cm^3$ voxels for most volume, $0.1 \times 0.1 \times 0.2\ cm^3$ near water/bone and bone/lung interfaces	EGS4/Presta, 2.0% statistical uncertainty, resolution: 1/10 of field dimensions with 0.2 mm bin thickness	DOSXYZnrc, ~1% statistical uncertainty, resolution: $0.2 \times 0.2 \times 0.2\ cm^3$ voxels
D-LBTE solver	Attila code	Acuros (Transpire, Inc.)	AXB of version 10	AXB of version 10	AXB of version 10	AXB of version 11
Dose distribution examined	PDD	PDD and lateral profiles	PDD and lateral profiles	PDD, lateral profiles, and 3D gamma evaluation	PDD	PDD and lateral profiles
Difference between D-LBTE solver and Monte Carlo simulation	Average discrepancy is 1.4%, with 2.2% maximum discrepancy observed at water/Al interface	For 6 MV, max. discrepancy < 1.5%, with DTA < 0.7 mm in the build-up region. For 18 MV, max. discrepancy < 2.3% with DTA < 0.3 mm in the build-up region	Discrepancies were within 2% in lung, 3% in light lung, up to 4.5% in air, 1.8% in bone, with slightly larger discrepancy (up to 5%) at interfaces	For 6 MV, average discrepancy of 1.1% in PDD and 1.6% in dose profiles. For 18 MV, average discrepancy of 1.6% in PDD and 3.0% and dose profiles	Discrepancies are mostly within 2%, with slightly higher discrepancy (up to 6%) at the air/tissue interface in the secondary build-up region	In general good agreement between AXB and MC, with an average gamma agreement with a 2%/1mm criteria of 91.3% to 96.8%

Some of these studies also compared the accuracy of AXB with AAA [29–31], one of which performed the comparison with CCC as well [28]. All of them observed considerably larger differences between AAA and MC than those between AXB and MC in the presence of lung, air, and very high density objects especially near the interfaces. It was found that AXB could improve the dose prediction accuracy over both AAA and CCC in the presence of heterogeneities. It should also be noted that the depth dose profile data presented by Han et al. showed that CCC produced slightly better agreement with MC than AAA in both lung and bone regions [28].

VERIFICATION USING MULTIPLE CLINICAL SETUP FIELDS WITH HUMANOID GEOMETRY

Verification by Comparison with Monte Carlo Simulation

Some investigations were performed to examine the accuracy of D-LBTE solvers by comparison against MC methods for clinical setup fields [24, 25]. One study compared the dose distributions from one prostate and one head-and-neck clinical treatment plans calculated by Attila to those calculated by MC using the DOSXYZnrc program. Both plans were generated using the CT image data set of the real patients using multiple coplanar open fields. 3D gamma evaluation showed that 98.1% and 98.5% of the voxels passed the 3%/3 mm criterion for the prostate case and the head and neck case, respectively.

Another study compared the dose distributions from a tangential breast treatment plan calculated by Acuros (Transpire, Inc.) to those calculated by MC using the DOSXYZnrc program. The plan was generated on an anthropomorphic phantom with two tangential fields using a field-in-field technique. Field shapes were defined by a multileaf collimator using both 6 and 18 MV beams. The 3D gamma evaluation showed that the dose agreement was up to 98.7% for the 2%/1 mm criterion and reached 99.9% for the 2%/2 mm criterion. The differences were mostly found in the air external to the patient and in the lateral penumbra on the inside edge of the fields.

In general, both studies showed excellent agreement between D-LBTE solvers and MC in all regions including those near heterogeneity and with the use of small fields. These studies indicated that D-LBTE solvers were able to produce similar accuracy as MC methods for complicated geometries. However, the achievable accuracy of MC approach was also limited by uncertainties of the particle interaction data, the geometry and composition of the field being modeled, and other approximations made in radiation transport. Comprehensive validations of D-LBTE solvers should also cover comparisons against experimental measurements. Treatment plans with more complex intensity modulated fields, such as IMRT and VMAT, were not included in these studies.

Verification by Comparison against Measurements

Verifications of AXB against measurements using IMRT and VMAT plans for various diseases were reported [30, 32–35]. Humanoid phantoms used include the Radiological Physics Center (RPC) phantoms, the anthropomorphic phantom (the RANDO phantom, The Phantom Laboratory, Salem, NY, USA), and the CIRS Thorax Phantom (CIRS, VA, USA). Table 2 summarizes some of the details including methods and results of each verification study. Regarding verification using thermoluminescence dosimeters (TLDs), all the calculated data matched with the measured data are within 5%, with an average discrepancy of about 2 to 3%. The positions of measurement included those inside the heterogeneous medium and near/at the interfaces.

Table 2: A summary of information on some previous experimental validations for the accuracy of D-LBTE solvers in predicting the doses in heterogeneous humanoid phantoms using multiple clinical setup fields

Published investigations	Han et al. 2012. [33]	Kan et al. 2013 [34]	Kan et al. 2012 [30]	Han et al. 2013 [35]	Hoffmann et al. 2012 [32]
Disease of interest	Oropharyngeal tumor	Nasopharyngeal carcinoma	Locally persistent nasopharyngeal carcinoma	Lung cancer	Tumor in mediastinum
Media involved	Water equivalent materials	Tissue, air, and bone	Tissue, air, and bone	Tissue and lung	Tissue, lung, and bone
Treatment technique used	IMRT, VMAT	IMRT, VMAT	IMSRT	IMRT, VMAT	A total of 11 different plans including opposing fields, multiple fields, IMRT, and VMAT.
Phantom used	RPC head and neck phantom	Anthropomorphic phantom (RANDO)	Anthropomorphic phantom (RANDO)	RPC thorax phantom	CIRS Thorax phantom
Measurement device	TLD and EBT film	TLD and EBT film	TLD	TLD and EBT film	EBT film
LBTE solver	AXB version 11 using both D_m and D_w	AXB version 10 using both D_m and D_w	AXB version 10 using D_m only	AXB version 11 using both D_m and D_w	AXB version 10 using D_m only
Observed results	For TLD, deviation within 5%. For gamma analysis with film, 88% passed 5%/3 mm criterion for both D_m and D_w	For TLD, deviation within 5%, with an average of 1.8%. For gamma analysis with film, 91% passed 3%/3 mm criterion for D_m and 99% for D_w	For TLD, deviation within 3%	For TLD, deviation within 4.4%. For gamma analysis with film, ~97% passed 3%/3 mm criterion for D_m and 98% for D_w	For gamma analysis with film, 98.2% passed the 3%/3 mm criterion for 6 MV and 99.5% for 15 MV

For the gamma analysis using EBT films, the passing rate of the 3%/3 mm criterion met the recommendation (should be >90%) set by TG 119 for the studies performed in the nasopharyngeal region and the lung, where heterogeneities exist. However, the one performed using the RPC head and neck phantom, where only tissue equivalent material was involved, could only produce a passing rate of 88% for the 5%/3 mm criterion [33]. The inferior results reported might be due to the larger uncertainty of the film registration method during analysis.

All experimental validations listed also compared the accuracy between AXB and AAA. The accuracy of both when compared to TLD measurement was quite comparable except for the investigation using intensity modulated stereotactic radiotherapy (IMSRT) in locally persistent nasopharyngeal. For the IMSRT cases, AXB demonstrated better accuracy near air/tissue interfaces when compared with AAA. This might be due to the very small field segments used in IMSRT cases with the presence of air cavities. For validations performed with films, the accuracy of AXB was in general shown to be slightly better than that of AAA. When compared to TLD, films could measure a much larger number of points in a single measurement and provided better spatial resolution. This might be the reason why films could better distinguish between the accuracies of AAA and AXB even when the difference was small.

DOSE IN MEDIUM AGAINST DOSE IN WATER

For external photon beam radiation therapy planning, the input data used for most conventional correction/modelbased dose algorithms are dose distributions and beam parameters measured in water. They usually report patient dose in terms of the absorbed dose to water (D_w) using variable electron density. On the other hand, LBTE solvers calculate the energy deposition considering radiation particle transport in different media and therefore report dose directly to patient medium (D_m). According to the recommendation from the American Association of Physicists in Medicine (AAPM) Task Group 105, MC results should allow conversion between D_m and D_w, based on the Bragg-Gray cavity theory, either during or after the MC simulation. This recommendation also applies to all other deterministic algorithms that are able to report D_m accurately for plan evaluation [39]. D_m calculated by LBTE solvers can be converted to D_w using the Bragg-Gray cavity theory by

$$D_w = D_m\left(\frac{\bar{S}}{\rho}\right)_m^w, \quad (4)$$

where $(\bar{S}/\rho)_m^w$ is the unrestricted water to medium mass collision stopping power ratio averaged over the energy spectra of primary electrons at the point of interest. It has been recently debated whether the D_m dose inherently predicted by MC methods needs to be converted to D_w. There are certain arguments between using D_m and D_w for radiotherapy treatment planning in the clinical environment.

Those supporting the use of D_w argued that (1) therapeutic and normal tissue tolerance doses determined from clinical trials were based on D_w as photon dose measurements and calculations were historically reported in terms of D_w, (2) calibration of treatment machines were performed according to recognized dosimetry protocols in terms of the absorbed dose to water, and (3) tumor cells embedded within any medium such as bone were more water-like than mediumlike. Those supporting the use of D_m argued that (1) the dose to the tissues of interest was the quantity inherently computed by radiation transport dose algorithms and therefore was more clinical relevant and (2) the conversion of D_m back to D_w might induce additional uncertainty to the final calculated dose.

Several studies proved that the difference between using D_w and D_m for predicting photon dose distribution mainly occurred in higher density materials such as the cortical bone. The dose discrepancy could be up to 15% due to the large difference between the stopping powers of water and these higher-density materials. For soft tissues and lung, the dose discrepancy was only about 1 to 2% [33, 35, 40]. An investigation by Dogan et al. based on the MC method found that converting D_m to D_w in IMRT treatment plans introduced a discrepancy in target and critical structure of up to 5.8% for head and neck cases and up to 8.0% for prostate cases when bony structures were involved [41]. Kan et al. also observed that AXB using *Dw* calculated up to 4% higher mean doses for the bony structure in planning target volume (PTV) when compared to D_m in IMRT and VMAT plans of NPC cases [34]. Figure 1 shows the difference in dose volume histograms (DVHs) between D_m and D_w for different organs at risk (OAR) and PTV components (both bone and soft tissues). They were generated by AXB using both D_m and D_w for a typical VMAT plan of an NPC case. It can be seen from the DVH curves that larger dose differences were found between D_m and D_w in organs with bony structures such as mandible than those with soft tissue such as parotids.

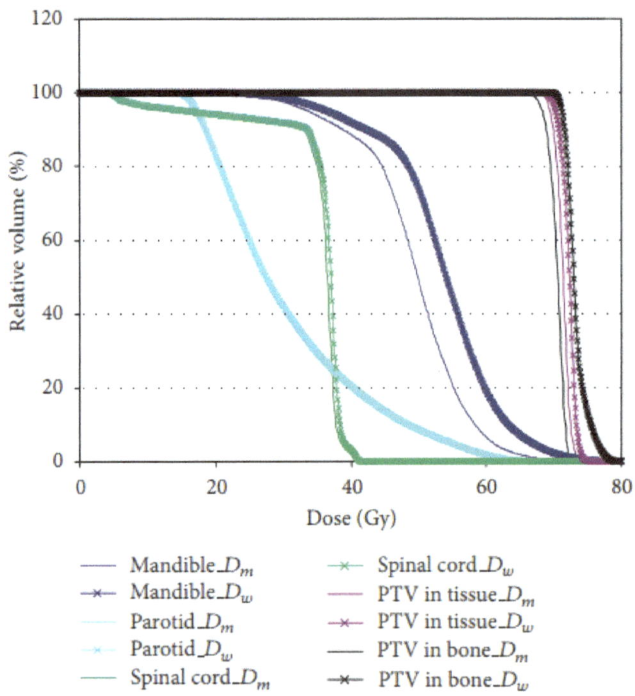

Figure 1: DVH curves for different OAR and PTV components generated by AXB with both D_m and D_w calculation options for a typical VMAT plan of an NPC patient.

Previous studies using Monte Carlo and AXB calculations proved that conventional model based algorithms predicted dose distributions in bone that were closer to D_m distributions than to D_w distributions [34, 42]. It is therefore better to use D_m for consistency with previous radiation therapy experience.

DOSIMETRIC IMPACT IN CLINICAL CASES

Various studies were performed to assess the dosimetric impact of using AXB instead of AAA for dose calculations in different clinical cases, including lung cancer, breast cancer, and nasopharyngeal carcinomas [36–38]. AXB calculations for these investigations were all performed using the D_m option, so that the capability of the algorithm to distinguish between different elemental compositions in the human body could be assessed. The grid resolution for dose calculation selected was 2.5 mm. In order to evaluate the dose differences between the two algorithms due to the issue of tissue heterogeneity, the PTV were divided into components of different densities and compositions during dose analysis.

Lung Cancer

The clinical dosimetric impact for advanced non-small-cell lung cancer was assessed using three different techniques: three-dimensional conformal radiotherapy, IMRT, and RapidArc (the name of the VMAT system from Varian Medical Systems Inc., Palo Alto, CA, USA) at both 6 and 15 MV [36]. The PTVs were split into two components, namely, PTV in soft tissue and PTV in lung. The dose prescription was 66 Gy at 2 Gy per fraction to the mean target dose for each planning technique. The results demonstrated that AXB predicted up to 1.7% and 1.2% lower mean target doses in soft tissue for 6 MV and 15 MV beams, respectively, and up to 1.2% higher and 2.0% lower mean target doses in lung for 6 MV and 15 MV beams, respectively. In general, AAA overestimated the doses to most PTV components, except for PTV in lung when using IMRT at 6 MV, where the opposite trend was observed. AXB predicted up to 3% lower mean doses to OAR. The observed trend was similar for different treatment techniques.

Breast Cancer

The dosimetric impact for breast cancer was assessed using the opposing tangential field setting technique at 6 MV [37]. Doses in organs were analyzed using patient datasets scanned under two different breathing conditions, free breathing (FB, representing higher lung density), and deep inspiration (DI, representing lower lung density). The target breast was split into components in muscle and in adipose tissue. It was observed that AAA predicted 1.6% higher doses for the muscle than AXB (version 11). The difference in doses predicted by both algorithms to the adipose tissue was negligible. AAA was found to predict up to 0.5% and 1.5% higher doses than using version 11 of AXB in the lung region within the tangential field for FB and DI, respectively. The authors comparing between versions 10 and 11 of AXB found negligible differences in the predicted doses for tissue and normal lung. However, they observed that, for the lower density lung in the condition of DI, version 11 of AXB predicted an average of 1.3% higher dose than version 10. This was mainly due to the more accurate dose calculation of version 11 for very low density lung achieved by including the low density air in the material list.

Nasopharyngeal Carcinomas

The dosimetric impact for NPC was assessed using IMRT and RapidArc at 6 MV due to the use of AXB version 10 compared to AAA [38]. The PTVs with multiple prescriptions were separated into components in bone, air, and tissue. AAA was found to predict about 1% higher mean doses to the PTVs in tissue, 2% higher doses to the PTVs in bone, and 1% lower doses to the PTVs in air. AAA also predicted up to 3% higher doses to most serial organs. It should be noted that AAA predicted up to 4% higher minimum doses to the PTVs in bone, where the gross tumor volume was located.

On the whole, the various investigations for different treatment sites listed above demonstrated that in general AAA predicted higher doses to PTV and OAR, when compared with AXB. The overestimation by AAA was mostly within 2% in soft tissues such as muscle and lung and could be up to 4% in bone.

DISCUSSIONS

Various studies showed that D-LBTE solvers were able to produce satisfactory dose calculation accuracy in the presence of heterogeneous media, even at and near interfaces of different material densities [22–35]. They were proved to produce equivalent accuracy to MC methods and better accuracy than convolution/superposition algorithms. These results are expected as D-LBTE methods model the radiation transport process in a similar manner as MC methods. There is still room for improvement in the latest version of clinically available AXB regarding accuracy in physical material assignment and calculation speed. For example, one of the limitations of AXB is the restricted material assignment range. If the CT dataset of a high density object contains HU values corresponding to a mass density greater than 3.0 g/cm^3, it is required to contain all voxels in a contoured structure with manual assignment of mass density. That means the mass density of the high density object must be known for accurate dose calculations. The validation of AXB by Lloyd and Ansbacher proved that it was able to predict the back-scatter and lateral-scatter dose perturbations accurately adjacent to very higher density objects (with density in the range from 4.0 to 8.0 g/cm^3) [31]. However, in reality, this would be difficult for real patient planning due to the misinterpretation of HU values of high density implants introduced by shadow artifacts in CT images.

When compared to MC methods, the use of D-LBTE solvers might result in relatively shorter calculation time as explicit modeling of a large number of particle interactions is not required. Previous studies observed that the earlier D-LBTE code, Attila, performed dose calculations faster than the general purpose of MC method such as EGS4 or the EGSnrc by an order of magnitude for both external beam and brachytherapy planning [22, 24]. Acuros, which was optimized for use in radiotherapy planning, was reported to perform roughly an order of magnitude faster than Attila for various clinical cases [25]. Furthermore, the latest version of D-LBTE method, AXB, was reported to produce 3 to 4 times faster speed for VMAT planning compared to AAA [36]. The above evidence indicates that D-LBTE methods can be a fast and accurate alternative to MC methods. However, it is in fact difficult to perform direct comparison of the speed between MC and D-LBTE solvers as it depends on the hardware and the efficiency of the coding used. The computation time of D-LBTE solvers might be further reduced in the future by implementation on graphical processing units and additional refinements. On the other hand, fast MC codes have been developed to improve the speed of dose calculation for clinical use. Examples include the Voxel-based Monte Carlo (VMC, VMC++), Macro Monte Carlo, Dose Planning Method (DPM), and MCDOSE [43–50]. Continuous development of more efficient MC codes in the future may compete with currently commercial available D-LBTE methods in terms of both accuracy and speed.

Although D-LBTE solvers were proved to be more accurate than convolution/superposition algorithms, significant differences were mainly confined to certain extreme conditions. These mainly include doses near heterogeneous interfaces when using single or multiple small fields. Up to 8 to 10% higher doses near interfaces were predicted by AAA compared with AXB when stereotactic small fields were used in the presence of air cavity [30]. Smaller differences were found when using IMRT and VMAT setup fields. Several experimental verifications showed comparable dose accuracy between AXB and AAA in soft tissues within complex heterogeneous geometries for clinical intensity modulated fields [33–35]. The studies assessing the dosimetric impact of using AXB on various clinical sites also showed only about 1 to 2% lower means doses in all soft tissues predicted by AXB compared to AAA [36–38]. Slightly larger differences of about 4% were found in bony structures due to the fact that AXB reported dose to medium as default while AAA reported dose to water as default. Most of these comparison studies were confined between AAA and AXB, as both of them are implemented in the same treatment planning system. Comparison between AXB with other convolution/superposition methods such as CCC for various clinical sites is not reported. From the single field study performed by Han et al. [28] in simple heterogeneous geometry, it can be predicted that CCC may produce a closer dose distribution to AXB than AAA for clinical multiple setup fields. It is because CCC predicts more accurate doses near heterogeneous interfaces than AAA for single fields, and, like AXB, it reports dose to medium as default.

Most dosimetric studies mentioned above indicated that AAA slightly overestimated the doses to target volumes compared to AXB. If D-LBTE methods are used instead of model-based algorithms for treatment planning, it is very likely that more doses will be given to the target volumes provided that the prescribed doses by oncologists remain unchanged. Whether such conversion will bring actual clinical impact to the patients such as improvement in tumor control probability for various clinical sites requires further investigation.

CONCLUSIONS

On the whole, grid-based D-LBTE solvers were evaluated by extensive investigations to be accurate and valuable dose calculation methods for photon beam radiotherapy treatments involving heterogeneous materials. They were proved to produce doses in good agreement with MC methods and measurements in different clinical sites using techniques ranging from relatively simple to very complex intensity modulated treatment. The use of D-LBTE solvers is highly recommended for cases with heterogeneities. However, users must be aware of the dosimetric impact on various treatment sites due to the conversion from using model-based algorithms to D-LBTE solvers.

REFERENCES

1. M. K. M. Kam, R. M. C. Chau, J. Suen, P. H. K. Choi, and P. M. L. Teo, "Intensity-modulated radiotherapy in nasopharyngeal carcinoma: dosimetric advantage over conventional plans and feasibility of dose escalation," International Journal of Radiation Oncology Biology Physics, vol. 56, no. 1, pp. 145–157, 2003.
2. W. F. A. R. Verbakel, J. P. Cuijpers, D. Hoffmans, M. Bieker, B. J. Slotman, and S. Senan, "Volumetric intensity-modulated arc therapy vs. conventional IMRT in head-and-neck cancer: a comparative planning and dosimetric study," International Journal of Radiation Oncology Biology Physics, vol. 74, no. 1, pp. 252–259, 2009.
3. E. Vanetti, A. Clivio, G. Nicolini et al., "Volumetric modulated arc radiotherapy for carcinomas of the oro-pharynx, hypo-pharynx and larynx: a treatment planning comparison with fixed field IMRT,"Radiotherapy and Oncology, vol. 92, no. 1, pp. 111–117, 2009.
4. P. Doornaert, W. F. A. R. Verbakel, M. Bieker, B. J. Slotman, and S. Senan, "RapidArc planning and delivery in patients with locally advanced head-and-neck cancer undergoing chemoradiotherapy,"International Journal of Radiation Oncology Biology Physics, vol. 79, no. 2, pp. 429–435, 2011.
5. R. A. Popple, J. B. Fiveash, I. A. Brezovich, and J. A. Bonner, "RapidArc radiation therapy: first year experience at the University of Alabama at Birmingham," International Journal of Radiation Oncology Biology Physics, vol. 77, no. 3, pp. 932–941, 2010.
6. M. J. Zelefsky, Z. Fuks, L. Happersett et al., "Clinical experience with intensity modulated radiation therapy (IMRT) in prostate cancer," Radiotherapy and Oncology, vol. 55, no. 3, pp. 241–249, 2000.
7. F. A. Vicini, M. Sharpe, L. Kestin et al., "Optimizing breast cancer treatment efficacy with intensity-modulated radiotherapy," International Journal of Radiation Oncology Biology Physics, vol. 54, no. 5, pp. 1336–1344, 2002.
8. C. C. Popescu, I. A. Olivotto, W. A. Beckham et al., "Volumetric modulated arc therapy improves dosimetry and reduces treatment time compared to conventional intensity-modulaed radiotherapy for locoregional radiotherapy of left-sided breast cancer and internal mammary nodes," International Journal of Radiation Oncology Biology Physics, vol. 76, no. 1, pp. 287–295, 2010.·
9. P. Zhang, L. Happersett, M. Hunt, A. Jackson, M. Zelefsky, and G. Mageras, "Volumetric modulated arc therapy: planning and evaluation for prostate cancer cases," International Journal of Radiation Oncology Biology Physics, vol. 76, no. 5, pp. 1456–1462, 2010.
10. I. S. Grills, D. Yan, A. A. Martinez, F. A. Vicini, J. W. Wong, and L. L. Kestin, "Potential for reduced toxicity and dose escalation in the treatment of inoperable non-small-cell lung cancer: a comparison of intensity-modulated radiation therapy (IMRT), 3D conformal radiation, and elective nodal irradiation," International Journal of Radiation Oncology Biology Physics, vol. 57, no. 3, pp. 875–890, 2003.
11. S. D. McGrath, M. M. Matuszak, D. Yan, L. L. Kestin, A. A. Martinez, and I. S. Grills, "Volumetric modulated arc therapy for delivery of hypofractionated stereotactic lung radiotherapy: a dosimetric and treatment efficiency analysis," Radiotherapy and Oncology, vol. 95, no. 2, pp. 153–157, 2010.
12. A. Ahnesjo, M. Saxner, and A. Trepp, "A pencil beam model for photon dose calculation," Medical Physics, vol. 19, no. 2, pp. 263–273, 1992.
13. A. Fogliata, E. Vanetti, D. Albers et al., "On the dosimetric behaviour of photon dose calculation algorithms in the presence of simple geometric heterogeneities:

comparison with Monte Carlo calculations," Physics in Medicine and Biology, vol. 52, no. 5, pp. 1363–1385, 2007.·

14. W. Ulmer, J. Pyyry, and W. Kaissl, "A 3D photon superposition/convolution algorithm and its foundation on results of Monte Carlo calculations," Physics in Medicine and Biology, vol. 50, no. 8, pp. 1767–1790, 2005.

15. A. Gray, L. D. Oliver, and P. N. Johnston, "The accuracy of the pencil beam convolution and anisotropic analytical algorithms in predicting the dose effects due to attenuation from immobilization devices and large air gaps," Medical Physics, vol. 36, no. 7, pp. 3181–3191, 2009.·

16. L. Tillikainen, H. Helminen, T. Torsti et al., "A 3D pencil-beam-based superposition algorithm for photon dose calculation in heterogeneous media," Physics in Medicine and Biology, vol. 53, no. 14, pp. 3821–3839, 2008.

17. C. Martens, N. Reynaert, C. de Wagter et al., "Underdosage of the upper-airway mucosa for small fields as used in intensity-modulated radiation therapy: a comparison between radiochromic film measurements, Monte Carlo simulations, and collapsed cone convolution calculations," Medical Physics, vol. 29, no. 7, pp. 1528–1535, 2002.

18. M. W. K. Kan, J. Y. C. Cheung, L. H. T. Leung, B. M. F. Lau, and P. K. N. Yu, "The accuracy of dose calculations by anisotropic analytical algorithms for stereotactic radiotherapy in nasopharyngeal carcinoma," Physics in Medicine and Biology, vol. 56, no. 2, pp. 397–413, 2011.

19. P. Andreo, "Monte Carlo techniques in medical radiation physics," Physics in Medicine and Biology, vol. 36, no. 7, pp. 861–920, 1991.

20. D. W. O. Rogers, B. A. Faddegon, G. X. Ding, C.-M. Ma, J. We, and T. R. Mackie, "BEAM: a Monte Carlo code to simulate radiotherapy treatment units," Medical Physics, vol. 22, no. 5, pp. 503–524, 1995.·

21. T. A. Wareing, J. M. McGhee, J. E. Morel, and S. D. Pautz, "Discontinuous finite element SN methods on three-dimensional unstructured grids," Nuclear Science and Engineering, vol. 138, no. 3, pp. 256–268, 2001.

22. K. A. Gifford, J. L. Horton Jr., T. A. Wareing, G. Failla, and F. Mourtada, "Comparison of a finite-element multigroup discrete-ordinates code with Monte Carlo for radiotherapy calculations," Physics in Medicine and Biology, vol. 51, no. 9, pp. 2253–2265, 2006. ·

23. K. A. Gifford, M. J. Price, J. L. Horton Jr., T. A. Wareing, and F. Mourtada, "Optimization of deterministic transport parameters for the calculation of the dose distribution around a high dose-rate 192Ir brachytherapy source," Medical Physics, vol. 35, no. 6, pp. 2279–2285, 2008.·

24. O. N. Vassiliev, T. A. Wareing, I. M. Davis et al., "Feasibility of a multigroup deterministic solution method for three-dimensional radiotherapy dose calculations," International Journal of Radiation Oncology Biology Physics, vol. 72, no. 1, pp. 220–227, 2008. ·

25. O. N. Vassiliev, T. A. Wareing, J. McGhee, G. Failla, M. R. Salehpour, and F. Mourtada, "Validation of a new grid-based Boltzmann equation solver for dose calculation in radiotherapy with photon beams,"Physics in Medicine and Biology, vol. 55, no. 3, pp. 581–598, 2010.

26. A. Fogliata, G. Nicolini, A. Clivio, E. Vanetti, P. Mancosu, and L. Cozzi, "Dosimetric validation of the Acuros XB advanced dose calculation algorithm: fundamental characterization in water," Physics in Medicine and Biology, vol. 56, no. 6, pp. 1879–1904, 2011. ·

27. K. Bush, I. M. Gagne, S. Zavgorodni, W. Ansbacher, and W. Beckham, "Dosimetric validation of Acuros XB with Monte Carlo methods for photon dose calculations," Medical Physics, vol. 38, no. 4, pp. 2208–2221, 2011.

28. T. Han, J. K. Mikell, M. Salehpour, and F. Mourtada, "Dosimetric comparison of Acuros XB deterministic radiation transport method with Monte Carlo and model-based convolution methods in heterogeneous media," Medical Physics, vol. 38, no. 5, pp. 2651–2664, 2011.

29. A. Fogliata, G. Nicolini, A. Clivio, E. Vanetti, and L. Cozzi, "Dosimetric evaluation of Acuros XB Advanced Dose Calculation algorithm in heterogeneous media," Radiation Oncology, vol. 6, no. 1, article 82, 2011.

30. W. K. Kan, L. Leung, and P. Yu, "Verification and dosimetric impact of Acuros XB algorithm on intensity modulated stereotactic radiotherapy for locally persistent nasopharyngeal carcinoma,"Medical Physics, vol. 39, no. 8, pp. 4705–4714, 2012.

31. S. A. M. Lloyd and W. Ansbacher, "Evaluation of an analytic linear Boltzmann transport equation solver for high density inhomogeneities," Medical Physics, vol. 40, no. 1, Article ID 011707, 2013.

32. L. Hoffmann, M.-B. K. Jørgensen, L. P. Muren, and J. B. B. Petersen, "Clinical validation of the Acuros XB photon dose calculation algorithm, a grid-based Boltzmann equation solver," Acta Oncologica, vol. 51, no. 3, pp. 376–385, 2012.

33. T. Han, F. Mourtada, K. Kisling, et al., "Experimental validation of deterministic Acuros XB algorithm for IMRT and VMAT dose calculations with the Radiological Physics Center's head and neck phantom," Medical Physics, vol. 39, no. 4, pp. 2193–2202, 2012.

34. W. K. Kan, L. Leung, W. K. So, et al., "Experimental verification of the Acuros XB and AAA dose calculation adjacent to heterogeneous media for IMRT and RapidArc of nasopharygeal carcinoma,"Medical Physics, vol. 40, no. 3, Article ID 031714, 2013.

35. T. Han, D. Followill, J. Mikell, et al., "Dosimetric impact of Acuros XB deterministic radiation transport algorithm for heterogeneous dose calculation in lung cancer," Medical Physics, vol. 40, no. 5, Article ID 051710, 2013.

36. A. Fogliata, G. Nicolini, A. Clivio, E. Vanetti, and L. Cozzi, "Critical appraisal of Acuros XB and anisotropic analytic algorithm dose calculation in advanced non-small-cell lung cancer treatments,"International Journal

of Radiation Oncology, Biology, Physics, vol. 83, no. 5, pp. 1587–1595, 2012.

37. A. Fogliata, G. Nicolini, A. Clivio, E. Vanetti, and L. Cozzi, "On the dosimetric impact of inhomogeneity management in the Acuros XB algorithm for breast treatment," Radiation Oncology, vol. 6, no. 1, article 103, 2011.

38. M. K. L. Leung and P. Yu, "Dosimetric impact of using Acuros XB algorithm for intensity modulated radiation therapy and RapidArc planning in nasopharyngeal carcinomas," International Journal of Radiation Oncology "Biology" Physics, vol. 85, no. 1, pp. 73–80, 2013.

39. I. J. Chetty, B. Curran, J. E. Cygler et al., "Report of the AAPM Task Group No. 105: issues associated with clinical implementation of Monte Carlo-based photon and electron external beam treatment planning," Medical Physics, vol. 34, no. 12, pp. 4818–4853, 2007.

40. J. V. Siebers, P. J. Keall, A. E. Nahum, and R. Mohan, "Converting absorbed dose to medium to absorbed dose to water for Monte Carlo based photon beam dose calculations," Physics in Medicine and Biology, vol. 45, no. 4, pp. 983–995, 2000.

41. N. Dogan, J. V. Siebers, and P. J. Keall, "Clinical comparison of head and neck and prostate IMRT plans using absorbed dose to medium and absorbed dose to water," Physics in Medicine and Biology, vol. 51, no. 19, pp. 4967–4980, 2006.

42. C.-M. Ma and J. Li, "Dose specification for radiation therapy: dose to water or dose to medium?"Physics in Medicine and Biology, vol. 56, no. 10, pp. 3073–3089, 2011.

43. I. Kawrakow, M. Fippel, and K. Friedrich, "3D electron dose calculation using a Voxel based Monte Carlo algorithm (VMC)," Medical Physics, vol. 23, no. 4, pp. 445–457, 1996.

44. I. Kawrakow and M. Fippel, "Investigation of variance reduction techniques for Monte Carlo photon dose calculation using XVMC," Physics in Medicine and Biology, vol. 45, no. 8, pp. 2163–2183, 2000.·

45. H. Neuenschwander and E. J. Born, "A macro Monte Carlo method for electron beam dose calculations," Physics in Medicine and Biology, vol. 37, no. 1, pp. 107–125, 1992.·

46. H. Neuenschwander, T. R. Mackie, and P. J. Reckwerdt, "MMC—a high-performance Monte Carlo code for electron beam treatment planning," Physics in Medicine and Biology, vol. 40, no. 4, pp. 543–574, 1995.

47. J. Sempau, S. J. Wilderman, and A. F. Bielajew, "DPM, a fast, accurate Monte Carlo code optimized for photon and electron radiotherapy treatment planning dose calculations," Physics in Medicine and Biology, vol. 45, no. 8, pp. 2263–2291, 2000.

48. C. Ma, J. S. Li, T. Pawlicki, et al., "MCDOSE—a Monte Carlo dose calculation tool for radiation therapy treatment planning," Physics in Medicine and Biology, vol. 47, no. 10, pp. 1671–1689, 2002.

J. Gardner, J. Siebers, and I. Kawrakow, "Dose calculation validation of VMC++ for photon beams,"Medical Physics, vol. 34, no. 5, pp. 1809–1818, 2007.

K. Jabbari, "Review of fast Monte Carlo codes for dose calculation in radiation therapy treatment planning," Journal of Medical Signals & Sensors, vol. 1, no. 1, pp. 73–86, 2011.

INDEX